Dedicated to

Mrs. Alton S. Winey

Everybody's

"Aunt Louise"

iv

This book is interesting, informative, relaxing, sad and reminiscent.

<u>WHO</u> will want to read it?   Teachers, principals, parents, relatives, pupils, friends, foreigners, and dropouts.

<u>WHY?</u>   Because it's about school years – years that form character, attitudes, habits, direction and strengths.

This book will sell itself – one reader to another.

INTRODUCTION

A substitute calls Substitute Office advising them she will be available to teach the following day. When called she arrives at the school office and signs in, then waits for a room and grade level assignment.

I carried two heavy satchels of supplies for various grades plus a portable record player and a few records.

Taking the room key and unlocking the door the substitute first locates the Attendance Book, then looks for a Lunch Money List and for a specific Lunch Eating and Leaving time. In crowded schools with small lunchrooms this is very important.

She puts assignments on the board, then taking the Attendance Book meets her assigned class of students, usually outside the building, and escorts them to their classroom.

Pupils remove their coats and hang them in lockers in the corridor or inside the room.

A substitute's day usually depends on her ability to start the day orderly. Either she or the rowdies will run the room. This can portend a pleasant or trying day. The culprits must sit down and at their own desks. The room must be quiet.

At this time I stand quietly, facing the class, then say, "I will be your teacher today, but I am NOT a new sub. I have taught school for twenty years right here in Chicago."

I have good, interesting work for you to do. When you finish it I have art work, music records, fun and thinking games. Here are some art samples. ("Ohs" and "ahs" follow seeing these.)

"But if you do not do the work and be quiet there will be NO art, NO records, and NO games. Instead there will be more work all day until closing. It is up to you."

Still standing in front of them I look around the room, up and down the aisles. "Hands up for those who choose to have a good day." Cautiously one, then another, then all hands are raised. I smile and point to my name on the board.

Our day begins.

Chapter 1

<u>Re-Initiation</u>

R-r-r-r-r-ING! It was Substitute Center telling me (at 8:30) to report to Truth School—my first substitute teaching job since retirement.

Quickly I left with two satchels packed with materials for grades one through eight, but because the school vicinity was not familiar to me I passed the street, then drove around searching for a parking place.

Signing in at 9:30 I thought of all those late substitute teachers I used to wait for. Maybe it hadn't been their fault after all. I felt foolish; two subs had signed in ahead of me, one at 8:30, the other at 9:00.

The clerk told me to go to a First Grade Room so my heart was happy as I looked for the elevator in the new school until I remembered that in schools you walk. But why the top floor for first graders? Two youngsters showed me which stairs to take.

Climbing I could observe the open classrooms, but spacious enough in between the groups, and the welcome air-conditioning was comfortably regulated.

Only a few youngsters were in the classroom. A soft-spoken teacher nearby explained there were no Lesson Plans as the teacher had not expected to be out. (I thought this was the purpose of such plans.) Before she left I jotted down the recess and lunch hours. Later I learned that pupils capable of learning to read had gone to other groups, that this was the lowest group, ready only for reading readiness – material I had not brought!

Thinking back to years when I had taught first grade I reminded them to sit up straight, place the paper at an angle before them, and demonstrated how to hold a pencil. As usual, a few were still clutching the pencils between their middle fingers. Explaining the two end fingers were to be bent in like "runners", "wheels", and that all we had to do was guide the pencil, which was resting between the thumb and the first finger, I captured their attention. Everyone started

1

making "pull-downs" for window shades, then circles, small and large, trying to remain on the line. All were happy and occupied.

Supplies were nil. Only crayons, a few pencils, and a meager supply of paper were found. The children were black, clean and dressed well, but without supplies. There were scissors; no paste; no drawing or arithmetic paper, the small amount of writing paper being all there was to use.

At 10:30 a Teacher Aide appeared so I asked her to borrow a record player from someone. She reported machines had to be ordered from the office by 9:00 "That was the rule". A piano was not far away, and on rollers, but with no music on the rack or in the seat. Music was another item I had not brought, and music is on the priority list for low first graders who are not yet ready for reading. Unfortunately, I did not have a singing voice but had bought records to compensate for this.

The class changed twice before lunch. Walking reading groups went from one group to another. Stragglers came and went, taking their own time. The floor was carpeted so the open rooms were quiet. Occasionally a teacher's voice could he heard in small exasperations, but not often, and not too loud.

The pupils were able to write satisfactorily and enjoyed doing this. They wrote two words, "Oh look" and then drew pictures of what they wished people to look at. Several were very good artists.

Lunch at 12:10 was good. The children had been trained to collect their trays in the cafeteria, the girls lining up at one side, the boys going to another entrance. They sat together in the large room. The teachers bought their food in an adjoining room. Fortunately, there was an extra salad for me as teachers had ordered earlier in the day.

The children enjoyed trudging up and down the three flights, but there was a little noise until I showed them how to take secret, quiet steps like Indians, walking only on the balls of their feet, so no one – no one at all – could ever hear them, and everyone knows that Indians ALWAYS kept their hands quietly at their sides.

We stopped at the washrooms again, where there was no paper for the children. I had to send for needed paper twice for some youngsters in need.

In the lunchrooms I had spotted a piano with two music books, so had copied a catchy, short melody, but after moving the piano across to our section, it was soon apparent that the children were a little restless and that my music talents were not strong enough to hold their attention without a record player. This did not surprise me. The records I had bought would have been perfect; all were catchy, fun and educational. We played a few games and had fun exercises.

In the morning I had distributed ditto copies of leaf outlines to be colored. In the afternoon another project was presented, which slowly grew into increasing disaster. First I showed sample copies of the art work to be done. Black strips of cut paper were to be arranged, then pasted, on to white sheets of paper; next, bits of colored paper were to be either torn, or cut, and pasted on to the trees; like leaves, with some falling to the ground. Strips of paper, arranged by color, were stacked on vacant desks to be used.

My downfall was caused by the paste. A neighboring teacher had loaned me a full jar. As there were six tables of youngsters, six at a table, I tore six pieces of paper and scooped paste with my fingers (no spoons) to supply each table. Although I told them to use but a tiny bit of paste on each strip, or leaf, in my heart I fully realized it takes much time and patience for children to accept, to understand, and learn this concept.

In minutes the paste landed on the strips, in fat globs, weighing the papers down, and I was surrounded with restless, noisy children out of their seats, their little fingers smearing everything in sight. Even the real artists grew restless; voices at each table grew louder. Paper, paste and crayons fell on the floor. Minute by minute more children lined up for paste, the supply growing smaller and smaller. For the first time in my life I found my eyes searching for the clock. I sensed trouble. I needed a record player, puppets, finger play books, all of which were at home.

A lady I had seen when I came in that morning walked around, looking at the unfinished work, the disarray, noting the restlessness. I sensed it was the principal and that she was not pleased. The class had been in delightful control all day until now, but this was when she came to visit. I could not move. I remained at the paste jar, frozen on my feet and dying a thousand deaths in humiliation. I could not help that situation, but I learned enough right then to prevent its ever happening again ever. A record player, liquid paste, scissors, fingerplays and thinking games were added to my supplies that evening, plus extra special emergency ideas to cover any grade level.

One child, with an escort, was permitted to go to the washroom and for the remaining time I was continually saying "no" to further requests. A teacher senses when the need is a true one.

At 2:15 the completed art work was collected, tables washed free of paste, all papers removed from the floor, board erased – mostly by the teacher, as the children appeared too immature to continue any job until completed. One, then several, would start to help, but soon ended playing and talking. Now, of course, the sitters of the afternoon were ready to start their art project, asking for colors and paste!

At 2:25 we lined up; by 2:30 there was a straight, quiet line. This was accomplished only by suggesting the talkers return to sit and talk AFTER SCHOOL. It was then I realized the girl who had repeatedly asked to go to the washroom really did have to do so. Other classes and teacher had left, and as we waited by the toilet entrance, I heard her ask for paper. I had hoped it would not be necessary. No paper towels were in the hand dispenser or in the individual boxes; no teacher washroom was nearby. I quickly returned to the classroom and brought her some writing paper saying it was all there was, and to hurry up.

At 2:30 I stood by the outer door, smiled as they passed me and wished them a pleasant evening. Thirty-one happy, smiling youngsters, left quietly, happily. One little girl pulled me down and kissed me – one of the hidden jewels of teaching, one that keeps calling us back.

Teacher, was I good today?
My mother wants to know.

Chapter 2

Same Class 3 Days

The call, at 8:00, was for a west side school, Lafayette. I signed in at 9:15 and was given a class of first graders to whom no reading had been presented. Lesson Plans left by the teacher indicated the day was to be filled with stories, finger plays, numbers. The plans were very informative about the times for toilet, luncheon trips, and recess, even specifying the times and numbered stairways to be used.

This was a very large, old school with anchored seats and meager, if any, supplies. I found some writing paper, none for math; a few pencils; no scissors, no paste.

Turning to the class I demonstrated how to hold a pencil, wrote some "1"s on the board and a few alert youngsters finished that assignment, plus another row of large and small "o's." After complimenting the achievers, the rest followed suit, everyone receiving stamped star papers.

Keeping them interested, and quiet, was much easier with the traditional seats which were fastened down, and after recess number concepts of one through four were reviewed and copied from the board. Lunch was early, at 11:30, and on our return another teacher entered to give them enrichment work of stories, singing, questions and poems. Her time seemed well planned and although I returned early she did not leave until her scheduled time.

Ditto sheets were given to the few children who had crayons and suggestions were given to outline the leaves, then color them. I hoped this would serve to bring in a few more individually-owned crayons the next day. The record player was set up in the back of the room. While I was selecting a record another teacher entered. She was testing them for speech enrollment classes, and took small groups outside into the hallway.

The record player played so softly that the class HAD to be quiet to hear anything. First, I demonstrated the actions for dancing the "Hokey-Pokey;" then they danced to the music; very quietly, because of the light music volume. Next I played the "Three Little Kittens" which we acted out. Six-year-olds really enjoy this.

On returning from afternoon recess, where I was "on duty" for the week, as one teacher told me, I noticed a new child, who had entered that day, was not present. Feeling a little smug about noting her absence, I quickly sent a note to the office, listing her name, and explaining that she was a new child. The fast results were surprising. In about 25 minutes two girls, about 12, came in with the missing child – plus another crying one. She, too, belonged with the room!

After recess I read poems to them, but they wanted to hear "Three Little Kittens" again, so the children took turns acting out the "mother" and "kitten" parts, as others sang the words.

At closing time chairs were put up quietly and as they left the building, smiles were everywhere. It had been a nice day for everyone.

As I signed out, a clerk in the office called out asking if I was to return. I was, and I was glad. Having read on the Lesson Plan Sheet that the teacher would be out the entire week, I asked the clerk if I could have the same room if I came early; she said this would be possible.

Everything was carried home again as even during the daytimes, I had been warned to leave the door locked at all times. Furthermore, most of the material I had brought was too advanced for children not yet ready for first grade work.

On the way home I stopped in a repair shop to have the record player amplifier repaired. My original machine had been taken years ago the only night I had forgotten to camouflage it. With this level of children I NEEDED a record player.

Once home I spent hours searching through a file cabinet filled with first grade material but I found all I needed. If the old ditto color and number book pages still worked on the office machine I would be in good shape, and with a Peabody Language Kit, several puppets, new ditto worksheets I had made up, plus a color chart, I was well fortified for the next day.

It was fun being back again with beginning first graders.

Before the class arrived the next day I made an Experience Chart about the school, and a duplicate, of which I cut off different sentence lines. In turn, each child was asked if he, or she, could match the sentence to another on the chart, as I read the words. Nearly all did it the first time; the others (with one exception) were successful the

7

second time. To me, this was a strong indication they were ready to start with stronger reading activities. Several similar cut-and-paste seatwork activity pages were distributed and most were completed correctly, a few upside down, but in the correct spaces.

One child came in a little late and promptly claimed the seat which had been given to a new child. As the first child's name was on the nameplate, which I had turned over and printed the new child's name, I checked in the attendance book. To my horror, this child was marked "Left" on Monday, but I remembered it had been before I had come in. Another teacher had taken attendance the first day. Apparently this child had transferred out Monday but returned Wednesday—without re-enrolling with her mother. This can cause endless confusion with attendance book figures, especially during the first school month in September. I informed the office and asked the girl to bring her mother in the next day; however, I had the distinct feeling this would require much persistence on the part of the teacher.

Later in the day the class completed the Fall tree pictures of cut pieces of paper that were quite attractive. As only one child had paste I found that tops of cottage cheese packages worked perfectly for distributing amounts of liquid glue which I had brought. First, I demonstrated how to use just a little glue here and there, not weighing the artwork down with the glue.

The room was blooming with bright colored art work and starred papers before the day was over. At closing time it was tidied quietly and quickly. And again all left with happy, smiling faces.

They had worked hard today, doing many varied types of work; qualities of leadership, dependability, and alertness were beginning to surface. The class had much greater potential than was at first apparent but a few days earlier.

On my third subbing day I again signed in at 8:30 at Lafayette School. It had taken about 15 minutes to make a left turn at one west side intersection, only two, one, or no cars moving at the fast light signal. I would not come this way another time. Another sub was signed in for my room, but it was given to me, thank goodness, as I'd prepared so much material for this particular level.

Two youngsters on the street had helped me carry materials into the school, and after leaving five ditto sheets to be run off with a clerk in the office, we took the other things to the room. While finding a suitable spot for the color chart I had brought, the greatest room problem was solved. A large, opened box of crayons, enough for a class of 30 pupils, was on a table by the window. I had brought a supply of scissors, and found another package of writing paper, so now the future looked bright with learning possibilities.

At recess I took the youngsters to the recess door and returned to collect the ditto work in the office. Here I found a long, handwritten note saying teachers were allowed 200 sheets of paper weekly – AND I HAD NOW USED MY SUPPLY FOR THE WEEK. Further, if I wanted more I would have to supply the paper myself. Although surprised, my first thought was that we now had a sufficient amount of work to last the week. I had planned to leave some for the next week so the teacher could continue the same routine if she so chose.

The note reminded me that when I started teaching I had bought my own paper to use and had a year's supply of word lists run off at a ditto company. I used to plan the semester's seat work of questions and run off the work during the first month of school as that was about the only time the ditto machine was dependable.

The lessons from the Peabody Kit were fun and educational as always. Not one child could name two of the ten animals – the donkey or the sheep. They did know most of the shapes, having learned them in kindergarten. The oval and diamond seemed new, or forgotten. The record player was sufficiently loud so all enjoyed "The Three Little Kittens" again – and again, acting it out. Work papers were starred and some good papers of seat work and coloring were put up to brighten the walls. A little time was left to introduce the puppets.

Noticing a box on the floor as I was leaving the building I commented, half to myself, half to another teacher, "I wonder what that child did with the coat he found on the playground. Well, at the time I did tell him to take it to Lost and Found."

"We don't have a Lost and Found Box," she answered. "It was stolen."

I had to laugh. Such a bare school. And yet stealing?

When I had signed in that morning, the clerk had asked me if I would return the following week. I explained that because I received Social Security payments I was allowed to work but limited days monthly, of which the next day would be the last. I sensed she was a little miffed about this, which proved to be true. As I signed out for the day there was no cheery comment or friendly smile, and nothing was said about my returning the next day.

Chapter 3

41 in Class
Scott Foresman Books

It had been difficult to find Belding School because the Expressway cut through a number of streets so the 8:30 bell rang as I parked the car, and on entering the Principal and teachers were already at the weekly Wednesday meeting. The clerk said I would have to wait to be assigned by the Principal.

Two upper grade boys monitoring the corridor entrance directed me to the third floor to see the paintings and gifts donated by graduating classes; these boys conveyed great pride in their school.

After the meeting I was assigned to a first grade class. Because of the many fine brick homes in the neighborhood I expected a class of high grade students but was surprised to see the usual variety of nationalities when I entered the room, and from past experience I realized it was a very low first grade group.

Three of the 41 students listed were absent. This was the largest class I had seen in years.

As it was already after 9:00 art work was given to the children so I could put seatwork on the blackboards.

It was surprising and pleasing to see Scott Foresman reading books being used as I had not seen them since I had taught primary grades many years before. Another surprise, also reminiscent of my first teaching years, was to see five students from other grades being brought in as there was no teacher for them. Daily, in former years classes without teachers had been lined up and divided into other classes. This I had not known to happen in 15 years. However, later I noticed a "Disbursement Sheet" on the teacher's desk, listing the students in groups of threes, so sharing classes without teachers must have been a common procedure here.

By recess time when I sat down I noticed the teacher had left several sets of dittos to be done by the class. In addition she had written much blackboard seatwork, all of which had taken much time to prepare, but it's easier to grade one's own assignments so I used very little of hers.

The class was an extremely low, but lovable one, and they tried to complete the work. All read slowly, many in preprimers, but they did try, and much of the board work was copied.

The day flew by as it always does with slow groups. They did really fine art work, which was left with their graded papers for the teacher.

On her desk was a plaque reading, "If you see someone without a smile, give him one of yours." This, plus the great seatwork she had left for a substitute, proved she was a kind, considerate individual.

The Principal, too, was kind and thoughtful, but on leaving I felt I had stepped back 20 years. Other schools might be facing this situation in the future, but to date they had not been confronted with it as all classes had had teachers.

If one math and one writing paper are done
pupils may have a turn feeding the baby alligator.

Chapter 4

Spanish Class
Starved to Read

At Stockton I was assigned to a Bilingual Class of 2nd and 3rd graders and told there would be a teacher aide there during the morning. The aide, however, unlocked the door for me – and left. I only wished I had known she was not returning.

The three front boards held assignments, the center one in Spanish, the first in English words and sentences. I erased the English section and printed six assignments there, plus crowding very easy work on the board by the door as the teacher aide had said the children sitting in the two rows by the door were the low achievers.

I wished I had not seen the aide at all as she was wrong and most of the students had to change seats. Further, no one used the Spanish work and I needed that space. Evidently the usual procedure was to have but two assignments on the board to be done – one in English (a simple "morning story" about the day's weather) and one in Spanish, which appeared to be fill-in sentences with words listed to be selected.

The children had entered quietly, with smiles. It was surprising to see their eyes light up with delight in seeing the many board assignments – instead of hearing the usual groans of dismay. These pupils *wanted* the work!

Not one of the 30 was absent; this too was unusual. The room was in the old school, being dark and dismal, with fastened-down, traditional seats and desks, but these children lightened up the atmosphere with their happy, receptive attitudes.

The board work was read, explained, and the top reading group called to read.

My heart fell. These "third graders" of 9 and 10 years of age, were starting to read the 1B Holt Company hard cover book, "A Place for Me," a first grade book; they were two and three years behind in their English education – and they had a teacher aide mornings! This saddened me. Six were in the group and they read like first graders. Later, when the board seatwork was graded one boy had written the

13

answers in sentences – indicating (to me) he had unused ability. A few wrote words for answers; some merely copied the questions.

The second group of three children were at Level 4, reading the fourth book of the six pre-primers, "Can You Imagine", which are to be read before starting the first grade hard cover book. They were eager, bright-eyed youngsters, so I had them finish half of the booklet, and their ditto pages, done previously, were checked and graded.

In the next group, reading in "Rhymes & Tales", Level 3, the first preprimer, only five children came to read. They explained the other eight students did not read. However, I had all of them come up and share books. Turns were taken, then each page read in unison. This group was very enthusiastic and asked several times if they could read again after lunch, which they did.

A few of the eight knew some of the words, which did not surprise me; they could have assimilated them in the classroom, or at home in books from brothers or sisters. What deeply impressed me was they so wanted to learn to read; they seemed starved and I wanted to help them. It had been my experience to find Spanish students learn to read quickly by sounding out letters and by syllabication – learning the meaning of the words was a slower process as I could not explain in Spanish.

It was a few weeks before Easter so samples of art work were shown and discussed before distribution. The majority had their own crayons and most did very good art work papers.

The teacher aide came in to say all were to have books on their desks for a 20 minute period around 2:00 so this was done but most had already completed the seatwork and art work before this time and all papers were stamped and returned.

Students were lined up and ready to go when the bell rang. About five had several boxes of candy to carry home from the annual school selling contests; two had won tennis rackets as awards.

It had been a very fulfilling day to work with this class. They were so quiet, so happy, so friendly to me and to each other.

Chapter 5

Halloween House
Spanish Class

At 8:20 the phone rang. Gathe School. I checked the school directory book. No Gathe listed; I called back. It was Goethe School, pronounced "Gathe". In 15 minutes I was on my way.

At 9:00 I checked in on the school record book. One other sub had signed in. The atmosphere in the office was friendly, calm and quiet. This time it was to be 2nd Grade, and I saw the children entering ahead of me as I approached the room.

In the room of the very old building the walls were already covered with art work papers; this was a working teacher. The 31 youngsters sat looking at me and smiled back happily when I introduced myself. But the blackboard words were all in Spanish. I looked at the class again and saw the youngsters were all Spanish.

After taking the roll, with only two absent, which again impressed me, I learned they had a large math workbook, and different Spanish pre-reading books – and I didn't speak Spanish. A Teacher Aide came in and took the class while I answered a call from their regular teacher. She explained they were learning two languages, that they had Spanish reading, and were now starting to learn the English soft vowel sounds. She was relieved when I told her I had taught first grade for ten years and would leave her a soft vowel-consonant chart with which I had always gained very good results with Spanish children.

The blends were put on the board, plus other 1st grade completion sentences which were read orally first. Most of the children did good, neat printing. After recess we had catchy oral math games and questions which they enjoyed, plus board work using owls and witches.

During lunch the little sharpies noticed I had two cartons of milk. Teachers pay for their lunches but the majority of children have free ones. They asked if they could get another carton. I answered they could try. I didn't look around but they returned with the milk. In a previous school such requests had been refused.

15

This had surprised me as where I had been employed extra milk was always offered to the free-lunchers – which the majority refused. I reasoned the refusal had been caused by the unusually large size of the school.

During morning and afternoon recess periods I visited the teachers' room and noted the friendliness of the teachers. Even in the hall different ones said "Hello" and smiled to me. Two or three times teachers stopped in the room, asking if there was anything they could do for me, which left a wonderful feeling. The last one informed me she was a teacher who roamed about the different rooms. I inquired if she could have two ditto masters run off for us, and this was done right away. She had first asked if the teacher had any white paper, but I had not seen any. White ditto paper is at a real premium in the schools. But even years ago when teaching I had all my word lists done at a ditto company and paid for this myself each year.

When talking for a second time to a friendly, very kind person in the hall as I waited for the children, I was surprised to learn she was the principal. This explained the friendliness of the entire school. A school always reflects the principal. Here the teachers came to the classes on time; left the teachers' room when the bell rang, children's work was seen on walls of each room, and classes entered and left the building quietly. This showed the principal was interested in people. She looked like a happy, likeable, well-adjusted individual.

Later in the afternoon we read and wrote Halloween words and then made a Haunted House. The teacher had told me on the telephone that I could use some orange paper. We cut windows and doors on the orange paper, stapled it to a dark green paper, then pasted ghosts, goblins, witches and skeletons inside the windows, writing warnings on the outside. This is always fun and provides learning values as well. Fortunately the TESL (Teaching English as a Second Language) Teacher, who was to start a project that afternoon, was able to help. She wrote the same words, and warnings, in Spanish for the children so they could choose which language to use.

The day flew by, and I was surprised to see the smiles returned to me as they walked to the outer school door at closing with questions as to whether I would be back the next day. I guess they, too, had enjoyed the day. Another beautiful memory. It's really wonderful to be a teacher.

But once I returned home I realized how tired I was and had to lie down to rest for over an hour. This had not happened before when substituting. These 2nd graders were forever whispering, and I was continually trying to quiet them; that must have done it. But it was the fun we had, the happy faces, and the good work, that I remembered. It had been a good day. I was glad they had a good teacher. The principal had told me she had never been absent the previous year and that her pupils didn't stay absent either.

Grandpa Frog accidently fell down on
stage but that was a hit with the audience.

Chapter 6

No Walking Reading
Open Court Books

R-r-r-r-ing! screamed the telephone three times before I reached the dinette. I looked at the clock. 7:25.

"Mozart School", District 3".

I thanked him and looked outside. Wet, raining, cold. Window thermometer registered 35 degrees. Perfect day to stay home in bed. Why did they always have to send me 3500 west? Plenty of schools around here by the lake. Oh, well. This time I'd take Fullerton instead of Diversey.

Fullerton seemed very slow but at least I didn't get lost. I signed in at 8:45. On the way my intuition kept haunting me about seventh grade. Each time I promptly answered quickly, "Oh no. I'm a primary teacher".

The school clerk commented they had three openings, two in 7th grade. I told her I was a primary teacher. She said to wait for the principal who came in shortly. He let me have a primary opening, a third-grade classroom.

The stairs seemed very high as I trudged up with two heavy satchels plus my portable record player. It was an old building. The room was very large, with moveable desks, which were arranged in comfortable groupings that offered a friendly atmosphere. Plenty of blackboard space to use; a small amount of orange paper; no black, and a school record player locked in the teacher's coat room; one small package of writing paper. I had asked about having dittos run off while in the office but received no encouragement. Was told the teacher aides who did that were on tight schedules, dittos usually being ordered a day in advance.

The class entered at 9:00. I could see right away any teacher would like such a class. Alive; interested; good potential. Talkers, but with ability of self control when admonished. The group seating would encourage talking. It was a self-contained room, which pleased me. No walking reading; no coming and going of students. And the reading book was one of the best, my favorite publisher,

Open Court. But the class was in the middle of a 2B book, already one year behind. Why? A few Spanish pupils, but mostly white.

The entire class was reading the same story, and they remained at their seats, they informed me, so they read silently looking for answers to questions, then orally by groups. Although they informed me they read but two pages daily, we completed the five pages, reading and answering orally all of the book questions. As the story concerned spiders, and insects, I suggested they write a Halloween story including some kind of an insect, and because I offered an award of two chocolate candies for the best stories, papers were received from nearly everyone.

I realized they were alert, and had ability, as while I took the roll I had offered a written contest of having them write as many words as they could in ten minutes that started with "br". Within five minutes three youngsters had called "twenty" and soon others did as well. Some had copied lists from books which I observed but as no rules had been specified I accepted these also. I had silently admired their ingenuity but later commented it was really not a learning process when copied this way. They knew what compound words were so I used a fun ditto picture work page that I was tired of carrying and not using. It had pictures of two objects, like a pie and then a pan, the answer being piepan. Most of them got 100 on this paper.

The principal had informed me in the morning that I would be on recess duty if they went outside so I had no time then to run off any more work sheets. Once we were outside at recess the children informed me we should have waited for their playleaders who came to the room for them. This sounded like a good idea to me, indicating it was a well-ordered school, one that cared about its students. We had arrived five minutes early so I let them go to the swings, although they told me it "was not their day". The 7th grade playleaders came shortly, one without a coat, and were glad to find their charges. They looked like frustrated mother hens when they first came out the school door but were soon laughing and happy. Not many classes came out so the youngsters were able to remain using the swings. Had the principal not told me I'd be on recess duty we probably would have stayed inside also – if the class had so voted.

It was at lunch time that I had my big surprise. I had learned from the class that they stayed in school until 3:15 so I knew they went home for lunch if they chose to do so. About one-third received free lunches; one third brought theirs, and the others went home. As I walked with them downstairs I found out there was NO LUNCH offered for the teachers, and we were already ten minutes late leaving.

I hurried back upstairs, took my coat, and walked two blocks to a restaurant. Many fine memories were recalled of the good old days when we had 45 minutes at lunch time. I used to drive home, or to the golf course to get an afternoon ticket to play, or stop someplace for lunch. But for the past several years most of the schools had changed to "closed campus" meaning the teachers remained with their classes at lunch times, and the school closed at 2:30 instead of 3:15. Both schedules offered advantages. The noon time was a fine time for many things, working in the room, etc., but the extra time after 2:30 offered a good many advantages as well.

The lunch I had was very tasty, but, with the tip, cost much more than school lunches. I was back by 1:45; the class returned soon afterwards.

A teacher across the hall came in and said we had arithmetic for 45 minutes; that she took the advanced ones. She took one or two from the room and a few others entered. I opened my folder and selected three sheets of oral questions and blackboard numbers, plus fun questions, and tricky listening problems. It is always fine for children to hear math from different viewpoints. After catching on, they learned the new concepts very quickly and everyone had fun. We covered all three pages in the workbook, concentrating on the importance of the decimal. They could tell me the number of tens, hundreds and ones in columns of large numbers I put on the board, which surprised and pleased me, but I found their weakness after that. Not one pupil was able to write any dictated dollar amounts. I think we started with "Five thousand dollars and fifty cents". I noticed that although I suggested they write the amounts in a column, with the decimals in a vertical row, not one did so. Each time I ended with writing the amount correctly so they could do the same. Within ten minutes they were able to write most of the oral amounts given, so everyone was pleased. It gives children great strength to master new concepts, to see their own progress. It is not unusual to see personalities completely change after a number of such experiences.

20

During the last hour we made haunted houses, cutting windows on the front of orange paper, stapling it to darker sheets, and placing scary Halloween objects in the windows. This they enjoyed. Half of the class needed glue and scissors, which I supplied. Each one wrote his or her name on a list to receive scissors, and each was returned by 3:00. At 3:10 we left; two offered to carry my heavy bags which surprised me. The art work was left for the teacher to see and use if she so chose.

The school was especially orderly. No fighting; no policemen waiting outside. Many homes were around the school; it was a quiet, residential neighborhood. Reminded me of a small town.

Afternoon oral reading is a favorite time.

21

Chapter 7

Taxes for Pilgrims?

Although the call came from Sub Center at 7:30, the caller hung up so fast after naming the school (Blaine) that I felt it was one far distant and unwanted. It was most surprising to find it was close to home. Visiting the different schools is very interesting.

This was a large, three-story, old building. Although a Patrol Boy nearby pointed where I could drive into the teachers' parking lot, it was filled, so I drove around to the front of the block near the entrance. In the back I had seen a number of demountables, one-story wood buildings, housing several classrooms, plus a number of mobiles, which are one-room units. The school was really over-flowing.

Five substitutes had listed their names to fill vacancies. Later I learned there were 55 teachers employed in the school. The interior atmosphere seemed to be one of learning activity. There were quiet, working classrooms; corridor bulletin boards had pupils' work displayed, and large reprints of top artists' paintings were under glass covered frames. The first and second floors had teachers' rooms in which book racks contained many fine, helpful books and magazines for the teachers' use. I noted the current magazines were already in circulation. The teachers appeared "working" ones – concerned about their work, interesting, congenial and happy. Pupils were a broad mixture of nationalities, Spanish, Korean, Orientals, white. Surprisingly, there seemed to be no black pupils.

During lunch the Assistant Principal told me the enrollment was 1168 students, down 125 from the previous year. The school had Open Campus, meaning lunch was from noon until 1:00, children either going home or eating in school; closing time being 3:15. When I commented the school had an "interested" atmosphere, and said the Principal must be absent, but enjoying his work, he affirmed this, adding some people felt he was "too interested." He added there were many programs offered, especially in tutoring.

My job for the day was to be a "walking librarian", meaning I was to go from room to room. A filmstrip machine and two filmstrips were provided. One was about Thanksgiving but needed a record as no words were provided, but the other, a Grecian Myth, "Daelalus and Ocarus," was of high enough interest to hold the attention of all the pupils from 4th to 8th grades.

The first class, one of 8th graders, was noisy and so I had a volunteer operate the machine, and turns were taken for the reading, while I moved about near the noise centers until it became quiet. After the first filmstrip we tried the next one. The noisiest girl offered to explain the pictures, and did an excellent job. No one else seemed able, or willing, to help, but she seemed to enjoy this. Afterward, questions regarding the meaning of Thanksgiving were presented, and it surprised me to find that only one boy knew the true, underlying reason for the Thanksgiving Holiday, which was very soon. I was used to this in the primary grades.

The next class, of 6th graders, was somewhat noisy too, but alert and seemed to be smart students. Five or six took turns reading the filmstrip, which they enjoyed doing. They also told the stories of the pictures in the second strip.

The third graders, next, in the newer annex building, were very smart, alert and good readers. Many offered to read.

The fourth graders were alert but only two boys volunteered to read, plus ten or more girls. The boys were mostly Spanish; others were English, Korean and Orientals. They were good at making up stories for the second strip. The behavior was also good except for one girl, who refused to apologize for continually making unnecessary noise, and later made herself sick and went to the washroom to regurgitate. Because she couldn't apologize I apologized to her, explaining that I long ago learned life was much easier for me that way. I hoped she could see the importance of this but felt she was much over-protected and this was an advance concept for her.

Later, when I found her still in the hall, I learned she had told the Assistant Principal about the experience, misrepresenting the facts. Again I shook hands with her. Later the Assistant Principal commented he did not want the mother to come in, which reinforced my feelings the student was over-protected. She would have to learn from experience later on in life; she was not ready now.

The next room of 7th graders was one of several noisy students but the interesting strip did capture their attention half way through. Again, only two boys volunteered to read, but many girls enjoyed doing so. Their teacher was a tiny Oriental one, and they became unbelievably quiet when she re-entered. Her voice was soft and she smiled and was most attractive. She must have been a truly good teacher to so command their respect.

As the boys in this class had not been good readers I had told them I could help them with reading and put the basic blends on the board, suggesting they go to the dime store and buy alphabet books to learn the sounds of the letters, then make up such blends as I wrote. I assured them they could learn to read; that reading was based on the sounds of the letters, plus a few skills that I had pointed out in the filmstrip. It was obvious they really wanted to learn; they were already old enough to know their handicap. Sadly enough, I have not known any teachers above third grade who know how to present basic beginning reading to non-readers. Primary teachers, of course, know these skills, but years ago elementary teachers were not expected to encounter this need and beginning reading skills were not included in their preparatory college curriculums. I surely hope that this situation has changed. Fortunately, the majority of schools now offer special reading classes to handicapped readers to improve this situation. The problem is difficult in that upper-grade students, usually boys, who need the beginning reading classes, hesitate to avail themselves of this opportunity as they feel they are admitting to their peers that they cannot read; this is a great problem to their personal self esteem.

During my last year of teaching special reading classes there was one group of six sixth grade boys with unbelievable severe behavior problems. All were reading at 1st or 2nd grade levels. They had been hand-picked by the Principal, so were forced to attend. However, once they realized I would give them a fair deal they settled down fast. I promised to have them reading at three or four levels higher in three months – IF they settled down. It was up to them. They made up behavior rules, and kept a record of who kept, who broke them. Star cards were awarded accordingly. It was the stars, not the reading that won them over. Behavior changed overnight; reading improved fast; they soon became fine, acceptable students. It can be done, and quickly. Older, mature students can grasp and apply basic reading skills much faster than primary children who require continual repetition.

The last class of third graders was one of alert children. Their Oriental teacher put three boys in different corners of the room, but they minded me and became perfectly quiet. However, the machine did not work so I told them the interesting story on the filmstrip and then presented a book on how animals sleep which was very interesting. This class knew more about Thanksgiving than any of the other classes; they were really informed.

Many adults don't feel children understand modern problems. They think youngsters of today are unaware of the economic situation. When I had asked the 4th grade class why the Pilgrims left England one girl quickly replied, "Because the taxes were too high". And to prove the Spanish are family oriented – The reason for the Thanksgiving Holiday is "to stay home and eat turkey with their families".

Circle of First Graders here

25

Chapter 8

Dream Classes
Good Puppeteers

The 7:25 call was for Perkins school, 6918 W. Strong Street. Feeling they would have their supplies I removed the box of 28 heavy scissors and the six boxes of crayons, leaving only four scissors – and four pupils needed them!

I took the expressway west on Hollywood Avenue, but that was a mistake. West-bound had but one open lane; Irving would have been preferable. However, I managed to walk inside the school at 9:02. The neighborhood consisted of brick one-story homes, and the school looked very modern, also one story.

The class was a primary one, there being twenty pupils in grades one, two and three. The room was beautifully arranged, light and airy. There were ten first graders; four at second grade level, and six in third. One pupil in third grade, surpassed all others in maturity. She took charge of various matters, like collecting and putting materials away, distributing supplies, sharpening pencils, washing the board.

The first graders seemed to be bursting with the joy of living and being in school, their eyes beaming with anticipation and eagerness to get started. The second graders waited quietly for instructions. The third graders silently followed through on assignments on the board. There was not one discipline problem.

Usually the pupils used math workbooks but I wrote work on the board which covered the three levels. This surprised, and slowed the work to be done, but eventually all were finished, and given stars, some with corrections.

Completion sentences and stories were also a new experience to them; stacks of graded ditto work was on a shelf, in individual folders but after some of the work was discussed most youngsters were able to follow through and complete the assignments.

In this school the children had an hour off from 12:00 to 1:00 for lunch so at noon I escorted them to the proper exit or lunchroom line, then returned to go to the lunchroom. It was then I learned that lunches were not prepared in the school for teachers. Fortunately, there were 45 minutes left of the noon period. I quickly got in my car and found a very nice restaurant a few blocks distant where the waitress obliged me by bringing my lunch quickly, so I had time to eat and be back at school before 1:00. Never again did I leave my apartment without a bag lunch, even though at times I ate the school lunch where I was sent. It was then I remembered once hearing a substitute comment she had been fooled so many times that she started taking her own lunch.

Later in the afternoon making Thanksgiving turkey artwork did not impress them, but once I brought out two hand puppets, interest became alive, and I found there were several pupils who were good puppeteers. The girl who was such a big help in general was especially talented in this area. Children always enjoy puppets, but seldom is any child a natural puppeteer. It usually requires much time to develop oral stories and actions to assure success with the puppets. At times a very quiet youngster will become active and interesting when working with puppets, forgetting the usual shyness.

I had put the shades up to let the sunshine in, but after the closing bell rang one child commented that the teacher always put them down at closing so people would not break in. I was surprised this precaution was necessary in this fine location but grateful to be warned in time.

After the class left I talked to the janitor for a few minutes. He said the school had one principal; three teachers; one head teacher; one librarian; ninety pupils. There had been 200 children when he started a few years earlier but now young people could not afford to move here so there were not as many children as formerly.

On the way home I stopped to call Sub-Center, signing up for the next day.

"You're two minutes late," said a crisp voice.

"It cost me 20 cents to call you."

"Just a minute." She let me hold the phone 3 or 4 minutes; then hung up.

Actions DO speak louder than words. Never again did I call in late.

Helping open the mail

I can't get the apple.

Quiet as Indians.

Fun at the Halloween party.

Students making papiemache fish.

Chapter 9

Noisy Free Time
Actress at 5

At Burley School I was assigned to a Kindergarten Class. My heart was both apprehensive and delighted as years ago when doing practice teaching in Kindergarten the experience was not impressive as the regular teacher didn't give me a chance to try things with them by myself. But this time it proved to be fun all day long.

As I entered the room a friend of mine was taking the class. She was teaching them a poem, one of my favorites, "First Snow". Nearby I saw a good record player which helped as I carried good action records. The teacher had left a good supply of ditto work to be done, plus time instructions and suggestions. The class was so lively, so active, so restless.

As they had sat nicely for ten minutes while I got organized and put my wraps away I started with body exercises. A snake, or fishworm – moving of hands is always a favorite, and they enjoyed it tremendously. Next, we did a color paper using the color BLACK which was the color for the day. As they had done a turkey picture the previous day they chose to color an Indian picture next. I did one also, showing them how to color the feathers different colors. (Several chose to make the feathers, head and face all one color though!) After three seatwork papers were completed (or at least started!), there were repeated requests to play with "the toys" so finally I agreed. The day was quite cold and we had been told over the intercom that there would be indoor recess.

The youngsters knew where the toys were, and all 28 of them made a big, noisy, sudden dive and scramble for them, fighting, pushing, yelling. Sometimes I called out a little, but the noise, and fun continued, and I went over to the greatest point of density in case I was suddenly needed. It really was wonderful to see all that activity and differences in individuals. One girl kept changing activity constantly, taking toys from first one and then another child. I finally did ask her to settle for some one toy for a little while.

The boys pushed others in wheelbarrows, drew them in wagons, or sat about on the floor joining plastic pieces into high buildings, or long ones on the floor. Everyone was occupied. There were dolls and dishes and tables, and noise, noise, NOISE.

The door opened and in came the Principal. I couldn't stop laughing and realized the noise was far too much in full bloom to stop quickly. His eyes had a painful look so after he told me the lunch and leaving times and left, I stopped the playtime and there was pin-drop quietness after the toys were neatly put away. It had been a beautiful few minutes that I always treasure in memory, even if the Principal didn't share in it. Next time I, too, would probably handle "playtime" differently. But this was a special memory. Everyone but the Principal had a wonderful time.

Fortunately, I had the class get their wraps ahead of time for leaving. I had forgotten how much help they needed. Nearly each one had to be zipped, scarf-tied, and mittens searched for. With first graders years ago I had told them to find a maid for help, which they had either done, or dressed themselves. But these youngsters, I realized, really were babies, needing individual help. But we made it on time, and quietly went down the steps "like Indians" as one never hears them. They were so loveable I didn't want them to leave.

There was a 20-minute break for a fast lunch until the afternoon class arrived, and I was back to greet them by the same outside door. This was an entirely different group. I realized at once this was the older group and was amazed at the difference a few months could make. This was a quiet, mature class. There was not the constant restlessness, movement and noisy talking. In fact, many of these produced work papers done as well as first graders.

After the work papers were starred we acted out the record, "Three Little Kittens", which they really enjoyed, everyone having a turn to be a kitten; they sang with the record naming the days and months of the year. I felt one youngster there could grow to be a great actress, as she was already one. I first noticed her taking care of a tiny boy, whom she explained did not speak English. He was sitting alone at a long table when I saw her go sit by him, taking him crayons and work papers. She took him cookies as well when they were served.

Later she came to me sorrowfully, pleading she "could not" do the work paper with the symbol "3" written on it five times. Her face was completely sincere, but I did not believe her; I felt she was pretending, even as I bent over and wrote the letter on the line instead of having it look like a bird. She assured me she simply could not do it, but I said anyone as grown up as she was, who could take such good care of another child, could certainly produce a good work paper. Some time later she was again before me, her eyes smiling, and she actually looked like a third child, a completely different expression now. Her paper was done very well this time. This child I would like to know better.

Suddenly I noted it was 2:10. Many of my school items were in various places in the room to be collected and packed, so I took out two hand puppets and asked who had puppets at home. Several had, so they took turns being puppeteers for ten minutes over a desk I had turned into a doll bed. Only one youngster had a voice loud enough to be really good as a puppeteer, but the class thoroughly enjoyed this activity and many had turns.

At 2:20 I told them to quickly, quietly get their wraps and take their folded, starred papers home. They lined up and softly walked down the steps at 2:25. I knew there was not enough time, but somehow everything fell into place. As we waited for the bell a mother told me the Kindergarten children left at 2:25 so they did, everyone wishing everyone else a happy Thanksgiving. It had been a beautiful day. Before this I had dreaded being sent to a Kindergarten room. Now I would look forward to it.

However when I arrived home I found my legs hurt so much I could hardly stand on them. I remembered I had stood up all day! Not one time had I sat, even to star papers. It was a full six hours before I felt normal again.

Chapter 10

Crawler; Jury Trial
Teacher, I Promise

At 9:00 I signed in at Swift School for a first grade class. The children were in the room, a student teacher with them. The teacher had left instructions in detail. "Not to write in the attendance book, but to list the names of absentees on her note slip; NO READING (which really surprised and puzzled me); papers were NOT to be collected but left in the pupil desks" (another puzzle as nothing was said about grading them). To me, seatwork is meaningless if not graded and returned promptly. Instructions for the day regarding time allocations were listed beautifully.

A poem was written on the board, read by the children, who seemed able to read quite well, and after looking at the seatwork papers on the bulletin board, I wrote some thinking math problems to be done. It was obvious that very few intended to complete any work, but just to sit and be noisy, so as soon as one paper was done correctly I took out my pad and star and stamped three stars on it. A few others then started to copy the work but it took much prodding, suggestions and warnings to start others. The puppets helped the most, a rubber frog and an alligator, both having large mouths.

A boy, whose chair was in the back row, was spending his time crawling on the floor from side to side under tables in the back. I had noticed his nameplate was missing from the desk-top so took a sheet of paper with me as I motioned him to his desk and walked back that way. The workpaper he showed me looked like animal tracks; I felt he was unable to print the words, so wrote his name on a paper and asked him to copy the first and last names if he could. As I stood there a moment he started to write from the bottom right side of the page, going backwards, from right to left, and upwards, instead of across on the lines. My heart went out to this child as I had seen this writing manner in so-called "retarded" children several times, as well as the crawling movement on the floor.

When I showed him the proper way to proceed he completed the sheet with good printing, which surprised me. Later, I again noticed he was unable to copy simple arithmetic work from the board; this also sometimes seems a great hurdle for retarded youngsters. I copied the work, asking him to write the answers. This he was unable to do as he could not tell me the answer to two plus two, nor could he write the numbers. I then wrote them (1 to 6). Later when I checked the paper he had filled the page with "1"s. Again I showed him he was to write the numerals and he managed all but the "5", which again, often seems a great problem to retarded children. The joy of his two star papers was reflected in his shining eyes the rest of the day.

There was inside recess because of the continual snowing which had piled up about a foot. Returning from the washroom there had been a fistfight so we had a prompt jury trial, the teacher being the judge to save time. First, two witnesses described the events, then the two boys. It seemed one had stomped spilled milk on the other, who then hit the first child in the eye. In turn, each agreed to apologize, which was done, and then they shook hands. Case was closed; everyone was satisfied. There had been no black eye, or severe fight, but the behavior did require discussion and erasing from memory.

We had two groups for reading who read from one book, "Rudy the Red Nosed Reindeer", and another from "The Little Engine that Could". I held the books in front of me, facing them, following their oral reading upside down myself. The group was constantly noisy, moving about, but quite good in reading, and for this I could somewhat overlook the noise. By lunchtime most youngsters had earned six stars on their papers.

I had called in the morning and learned there was no lunch provided for teachers so had taken one. Some pupils had "bag lunches" provided (a sandwich, banana and milk carton); one third went home for lunch; others brought their own. All children with lunches went to the auditorium to eat, our class sitting in the back. I sat with them. It was a little noisy, but about six teachers walked up and down the aisles keeping order as the large room was filled.

After eating I returned to the room; the children played outside for another half hour. I put a Christmas poem on the board and some easy arithmetic computation. When they returned we read from the storybooks again; I starred papers for nearly everyone, and art ditto papers were given to pupils who had completed their work. These contained two angels to color and decorate, a bell and a stocking.

Later in the day I read three Christmas stories, "The Night Before Christmas", which always brings primary children to absolute stillness; "The Little Lost Angel", which they remained quiet for and seemed to enjoy and understand; and "The Little Engine that Could". Next we sang Christmas Carols and used Christmas cards were given to youngsters who had tidy desks and floor areas; this worked like magic as all papers disappeared at once. All were smiling as they left.

The face and words of one little sharpie remained with me for weeks. He had been a continual source of aggravation all day and I told him he would have to remain after school. Later, as the class was getting their wraps this handsome little fellow came to me with the words, "Teacher, when you come to this school again I will be good all day." I smiled. The reason for this bright tinsel promise did not surface until hours later when all were safely home and some of the events of the day reappeared. I recalled the tall fort he had built with chairs in the back of the room during the afternoon when others were completing assignments. (I had learned he had no father to whom I could report his misbehavior.) And it had been there, in self isolation he had prepared his verbal deliverance from the after-school penalty, which I had forgotten.

One little girl, an Indian child, had enrolled at noon, transferring from another state. Her mother had said she would return for her but she had not arrived so I told the child to wait outside for her friend who had come to talk to her at lunch. After I signed out and was leaving by another door the mother was outside the door waiting, and with the other "friend". We all went to the other door exit, and there was the child – standing, crying alone. By the time we reached the street corner the tears were gone. I told the mother what a good reader she was, and that the other door was the one the class left by at 3:15.

It had been a good day – a full day.

Chapter 11

Problems Here

When the telephone rang at 7:45 I was pleased to learn the assignment was for Audubon School as I thought that was one of the choice schools. What a surprise was in store for me!

Signing in I noticed three other substitutes had arrived ahead of me. I mentioned to the clerk I was a teacher for primary classes and would appreciate the lowest grade she had available, whereupon she told me to take the Library Assignment, where I would have all the primary grades.

But shortly the principal told me to take a fifth grade room as that was more important. I carried my things to the room, where another teacher was busy yelling at the pupils there. She continued talking very loud for another 25 minutes to two children who were to handle the lunch money and tickets. It was easy to see this was a room filled with problems. The students were very restless and noisy so while I took the roll I challenged them with a quick assignment – to write as many words as possible that started with the letter "o," but the class was sharp, and used dictionaries, compiling 25 words before I finished, so I suggested they list words starting with "br" from their own thinking.

I saw the teacher's desk was piled with ditto work to be done but I felt a dictating letter experience would be worthwhile and interesting so I dictated while they wrote as "secretaries". This was graded orally and corrected by the writers. To me there is great learning value in this as such papers reveal their progress in thinking, grammar, writing and spelling.

There was constant turmoil, talking, moving about, with little accomplished before the 10:15 recess. Fortunately, the office did run off three ditto pages for me, so I explained an interesting one which used ten different meanings of ten words which were to be put in their proper sentences on the page. Three pupils did very well with this work, which involved real thinking; several had many errors, and only one completed the English work of correcting a paragraph. One girl had a perfect paper except for the apostrophes. Many just sat, causing continual disturbance.

At 11:30 I had corrected the papers, distributed another more difficult one, for which dictionaries could be used, and as their English seemed so poor, I decided to use the Milton Bradley Bingo Game which is popular with children. It reviews and aids in learning the abbreviations and contractions. The cards were passed around and they enjoyed this activity. But constant disturbances continued among the girls as well as boys. The gym teacher took two girls and one boy which helped tremendously.

After the lunch period I realized many had not returned so carefully took roll and a note was sent to the office, whereupon the Assistant Principal returned with four students who had been in the building someplace.

They did enjoy a page of thinking, oral questions I had made and after the board work was finished we started the Bingo Game for which they remained somewhat quiet. In fact, if the boys made noise their side lost a winning point; girls likewise.

At closing the class again became unruly so at 3:10 I sent two pupils to ask the gym teacher, next door, to come in but he was not there. By the time they returned the class was really wild. Several tried to rush out the adjoining closet hallway but I walked through the classroom and stood at the entrance to both doors. Four other girls were out there from a 7th grade room. One caused quite an uproar asking why I had hit her sister. I had hit no one but in this profession such an accusation is serious so I had to take time out for long discussions, which accomplished nothing.

After going down one flight of stairs most of the class quickly turned and darted out another door leaving the building. Two 7th grade girls took the others down to the proper exit.

I returned and collected my things. This was the first such experience I had had while doing substitute work. It did surprise me as I was known to be a strong disciplinarian. I felt certain this was a room that enjoyed taking advantage of any substitute. In fact, several of the girls in the room had admitted that many in the room caused continual disturbances even when their regular teacher was there.

As I signed out I told the Clerk it was the only time I had ever had trouble. The Principal had left but I saw the Assistant Principal talking to someone and I said I wanted to talk to him. I wanted to explain about the child who said I had hit her. The Clerk told me not to bother him with it; that he was very busy, but I waited anyway. After about 15 minutes, when the Clerk was leaving she informed me they were well acquainted with the girl, and her sister, and knew their word was unreliable, that no one believed much of anything they said, even their mother. This was a great relief to me. She added that she knew this was a problem room and that she had tried to give me the library assignment. She added the Principal had had to help in the 8th grade room that day, and said that all rooms were difficult in this school.

As we left the school together a car slowed up near us, with a child from the room I had been in. Her father was driving and wanted to talk to me. The girl was crying and I remembered her as one of the chief agitators throughout the day, talking, belligerent, spiteful. She told her father I had choked her. I said I didn't but saw he was not impressed. I told him she had tried to leave, with her coat on from the cloakroom, at 3:00 and I had stopped her by holding her wrist and insisting she remain. Her father turned to her angrily about this; she just as quickly offered many explanations in Spanish. They seemed to be carbon copies, both likable, highly emotional, reacting swiftly with loud, fast verbal retorts.

We talked five or ten minutes but he remained emotionally upset so I suggested he come in the next day and we could resolve the situation. Once home I remembered that when I brought the girl back in the room at 3:00 she had defied me and constantly stood up, talking very loud, so I had put my hands on her shoulders to force her down into the seat. This is what she must have been referring to.

I was glad the day was over. When I called Sub Center and said I would be available the next day I inquired if it was possible to refuse a school assignment and was told a teacher could do this. I felt I did not want to return to Audubon School. During the lunch period I had talked briefly with another substitute who was teaching a third grade class but was an elementary teacher and preferred a higher grade. I would have loved the 3rd grade. Without doubt all this difficulty could have been averted had the school asked the substitutes which grade level they had been called for. To me, this seemed to be a very weak point in the system. Two teachers and two classes of children would have benefited greatly with correctly assigned teachers.

Chapter 12

Noisy Mothers

At LeMoyne School as I was assigned to a Pre-School Class the clerk commented, "The thing you have to do in that room is put up with the noise."

Walking to the room I wondered how little pre-schoolers could earn such a reputation. I had taught in the room many months earlier and had later met the teacher who was quiet and interested in her pupils.

A teacher aide was already in the room preparing food for the children. Two or three mothers were there, and all were talking.

Amidst the noise, and adding to it, was a lady using the telephone constantly. She stopped long enough to tell me she was there to inoculate all the children that morning, and was using the telephone for that purpose. She was probably calling parents at home between talking to those present, as she said it was necessary for the parent to be present when the inoculation was given, as well as sign the required forms. It looked like one child was finally walked down the hall, with his mother, for this purpose, but most of her time was spent talking on the telephone for an hour.

By 9:00 there were 6 or 8 mothers talking in the room. Loud, fast talking. It was awful. I had seen a notice on a door nearby about a parental meeting and learned it was this day. That was why so many mothers were standing around talking, talking, TALKING!

The floor was not carpeted so I had put chairs for the youngsters in a circle so I could take roll, but with all the talking of the mothers I knew roll taking would be impossible. Besides, some little ones kept running to their mothers and back again. One or two had crying turns. If left alone they would have become interested in the group activities, but each time they cried either the mother, or the teacher aide, would pick them up and hold them, so this was repeated many times for about 30 or 40 minutes.

With all the other noise I had to erase the crying episodes from my thinking and concentrate on the welfare of the group. In desperation I put the attendance book down. (The teacher aide later wrote down the names of those present, both morning and afternoon.) I located the record player – under a few mothers' coats – and turned it on good and loud. I played a child's Polka exercise record and had the children stand to follow the directions given on the record.

The noise was about even between the loud talking of the mothers, the telephoning, and the record player. At one time the loud music got through to the Teacher Co-ordinator (between teachers and parents) and she turned it down, but then the children could not hear the words so when she left I turned it loud again.

The teacher aide had prepared food and the tables were set and ready so the children sat down to eat. There were peanut butter or jelly sandwiches, sliced peaches and milk. A few children did not want any food as said they had eaten at home so they sat quietly at the tables.

By the time the youngsters finished eating the mothers had finally left for the meeting. I had counted 12 present at one time but three or four others were later left in the room to remain until after the meeting, plus one there "on trial" to see how he conformed with the group. He looked younger and much less mature than the others and throughout the day continued to have individual inept experiences.

While the children were still at the breakfast tables, and it was quiet, I explained we would do some seatwork papers to take home. The correct way to hold a pencil was demonstrated; samples of the printing to be done were shown; paper and pencils were passed out, and each child was soon busily engaged in drawing lines and writing the letters "O", "h" and the word, "Oh".

The teacher aide, a very likeable, and helpful individual, who obviously loved children, had cleaned away the morning food extras, equipment and mishaps and was writing the letters for the children. I tried to get her to stop, saying they could do it, but she must have felt they needed her help, and some starred papers were of her work.

Papers were reversed and the number "1" and "2" were written on lines they drew as I had found no primary lined paper and was using 9 x 12 unlined white sheets. Several surprised me by writing very good "2's"; a few made them backwards; some scribbled, and some sat. All papers were given star symbols, a bunny star on one side and a big star on the other. One mother, who had remained in the room and whose child did work as good as a first grader, asked me if the star

symbols signified acceptable work. She and the boy appeared
Oriental and she was deeply pleased, and grateful, to feel her child
had done good work.

Plastic art forms and more paper were given out and the
youngsters shown how to trace the forms on the paper. It was
explained they should hold the forms down with one hand and trace
with the other.

When finished, children were asked to fold all their papers and put
them in their coat pockets to be taken home.

The teacher aide had prepared a hot chicken dish that had such a
savory smell that everyone ate some of it. In addition to the chicken
there were mashed potatoes, mixed vegetables and milk. I helped
distribute the food and cut up chicken for some youngsters.

After lunch a finger-play exercise was taught, a story, "Curious
George", read and oral thinking questions at Kindergarten level asked.
They were quiet and doing well answering these until the parents
started coming back in and the noise was rampant again. The meeting
in the other room was obviously over.

I gave up with the oral thinking exercises and started a ball rolling
game. The children sat on the chairs in a circle, rolling a partially
deflated basketball across the circle to each other, in turns. This
seemed to interest them and was a quiet, orderly game. At various
times throughout the morning a few youngsters had started getting
toys out of various places to use, but each time I had returned them as
felt a free-play period could become too undisciplined and should be
offered only under the eyes of their regular teacher.

The parents' talking continued to be such a disturbance that I
again turned on the record player nice and loud. This time the
children acted out the "Little Teapot" and "Three Little Kittens"
records.

After this it was about noon and some children were leaving and
others coming in for the afternoon session. All chairs in the room
were filled; some youngsters had coats on ready to leave; others had
just arrived and removed their wraps.

Fifteen were in the afternoon class and the procedure was the
same as that of the morning program. There was one little
nonconformist, a girl who was strongly attracted to aluminum pots
and pans. Although I called her several times to join us after she had

done the required paper seatwork, this child persisted in remaining in the back of the room and noisily putting the pans, one by one, into a sink, then taking them out again, and stacking them back on top of each other. At closing when an older boy (her uncle, age 10) came for her, I told him to tell the mother the child had only one interest in life – to wash dishes. A mother then told me this youngster was new to the class – and was only three years old! But that little tot had stayed with the pans; she had been adamant about that and had enjoyed the day in her own way.

At closing only one youngster came for help in fastening a coat zipper. They had really learned a great deal in six months. Everyone had asked for help when I had been there before.

I drove home and was so tired I went to bed for two whole hours! It had been an exhausting – but enjoyable day.

Chapter 13

Holt Reading System

When the telephone rang so early at 7:13 A.M. I assumed the call was for a south side school as they start at 8:00, whereas the north side schools start at 8:30 for teachers, pupils arriving a half hour later at 9:00. The call was for Brennemann School, not far distant.

The assignment was for fourth grade, a "low class", which I quickly surmised by their behavior and attitude. There was a mixture of races, one-third black students, one third Spanish, the others white, Korean, Oriental. They were alert, verbal, and ready to offer me a very difficult day, but knowing two of the teachers I quickly exchanged three students with them to separate the ringleaders. This made a great change, leaving but one major problem, who managed to quickly ring the office intercom bell, after which he was told to take his message there. When he remained in the hallway instead I reasoned someone would come for him, which happened very soon.

The problem class then turned into one of growing cooperation and appreciation. Being a substitute for one day only it was much easier to be relaxed and enjoy the students, regardless of their behavior. A regular teacher is under constant strain of improving reading and math skills, plus mountains of paper work to be completed; she really needs three days to complete one day's work. In this class of 41 pupils about six had already moved; ten were absent; the reading level was at beginning 2nd grade, as was the arithmetic. Their workbooks indicated they were working on contractions and abbreviations so the Milton Bradley Bingo game on these subjects was perfect and one that held their attention.

After the regular teacher's assignments were completed, those who chose to do so copied work I had put on the board which consisted of a Christmas poem, followed by twelve questions pertaining to it, covering comprehension, work attack, and utilizing the thinking into their daily lives. Pupils who completed various papers became teacher-aides and graded the work of others. This honor prompted others to hurry and finish.

This was a "closed-Campus" school where students and children ate together and school was over at 2:30. Their lines to and from the lunchroom were very good but they were far too noisy while there. "Walking Reading" (students joining groups at their own level) lasted for an hour after lunch during which time I had two groups, one of beginning reading, the other at 1A level, which is first grade, second semester.

Brennemann concentrated on the Holt Reading System wherein children progress at their own rate, the only difficulty being that the series is a difficult one. However, it is very complete and as long as a school follows one system, that in itself, is certain to produce benefits. In Holt skills are repeated continually so most youngsters are apt to master them eventually.

Poor readers are nearly always very good in art work and this was true here. In the last period two kinds of Christmas art was presented while a record of Christmas Carols was played. Four boys who did not want to participate were allowed to quietly read books of their own choice. Some of the art was so exceptional they let me have samples to show other classes, and I gave them duplicate papers to work with. Most likely it was the art work (and Bingo games) which prompted many of them to ask if I would come back again the next day, but I explained I preferred to work in different schools.

The teachers were impressed with the fact I worked but a few days monthly. It sounded like Heaven to them – and to me too. I had dreaded mandatory retirement, but was surprised to find it pleasant. Although I had thoroughly enjoyed teaching a regular class it had been a 24-hour job with me, and now that I was away from all the pressure it entailed I had time for other interests there had never been time for previously. My time was still completely filled, but without pressure, so I found retirement very satisfying.

Chapter 14

TESL Class
12 Pupils Per Class

Morris School was a gem – and in my own neighborhood, ten blocks away, but I had not known of it as it was not located on a main street.

Two substitutes had signed in ahead of me, one at 8:30 and I resolved to do the same thereafter as the only opening left at 9:00 was 8th grade. I commented I was a primary substitute but guessed I would survive. The clerk spoke to the principal in another room, and when returning told me to take TESL (Teaching English as a Second Language) instead, whereupon I informed her I had had courses and experience in this area.

The school was quite new, having been used but a few years. The three-story building was carpeted throughout, corridors as well as classrooms, but one could sense the quiet and orderliness at once when entering.

I took the key to a third floor room and noted the interesting, colorful bulletin boards on each floor. One on the main floor portrayed the Reading Book Series, month by month. The majority of bulletin boards were of Christmas holiday material; classroom décor seemed varied and interesting, showing the teachers were interested in their work. Three different times as I walked down the corridors and stairways during the day voices of teachers and children were never heard.

The TESL room was of regular room size and abundant with educational supplies and equipment aids. The room was well lighted, windows on one side of the room; four groups of student desks and chairs were attractively arranged. Blackboards covered one wall; charts, posters and informative materials were on the other. It seemed a dream-come-true with everything needed, except PENCILS! The three tiny stubs on the teacher's desk were promptly carried off by the first pupils who left after their reading period.

Seven pupils appeared for the first class; they were from grades 4, 5 and 7. I wrote fifteen Christmas words on the board, which were read together, then individually. Next, the five vowels were presented, the *soft* sounds, voiced, then their blends with the other consonants. Several wanted to copy these blends to do further study at home and help their parents as well. The blends are

ba	be	bi	bo	bu
ca	ce	ci	co	cu
da	de	di	do	du
fa	fe	fi	fo	fu

through the alphabet. I explained this was one way to cut the words into pieces (syllables) and sound them out.

The storybook, "The Night Before Christmas" was presented and they voted for me to read it instead of them doing so. I held the book up facing them and they sat close by, watching the words as I read the lines; all could read a little following my oral reading.

Next, I played a large record of Christmas carols and showed a Christmas Tree picture drawn by a 7th grader in modern version, sort of ceramic design, done with crayons. Each wanted to make similar ones and they were very good artists, which did not surprise me. Later I gave them ditto copies of other Christmas art work to color and cut out for their trees, and chimneys and Santas.

Several other classes entered during the day, most having about twelve pupils, and a similar program was followed.

At noon I went to the lunch room and ate with the children but I had brought by own lunch. Three classrooms were eating there; the Assistant Principal walked about, maintaining order and quietness. When returning I visited the children's washrooms and found there was paper in the containers which was not the custom in most schools I had been in; often only teachers' washrooms had paper.

As I signed out at 2:35 I again looked for the Principal. I felt this must be a very fine person as such interest, quietness and orderliness permeated the entire building, and this reflects an interested, capable principal in charge. I had looked for her in the morning, at recess, at noon, and now as I hesitated she came from her office into the outer office where teachers were signing out. Being close by I smiled and she stopped and talked a moment. As I had expected, she was gracious, pleasant, smiling, quiet and interested. I conveyed my

47

compliments on the fine school atmosphere, whereupon she softly mentioned she had heard a little noise from the 8th grade that afternoon.

My heart went out in sympathy for the individual sent there instead of myself for the day, and I was again grateful for the wonderful day that had been experienced. I reminded myself to arrive early in the future to have a better opportunity to be assigned a primary grade, one for which I was qualified.

Soft Vowel Sounds

ă	ĕ	ĭ	ŏ	ŭ
ba	be	bi	bo	bu
ca	ce	ci	co	cu
da	de	di	do	du
fa	fe	fi	fo	fu
ga	ge	gi	go	gu
ha	he	hi	ho	hu
ja	je	ji	jo	ju
ka	ke	ki	ko	ku
la	le	li	lo	lu
ma	me	mi	mo	mu
na	ne	ni	no	nu
pa	pe	pi	po	pu
qua	que	qui	quo	qu
qud	que	ri	ro	ru
ra	re	si	so	su
sa	se	ti	to	tu
ta	te	vi	vo	vu
va	ve	wi	wo	wu
wa	we	xi	xo	xu
xa	xe	yi	yo	yu
ya	ye	yi	yo	yu
za	ze	zi	zo	zu

Chapter 15

No Lunch Ticket
Well Behaved Class

At Brentano School I was given a 4th and 5th grade class. I had arranged to arrive early, but this was the lowest grade needing a sub; three other rooms of higher grades were waiting also. However this was a wonderfully well-behaved class; they were quiet, well-mannered, and appreciative.

The teacher had left detailed suggested plans for the morning, noting there was an assembly for the afternoon. Only one child was absent and there was no problem with the lunch tickets – until lunch time, which will be noted later. Having arrived at 8:45 I had plenty of work on the board to be done before they entered – written work and questions to be answered. In addition, I listed the work the teacher requested.

Reading groups were taken for both grades; this was done in English workbooks and the working pages were on pronoun substitution for nouns, which was fun to do orally in groups. By the time we finished they all seemed to understand how to make the substitutions which was familiar with but a few in the beginning. This is a concept introduced yearly by teachers but not an easy one for students to master.

During indoor recess there were physical education exercises, and one of the girls was exceptionally good as a leader. She must have practiced the exercises she saw on the TV yearly school competitions.

Next, we played the Contraction and Abbreviation Bingo game by Milton Bradley. I tired of it before they did but it was a close game between the boys and the girls. One boy, an obvious bookworm, completed all the assignments before joining us. I had expected the assembly to last about 40 minutes and we would have time to complete the other work later in the day.

As we lined up, with coats on, in the hall, one girl declared she had no lunch ticket. We returned to the room, sat down, and I called each name that was written for a ticket. Each one lined up; that girl had never signed up. She had not listened to much of anything all morning, but gone ahead doing other things and then wanting to ask questions. She said she would go home for lunch.

The class was orderly going down the three flights of steps, and the Principal was noticing them. I commented this was a good class and she added they were the best on the third floor. It was "Open Campus" meaning pupils had a choice of going home for lunch, bringing lunch, getting free lunch, or buying lunch in the school. I had brought mine but stopped for milk and joined another teacher to eat. It was such a very large, old school, with so many stairways and corridors that I felt I might get lost by wandering around. After eating I returned to the room but was surprised to see it was ten minutes to 1:00. On the way back I had checked the girls washroom and found toilet paper was available. It was on a roll hanging on wire loops, not sheets in metal containers.

At 1:00 I went down to get the class again and we returned. The flights of steps did not bother me but some of the girls said they got very tired climbing them. After taking roll, we went to the assembly and it was a truly delightful program. It consisted of primary through eighth grades and lasted an hour and a half. I had seated the pupils apt to be restless near me so was able to keep everyone well behaved, having just a few changing seats at times. It was truly a wonderful memory to keep over the holidays.

In the morning I had mentioned I would give everyone a Christmas Card which they remembered and requested. Each child received two cards and everyone seemed pleased with them. They left quietly and went happily down the stairs. As only one boy had completed the board work I thought the teacher might like to use it so left a note explaining this and did not erase the work. And the Christmas Tree art papers had been barely started before the close of the day; these also should have pleased her when finished.

The teachers seemed happy; the school was quiet and well organized; one could tell there was much learning being accomplished. Here was another school I would like to return to. It was a very old, brick structure, but the atmosphere was one of happy learning and discipline, the latter being enforced by the principal. This was a perfect example of a well-run school reflecting the planned organization, interest and discipline of the principal. Her size was small, but not her interest.

Chapter 16

Church Classroom

At 9:00 I signed in at Trumbull School and was assigned a third grade room. It had taken me five or ten minutes to drive around the area to find a parking space. The small teacher's area appeared to be filled and I hesitated to park there as I would be blocking the already-parked cars. The spot I chose seemed two blocks distant, but when I learned I was to teach in a church building next door, I then realized I could not have chosen a closer spot to park.

In the church, or in that section of the church, there was one other class with a teacher. Three impressions greeted me simultaneously as I stepped inside; the awesome quietness, although there was no actual room divider; the vastness of the interior with the extremely high ceiling, and the sixty-five degree chilliness. Fortunately for myself, cold weather seems inviting, but I wondered about the children. The sweater I always carried solved the problem for me, but intermittently during the day, youngsters asked permission to obtain their coats for themselves.

The class was well-behaved and I could quickly understand the reason many teachers had often voiced a preference for third-grade classes, saying "you could do more with them". Most were reading at third grade level; four were at first grade, and one lone child had recently arrived from Greece, who did not yet know the English Language. Luckily for her another girl in the group knew the Greek Language and was able to help. I had the newcomer sit by me in reading but no word seemed familiar to her.

Supplies were minimal. The other teacher informed me there was no ditto paper to run off any seatwork; however, I had brought two prepared ones to use. I prefer to write work on blackboards as feel pupils need practice in writing daily, but it was already nearly 1:30. Further, the three improvised "blackboards" did not look dependable; the light in the interior was not good, and the boards had green surfaces on which the work from the previous day did not appear very distinct.

This was an "open campus" meaning there was a fifty-minute lunch period, the school closing at 3:15. During the lunch period I did fill one board with arithmetic work and one with a poem written in cursive (longhand) as this is often a new activity for third-graders, and so it was with this class. The morning papers were also graded during the noon period as I had brought my lunch. There was a lunchroom in the adjoining school, but it would have taken the entire period to walk over there, eat and return.

By the time the children returned I was ready for them. The first period was for mathematics and some students were exchanged with the other teacher. I had written computation for abilities from 1st through 4th grade on the board so all were able to complete some, or all of the assignment. Later papers were exchanged and the students graded them from the answers I then wrote on the board. Morning papers were also returned.

Next, we used the Milton Bradley "Contraction" and "Abbreviation" cards. This game has great learning values, and is also great fun. The children asked where they could purchase it. After the girls won four times I noticed there were but a few boys in the class so we changed the contest to one half of the room against the other half. Contests always heighten interest but I was glad it ended in a tie as this was such a good group of children. No doubt the good behavior was because of the small number of boys. But the church atmosphere could have had an influence as well. On entering I felt to enforce discipline no words would be necessary. Just looking upward should be enough.

During the day one child had announced it was her birthday and had asked permission to pass out cookies, which she did, while we sang a song to her. She was nine years old, and the only child who had completed both dittos nearly perfectly. She was also one of those who had helped grade papers before the lunch period.

The last hour was spent doing art work, quiet games, and some oral thinking contests which have been collected from various sources. It seemed a pleasant, meaningful day for all of us, and during the last hour even the huge room began to warm up to a comfortable degree.

Chapter 17

Princess in White
Good Workers

Goudy School had 50 teachers, about 1000 students, many teachers offering extra programs in the school. Some classes attended in nearby buildings. Although there was uncontrolled noise as the children entered the building in the morning, the school atmosphere was one of planned learning. As one walked down the corridors and looked into the rooms interesting, worthwhile work appeared on the classroom walls, and the pupils were busily occupied. Teachers smiled but attended to the classes. Substitutes commented it was a "good school" and when asked to explain this added there were interesting programs offered, with extra teachers helping in various projects and sufficient supplies were available.

My morning room assignment was a Kindergarten Class. A teacher, who was already in the room, explained she took part of the children and that there was a Spanish Teacher Aide. I was to have the non-English children who were mostly Spanish. As I did not know Spanish this surprised me for a moment, but I soon felt that they would understand English more than most people realized. This I had learned twenty years earlier from a first grader (Spanish), who pretended he did not understand, but after two months I discovered he actually understood a great deal and could even read a little.

Twenty-two youngsters entered quietly – not like the older classes who were very boisterous when entering the building. Four others came in a little later. I watched silently as they removed their coats and sat at tables, and was particularly interested in seeing them care for one tiny girl, dressed completely in white – dress, boots and gloves. She stood, saying not a word. Various children came, like maids helping a movie star, each one removing a coat, a hat, gloves, and hanging them up. The child in white said not a word; she was very beautiful, with long black hair. In mentioning to the other teacher how helpful these children were to the tot in white, she said the girl was a new-comer, and that the class does help new children – if they are little. The picture of their helpfulness was very sweet, and

53

remained in my memory for days. The little "queen" remained aloof all morning, silently observing activities of others.

The absent teacher had left an easy-to-follow program for a substitute, and one that covered the time very well. Work was explained, and completed, in three workbooks. I was surprised to note that they were familiar with counting to ten, and able to write the numerals through the number five. Two of them had the threes flying like birds, but many first graders do likewise. The number "5" for the day seemed to be familiar to each child, and all but two wrote it correctly. Before writing in the workbooks I had handed each youngster a piece of chalk and let him, or her, have a turn printing it on the board as I had demonstrated "down, around, with a cap on top". Correct writing of numbers and letters is a part of the Kittle Printing which is used in primary grades and this system has a beautiful fluency if done correctly.

During the recess break I walked upstairs to the Teachers' Room. On the stairway walls, on each side, there was a large mural of the children, so beautiful it was astounding. It continued from the first through the second story stairs, on each side. As I returned I stopped to note that it was sponsored by the Southern Culture Exchange, the Uptown Educational Center. I had spent too much time absorbing the beauty of it, so did not write down the name of the individual artist who supervised this project, but it was to continue upwards through the third floor walls. My only regret was that it had not been done in a more noticeable location like along the front corridors instead of on a far side stairway. The children on the mural were in color, and life-size. It was truly impressive, and was most likely of children attending the school.

The morning flew by, quietly and busily. At 11:30 the children left and I collected my things and reported to a nearby building to take a third grade.

I entered a noisy, boisterous classroom and the laughter grew so high that I stopped it at once with, "I beg your pardon!" in a quiet but firm voice. The Spanish teacher there seemed to be in trouble with them, but they stopped at once when I spoke. This was a class of about 35, mostly Spanish, and 70% boys.

Slowly and quietly I informed them I had good records, good art work, and very good games and other material to use – IF THEY

WERE QUIET. However, if they were not quiet, I also had much work that could keep them busy every minute, even after school. They agreed to remain quiet, and were so with a few reminders during the afternoon, except for two boys who sat on the carpeted floor until they remembered to be quiet.

We had music during the lunchtime; they got their hot lunch in the hall and returned. Next we had oral thinking math and globe questions. After reading we used the Milton Bradley Contractions and Abbreviations Bingo Game. Here each child has a card. Even the non-speaking Spanish children were quick to learn to recognize and punch in the correct words and several of them scored for their teams. In fact, they voted to continue this after I tired of it.

During the last period I let them choose the ditto butterfly picture they would like to color and was surprised to see each one select the large, but finely detailed butterfly. I had assumed they would select the six smaller ones. I was not surprised to see the elegant results but wished I had extra dittos to exchange with them so I could have a few samples for future classes but we used each one.

As they left several asked if I was returning the next day, probably because of the butterfly sheets. I think I listened to the music more than they did, but they also enjoyed the challenging thinking work, and the contraction-abbreviation game, and I felt good that so many of them, being Spanish, were able to win in the game. Primary children need much reinforcement in these two areas and this is a painless way of review and implementing words.

It was now easy to understand why teachers often prefer third graders. They do have much unused abilities, and are also teachable. One youngster would have liked to be a tyrant (seated by the teacher's desk) but his interest was early captured by the work that was offered, so there was no trouble at all. The many hours I had spent in preparation during the Christmas Vacation had paid dividends today.

Chapter 18

Acrostic Fun

There had been several days of zero weather, plus much snow on top of icy pavements, so I drove very slowly to Swift School, and although a space in front of the school was available the icy edge there required extra time in getting the car properly parked.

It was 9:00 when I signed in and eight or nine people had already signed in on the sheet, leaving but two blank lines. The clerk said there was a 6th and 8th room available. With a sinking heart I asked if I could have a ditto run off; the clerk took it, saying she would do it within the hour. I signed in for 6th grade.

The three flights of stairs to the room did not tire me and I entered the room as another teacher was finishing taking attendance. Here children either brought their lunches or went home; they ate in the auditorium, which had stable seats, slanting down toward the stage.

The pupils looked happy, alive, interested, and were already noisy. After explaining we could have an interesting day with various materials if they were quiet, or heavy seatwork if they continued to be noisy, most of them quieted down. Knowing they had a gym period in twenty minutes I introduced two word contest games for the short intervening time. By the results I knew this was a really smart class of students – the most advanced I had had while substituting. However, they seemed very likeable and friendly and there was no fear on my part.

While they were in the gym I walked about the building. It was very old with high ceilings. No one was in the halls. On the first floor I got the dittos, some coffee, and returned to run off two more dittos myself of much more advanced work. This material would keep any class well occupied for quite some time.

When they returned some wanted a drink so all went for water, which was close by. It was difficult to establish and maintain a quiet atmosphere, so it was necessary to move a few of the boys up near me, but as the day progressed this difficulty was overcome to a great extent. After the regular reading work was completed I used ideas as they came to me. My intuition told me they might be weak in English so I suggested they become secretaries and write the business letter I would dictate. This must have surprised them as everyone was quietly and busily occupied for several minutes, although it was a short letter. The papers were exchanged twice, after which I wrote the letter as it should have been done on the blackboard, explaining in detail each required punctuation mark. Several questions were forthcoming, which seemed to convey their interest. The papers were then returned to the original writers. There was no perfect paper. One said he had only one mistake. I had explained the open or closed punctuation method, advising either could be used but it must be followed the same way throughout. I asked if they wanted to try another letter but there were a few dissenters so it was not repeated.

One boy was causing a disturbance so I assigned him a ditto advising there were more difficult ones to follow, if necessary. Meanwhile I distributed cards of the Milton Bradley Homonym Game. They seemed to enjoy this, but one pupil was always giving them the answer words to search for. As they were slow in adapting to the game I felt this was a help so overlooked it. However, the boys started to become noisy so they were warned that each time this occurred a point from their score would be erased. One boy caused seven points to be erased; after that he sulked for most of the day. The boys won that game and I tired of it before they did but it was soon lunch time.

During lunch I took the regular teachers' duty in the auditorium maintaining quiet and keeping them seated. The entire auditorium of children seemed easier to keep quiet than the smaller, but older, sixth graders, but there were four teachers on duty walking the aisles.

After lunch I introduced Acrostics by writing the word SCHOOL on the board in a vertical column. I explained that each letter must start a word pertaining to the word that was listed vertically. I suggested other words like "Pets", "Chicago" and "Boys" and "Girls". The last two took hold like electricity and interest was intense. Children were popping up continually reading their acrostics, especially for the "Boys" and "Girls". Some were flattering, most were not, but all were in fun. Once Acrostics are started it's like popcorn; everyone found it hard to stop and very good results were completed. One girl gave me her paper to keep; it had eleven good ones.

<u>S</u>tudy
<u>C</u>hildren
<u>H</u>istory
<u>O</u>rganization
<u>O</u>bedience
<u>L</u>earning

Some of the children had chosen to write crossword puzzles from words in the glossaries of their books instead, and several turned in very interesting papers.

About fifteen prefixes were written on the board in one place and that amount of suffixes in another group. I explained that the Leader says a prefix or a suffix as he points to a student; then he begins to count 1 to 10. This was a game I had always wanted to play but had never had a group able to do it. The class could and there were good leaders to keep it going. But again the boys won as many of the girls were Oriental and appeared too shy to respond to oral activities. I had wanted to divide the class in half feeling this might happen but some pupils had preferred another battle of the sexes.

After this they were ready to complete the regular teacher's work satisfactorily and there were no further discipline problems.

At the end of the day quite a number commented they wished I would be back the next day which strengthened my confidence somewhat regarding upper grade assignments. Having worked with primary levels for years I felt at ease and assured of success with them, but wider horizons are always inviting and challenging.

Chapter 19

Good Class
Noisy Washroom

The call came later than usual, at 7:45, and I was glad I was nearly ready to leave as it was for Audubon School, where I had previously had a difficult grade. As it seemed to me the first substitutes to appear were given the lower grades, I decided to arrive earlier, at 8:30 instead of 9:00 or later, and in this particular school even earlier.

At 8:20 when I signed in there were but two vacancies left, one a second grade, which was given to me, and the other a split sixth and seventh grade. During the lunch period I spoke to the substitute who had the higher vacancy, who told me what a trying day she was having. She had arrived at 9:45. Feeling sorry for her I shared some top ideas I had used with success with other 6th graders.

The 2nd graders I had were a dream class. They were inclined to be somewhat noisy, especially in talking, the only problem, and this was easily solved. The cloakroom was in the back, where the noise really boomed, so I stood back there until everyone was seated.

"My Three Wishes" was the heading of a large bulletin board, and from the stories there I knew this class was a good one, probably advanced. The stories were charming; unfortunately, I had time to glance at only a few.

The teacher had indicated this was an "SRA" reading day, of which the students reminded me, but I did not want to leave work for her to grade, so used my own method. The teacher had many dittos of all aspects of reading skills, but I used my own.

A poem about "Birds in the Snow" was written on the board, with fourteen questions of seatwork to complete about it. Meanwhile, three reading groups were taken, one at a time, for silent and oral reading, the last, slower group reading two stories. One little fellow was a painfully slow reader, although he did read correctly, so I suggested he obtain a library card and ask the librarian for 1st grade books. However, later when the class went down two flights of stairs to the washroom, I noticed he slowly trailed the boys, arriving as most were leaving the toilet, so he turned at the door and rejoined the group, so most likely he is one of those who do all things slowly.

Two girls completed the seatwork before lunch; their papers were starred as both were correct. Next, the entire work was completed on the board, and we turned to arithmetic. They were unfamiliar with 2nd grade carrying and borrowing so ten such number computations were put on the board, samples of each completed to help them. Then it was lunch time. Some went home; some ate in school.

After lunch one little boy asked to go to the washroom so everyone went. As the boys entered their toilet there was such a tremendous, vibrating war cry that I darted inside to catch the culprit. I was surprised at the hugeness of the room, with boys facing the walls on two sides, busily occupied, but they pointed to the boy who had just entered, near the door. I left at once with him, and outside questioned him about the loud yelling. A few minutes later as we were lining up some way away from that door, I noted the Principal leaving the washroom.

After lunch we used the Bradley Abbreviation and Contraction Game and again my intuition was correct as it took a good half hour for them to begin to learn to use this game easily as these skills were not yet engrained too firmly in their reading. Contractions should have been easier for them as that is introduced in first grade, but the abbreviations are a 2nd grade concept. I walked along the aisles, helping them, and was glad when a 7th grader came to offer her assistance for a half hour; by then they were able to work the cards quite well. Several commented they enjoyed this better than their own Bingo game. Children always enjoy educational games that offer good learning skills.

Next, I went over the subtraction, with borrowing, and adding, with carrying, again and again and again, until most of them were able to tell me what to do with the problems on the board. This would require reinforcement, of course, but at least it would be easier to many of them the next time, and they appeared capable of learning this at their present stage. This was an alert class.

During the last half hour we had music and art work, which all seemed to enjoy. Nearly all had their own crayons or felt pens, and their work was attractive.

It had been a pleasant day, both for them, and for me, and I left with a much improved memory of this school. This had been a delightful class to work with.

Chapter 20

Jehovah's Witness
Little Teacher Helper

At LeMoyne School the Kindergarten classroom in the basement seemed a little chilly; the building was warmer on the first floor and much warmer on the third. The school was large, old, the stairs long and high, but the school was very neat, and quiet; only messengers were seen in hallways except at school opening and closing times.

31 pupils were enrolled for the morning class; four were absent; eleven had already transferred out. 22 were present in the afternoon, two absent; ten had transferred, and this was but the fourth month of the school year. The youngsters were neat, loveable and interested. I recited two poems, after which they chose to learn one. Next we acted out the movements for the record, "The Three Little Kittens", everyone having a turn. Each child was given a used Christmas Card as we sat in a group, and the youngsters tried to explain the meanings of the pictures to the class. Only one little girl seemed to understand the meanings of the cards, so she helped the rest tell their stories. She seemed to be a self-appointed teacher-helper, as later after the class had completed the writing and arithmetic work, she finished her chimney with Santa entering and announced she would help others. Many just sat and she helped them as I was doing.

The afternoon class was much more quiet, but their art work did not seem as impressive as that of the morning children. Soon after arrival they were taken to the Library and I relieved a first grade teacher, where I was asked to read two Christmas Stories. But when the Kindergarten Class returned, after a 35 minute library visit they said they had heard but one story so I read two more to them, "The Night Before Christmas" and "Frosty the Snowman". Strangely enough, they seemed to like Frosty better. After this there was time for coloring angels on ditto pictures, which they took home to cut out.

Having had a Kindergarten class about a week before I had learned NOT to stand up ever minute so my legs did not hurt when I returned home. The beauty of the day was the quietness. Two 7th graders who came from the office to ask if there were any messages, had offered to take the youngsters to the library. One of these boys had a magic way with little boys and girls and the lines were so straight as they followed him, so very quiet, that it was a joy to watch, and when going up the long stairs he stopped repeatedly and waited for the slower ones to catch up.

LeMoyne seemed to be a well-organized and managed school. I saw the Assistant Principal a few times during the day and learned the Principal was absent. When signing out I noticed six different sheets for teachers to sign in and out on, totaling at least 60 names. Eight years before the school had appeared to be noisy and unkept, with teachers teaching in the halls and on the stairways as there were not enough rooms, but this was not true at present.

During morning outdoor recess one little girl was brought in with a large surface-skinned leg. It was about an inch wide and two inches long, the top skin being off, and lightly bleeding. While not crying and sobbing like most children, her eyes were filled with tears. Her parents were notified, and when the mother came for her I mentioned the child had explained to me she had not participated in the morning exercises of saying the Pledge of Allegiance or singing the country's song, "Our Country 'Tis of Thee" because she was a member of Jehovah's Witnesses. The mother told me that was because "if we go back far enough in history we see that..." We were interrupted here by an office inter-com announcement so I never got the explanation. The child had not been hesitant about it, and I had admired her confidence and ability to be independent.

The day had been pleasant and quiet, one greatly appreciated.

Chapter 21

8th Grader Trouble

The call from Sub Center had come at 8:00 but I managed to sign in the school at 8:40. It was Audubon School; the assignment was for the Library, for all grades, which I thought would be a pleasant change.

There were no Lesson Plans, or room schedule, but this, too, could be a surprise. The first class was of kindergartners, then another one joined them who looked like first graders, but had grown that much since September. They were quiet, interested, refreshing to be with. The Librarian had a supply of storybooks on her desk, but I opened my own satchel. I told them we would have a story, or two, but first would have some fun questions. The room of children was divided in half, and they enjoyed the thinking questions that had been selected from a variety of sources, a section having been grouped for kindergarten classes. Next I read a storybook called, "Nothing to Do", which they had not heard. And last, they enjoyed the book, "Happiness is a Sad Song", a book about Charlie Brown.

For the next group of first graders I divided the time between the book, "How Animals Sleep" and the Bradley Contraction and Abbreviation Game, using only the contractions. Oral word games and questions were also used. This was a lively class and the time flew by too fast for everyone.

The fourth graders, who entered next, were the first ones I had ever been with. They were a quiet group and chose to play the Homonym Bradley Game. But the game progressed very slowly and there was only a little time left afterwards for some oral fun work.

The seventh graders overwhelmed me with their size, in such direct contrast with the primary children; but they were well-behaved, and accepted the acrostic word games I offered after we had had fun with the higher level oral word games, which they had enjoyed.

During the lunch hour I was "on duty" in the upper hallway, where I was kept busy keeping fifth graders from sliding down the back stairway. Evidently this group was being kept waiting their turn to proceed downstairs to lunch, and they were located between two upper stairways until there was room for them below. Fortunately they had to wait only about fifteen minutes.

During the lunch time that was left I listened to two young substitute teachers tell of their troubles with 7th and 8th graders, and also about their frustrating attempts to be assigned to a school of their own. The future seemed to be one of a long wait, and one was seriously considering entering the stock market field as a broker. Both appeared to have much to offer any field they chose.

After lunch a first-grade class came to the library, and after returning their books, said they preferred to spend the time selecting others to take. They wrote their names and room numbers on the books they chose and were content to silently read them and enjoy the library.

Second graders also returned books but did not take another supply. I showed the pictures of the book, "How Animals Sleep", reading some of the chapters. Part of the time was spent on the Contraction Game. A 7th grader stopped in to help and it was appreciated as this group needed help in playing this game. But before their departure time they were really enjoying themselves with it.

The next class was one of 8th graders. They were tall, husky, sturdy, and very noisy. Some of the boys started tapping pencils, stomping and acting silly immediately. I suggested making acrostics, with which they seemed unfamiliar, but most of them accepted this idea, and progressed well with it. However, some of the students in the back persisted in making noise and talking loudly all the time. This increased as the period continued. The idea of being with 8th graders overwhelmed me. Two of the girls started throwing paper wads, wet ones. The noisy boys had been folding and tossing paper airplanes since entering; now the spitballs. The wet balls grew into the size of oranges, covering the floor. Then one of the girls threw a hard sucker and pieces of hard candy. I saw a small, hard object fly across the room. Several students were out of their seats. The door behind me opened and the adjustment teacher stood there. I commented I wished she could do something to help. She closed the door, but in about five minutes the Assistant Principal came quietly in the other door. A few students did not notice he stood inside by the wall.

When he did make his presence known, and after he had reprimanded them, I was so disgusted with their behavior that when he asked which ones were the culprits I quickly pointed to five of them, two boys and three girls. It all happened so quickly. He removed them, saying their parents would be contacted. The room was an orderly one after that. Later I was amazed to think that five students could have created all that trouble and that the majority of the students were good, orderly ones. It was really unfair for them as they were good, well behaved pupils.

The last class was one of second graders and we used the Contraction Game which they liked a lot. One of the 8th grade girls had remained as another girl had threatened her as the class left so I had asked her to stay. She helped some of the slower ones to play the game. While she was still there a note was brought in from the Assistant Principal listing four of the culprits' names and asking me to stop by his office when leaving. I wrote the name of the other boy on another sheet of paper, and asked the girl from their class to tell me where they had sat; I then jotted down some of the things they had done to cause the disturbance. At 3:15 I had a full sheet for him which he needed, and as I left I saw the pupils standing outside his office waiting to see him. They did not look so arrogant now but as the Assistant Principal had told me they were continually being reported. I did not feel sorry for them.

Chapter 22

Air Conditioned School
Slow in Reading; Math ok

At 7:30 the call came for Brennemann, which was a Kindergarten to 6th Grade School.

I was given a third grade class in which all the students were Spanish, the regular teacher also being of Spanish origin. This did not worry me as in the school they were taught English. I ran off two dittos for art work before going to the room. There was a Teacher Aide there who told me she would be present during the morning, and that it was a very, very slow class, so I did not put the work on the board I had in mind.

I wrote easy first grade work on the board, completion sentences, and two other fill-in word assignments, plus two poems. The children entered smiling but looked quite surprised at all the board work until I explained that for every completed paper they would receive a star symbol – whichever one they selected from a box of eight stars which I showed them. This pleased them, and as one group came up in front for reading, the others worked on the board work. The Teacher Aide said she took the slowest group; she was also of Spanish origin. Most of the pupils were reading in first grade books, but they did do the seatwork rapidly and correctly.

This school was one blessed with sufficient supplies and two teachers gave me some master dittos which I really needed as mine were coming out too faintly on the reproduction machine, having been used so often. The teacher had a record player so I knew we would have a pleasant afternoon. I always carried a supply of records.

The children all ate in school as it was a "closed campus" school, meaning the teacher and class remained together all day until 2:30 when school was out.

After lunch I put arithmetic on the board and many were able to do second and third grade work in this area, which I had expected. However; only one or two got all of the work done correctly the first time. I put three other short assignments on the board for pupils who like board work. The Milton Bradley Contraction and Abbreviation

67

Bingo Cards were distributed, and explained, but they were not advanced sufficiently to be able to enjoy this game, so the cards were collected and art work given out. Samples were shown first, and many youngsters did very good work in this field. Most Spanish children seem talented in art, dancing and music. We had music while the art was being done. Some did two pictures. I left all of them for their regular teacher, feeling she might want to use them on a bulletin board.

While outside on the playground on recess duty I looked around and could understand why teachers liked to substitute in this school. The structure was comparatively new, one story high, and was located amidst other interesting and beautiful high rise apartment buildings, also quite new. All this contributed to giving one a good, refreshing feeling. Inside, each of three long corridors had a front section of glass see-through walls, enabling one to see green trees, grass and flowers growing between the corridors of the building.

The classrooms were different from those in other schools in that there were no windows on the walls. This left plenty of space for front and back blackboards, and the bulletin boards on the third wall. The fourth side had coat racks and cabinets for supplies. All rooms were beautifully lighted by multiple rows of florescent electric lights, arranged across slanted ceilings, making a most impressive and attractive room interior. The school was air conditioned and had a parking lot for the teachers. There was no auditorium, the gym being used for special school events, and the library doubled as a school lunchroom both early mornings and noon times. The exterior of the building looked like three long two-story camel humps, and without the colorful front bulletin boards, one might not think it to be a school building. It was, indeed, most different from all other buildings.

The teachers had been friendly and helpful, and as I waited for children to leave the building at closing time I observed a mixture of Spanish, white, black and Oriental pupils in orderly dismissal lines.

Chapter 23

North Side Class
Starved to Hear Story Read

McCutcheon Branch was a comparatively new school, one story high, the main school being a few blocks distant. The area was a highly transient one, low economic background, a true melting pot of many social backgrounds – Appalachian Whites, Mexicans, Koreans, Puerto Ricans, Blacks, Orientals.

The assignment for the day was that of Resource Teacher, meaning I was to take small groups of pupils from larger classrooms for individual help in another location. The program handed me indicated the periods were for thirty minutes throughout the day, except for two periods of 45 minutes for library time for classes.

I wrote seatwork on the blackboards in advance, which ranged from beginning to advanced primary assignments. Five blocks were filled in on the board, all of reading work, which could be read, then copied and completed. Some was for completion work. The advanced work was for silent reading of art work to be done on the paper, a continuous and interesting project of several things to be outlined. (1. Draw a big tree. 2. Put apples on the tree. Etc.)

The first group, of five youngsters, was barely able to read, or write, but they were very sweet and did try. We read all the work together, and the papers that were copied were starred, which really pleased them.

The next group were second graders, who were able to read the work; one tried the silent project, finishing a little of it. Both groups had been very quiet.

The following group was from a third grade; they enjoyed reading all the work, and completed all the comprehension work. Had they not been separated on entry they most likely would have been noisy and playful, but the work did seem to interest them. There were but a few questions regarding the words.

It had been too good to continue, as I well realized, and the next group was a greater challenge. Although there were but four, each one needed special help and reassurance. Once seated, and well

69

distant from one another, three of them did start the work, and completed two or three papers. One boy persisted in continuous talking; did not pick up a pencil; did not settle down to work at all. I took him to another side of the room and reviewed the sounds of the alphabet, using a colorful book, then alphabet cards. He needed repeated review but seemed to enjoy the individual attention and did learn a few of the sounds. We then continued with an alphabet card game to reinforce the sounds and also learn a few words given in the game.

The following group of five were noisy all period, resulting in very little work being completed. Again I had a talker who flatly refused to pick up a pencil and do any work at all – or remain silent. I finally handed him a large book about a Space Man, saying I hoped it wouldn't frighten him. This worked and he became quiet, looking through the book. The others were really proud of the star papers they carried out.

The last group before lunch was REALLY noisy. In fact, their entire classroom was one of the noisiest I ever heard so I was not surprised I had to line them up in the small corridor and remove a hat from one. Again, they were separated in the room, several desks apart, which did invite quietness in a short time. Once quiet I told them they had a choice. They could leave with papers with six stars, or they could sit like statues with folded hands all period. I folded my hands and sat facing them with a very sour face. After a few giggles the noise lessened, and soon pencils started moving so that each child kept occupied throughout the period.

After lunch there was a group of four, one girl and three boys; all black. They were very noisy until the rule was voiced to them. Stars or sitting, hands folded. Pencils started moving. This group was able to do all the work so we concentrated on the blends which seemed to interest them. All left with several star papers.

The next 45 minute period was one for library but the teacher needed the children in the gym to practise for a future assembly program so I helped. All the rooms came in and I spotted the problems I had had and seated them near me to maintain order. As I had expected, the ones I had had in reading had been the school's behavior problems. I also noticed that some of them were now able to control themselves, although they kept watching me.

The last period was one for library for an entire class. After separating a few talkers, mostly girls this time, I was really surprised to note the interest of this group in the story. I could feel their starved attitude because the story was not that great to overwhelm them. Obviously this was a smarter class than the others, and the story, "Nothing to Do" was one I felt would hold the interest of lower-graders than this third grade class. But they listened eagerly, not a normal quietness. Of course I had explained in advance that they could use the secret in this story to quiet a younger brother or sister who was bothering them. But I felt their starved interest as they listened for every word. The bell rang before I had finished the last two paragraphs and no one got up to leave or made any disturbance. Their unusual receptivity made a great impression on me probably an indelible one.

I felt I would like to contribute some books to this group. The library supply of but a few shelves looked so meager in the hall. I had about fifty little primary books at home by Rand McNally, Whitmore and Golden Press and felt that when I finished substituting I would give them to this school for their library. The paperbacks there looked like take-home books.

Of all the schools in which I had substituted this school seemed to be the lowest of the north side. I realized I had had the lowest achievers that day, but some of them were far too low, some not knowing the letter names, several not knowing the consonants. Probably they were from families who had moved a great deal, most likely all were absent often. I was returning to the school another day so would take specific work to help them.

Chapter 24

Little Terrors

In a Second Grade class at Stewart School I had one of the worst days a substitute could have. Many in the class were unbelievably undisciplined and displayed impossible behavior.

There was an abundance of seatwork on two long blackboards on two sides of the room when the class entered. The teacher had left sufficient ditto work for a week in folders labeled for five days, but it requires much time to grade this, which students can do quickly, and is easily copied from other pupils' work, so I prefer to use board completion assignments. These I can grade at a glance as am familiar with them, and the pupils also have practise in writing.

The first child to enter was a very, very small boy. He ran in, started yelling at the top of his voice, and kept darting about the room when I tried to catch him. He was followed by others who reinforced the noise with loud yells and talking. This did not surprise me too much as I had previously substituted in a room nearby and had noted the constant turmoil in this room throughout the day and had wondered why it was permitted and how the teacher could endure it. I recalled she had been pleasant, smiling, and seemingly unaffected by the disturbance. She was not a newly assigned teacher, but appeared to be one who had been in the profession for some time.

I finally managed to capture the noisy boy, but his strength amazed me; it was very difficult to hold him still, and his body and mouth continued great resistance to anything I said or did. Meanwhile, the other pupils made such noise both in the room and in the adjoining coat room that I had to release the one child and try to stop the overwhelming uproar. This took some time to accomplish.

At last when the class was finally seated, the desk of the little culprit was pulled up in front near the board, with him seated at it. A mother and the Assistant Principal appeared. She was reporting this same child's behavior with her son. I told her I was already aware of the trouble he caused but assured her it would not continue as no further disruptions would be permitted. This I soon learned was a very difficult promise to maintain throughout the entire day.

As soon as she and the Assistant Principal left her son immediately became one of the worst offenders. Nothing impressed him. It seemed he had no father. And when I threatened to call his mother, checking first in the attendance book to make certain there was a telephone there, he promptly replied she was not home then. He had a loud mouth and it did not stop then or much of the day.

Because of the noise and confusion it had not been possible to record the names of students present before a new group started entering for "walking reading" and the uproar started all over again. An attractive, neat and well-dressed black girl refused to become quiet, or to sit down. She kept laughing, yelling, and running about, calling out obscenities. When I managed to get hold of her I took her outside and had two boys take her down to the office with a note she was disrupting the class. The two boys could not control her so a third joined them and I did not see her again until the last period. During the recess break I learned she was one of the school's worst behavior problems, which was obvious. And she was but a 2nd grader!

After she left I noticed a small girl taking my first problem by the hand and leading him out of the room. On questioning her I learned she was his sister (a year older). A classmate had told her of his classroom behavior, and she had come to take him to the office. She was very upset and said she would tell his mother of his actions. This I said she could do, but added the Principal already knew about him, and I felt he was going to control himself the rest of the day – which he did try to do.

The new "walking reading" group was to remain for about an hour and a half. Talking was continuous and as the desks were arranged together in three groups, the first thing I did was to separate them.

The board work was explained; star symbols were shown that would be imprinted on finished papers, and reading was started, but not much work was even started for quite some time. I noted several did not appear to have pencils but I hesitated to loan any as felt practically everyone would line up to receive them, so I waited until later on when seven were given out.

Five in the top reading group were good readers; three could not read the book at all and it really hurt my heart as these were quiet children, really needing much help which could not be offered in all

73

this confusion and constant turmoil. There were so many interruptions that I did not stop to write the names of the reading books.

The next group of readers followed the pattern of the first group; some could read; about half could not; one was not able to read any of the words. At recess when an older brother of one boy came in I asked if he could read and told him his brother really needed his help. After the pupils had had turns reading I tried to have the better readers offer to help the needy ones at home, but none seemed to live close together, and there appeared to be no interest in helping one another. In many school classes a friendly, helpful attitude toward others existed but it seemed lacking here.

After two or three children brought up one completed assignment I stopped and starred it, which did prompt many others to do some of the work. In other classes I always had pupils keep their work together to be graded later at one time. But in this class only a few were producing anything. The atmosphere was deplorable, very antagonistic to learning.

Because of the behavior problems we never got to more reading groups. In the morning I had seen some beginning first grade work on one board so had put up special easy work in one section. And during the reading groups I had noted three or four of the large boys doing this work but they never brought up any work for stars.

At lunch time the home room class returned but we left ten minutes late as I refused to leave until they became orderly and stood up in quiet lines. On the way we stopped for washroom visits, the boys waiting while the girls went in, and vice versa.

They were quiet and orderly at lunch. This was especially obvious as at a nearby table were many of the unruly students that had been in our "walking reading" class. Their male teacher really had a most unruly class. He rose several times attempting to manage them but was not too successful. It was an extremely difficult group of both girls and boys. I told him I certainly would write a "blue slip" for one girl, which he said had already been done. (She had been in our room for reading and had been utterly impossible all during the period, but I had sent one to the office and this one was but a few shades worse than others present.) A "blue slip" indicates a child is considered an applicant for a special class because of behavior.

After lunch there was "walking math" so again noise and confusion prevailed. Those who entered glared as I erased work that had been done and put problems on the board. No one moved to do any work until I put even easier problems up – first grade ones, but I doubled the quantity, and handed ditto math sheets to those who did complete any board work.

The afternoon was much more quiet and orderly. Possibly we became more adjusted to each other, but the majority of the math children were new ones, smaller and less belligerent.

At the end of the math period when the home-room students returned one asked to go to the washroom so we all went. The washrooms were down in the basement and as there were large room sized waiting areas, on concrete floors, with no other classrooms nearby, I had the boys do physical gym exercises while they waited for the girls. They skipped, ran, jumped, and jogged until they literally looked exhausted. Experience had taught me that the worst classroom behaviors usually try to avoid any organized group physical activities, saving their "talents" for continued classroom disruptions (which several attempted to do by sitting down on side benches – the first being the tiny problem that had first caused trouble that morning) but I was beside them at once, urging them to join in the exercises. The same exercises were repeated with the girls as they waited for the boys.

As we then went up the two flights of stairs I felt their excess energy was used up, and it could very well have helped a great deal as there were but a few more discipline problems to be handled.

In the room good art work was shown before papers were distributed. At this time I noticed the girl was present that I had taken to the office early in the morning. She had been told not to return. I gave her an art paper to do, feeling that she might have talent in this area and display better behavior, but after but ten minutes she was again acting up and I told her to leave. After slowly wandering about the class, causing more disturbances, and after repeated demands to leave, she finally did so. In about five minutes a man opened the door informing me I could not have the girl in the corridor but had to keep her inside, that I was responsible for her.

Helen Marie Prahl

"Oh, no!" I replied. "She was sent to the office this morning and was not to return here!" With that he left and later returned saying she was not supposed to be in the room at that time.

At closing time I refused to leave until all the chairs had been put up, which took some waiting to accomplish, but after that they went down the stairs without further disruptions.

The office clerk had sent a note asking me to return the following day "for the same class" but I told her I was taking the rest of the week off. In fact, three days later I still did not feel interested in reporting for work after Christmas. This class had been too, too much!

And the school too. The noise and uproar in the halls as classes were changed, both mornings and afternoons, was unbelievable. Loud talking, yelling, running about, pushing, pummeling! I had never seen, or heard, such disorder in any other school and wondered why the principal allowed it. I knew I would never return again.

Chapter 25

Abundance of Equipment
Left My Car Where?

The telephone did not ring at 7:30, or 8:00, or 8:15 so I felt I would not be called, but at 8:30 the call came in for Jahn School.

A young 8th grader girl, a teacher-helper, was in the First Grade room when I entered, which was a great help as she showed me where the cloak room was for teachers, as well as the chalk and writing paper for the pupils. I asked her to take the roll and collect the lunch money which was listed on the board but she said one-third of the class was in a Spanish Class in a mobile and would return at 10:30 at which time the teacher collected the lunch money and took the roll. She also told me this was a very, very low achievement group.

They entered quietly, were very little, and took their seats. The helper had a few at a time hang up their coats; she passed out paper while I wrote material on the board. I wrote three short poems to be copied, one completion, one of sentences, and one with thinking directions of what was to be done, a fun assignment. The helper then left and the class read the work on the board and started working on it.

The teacher had left excellent instructions, clear and easy to follow, even designating the pages for the groups to read. The first group was in a 1B book and surprised me with their good reading; each child read a page without a mistake. The second group read with confidence in a third preprimer but read very well; the third group read more slowly, but well in a 2nd preprimer. Preprimers are the soft cover books before starting a first-grade reading book with a hard cover. Usually first graders read at least one hard cover book by Christmas and another hard cover one before June, plus other books for faster students. There were two groups the teacher suggested not calling for reading.

At 10:10 we got ready for outside recess, and not wanting the children to lose their lunch money, I collected it then. Later I learned it was inside recess. Three bells advised this which I did not know.

The board work was explained to the Spanish pupils and before lunch they, too, had an opportunity to read. They loved having the books and read for quite some time. I invited anyone who desired to join the group.

At lunch time only two children went home; most ate at school. Twelve had free lunch tickets, ten had paid for the day's lunch. I walked with them downstairs; they were a quiet group, and so very tiny. The bigger, older children let them pass on to the lunchroom as we were a little late getting out.

I had brought my lunch so ate in the room and changed the board assignments for the afternoon as a few children had finished all of them. Again I put up some easy work to do, some with thinking required, and some short sentences to be completed with fill-in words.

I was impressed with all the equipment in the room. Two 4-drawer file cabinets; two cabinets, well filled with supplies; two other cabinets in the side coat room. All were locked but I opened them with the keys and found all were filled with supplies, one had electronic equipment. The record player was out in the room, not locked up, which also surprised me. This had to be a teacher who had been there some time, and was really interested in her work, to have collected all these items and equipment to store things in. There were also book shelves with books in a little alcove by the entrance, a good supply at various levels.

After lunch the new work was read by everyone and more stars were earned by most. In a little while the Spanish group asked to read again so I invited any who wanted to to join us again. They read for over a half hour without tiring of it. First graders are a true delight to be with. Their printing was beautiful, but I did notice that many copied without understanding. I filled in the blank lines and corrected the errors, stamping on the stars for each paper anyway. But a few could do the work correctly and did so quietly.

Arithmetic was on the board and everyone did that as well, so I played songs and stories on the record player while they enjoyed some special art work I had brought. We danced to the Polka record and did gym exercises for a short time. Everyone had a pleasant day and after they left I returned to wash the board. There was no sponge but a teacher loaned me a cloth.

The principal asked me to return for a 2nd grade class the next day. Usually I prefer to skip a day in between working but he was so nice and this was such a pleasant school I was happy to return.

The building seemed to have several exits and I must have left by a different one and I was not certain which one I had entered. It took a very long time to locate the car which taught me to note the street names on adjoining corners in the future. Later I learned this had often caused problems to newcomers to the school.

Chapter 26

V.I.P. Visitor

The Principal at Jahn School had asked me to return the previous day, so knowing it was for a 2nd grade I took materials for that level. Also included were two small pails and a good sponge to clear the blackboards. Although I signed in at 8:30 the boards took a very long time to dry as it was necessary to wash them twice to remove the chalk. The erasers were so calked with chalk that I asked two boys if they would go outside and dust them by hitting them together, but they did not get much of the chalk out; younger pupils would have done a better job. Later I learned from the Principal that the school had an electric eraser cleaner and did clean them on Fridays. I wondered what system was followed. Were they collected weekly from all rooms, or did some teachers not avail themselves of this service? The room I had been in the previous day had erasers with over a half inch of chalk on, plus the same amount on the ledges, the air being filled with it all day. I had removed some of it after school but the teacher from whom I had borrowed a cloth came for it before I could go over the ledge again. She locked her room when leaving so I could not re-borrow it. This is why I took my own sponge and pails the next day.

Two ditto machines would not work and after trying a third machine I realized my ditto was worn out and not reproducing any longer. By then it was 9:00 so I ran off two art sheets for the class instead. Fortunately experience has taught me not to depend on machines entirely for much of anything so I had brought two other good sets of run-off work papers in case I needed them.

When I returned to the room some children were quietly entering. The teacher next door soon warned me the District Superintendent was visiting the school that day. The desk was a mess of papers, left by the regular teacher; there was no work on the nice clean board. It wasn't at all representative of me to be messy, or to have blank blackboards, so I figured he would come right in. I refused to be upset when two men entered, one with an outstretched hand. Mine was full of chalk so I put forth the left one, explaining. He was a handsome man, smiling and pleasant; within five minutes he was gone. Quickly I asked the class if they would like to write him a letter and when they agreed I found him nearby and told him that if he would chat with the children a few minutes they would like to write to him. He seemed pleased, returned, and asked them to be sure to write.

Some messages were fine; a few were catchy and very good. I asked them to decorate the notes with flowers, like stationery. Many mentioned his two dogs he had referred to, plus thoughts about their own and other pets; some wrote of his good job, and their fathers' jobs. I asked one little fellow to please copy his letter for me. He wrote, "Dear Mr xxx. I like your joB mayBe when I get biger I will do what you are doing I will like to met your dog's love John" There was only one hint at punctuation – an apostrophe in the wrong spot. But I loved the entire letter. His art work was tops. A large mailbox plus a person walking to it with a letter in one hand.

The letters were done first of all. As they were requested I wrote 21 words on the board to be used in spelling but changed no spelling on the finished work. To me that was part of their charm. I did help a few shy and Spanish pupils to compose a few sentences. But it was not the all-day job it would have been in a first grade room. Meanwhile I had managed to start covering the board with work for the faster students, and several kept up with me in doing it. This was, indeed, a good class, as the Principal had told me the previous day.

There was outside recess so I was able to complete the board work during this period, as well as run off more ditto papers. It was one of the few schools to have ditto machines available so readily for teachers; however, there was no ditto paper, but I had brought a good supply of my own.

After recess I distributed an interesting, fun ditto page for everyone to do. It listed pictures, plus letters, which called for name answers. For example, a picture of a cat, plus "ch", the answer to be "catch". These I later took time to grade, and about eight received 100's, ten "very good", fifteen "good", and five showed no ability without further help. Many had errors in putting the instructions backwards, as writing the "ch" before the "cat". But all this was good experience for them. Although I left the papers, plus their good art work, for the teacher, I called them to see their errors as I graded them, which surprised me in taking quite a long time.

In oral reading every child could perform well; there were four groups, but each was in a second semester second grade book; all could do second grade arithmetic computation as well. Later we did try the Milton Bradley Contraction and Abbreviation Bingo Game cards, but only twenty minutes were left and this was not enough time for them to master this new presentation. Had we had an hour most would have caught on to it and really had fun. As it was, one boy won and one girl evened it.

They surprised me by requesting homework so I suggested they write their teacher about the day's experiences.

At closing I walked down the stairs with them. They had been one of the best behaved classes I had had, even leaving quietly, and everyone was smiling.

I returned, washed the boards twice and left.

Chapter 27

Little Beginners

Having been asked to return the previous day by the Principal of Jahn School, and knowing it was a slow first-grade class, I prepared for the day by taking a great deal of new beginning first grade work material. I spent the time running off ditto art work before they came in as felt they might not be able to do any board work.

At 9:00 the inter-com of the school played the National Anthem after which we said the Pledge; attendance was taken, and milk money was collected. Next I showed flash cards of the names of the weekdays, the months, and names of numbers, one through twenty. Sometimes they needed help with the first set, but once started, could say most of the words, and with repetition by mixing them, they were capable of reading them. This made me feel they would be able to do the work from the board.

Next we cut small one inch paper squares which were distributed, ten to each child. As I wrote numbers on the board, like 4 plus 2, I asked them to arrange four squares in one row, with two squares beneath them. This took a little time to check and have each one put them in parallel rows, but soon all were arranging them correctly, and then "adding" them. The addition exercises seemed easy enough for them. However, when we started the subtraction, after recess, many had difficulties. This would require much repetition. Later I left the math problems on the board the teacher had there, just changing the top numbers. The pupils would be familiar with her work but I did not know if this was new or completed work.

At recess I put simple poems on the board, which they copied. Also I put some sentences with blank spaces where words were to be inserted. This was too hard for them; they just copied the work.

They were reading in pre-primer (soft cover) booklets and each child was able to read all the words. They read individually, and in unison, taking three stories in each reading group. After this I went over the board work with them, showing them how easy it was to put the words in. I wrote new sentences, using words from the booklets from which they had read. Again, the hurdle seemed too great at first.

83

A few cried as they felt it too hard. But I kept assuring them they really could do the work as it was of the words they had read to me. And little by little, one at a time, a few did complete the work; others just copied, or sat.

During the lunch hour, this school being Open Campus, where there is a lunch period of 45 minutes, I starred all papers left on desk tops as requested. A color work paper from the absent teacher had also been distributed, which they were used to doing, so most received stars on that one. I put a star on every poem that was copied, for the effort entailed, and for good quality printing put two or three stars. About eight sentence completion papers received three stars; three math papers had three each, five neatly done color papers, and two beautifully colored butterfly art papers were pinned on a front bulletin board. This pleased them and encouraged better effort in the afternoon when more completion work was put on the board.

In the afternoon each group read two more stories, did the board work, quietly joined in a surprise fire drill, and did more arithmetic work. There was barely time for special art work and a little puppet show. I had brought a number of puppets for this and they reminded me of them, as I had requested in the morning; I was pleased they did as I would not have remembered them. Children love puppets, and when the bell rang they quickly cleaned the room, lined up, and left smiling. I told them the next day I came they could be the puppeteers.

Chapter 28

Little Charmers to Principal

The call was for Audubon, a school where I definitely did not want to arrive late and have an elementary grade, so I started very early. But as there had been two or three inches of new snow on top of piled up old snow and ice, the bus was very slow, and after waiting 25 minutes for it I returned home and drove to the school, signing in at 8:30.

Once there I sat and waited another 25 minutes for the Principal to call in so I could be assigned a class. There were four vacancies for substitutes on the sheet, but as I was the first substitute to arrive I felt my chances were good for getting a primary class, which I did, a second grade. Besides, no other substitutes appeared.

There was time to put but two assignments on the board before the children arrived. What a relief it was to be with primary youngsters again. 22 were present, 7 absent; there were 12 red marks through listed names, indicating this must be a transient neighborhood. Three paid for their lunches; 16 received free tickets; the others went home at noon as this was an Open Campus School, having an hour for lunch and closing at 3:15.

A teacher of Spanish children brought in two shy little girls explaining they were afraid to come in as had forgotten their books. She said they came to her for reading at 10:30.

After putting more work on the boards I took the Spanish children for reading first. Two could read the English slowly; then we read in unison and I noticed the two who had not read individually could read much of the material.

There were three other reading groups but all read from the same first grade book, "Seven is Magic", by Ginn & Company, a Level 6 book. Only a handful read easily but those did little seatwork.

Most of the class were age 7; six were 8. Few were able to do simple first grade seatwork; most merely copied the work. But with a few reminders they were quiet.

When doing the simple first grade adding and subtraction work several came to the desk to borrow plastic chips to help them figure. I showed them how to put tiny circles by the numbers to add, or cross them out in subtracting, but they were used to the chips.

During the lunch hour I erased the first assignments and printed three easy poems to be copied for more stars, and when they returned from lunch records were played while they completed more work and all the papers received stars. A few youngsters had copied all the work. I had a box of eight star symbols which primary children always appreciate, and for each assignment a student received a stamped star. The box contained a Bunny, Pumpkin, Turkey, Flag, Santa, Lincoln, Washington and a big Star. There were probably a dozen short assignments so there was much starred work to take home. Although I had them continue the work on but one or two sheets of paper, each completed assignment received a star symbol.

Some Hans Christian Anderson Stories were heard from a record and a child's Polka exercise record was enjoyed, as well as catchy educational records about the vowels, time and months.

Children who had finished the work received art papers and most were surprisingly fine little artists; they had a choice of butterfly or sunset pictures to color.

The teacher had left a set of sheets from a reading workbook to be done in the afternoon which we did together as she had suggested. It was a page with three-line stories, followed by questions; the reverse side listed questions to be answered by putting crosses under "Yes" or "No". Nearly half the class crossed out the top "Yes" and "No" instead of putting their crosses on the specified lines, as directed. Listening and following directions is something they needed much practise in, but eventually everyone ended up doing the work correctly and receiving "100" on the pages.

After lunch the two little Spanish charmers, who had come in late in the morning, said the Principal wanted them in his office at 1:00 "to do some work". I said that was too bad as we would be having records and art work but let them go. In a few minutes they were back, explaining he said they should return after the music and art hour. I had told them to tell him they were my little valentines and he should not be stealing them, but they had not told him. One was truly a little heart stealer. Later when they did leave they returned for "work to do". I felt he wanted to help them and was glad the teacher had left the page from the workbook; he would enjoy that as we had, and it was one with much learning value for the children.

There was time for two stories, one, "Curious George", and one about the Statue of Liberty. Surprisingly enough, four students had visited the statue and they related their experiences; all had walked up the 168 steps to the top. After a few oral word thinking games it was time to go home. The boards were washed and all quickly and quietly put on their wraps.

It had been a most pleasant day but driving was so slow and the car slid on the ice so many times that I drove very slowly and did not arrive home in time to call in to work the next day. I should have called from the school. I would not forget again. I, too, had learned a lesson that day.

Chapter 29

Taped Reading with Workbooks

The call came at 7:50 and I signed in at Morris School at 8:30. There was but one opening left, of four, and it was for a 4th grade class. I had been wishing to have a 4th grade room as this had been my favorite grade in school as a youngster.

The stairs seemed high as I climbed to the third floor but the building, which I had been in previously, was a very new one, and a pleasure to see and work in. The wall-to-wall floor covering made the biggest difference, offering a quietness that is most welcome in a school building, and although the stairs were not carpeted, their content, not being marble, did absorb 95% of step noise. They also seemed to offer more foot security, the surface feeling like it contained a heavy cork substance which would restrain sliding or falling. However, the rail banisters did have round, glossy (inviting) tops and I did see children sliding down on them a few times.

The room I was to work in had brown blackboard space and only on one wall, one side being of windows, one of cabinets and coat hooks, and the back one of bulletin boards. And to make the brown board an added problem, the only chalk I found was of a texture that did nor mark clearly; it was like a #3 pencil. Later a Teacher Aide brought me a few chalk sticks, which were of a soft texture and wrote very distinctly for all to read.

For seatwork I chose a poem about cars with ten questions, adding five more of current interest. This boardwork was waiting as the pupils entered. They displayed the usual special noisiness for a new-appearing substitute until I assured them I was an experienced teacher and well knew how to handle roudiness. Nonetheless, it took a good fifteen minutes to subdue everyone and get them working. Most did have their own paper, and there was none in the room except unlined, which they did not care for. Some borrowed from friends.

They were a good-appearing group, and I assumed they were at a high third-fourth grade level, which proved to be somewhat correct as the day progressed with completed work activities. The class was primarily white and Spanish, with a few Blacks and Orientals. Only one child was absent; most had free lunches; it was a closed school campus, meaning lunch lasted but twenty minutes and school was out at 2:30.

"Walking reading", meaning groups from various rooms walked to other rooms being of the same reading level, started at 9:05, so there were changes right away. The children quickly informed me that this was a day they used a taped reading session, which proved to be very interesting to them, and to me. The pupils had workbooks to follow as the taped lesson was heard; I wrote a list of nine words on the board which were being studied, and after the taping ceased in about 20 minutes, they selected the correct word from a multiple choice of three sentences, one of which gave the correct meanings for the listed words. As they completed the work and brought it to me I quickly graded it and then had others whose papers were graded help in the grading. Meanwhile I had taken other notes to question them about from the taped exercise; they enjoyed this as it was turned into a contest by rows, and it also helped them in determining the correct answers for the exercise. While they finished the exercise arithmetic work was put on the board, ranging in difficulty from first through fifth grade. Most were well grounded in this computation and received high marks.

As the playground was not yet ready for use there were inside activities of gymnastics, mostly by room volunteers, but later a primary grade activity was started which turned out to be lots of fun, more so for them than for younger children as they were capable of thinking of better ideas and acted on them more quickly. Originally, I chose a student, telling him to rise and drive his new car over to another child's seat. As he sat in the new seat he was to instruct the removed child to travel to another's seat, specifying how (by bike or car etc.). Very quickly the "how" changed to an animal, as "be a frog, monkey, Dracula, Spaceman" etc. Enjoying this, their voices, and actions, made it fun for everyone.

The board work, plus three special think-reading dittos were completed by many before lunch, and graded as handed in, by the teacher and helpers who had already done the work, so everything was up-to-date as we left for lunch. About seven of the class finished all the work; nearly all turned in at least the two board papers.

After lunch the Milton Bradley Homonym Bingo Cards were explained and given out. They understood these readily so the interest was heightened by a boy-girl contest. And to keep the excitement under control a rule was enforced that for any boisterous noise a point was deducted from the score of that gender on the board. Once enforced, the noise disappeared throughout the playing of the game. In fact, they voted to continue the game longer than intended, cutting down on the puppet, record and art time left. But there was much learning value in the game so it was prolonged as they desired.

Twice during the Homonym Game period (Homonyms are words that sound like other words, but are spelled differently, like "to" for "two", "see" for "sea") two different teachers had come into the room for items in the teacher's desk folders. How grateful I was for this interesting and worthwhile material, that I had spent so much time and money searching for years ago. And although it had not been used much in the room I had before retiring, so much of the data I had collected was really invaluable in substituting at various levels.

For a short twenty minutes the students chose their activity and the room was divided, one corner with puppets and two puppeteers, one listening to records, and the majority doing art projects.

At 2:25 they lined up quietly enough and by 2:30 were leaving the building. As I had anticipated, fourth grade had been a pleasant grade to work with. And there had been no serious behavior problems, which helped to enhance the memory. Several told me they had enjoyed the day, so it was a good day for everyone.

Chapter 30

Tunnel Punishment

For two days there had been no call from Substitute Center so I called in to work on Wednesday, a day I prefer to use for personal interests and activities because it is in the middle of the week. It did not surprise me to receive a call at 7:25 as the few times I said I would work on Wednesdays, even preferring not to, a call had always come in. The assignment was for Burley School.

Having thought the school to be another on the same street in which I had worked I drove around a long block expecting to park in their parking space. However, there was none and with the extra long blocks, one way streets and busy intersections, I got lost twice so finally arrived at 8:30 instead of 8:15 as planned.

Two other substitutes had signed in ahead of me, leaving but one other opening for me, which was a Kindergarten Class. As I walked into the room a friend called, "Hello" and I realized I had been in this school a few months previously, and I was to have the same grade again.

Kindergarten classes have a morning class that leaves before 12:00 and a second afternoon class that arrives shortly after 12:00 This teacher left excellent emergency plans and ditto work for substitutes so I looked through the material until the class came. As Kindergarteners aren't able to copy board work there was nothing to put there.

I noted there were papers on which they had been copying their names, so I took the attendance book and wrote their first names on writing paper with a red flowmaster pen. That paper, plus a counting and coloring one would interest and occupy their time for awhile.

They came in reasonably quietly at 9:00 – 38 youngsters, eleven having moved; five were absent. My friend later told me the regular teacher felt there were too many in this class and some should be changed to the afternoon class. From the experience I had had in other schools it was unusual to see this large number in a class without a Teacher Aide, but I told my friend I had had in my first grade class when I started teaching years before I had thought nothing of the number.

When we said the morning Pledge of Allegiance I noticed all did not appear to know all the words, and in singing the National Anthem this seemed to be true also, but they were just little ones starting out to learn all these things in life.

The name papers were given out and as they wrote them I wrote some of the alphabet letters on the board, showing them how easy it was to print them. These they copied on the back of their name papers.

I noted one little fellow persisted in sitting and scribbling, so I felt his name of seven letters could be too great for him. I cut it to a nickname of four letters, telling him that would be much easier. He did copy this page so maybe that was his problem. But with a second paper he just sat, really scribbling over it with a crayon. Perhaps he needed more individual help, but there were too many in the class to keep up with and keep them all busily engaged, so I was not able to get back to him a second time.

The number dittos of 6, 7 and 8 digits were next to be done. There were rows of pictures; the children were to count these and place the correct number in the right hand column, then to color the pictures. Later, in grading the papers, I noted some had merely written a number without counting, or did not yet know how to count correctly. However, I put a bright red DUCK stamp on every completed paper, changing the incorrect numbers in pencil. The cheery duck stamps pleased the youngsters, inspiring all to turn in papers.

At recess time I took them down to the washrooms – after having tied several shoes and zipped up a few jackets. As the boys waited for the girls to come from their washroom, two little girls, about 3rd graders, appeared saying they were to take the children to the toilets and to recess, so I left. Fifteen minutes later when I looked for the class outside, the Principal told me they were in the "tunnel". Finally I found out the "tunnel" was the basement corridor in the building where I had left them. The boys had been naughty and fighting in the washroom, and the little girl monitors had not been able to control them (or most likely, not wanted to enter the boys' toilet room), so the children had not had recess. The Principal said they could go out for ten minutes after the other classes came in so I hurried and put on my coat to take them outside. Recess seems so important to youngsters and I enjoyed seeing them run about the small area.

After recess there was milk for the ones who had names listed to receive it. No one mentioned cookies and I didn't think of them until afternoon when I opened a tin can on the desk out of curiosity and saw a few crumbs. The class informed me there were cookies only when they brought them. This surprised me as in the two schools where I had taught teachers, including myself, had always supplied such treats for Kindergarten and first grades, and often for second and third as well. Obviously the young teacher here did not feel like spending her own money this way.

I drew a picture on the board of a kite and a boy flying it for those who cared to draw while I starred all the work papers. A story record by Hans Christian Andersen was put on for the children to hear who had finished their work. Next, we had a dance record, "The Polka", with exercises which all youngsters enjoy. A few songs, "Doggie in the Window" and "I'm a Little Teapot" were played. Then, to have a quiet group leave the building, after their wraps were on I played "The Three Little Kittens" while we acted it out. Primary youngsters love this record, and it calms them down in a lovely way so we had an orderly, subdued group leave to meet their parents at 11:40, and everyone was pleased with the day's activities.

As I ate my lunch I printed on work papers the names of the afternoon class, noting there were 36 listed in the book. However, nine were absent, the class telling me most of these were attending other schools. A number of the absentees were marked absent for a number of weeks so this could have been true, but one can never accept a child's word as reliable information. Ordinarily a teacher refers absentees to a Truant Officer on the third day's absence. It was unusual for so many to be marked absent for such prolonged periods.

Ten less in the afternoon class (27) did make a remarkable difference. It was much easier to teach, fewer disruptions and noise to control, so more work was accomplished by them. A thinking discrimination work sheet was explained and done by most; however, only two had completed it correctly in every instance. To me, this indicated these were the ones best able to start reading soon as they were able to discriminate between likenesses and differences in

93

printed symbols. Most likely the rest of the group would learn this before school was out in June.

The afternoon schedule followed the morning one and they left at 2:25 a little in advance of older, larger students. It had been a good day, thanks to the good plan schedule left by the regular teacher. Usually they are so jumbled I plan my own time. But with a Kindergarten Class I appreciated having had a practical, readable one with useable worksheets.

Chapter 31

Lunch Tickets
Car Notice – My Car Towed!

For a Fourth Grade at LeMoyne School I selected an interesting poem to write on the board and listed several questions about it. One board was covered with arithmetic ranging in difficulty from 2nd through 4th grade, one of science about the earth, and one relatively easy categorization of a list of thirty words. I felt I was well ready for them when they entered.

How wrong I was! They came in noisily, disinterested, throwing caps and jackets all around, shoving desks, looking disgusted. "Man!" they cried. "Do we have to do that!" Nearly all were Spanish or Black, a few white and Orientals. It took fifteen minutes to quiet them. Before they entered a neighboring teacher had stepped in, smiling, saying if there was trouble to send such students to her, so I marched the seeming leader to her room. She kept him a while and he was much improved the rest of the day, but there were many others.

As I completed the roll and collected the lunch money from four pupils the Assistant Principal entered. I asked him if I should accept their word that they had free lunches, whereupon he promptly asked them to stand to be counted for tickets. Fourteen stood; I ordered fifteen, feeling someone might come in late. I wanted to list the names as always, but a lady came in to collect the money and gave me the fifteen tickets. The Assistant Principal had said they had library at 9:30 so they then lined up to leave and I walked with them to the other room.

I was to relieve another teacher in a Spanish Class while my group had their library period. The class was one of about twelve youngsters, five years of age. I was at a great disadvantage as all my material was in the other room. We started with thinking games but the two other Spanish teacher aides in the room kept talking to each other with such loud voices, in Spanish, that I gave up as the wee, little voices of the children could not be heard. Exercises and songs were introduced which they seemed to enjoy.

After the library period I finally managed to get the fourth graders started doing some work. Interesting, fun activities were promised for the afternoon. To their seeming dismay oral reading classes were started in one corner, and, as I expected, they were reading in second grade material, many not able to do this. There were four groups and each read a story, taking individual turns.

Two boys continued to cause much trouble, refused to come to reading, and as they were not doing any seatwork I finally took them to the teacher next door. One look at them and she told me – in very loud terms – to take them to the Assistant Principal, saying she knew them, and if I did not follow through right away I would have much worse trouble in the afternoon.

The Assistant Principal was in the lunchroom. He told me to have the boys "get their coats" and come to him. When I returned to the room the entire class was standing outside in the hall, a Spanish individual talking very fast in Spanish constantly. The class told me they were to have lunch. The Spanish teacher was getting more excited by the minute. I opened my purse and took out the tickets, but would not move until the classroom door was locked as all my material was in there, three satchels full.

As I distributed the tickets I expected the worst – and got it. I didn't know one hand from another that was shoved in front of me so about five had no tickets. But I felt all would manage to obtain lunch which was true as no one complained later. I ate with the teachers in a room upstairs. Two tables of teachers were sitting, eating, without a single word. I commented on the lovely quiet, to which they smiled, saying it just happened that way for the moment. However, they were never noisy, but spoke softly when they did so, which was not often. They appeared pleasant, happy and relaxed.

After eating I returned to the room and put another fun assignment on the board, a Secret Code Letter, which was explained, and several decoded it, many others thereafter copying it to use.

After seatwork was starred oral thinking rhyming games were introduced which they thoroughly enjoyed. The boys won, but two-thirds of the class were boys. Next we had the Milton Bradley Contraction and Abbreviation Games of bingo which provided painless review. I doubted they knew the abbreviations so told the answers as the game proceeded as there is great learning value in seeing the correct answers on the cards. This held their attention for some time until one girl remembered art work had been promised.

There was a starved feeling in this class for art work, and seeing the blankness of the room I could understand it. Usually classes two and more years behind achievement levels are very good in art. After distributing the work I was surprised that little talent seemed to emerge, although excellent samples of work done by others in lower grades had first been shown.

About seven papers were bright, cheery and interesting so I put them on the top wall with a bit of mystic tape in a location suggested. Another cautioned me papers were not allowed on the walls. This is true, but I told her I had used just a bit of mystic tape and her teacher could move them.

The class left happily and quietly, admitting it had been a nice day and that I had been a good sub. I asked if they had a lot of subs which they said they had – awful ones. I asked if they hadn't forced the subs to be that way, and after considering this they agreed. Most likely this was a problem room in the school.

I walked on to my car which had been parked in the school lot. It was sprinkling a little so I removed a notice on the windshield, placing it in my purse. Later, at home, I read it and learned I was being warned; that this lot was not for the public; that the next time I parked there my car would be removed by a towing company!

At first I was angry. Then the smiling, happy faces of the children as they left, and the nice comments they made when leaving soon replaced the annoyance. After all, schools are for children, and difficult as the day had been, I had come through with happiness and had offered a number of educational endeavors that might leave an imprint on some of the class.

Chapter 32

Gym Wrestling

At 8:20 Substitute Center called me for Lafayette School. I signed in the school at 9:00 for a class of six year olds, having been told the school did not have grades, but levels.

At the office counter, when signing in, I had observed eight pads of signing in sheets for regular incoming teachers, and felt this must be one of the largest schools in the city; usually there had been but one sheet for signing in in the schools where I had been. Substitutes sign in on a separate record, and here again, instead of one to four vacancies to be filled for the day, eleven were listed. Later, when leaving, I noted that two vacancies had not been filled; also that four other names had been written on the sheet, evidently being teacher aides, or teachers of extra-curricular subjects.

In the room a TESL Teacher was taking the roll, which I appreciated. She also wrote a morning story on the board while I hung up my coat and got my supplies out. "TESL" means a teacher who teaches English as a Second Language, and I saw each child here was of Spanish background. I also saw a special sweetness in this class; each child seemed to radiate loveliness. The teacher told me that but a handful could do a little reading, which did not surprise me; somehow I had expected them to be at a level between kindergarten and first grade. Nineteen were present, ten being absent, but it was a cold, damp day and one on which very young children were often kept home.

I wrote a simple, short, happy poem on the board for them to copy. Next I borrowed a reading book from a child and wrote a seatwork story of those words to be copied. The pupils read it orally and all copied the three board papers, plus some simple adding and subtraction work. It was soon apparent they could add but not subtract so I drew tiny circles by the top numbers and explained the bottom number told them how many to cross out. Some did it correctly after this, but most at least copied the work. What a difference in attitude to seatwork compared to the 4th and 5th graders I had had recently.

The class said gym was after recess and as there was no time schedule to be found I sent a note to the office asking for the gym time, lunch time, and for six pencils. An answering note indicated gym was at 10:05 to 10:35, lunch from 12:00 to 12:25 and "We don't give out pencils". Searching my purse and the desk I found four which were needed, the other two having been requested as extras, so everyone had materials to write with. The extras were intended for those who lost theirs during the day – a usual experience in primary grades.

Many finished one or two papers before the gym period. Gym was on the third floor. As I entered the gymnasium I felt a great sense of airiness and being lifted up of joy and freedom. The room was so vast, the size of four classrooms, or more. The brightness of the outside came in through three sides of windows, explaining the sense of lightness. This was wonderful; so different, I wondered why all modern buildings had gyms in the basement. But gym is so important to children, such fun, that the location is not too important.

Before the end of the period I returned to observe what they were doing. As I entered it must have been a free period as many children were all over the gym, doing their thing. Hoops. Jump rope. Hopscotch. Piano playing. Balls. Four were sitting watching. All were girls. I saw a young female gym teacher, who explained to me that two classes were here having gym together; that the boys were in an adjoining room, having wrestling. Opening the door carefully I saw two lines of boys, ready to leave, but I asked if I might see some wrestling as I had never witnessed it before. The male teacher agreed and called two youngsters, one from the room I had brought up.

The boys faced each other, and as he blew a whistle they darted to each other, and went down onto the mats, arms about one another. The teacher was bending over, watching closely, and soon it was over. To me it looked like a normal, every-day fight that teachers and mothers see constantly. The gym teacher agreed, adding they were too young to follow much of wrestling procedure.

After gym, the toilet stops, about seven came with first pre-primer booklets for reading. Pre-primers are little soft-cover booklets that are the first ones used in reading classes. The number of the booklets varied with the book publisher. These were by Banks Company, who offer many such booklets, which to me, seem to be one of the easiest sets to use for beginning readers who have problems with reading, as in this class, a different language being used at home. Obviously, these pupils had had two of the stories and read the words well, individually and then in unison as each page was read. We added another story, using the same procedure but did not do work in the workbooks as I felt that should be supervised by their regular teacher when she was present.

Many students had completed all the work before lunch time, and the papers were all marked with stars. Luncheon was one they liked – pizza, corn, fruit salad and milk. After lunch a Spanish Teacher Aide entered explaining she would be there until 2:00 to help; however, she left at once. I looked for her as I wanted her to find a record player for us and saw her talking on the hall telephone. She remained there for half an hour so I finally went after her. She didn't seem to want to look for the music player, so I left her with the class and searched for one myself. Fortunately I located one, but it only worked on the 75 speed, of which I had but one record, "The Polka", to which we danced. I returned the machine and borrowed another one, but with the same results. Possibly the plug-in socket was not working properly. I don't know. Both teachers looked at me as if I had damaged their machines.

Returning, I had the class sing songs, and one was especially entertaining, fun and well done. It was about riding on a bus, and they sang the different sounds they heard there. Not being gifted with a musical voice I always carried records to offer as music and storytelling as well. I distributed colored papers which we folded into squares and with crayons printed the alphabet letters, capitals and small letters, putting a picture of the sound of each one in the appropriate square. Somehow these did not come out very neat or desirable for bulletin boards so I passed out other art outlines I had brought, first showing samples of how others had colored the papers. A few of these were quite nice and I left them on top of the desk for the teacher. She already had a colorful, inviting room, but these were very nice to use also.

The sweetness of this class lingered with me for hours, and my experience from traveling from school to school had taught me to reason that much of a class attitude and behavior was determined by the regular teacher; I felt theirs must be a very nice one.

Although very immature (many lost their pencils during the day), they were relaxed, very complimentary (many complimented me on my rings and bracelets when we ate together at lunch time), and their printing was progressing very nicely. They also knew the alphabet and the sounds of the letters; to me this was a very important step towards reading. Reading is based on sounds, not the names of the alphabet letters.

I had a good feeling about this class – that most of them would be ready to make progress in the fall and that all would become good readers. It was a fine feeling to be with such a class of youngsters. And they, too, seemed to enjoy the day. Most waved good-by to me as they left the building.

Chapter 33

Sick Attendance Book

Not being called by Substitute Center until 8:30, I entered a 2nd grade classroom about two minutes before the children did. A fifth grade boy was there feeding the fish. He started talking and did not stop, although I asked him to leave and said the class would feed the gerbils, a duty he said he was to do. However, it took me 25 minutes to manage to get him out of the room, and all the time he talked incessantly. When I finally gave up and walked him out, he still returned, stood inside the door, talking, saying he would be back at 10:30. He returned at recess, was not admitted, and was back at closing to get his brother. I suggested he walk beside him but not break the line until the class was outside the building.

Meanwhile little children had come in; they seemed so very little, even smaller than usual first graders. It was an extremely slow group. There were one-third empty seats, which the class explained was due to children being other places, saying they would return after recess, so I postponed taking roll until that time.

The side blackboard was mostly covered with art and teaching skills; I removed a few items not taped down and wrote some completion sentences. On the front board only a small center section could be used for assignments. All the work was read and explained. Four pencils were given to youngsters who had none; later I found two others had just sat, having none.

When reading I learned they were in the first soft-cover pre-primer booklet; many had left their books and workbooks at home. All seemed very immature, fidgety, inattentive.

When not in a circle reading the pupils seemed to be constantly moving about, often sitting together. Being so little there was sufficient space for two to sit together, but I wanted to know what they could do individually and continually requested them to sit in their own seats. But every time I looked up there were empty seats as the children had moved other places or sat with a friend. They never gave up, and neither did I. And of course this fanned a constant flow of conversation on their part. Everything was going fine until three loud-mouthed girls from an upper grade wandered in, talking loudly. I told them we were staying in because we needed the time, and asked them to leave, but it took most of the recess time to get them out and have it quiet again. They kept talking about papers, saying something about taking the papers. (Later I felt they may have come to grade the day's work, but I do this to ascertain the progress of the children.) I told them to return the next day and finally ushered them out, one by one.

The door on the room did not close, but was a swinging door, without a knob, so they stood outside, talking loudly for some time, pushing the door open, so I got out the Polka record and had the class dance and then do exercises. Finally the girls left.

The attendance book was really a dilapidated looking one. Usually teachers keep them covered as this is an important record that is kept permanently by the school. Not covered, this was torn in two places; inside it was a real scramble as well. Attendance had been recorded throughout in pencil, as well as the month-end totals. One third of the names were in soft pencil, barely legible.

As I called the roll I was told several had moved, or changed schools. It developed that of the 42 listed in the book, thirteen had left. Two were absent.

Three paid for lunches; twelve had free tickets, others went home as lunch time was from 12:00 until 1:00. I ate in the teachers' room in ten minutes and returned to the classroom. About seven upper-grade pupils were there, banging on the piano, mulling about the teacher's desk, talking loudly. I got them all out explaining I needed to plan for the afternoon. After erasing the board, it was replaced with easy poems to be copied.

When the class returned we had adjusted to each other much better. The poems were read and the box of seven star symbols shown to them. Any papers completed were brought up to be starred, which acted as a stimulus to start others completing their work. One tiny boy did most of the work, all done correctly; others were busy trying to borrow pencils.

By mid-afternoon most of the papers had been checked and starred, and art work was given out. About this time, in wandered the noisy upper-grade girls again and the morning experience was repeated.

At one time I noticed one little fellow was not in his seat, or in the room, and learned he had left with another little boy – through the cloakroom door which opened only from the inside to the outer corridor. I was not aware there was a door there. When they returned in about fifteen minutes I said they needed a pass from the office. But they had already been there, explaining they had wanted a drink!

I told them I intended to call their fathers and opened the attendance book to write their home numbers. One said he didn't care as his father wouldn't do anything. I felt he was probably right. He had been one of the worst wiggle worms about moving from seat to seat, talking, and fighting in the cloakroom all day. I felt he was a smart child but his behavior was keeping him here.

At one time the Principal quietly appeared, asking for one girl to come to him, whereupon he asked her how she felt "after falling down". He explained it had happened the previous day in the classroom. She was a larger girl than most, very active, and a loud talker. It seemed she had fallen in the cloakroom, being tripped by a boy. Her mother had come and the Principal had carried her down to the car. This day she had been very active so it had been a minor injury.

This girl had defied me by leaving the classroom during the morning, reacting to a minor occurrence in which she was not even involved. She, and the boy who had left "to get a drink" in the afternoon, had left in the morning as well because I refused to star a paper he brought me. It had not been his, but another child's that he had picked up from the floor. I noticed the difference in the printing of the name and the work on the paper. Their departure seemed to be a climax to the morning noise, movement and confusion and I felt their purpose was to have me go after them. Although concerned about their leaving, knowing I was responsible for them, I decided to defeat their purpose and wait their return. In about 20 minutes the door opened slowly and both came in. I continued with the reading and said nothing as they went to their seats.

Toward the end of the day the two little fellows who had left the room continually came to me, giving me interesting compliments about how much they loved me, what a good teacher I was, how pretty I looked, etc. and always ending by asking if I was still going to call their fathers. I replied I was still thinking about it. Two days later I was still thinking about it. But I didn't. The responsibility for the class was with the regular teacher, not me.

Chapter 34

Too Many Teachers

When called to substitute at Goudy School I had my first experience with serious parking problems, driving around searching for thirty minutes.

The clerk said I had a first grade class and it was 8:50 as I entered the classroom. Two adults were there, speaking rapidly, and loudly, in Spanish. I surveyed the room; the floor was carpeted. One side was completely windows, one was of cabinets for coats and supplies; the front and back of the room had blackboards, but they were mostly covered with taped-on materials, which always infuriated me. Blackboards are supposed to be used for teaching. There was a movable blackboard in the back-center and this, too, was half covered with taped on paper.

After hanging up my coat I started putting printing material on the front board to be copied. A Spanish teacher aide tried to stop me, saying I was never to write on the board. I explained I had taught first grade for twenty years and completed the poem to be copied, and before the class entered I removed the paper taped on the center board and covered both sides with work.

The children were adorable. They came in smiling merrily and chattering loudly in Spanish. There seemed to be three groups according to the arrangement of three long tables – no desks. The Spanish teacher aide said she took one Spanish group of twelve for the entire morning. All their work was done in Spanish, reading, writing and arithmetic. Later in the afternoon I was surprised to find another Spanish teacher in my part of the room; she insisted the room was hers for an hour, and she taught arithmetic to the entire class, using workbooks. The smaller group of twelve had no English work all day.

In the morning I took three reading groups, the children promptly coming to the back section with books (some of which were at home!) and workbooks, and each group read two stories, individually, and did two sections of the workbooks. All were in hardcover, 1A reading books, and all read very well. They also completed the workbooks correctly, the smarter ones trying to pretend ignorance and needing help, which I secretly enjoyed, but pretended not to notice. While they read the other groups copied the board assignments which I was glad I had put on the board. However, all did print very well, so the teacher had somehow taught printing without abundant board work, which really did surprise me. Having been a secretary in the business world for years and working for top executives, many of whom could not read their own writing, I felt it a teacher's duty to teach pupils to write legibly as well as learn to read and understand arithmetic.

At recess time the Spanish teacher took the girls to the washroom; I took the boys. Then 7th graders came in and took the class for exercises and games. It was fun to watch them enjoying themselves. A favorite game, one new to me, was one of competitive relays between two students, who ran to a chair, built five blocks on top of each other, then ran back to the starting place. Sometimes two additional blocks were added, making it very difficult, but everyone had fun. Next I played the Hokey Pokey record, which everyone danced to following instructions on the record. Primary children always enjoy this.

At 11:30 math was put on the board, and they finished this as I starred papers. At 11:50 all lined up for the washrooms and lunch, which was served in the corridor outside the room.

When all returned with filled trays another Spanish teacher aide told me she came in for ten minutes and I could go to the teachers' room for lunch, which I did – to get away from the N O I S E. The children were smart, able to read, and do math, but they were the noisiest class I had ever been with. Of course, much of this was from the other Spanish teacher aide in the room, who had talked loudly to her group all morning. In fact, most of her class kept talking loudly to each other all morning. Her children were adorable, vivacious, talkative, but always up out of their seats, moving about, constantly yelling at one another.

Just before lunch I had tried to present two beautiful Easter Ideal Poem books to my group, but it was not too satisfactory with all the noise from the other part of the room. Poems, even with the beautiful Ideal pictures, are to be enjoyed in a quiet atmosphere.

Returning to the room after lunch another Spanish teacher aide was there, one with authority, who insisted this was her time. She maintained she would have the class until 1:30. Due to this we were not able to complete the Easter Story Books. This was a good teacher; the class was noisy, but she kept trying to control them.

In about 40 minutes the Spanish group of twelve had completed two pages in their math workbooks so I showed the teacher, saying I would star them. Then I distributed ditto papers of Easter Eggs to be colored, after showing them samples of good art work of the eggs. Little by little the other two groups finished their math and also colored the egg outlines after studying the sample pages. There were some very, very good artists in this group. We had time to make an art card to take home with the Easter Poem seatwork folded inside. There was no glue or paste to be used and we needed to attach a folded egg to the card, so I took the teacher's stapler, showed the Spanish teacher aide how to staple the yellow folded eggs to the papers, but she refused to do it and sat down, watching. This surprised me, but I continued going from one group to another, showing and explaining what to do and then stapling the papers, keeping one eye on the clock as we were racing to finish before closing time. Somehow all did finish and left happily.

I left a note complimenting the morning teacher. This had been one of the two best achieving classes I had been in all year at first grade level. These children were being *taught* and it left a very good feeling with me.

Chapter 35

Top Art Teacher
Music Student Directed

Alcott School was a three-story brick structure, relatively new looking and inviting on the outside. After driving around the entire block area, I was delighted to find there was a school parking space as well. The inside was equally new looking and I later learned it had been repainted and decorated the previous summer. The walls were a yellow-cream, hall lockers a golden brown, all floors polished and glistening. The washrooms had new white tile, with orange toilet doors. The hall bulletin boards were most attractive, all three-dimensional; many boards displayed children's composition papers as well as art decorations. Classrooms were fully carpeted. It was a beautiful, uplifting school to be in.

The third graders assigned to me appeared to belong in this school, looking alert, interested, well-behaved, and noting the three isolated seaters, I quickly assigned extra cherished duties to them. One constant talker seemed unable to stop talking, and I later learned he had spent half his school days for the past two years attending Children's Memorial Hospital to overcome his difficulties. Having had many such children while teaching I did not inquire into this, assuming it pertained to his personal background. Toward the end of the day he was somewhat subdued, or in control. I felt adjusting to a new teacher probably over-stimulated him.

As I had arrived about 8:15 I had had time to fill the blackboard with work to be done and had studied the time sheet and teacher's suggestions. It was the most organized school I had ever been in. The teacher's notes indicated the attendance book would be picked up at 9:05 and lunch records, with money, at 9:15. The students advised me to place the attendance record outside the door, where I then noticed a large paper pocket was adhered to the outside of all classroom doors. These arrangements eliminated the usual morning interference during reading periods of children, or teacher aides, entering and leaving the room to take care of such duties.

The only difficulty encountered was having many children copy and complete the board assignment; strangely enough, about one-third chose to sit and do nothing. This I did not realize for some time as they remained quiet. Although I had said none could enjoy recess until some of the work was done I could not keep them in on such a fine day, so after five minutes let all go outside.

We had three reading groups before recess and all read at their grade level, able to answer questions, three of the talkers wanting to impress me with their reading ability. There were different sources of reading material in the room, and most youngsters had brought their own pencils; some had their own paper to use.

At 11:00 an Art Teacher entered and this proved to be a most interesting period, to me as well as the class. She showed colored slides of different types of art on a screen, eliciting comments, descriptions, and explanations from them about the work. It was not a lecture, or art talk and her method held the interest of the majority. Her questions kept them thinking, which children enjoy. I noted the inattentive ones, whispering, and expected them to follow through in such manner throughout the day, which they did. But the teacher had a soft voice and continued as if not noticing them; she was very quiet, undisturbed. Her questions and the answers of the class were really interesting. Many pictures were symbolic, some modern, some realistic by old masters. Some comments were, "It's hard to look at"; "It's bright", to which the teacher answered, "It is." This was pertaining to a very brightly painted painting, which she later said was waters; it had been of yellows and orange and whites all mixed and bubbling, or so it seemed to me. There were works of ancient to modern times. At 11:30 she said Picasso would be the subject of the next visit.

As I observed the class I noted nameplates, printed by the teacher and decorated by the students, had been attached to the front of the desks, thus enabling any teacher, or visitor, to know the names of the pupils. The art on the cards was very attractive. (In first and second grades nameplates are used on the tops of desks to help children print them correctly.)

This was a closed-campus school, meaning all the children ate in school, the school closing at 2:30 PM. At lunch I started to eat in the teachers' room, next door, as the small children's lunchroom was unusually noisy, but when I questioned who stayed to supervise the youngsters, I was told the classroom teacher remained with them, so I returned and joined the class. Although I had brought my own lunch, as usual, the chicken looked so good that I ordered that instead, and it was even better to eat. I was very surprised that it cost but 75 cents as in most schools this would have been $1.25 – and not been half as tasty. Even the carrots were cooked just right, having a true flavor and not being overcooked. Everything about this school was very impressive and inviting.

After lunch the pupils insisted they had a music period on that day in another room, which proved to be true, the teacher expecting them. I learned I was to remain with the class. Again, the period was very interesting. As we walked up the stairs I noted there were about two-thirds more girls in the class than boys, which was unusual. In the Music Room there were paint jars on a long table, and paint edgings on the floor, as if they had come from edges of painted papers; the room was probably alternated for art and music classes. The singing was very good. The children sat where they chose and took turns in directing the session. They sang to the teacher's piano music, sometimes using books. A song I especially liked was "Kum Ba Yah" in a book by Follet named "Discovering Music Together".

Returning to the room there was an oral math period, then written board work while the other reading group had reading. Last was art work, using ditto butterfly papers I had brought. This paper activated many sitters to produce a work paper whereby they might also receive an art paper to color. Before closing time every child had started to produce some work even though several had been very late self-starters.

It had been a pleasure to be in such a school. The teachers, as well, had been friendly and helpful. Those teaching primary grades were greatly concerned they might be re-assigned as the enrollment seemed to be declining. But it was in a good location and this could change at any time. For the sake of the school, the teachers, and the pupils, I hoped the situation would soon improve.

Chapter 36

Clerk Anywhere?
Water Sprinkler

Substitute Center called me at 7:30 and although I arrived at Ravenswood School at 8:30 it was necessary to park a full block away from the school as there seemed to be no area for teachers' cars and all street spaces were filled.

There was no one in the office, no clerk. After waiting several minutes I signed in on the one empty space left for a substitute. Two other subs had already signed in. Two teachers coming in informed me it was for a first grade room. What a relief. During the recess period I saw the two other substitutes and learned one had an 8th grade room and one a split fifth and sixth class.

The Principal came in soon and gave me a key for the door, which I had to return right away to him as none had been left in the key box. The clerk had not returned; I felt she was absent, but at recess time one teacher commented the clerk "was never in the office". This was most unusual as school clerks usually have so much clerical work that they barely have time to eat lunch, and teachers are always needing them for details about children from the office files.

Although it was a hot day I had been assigned to a cool basement room, once the high windows were opened, and the door left open. It was a delightful class; one that remained quiet without more reminding. Eight written assignments were put on the board and there were eight star symbols to stamp on completed papers. It was explained to the class that they could select any symbol they wanted for each completed assignment.

The first reading group proved to be good readers, reading in a 1A book. The second group was not as steady in reading, but were in a 1A book also. The city neighborhood librarian came in during the second reading group so she talked to them about coming for library cards and to use books during vacation times.

Shortly after this two seventh graders came to take charge of the class at recess. As it was so hot outside they decided to have games in the cool room. I learned there was no coffee sold to teachers, but a friendly teacher aide told me to follow her. She showed me where the teachers heated water and loaned me a cup and some instant coffee. When I returned to the classroom the two helpers were teaching the children a song. They seemed to really enjoy their work of being with the children, so the class appeared happy with them as well.

After recess the second group finished reading. Four in this group needed much special help and much practise as they really could not read the material. The third group were in beginning reading books, meaning these six would be a year behind in reading at the end of their first school year.

The outside sprinkler had been turned on about 10:50, and although I saw the water entering through three windows I left them open as felt it would become too hot if they were closed. The children sitting near those windows moved to other seats. When the class left for lunch I got a school mop and tried to mop up the water. But it had become very deep through two rows so all I could do was even it throughout the entire room area. Fortunately, my shoes had half inch thick rubber soles. As I was putting the sopping mop away a janitor was in the clean-up room. He then returned to the room with a pail that had a wringer attachment and really removed the water. This was a very pleasant janitor, not at all upset or angry, but smiled often and said this was his job to do. This school was indeed fortunate to have such an employee, so cheerful and helpful. During this time I discovered a long pole and figured out how to open the high windows by lowering them from the top, so the lower sections could remain closed. About then, the sprinklers were moved farther away.

Most of the students went home for lunch, just a few eating in the school; this was a school having "open campus" meaning it was open until 3:15 because of the going-home lunch hour. More seatwork was on the board for the class at 1:00 when they returned. All the assignments were short ones, usually of four lines.

Among this work were two poems which I read to them from the board after which one little girl exclaimed, "Where did you find poems like that!" Her eyes were beaming, and my heart ached because she was one of the slowest group, hardly able to read at all at the end of her first year in school. I smiled, explained I enjoyed poems and was glad she did, adding I found most of the ones I liked best in children's magazines in the school and in the Public Library.

And inasmuch as the class was having their public library cards processed at this time I suggested she ask the city librarian for some books of poetry when her card was ready as there were many fine books of poetry for beginning readers, especially the Mother Goose Rhymes.

After PM reading all papers were stamped, with whichever symbol the child selected. The package of eight symbols seemed to encourage more work being completed. These first graders chose the Bunny Stamp, the Santa, and the big Star most often. Later I learned second and third graders preferred the Flag, the big Star, Washington and Lincoln. Other stamps were a Pumpkin and a Turkey.

After reading we had a short puppet show, using two rubber open-mouth puppets, an alligator and a frog, which they liked. A story was read about the Statue of Liberty, and children told of trips they had made to visit this statue. Others then told of summer vacation plans. As various pupils told of planned trips to relatives we seemed to travel from California to Missouri, New York, Virginia, Florida and Alabama. It was nice to have so many relatives living all over the U.S. that we could enjoy hearing about.

It had been a pleasant day for everyone. Before leaving a messenger brought a note from the principal asking if I would take a 2nd grade room the next day, and although I had other plans, somehow this school with its friendly teachers, and happy children, seemed really inviting, so I agreed to return.

I recalled another friend of mine always said 2nd grade was a teacher's paradise. Now that I had been subbing nearly a year I was inclined to agree with her but only pertaining to substituting and being in a room a day or so. The 2nd graders were "broken in" to academic work and able to follow through with assignments. But First Graders still had a very special place in my heart as that had been my first regular teaching assignment for several years and it remained a cherished memory.

Chapter 37

At Grade Level
Workbooks Graded by Students

At Ravenswood School a 2nd grade teacher asked me to take her class the next day so the principal asked me to return.

It was a pleasure to know the grade in advance so I could take work especially geared to that level. However, the time somehow got away and I arrived to the school at 8:45. Fortunately, it was a "late day", meaning the pupils entered at 9:10, so I did have time to prepare board work before they arrived. I was surprised, and pleased, to find a boy from the class already there busily opening the high windows from the bottom and the top with a long pole. He also watered a geranium plant which needed water.

The outside weather was 70 degrees but it was over 80 degrees, and stuffy inside, so his help was especially appreciated. It took him 25 minutes to complete the job; in fact, we both finished just as the class came into the room. I had written a short poem, with ten questions about it, plus five rows of mathematical computation problems to be done; these ranged from easy to more difficult 2nd grade work.

The youngsters appeared happy, and cheerful, but proved to be constant talkers and up and out of their seats, visiting other children. This continued most of the day, with repeated reminders that such behavior was not acceptable. Only one boy was absent, and the children were interested, and able to perform good work. However, by the end of the day I realized that a minimal amount of seatwork was being turned in. The eight star symbols had been displayed after the roll was taken, with the explanation that stars would be given for each paper completed correctly.

The first reading group proved to be the largest, encompassing most of the room. This group was reading 2A work very well. This was the day to grade the workbook pages done previously so each child stood, by turn, and read the selections, with corresponding correct answers. The workbooks had been exchanged in the group and were marked by other pupils. They explained that if a child had more than two incorrect answers to a page the mother was asked to visit the teacher for an interview about that child's progress. Some pupils had not completed the work so the grader wrote "DO" on the pages. They had been well trained to handle the grading and watched it conscientiously, as well as trying to watch how their own work was being handled.

The next group of eight youngsters also brought workbooks to be graded in the same way. They were at 2B level. There seemed to be a little difficulty here in wanting certain others to grade their work, or trying to retain the pages themselves, but the books were finally exchanged.

The reading groups had been timed well as two groups had finished before uppergrade class pupils came to take the children to the washrooms, then to recess play.

After recess the third, and last group, came for reading. This was a group of six boys and girls, all carrying 1B reading books, but only one was able to read in it, so I had the one read, the others watching. But the book was so advanced that they were not able to pay attention, so after the one child read a story, I got some preprimers for the others.

However, no one was able to read in this one either, so I turned to letter sounds. Two knew these: five did not. These five were inattentive, squirmers, very mobile throughout the day, quickly moving about to visit, or just keep on the move. My heart really ached for them as they needed so very much special help to get started in reading. I felt they had the ability. Having taught in the public school for many years I knew there could be any number of explanations for their lack of progress, but I still wanted to do something.

At this time the art teacher entered, telling me she would dismiss them at lunch time. I felt she meant I should leave the room so I made up some ditto sheets for the slow learners to use to learn the sounds of the letters and the blends. Then at lunch I drove home and got a Milton Bradley Homonym and Antonym Game, a word bingo game, two mix-and-match picture card boxes, an alphabet picture book and some alphabet flash cards and blends to use.

The afternoon seemed a little more harmonious as everyone was more involved at his own level. The slower learners used the matching game cards, which they found to be fun, plus needing some thinking to figure out. Some enjoyed the alphabet picture book. Most liked the homonym card game, which proved to be a close one in score between one half of the room against the other. They had been studying homonyms for some time and liked this activity.

Next there was art work and all papers of the day were stamped with star symbols. Some collected many stars; some brought up but one or two papers. It was then I realized so fully that many had been sitting without working much during the morning. They were obviously used to working with ditto worksheets as I had seen a big box of these papers by the teacher's desk, but I like to assign lots of handwriting work as feel children need it. However, many of the papers that were completed did have truly beautiful printing on them.

Even with the talking it had been a pleasant day. The children were very likeable, alert and fun to talk to. It was really wonderful to be with a group of youngsters of this age, so eager and active. Even their names had been of unusual interest as I read the roll call. They were a truly cosmopolitan group, from all nationalities and ethnic groups, all beaming with joy and interest in life.

Chapter 38

Quiet Class
1st Absentee in 3 Days Here

The Principal of Ravenswood School had asked me to return the previous day to take a 3rd grade room so I was able to again take material specifically for this grade level. But from previous experience in the school I also took beginning 1st grade level material as well, which proved to be very useful.

The children in this classroom were very quiet, which was a great relief, and we were able to accomplish much more than would have been possible otherwise. Later I learned the regular teacher maintained a steady quietness in the room. This teacher had left an excellent Lesson Plan Sheet of suggestions for the day and her desk was in top order, both on top and inside.

The attendance book indicated 34 pupils had been in attendance, but ten had left so there were only 24 at this time; one was absent. For the three days I had been there, in three rooms, only one had been absent, so the school must check absences very carefully. This room had stationary seats for pupils, something unusual in my experience in various schools; in fact, the other two rooms I had taught in here had had moveable desks.

The only problem with the stationary desks was in oral reading as there were no extra desks to move to the front. The children informed me there were but two reading groups and that they remained in their seats. I asked those in the first group to stand to see where they were and was surprised to see twenty children stand. I had them read row by row, watching the lips, and listening to the voice of each child. If one read much faster than the others I had that child stop and read later, until I checked the entire class. The book had very interesting stories and was a third grade level, and each child read satisfactorily. All were able to answer questions about silent reading as well and to enjoy the activity.

One little girl seemed unable to do any seatwork and although she copied the math problems, all the answers were wrong, so I made up some 1B work for her, using tiny circles by the numbers to be added,

117

or to be crossed out in subtraction. She was able to get most of the adding correct, and received a star which pleased her. She was Spanish, having arrived a month before, and attended a Spanish reading class in the school, where she told me they read in Spanish, not English – as others in the others grades had also told me.

Washroom visits, recess, and a Library Period visit took a great part of the morning, leaving just enough time for the three other boys to read a little while. They, too, were Spanish but could read a little from a first grade book. I gave the girl a word book to study with usable, everyday words and pictures, but she didn't seem to be interested in it.

After lunch there was a little time to complete seatwork I had put on the board in the morning, and after seeing the interesting star symbols being put on student's papers, others became stimulated to turn in some work to obtain these symbols on their papers. In the past I had inked the pad daily, but had not done so for over a week and discovered the imprints were much clearer than when moistened daily. One student completed all the board work, three most of it; nearly all were able to take home one or two papers. This seatwork had been lots more fun than that for lower grades as the higher level was capable of more interesting work. However, first graders enjoy doing everything as everything is so new to them.

At 1:30 we played a Milton Bradley Homonym punch-card game, followed by one of Synonyms and Antonyms, which everyone enjoyed, the boys winning both games. I had brought two sets of "Put-Together" thinking cards for the children of lower-level achievement, so they were happily occupied as well. Next we had oral thinking activities but this class was not sufficiently alert to have much success with them so we changed to rhyming and sounding oral puzzle games. Last was art work, some of which was very good.

All boards were erased, windows put up, papers picked up, and as they walked quietly down the steps at closing everyone, including the teacher, was smiling. It had been a pleasant day.

Chapter 39

Slow Class; Slow School

The call from Sub Center did not come to me until 9:25 so I called Bethune School to ask if I should come in so late. The clerk said they had called in late and that I should come.

When I arrived I sat in the office and waited 35 minutes before being given instructions as to what room to go to. Another substitute came and sat also; she said she had been called late too. At long last another clerk came to show me the room; she walked and talked SO SLOWLY, like in a trance.

The room was for a 2nd grade class. The children were all black; there was a Teacher Aide there, black also, who remained all day, every day. The room was drab, with no work papers or any décor of any kind. Stacks of marked work papers were on one table. Obviously the class had been given lots of work re letter sounds. But they were unable to read – and with two teachers daily! They seemed eager to learn, and mannerly, but were reading in a 1st pre-primer! Already a year and two months behind in even getting started.

They could print a little but had no math skills either. During the day the Teacher Aide returned seatwork completed the previous day, calling the pupils to her individually for help. Possibly this was part of their trouble as I had always graded and returned seatwork done by primary pupils the same day it was done; otherwise the learning value seemed lost. It was difficult to do but teaching has never been an easy job. Occasionally some classes do appear to be listless and dull, but students must go forward, not stand still, and if there seems to be no fire within, then a teacher must somehow kindle interest to get the fires of learning started.

The class had had a Thanksgiving Unit two days before my arrival so my Thanksgiving stories were flat. We made Indians instead of turkeys to capture some interest but although samples of colorful Indians made by first graders were shown to them, theirs were sadly dull and without interest. They seemed to be so sweet, such heart-stealers, but completely listless.

The Teacher Aide left three times during the day for about 45 minutes. One time I noticed her talking on the hall telephone. She returned when she saw the class was leaving for the day, stooped over and kissed each one good-by – breaking up the quiet, orderly line.

The love between them was beautiful to witness, but I felt they were not receiving a fair deal; they were here to learn the three R's, the basic skills of reading, writing and arithmetic. There was no language barrier to overcome. Surely an honest love would have removed the apathy, then stressed and instilled the fundamental skills to ensure their future.

I left with a sad, empty, depressed feeling which never stopped haunting me. A teacher, plus a teacher aide, all day, every day – but still in a 1st preprimer in their second school year. Sad, so very, very sad.

Chapter 40

No Attendance Book
Class OK

Although I found a parking space very close to Audubon School a lady, in a nightgown, standing part way down the side steps of her apartment building, yelled at me to move my car further away from hers, which was directly behind mine. I had checked the open space behind her car and explained there was a five-foot area there. Nevertheless, she snarled, "We'll see about that", before turning and going back upstairs. A driveway in front of my car prohibited me from moving the car forward. But the tone of the woman's voice made me uneasy about leaving the car there so I moved it.

Changing parking places took fifteen minutes but I managed to sign in at 8:45, ahead of any other substitute and was assigned a 4th grade. Climbing the stairs I put two assignments on the board before the class entered. They came in reasonably quietly, a little surprised to see a different teacher.

There was no attendance record to be found and the class said the teacher never took roll but that she took it from the work papers turned in daily. There were lists for free lunchers and the 20 cents and 40 cents ones so these duties were quickly handled. Some pupils persisted in talking and whispering so another child was asked to list such names, which helped a little.

The class looked to be average in ability so I took some more interesting work to put on the boards. One boy won the first word contest and was given a money saving card folder.

The five board assignments were explained and the children told they might select any of them to complete, but that each pupil should do at least two papers during the day. Either they were lazy or the day's expectation had not been emphasized enough as not many finished papers were turned in for stars.

At 10:00 the office clerk reminded teachers the attendance totals were to be sent to her by that time. I was concerned about this as there was no attendance record to check by but sent her a note saying only two pupils were absent, which information was acceptable to her.

During the morning three students said they were "Messengers" and were to go to other rooms to help. I told them to finish the work first, but shortly a voice on the inter-com requested them so they left. In the afternoon three different children said they were then messengers so I let them go. One returned saying he was to bring work to be done; I told him to explain the days's assignments were all on the board; he left and did not return. It seemed two children had gone to the school office to help and one to another official. Later in the day, when seeing the work done by the children, I felt helpers should have been selected from a more advanced room.

Prior to the noon period there had been an announcement that teachers were invited by the PTA to come to the library. This is a usual Fall courtesy extended teachers by their local PTA, so after eating part of my lunch I went to the library. A long table was covered neatly with rows of pastries and one very attractive young mother was there – just one, which surprised me. I sat with the latecomer sub and a 3rd grade black teacher who was especially nice. She told me I might obtain ditto paper in an adjoining room and that if I didn't receive any she would share her supply of last year with me, a most unusual offer as in the schools ditto paper is nearly non-existent and highly guarded, even by principals. The Assistant Principal gave me enough paper for one ditto so I ran off one to use in the afternoon.

After lunch the 4th graders returned quietly and math was a new assignment as some pupils always choose to do this work. After 45 minutes we used the Milton Bradley Contraction and Abbreviation Game, which really fascinated them. They never wanted to stop playing it, once they caught on, which took a good 25 minutes. Although the room was evenly divided between girls and boys, the boys won repeatedly and ended up with nearly one-third more winning points. The oral contest games proceeded slowly, without much reaction until the end as well; this was not an alert class.

Work papers were starred, art work distributed, and students with the most stars on their completed work erased and washed the boards, forever cherished activities. The class was well programmed in knowing the different times they were to leave to be messengers throughout the day, mornings and afternoon; however, leaving a classroom for any reason, at any grade level, seems to be a special activity for pupils.

The room was in good order as we left together quietly. They mentioned homework and were told they could write their teacher a letter about the day's activities if they so chose, or why they wished she would not be absent. With the minimal amount of work received I was not surprised to be asked if this was an expected assignment, and to hear sighs of relief when hearing it was not mandatory, but by choice.

They were a likeable class with no major behavior problems – a great pleasure to any teacher.

Chapter 41

Bradley Contraction Games a Hit
Librarian Helps

In spite of the slow Fullerton traffic I managed to sign in the Pulaski School at 8:30 and was assigned to a 3rd grade room in their Modular Building, next door to the regular school edifice.

The building, and classroom, being quite new and modern, were a delight to be in. The room was well-lighted and cheerfully decorated with new, glossy, brightly colored cardboard educational teaching aids, yellow being one predominant refreshing color. These covered two walls and bulletin boards, one side being windows, one of blackboard space. The floor was carpeted, the desks moveable.

The children lined up in the carpeted corridor outside the door, receiving a substitute's presence without obvious objection. Several inquired where their teacher was, and when I said she stayed home to watch television all day, they laughed. They were friendly and smiling continuously throughout the day – also talking.

About half of the board space had been filled with work before they entered, and after introducing myself, taking attendance and lunch records to report, I finished covering the board with more seatwork, which was explained and read in turn by the various groupings of children. This required some extra time but insured their understanding to complete the work, as well as assure myself they were capable of understanding it.

However, although it was quickly apparent they were able to read, the soft talking and whispering continued so constantly that I rearranged the groupings into straight rows, placing quiet children near the talkers. This, too, took extra time, but the difference in quietness, and in work performance was immediately discernable, and even the children agreed they liked the arrangement better. Changes in seating arrangements are always a welcome change to classes at any time during the year, the refreshing newness often resulting in renewed work impetus as well.

The morning seemed to fly by although everyone kept busy; there was time for only the slowest reading group to read before lunch.

This group of eight youngsters was reading slowly in a 1B book; the next group of ten read after lunch in a 2B book, and the last ten were in a 3B reader.

After lunch one boy kept walking about the room until I finally asked him, "Don't you have a pencil?" to which another quickly responded, "I'll borrow him one."

The class appeared to be primarily Spanish, Vietnamese, Philippinos and whites, no blacks. Only one boy was absent; two had moved, by the third school week in September. All were neat and courteous, the boys having been trained to let the girls leave and enter the room first. Only two requested pencils; one paper; all seemed to supply their own. Later in the day only two admitted having no crayons for art work.

The highlight of the day was using the Milton Bradley Contraction and Abbreviation Card game. It took quite some time for them to understand and be able to use this but even in the beginning they seemed fascinated with it. The game offers tremendous learning and review values in reading. The teacher calls, "can not"; the pupils search for "can't"; "Avenue", they look for "Ave.". Each card is different, and the children punch in the words they find that are called. Once punched in both words are visible, "can not" and below it "can't". As this class seemed so slow in catching on to using the game I told them the correct answers to look for in the beginning, and helped a few who were having difficulty, but after about 40 minutes most seemed at ease with it and the game went much faster. The cards worked like bingo cards to win, having straight or horizontal lines punched in.

The children chose to continue the game instead of taking their library visit and when the librarian came in she helped a while in calling the words as I assisted the slower pupils.

As this was a closed campus school and out at 2:30 there was barely time to check and star the work papers, and distribute some art work before closing time. The art work was not finished by closing time but they were doing very good coloring work on them.

Most likely it was the Bingo Game that caused many to ask if I was returning the next day. It had been a fun day for everyone, children as well as teacher.

125

I realized throughout the day I was working very hard, standing most of the time, and continually watching to keep youngsters working, and quiet, so once home was not too surprised to find I needed to soak in a hot tub to relax from the day's tension. It had been really wonderful to be working so hard again, but a substitute's responsibility does not continue and grow into a constant burden as with a regular teacher as the substitute usually leaves at the end of one or a few days, whereas the regular teacher must watch and constantly promote progress with each child in the room for a ten-month period.

For substitute work I carried three heavy satchels of materials to be used for whatever grade I was assigned but my responsibility for any class ended when I left the building, even though specific memories of children needing help remained with me forever. This day I felt I had contributed a great deal to the learning of the children, and I had enjoyed their youthful exuberance as well.

Chapter 42

Good Class; Sad Class

At Manierre School there were eight or ten sign-in sheets for teachers instead of the usual one or two. After a 20-minute wait for the absent teacher to call in I was assigned to a 2nd grade class. Fortunately there was time to put the board assignment on the board before the 9:00 o'clock bell rang.

The children were neat, clean, well dressed. All were black; they were polite, intelligent and reasonably quiet. 27 were present, 2 absent; all received free lunches.

A black teacher aide was present all day. She was quiet and helpful, one of the best I ever worked with so it was refreshing to learn she was studying to become a teacher. After I took the roll she quietly motioned pupils (by rows) to come to sharpen pencils and had two students pass papers after the board assignments were explained.

The three reading groups took turns reading from Lippincott Basic readers. The first group of ten first read silently and answered thinking questions; they were at ease in oral reading at Level F. The second group of ten could also answer thinking questions and read easily at Level E. Seven in the third group at Level C were a little weak in reading and read much more slowly. They were three-quarters into the reader.

Before leaving the group one little fellow asked, "What do you do for a living sometimes?" As I thought about this he continued, "You can have a store. Then you would not have to go to the store and you could have your own candy. You don't have to have anybody hire you."

The aide helped grade the seatwork throughout the day and during art period these were finished and put in their folders.

It was a pleasant surprise to be sent to the same school the following day to another 2nd grade class—one very different. Shortly after I entered a teacher aide entered. I asked if she would like to erase the board.

"That's not my job!" she retorted. "I don't erase boards!"

I erased the boards and covered them with seatwork.

The class entered, with smiles, and loud chatter, but not as noisily as the aide talking and calling out to them.

While I was explaining the board seatwork the aide had a child start passing paper. This distracted pupils so I asked him to sit down until the work was explained. The aide angrily snatched up the papers.

Several children needed to sharpen pencils. The noise in the room, from both the pupils and the aide, was still at a high level so I said ONE at a time could use the sharpener. The aide, however, kept lining up four and five behind the sharpener, talking to them all the while.

Nine children had no pencils. When I asked the aide if the teacher had any she said, "No, let them borrow from someone." I had them line up, write their names, and loaned pencils from a supply I carried.

When one boy was repeatedly naughty I finally said, "If you keep that up you can go to the office!" This was but a threat, one seldom followed through on my part. But when the aide promptly said, "You don't have to go to the office," I said I'd be back in a minute and went to the office myself. I asked the person who assigned me if it would be possible to find something else for the teacher aide to do. Later an Assistant Principal talked to her and the hostility and loud talking diminished.

The room itself, as well as the teacher's desk, were completely bleak; whereas the walls and desk of the other 2nd grade displayed colorful educational charts and bulletin boards. This room had but one dismal pen-written calendar.

No one was able to do the work on the board so I erased it and put up very easy poems to be copied.

The children's reading, writing and math were sad examples but without discipline and a quiet and activating atmosphere learning is often elusive.

Chapter 43

Like Private School
Science & Art Different Rooms

As I entered Hayt School a large greeting from the Student Council welcomed me. It was in large letters, red and black, reading

Cherries are red
Licorice is Black.
KEY KIDS
We welcome you back!

The first grade room assigned to me was a very large one, newly painted in yellow and white, and most attractively arranged with the desks and chairs arranged in four small circles. An upper-grade room helper, already present, erased the blackboards on two sides of the room, and the specific time schedule left by the regular teacher for the day was very helpful.

Three children were absent from the usual motley group of various racial backgrounds – primarily white, with Oriental, Indian, Spanish, and one black boy.

After putting beginning first grade seatwork on the two blackboards I worried it might be too difficult when I noticed the only work on the bulletin board consisted of name-plate copying. However, the work was read easily by the class, with but a minimum of help. As several youngsters were holding their pencils between their middle fingers I showed them how we usually hold a pencil, resting it between the thumb and forefinger, using the two last fingers as runners, or wheels. This impressed them enough to try the new method as their habits had not yet been too engrained at this early stage of the school year.

There was "walking reading", meaning pupils walked from home rooms to their reading levels, the group in the room being of at least average ability as all were reading in a first pre-primer booklet. However, when I called for Group I to come for reading no one moved. The teacher had a reading record book, neatly prepared in detail, listing the reading skills to be covered, with Group I, II, and III written at the top. Seeing the reading booklets I held up one, asking, "Who reads in this one?" to which nine rose and came to the front. Later I learned all in the room were reading from the same books, at the same place. Each child read one line, in turn, and nearly all were able to do this without much help. It was sweet the way they waited for the slower ones to think of the words without telling them, which is difficult for children in higher grades.

A very friendly first-grade teacher across the hall, who had come in several times offering help, at recess informed me she took the boys and I took the girls to the washrooms on their way to outside play. When they left I walked upstairs to the teachers' lounge, where my friend had told me I could find heated water for coffee. I had learned to bring a plastic cup and instant coffee. The three teachers there were friendly and commented they wondered why they had not seen me before. I was happy to be there as felt at home in this neighborhood in which I had formerly lived.

After recess I read a short story to the class and had time for a music record.

At 10:45 it was "walking math" time, my friend advising me in advance that my group was the low one, and that the teacher had been working with plastic numbers in groups, which could be seen on a flannel board in the room. I wrote different numbers on the board, which they were able to name, then called out numbers asking them to hold up that number of fingers, which most were able to do. Next, I called out numbers, asking them to take away the second number of fingers, telling them this was called subtraction. I wrote the numbers four and two on the board, asking they add the numbers, but only one child could do this, so different groups of items in the room were added, ending with guessing the total of buds on a pussy willow stem, one group guessing twenty-two, the exact total.

The last morning period was one in science, four primary classes meeting in one room for this, where a student teacher presented a Farm Movie Unit, emphasizing the care of cows – their being washed, milked by machines, the milk put into cans, etc. The children were too young to be still so long just before lunch, but with three teachers present they remained quiet throughout the movie and follow-up pictures and questions. As we returned and entered the classroom for wraps one tiny girl looked up at me asking, "Teacher, is it lunch time?"

My neighbor teachers stopped to tell me where the teachers ate their lunch, adding I would find them very friendly. There was hot water on a stove there, for coffee, and the teachers were friendly. The only problem was their conversation subjects, which progressed from the behavior problems of children to the number of teacher meetings, and was climaxed by one saying the previous year a teacher had killed himself by jumping from a third story window. Thank goodness, the teacher next to her explained she knew the man personally, adding he had been having treatments for mental problems for several months. I laughed, feeling the individual who had first mentioned the jumping was disappointed; I thought she liked to impress upon people the thought that teaching was very difficult, but actually I felt they all did enjoy the profession.

There was time to run off a ditto but no liquid, or paper, so I returned to the office to fill the container. The clerk said she had no paper, that it was given out only on Thursdays, but I had brought a supply in case this happened.

At 1:00 there was walking reading again. Another poem was added to the four items on the board for seatwork. The youngsters were good little readers. I called pupils to read first who had done part of the board writing, which caused others to do more work, and later all selected their star symbols for completed work papers.

Afternoon recess was followed by an art period in another room. Pupils were to bring their supply boxes and paints. This proved to be a most interesting period, which the teacher there told me was offered twice weekly. The children were given 15 x 24" art papers on which they had already drawn pictures. The majority had brought paints to use; if not they were told to use crayons or to share. The colors to be used were primary ones, red, yellow and blue.

One little boy was most unhappy all period; I saw no paints by him, and he sat glaring most of the time, finally crayoning his drawing in which I thought was inner frustration revolt due to wanting paints. During the last five minutes desire overcame pride and he borrowed a brush and paints from the pretty girl near him. But his painting was as sloppily done as the crayon work, so it must have been he needed a little help in this area. Nevertheless, from the look on his face all period, I felt certain he would have paints in school the very next day. As the period ended each child carried his painting to a dry space, emptied the water container, collected his supplies and lined up to leave. I was pleased to see this orderly, quiet procedure.

We returned to the room for wraps before leaving. Visiting different rooms for the different subjects had made it a very interesting day – like being in a private school.

Chapter 44

No Walking Reading Fridays
FBI Starlet

Arriving at Brennemann School at 8:15 I parked in the last available space in the teachers' parking lot. This lot was located beside the playground area and many children walk through the lot on their way to and from school. Because of this I preferred a nearby side street area, but due to heavy rain being forecast and the many school items I carried for use in substitute work, it seemed wise to choose the closest spot to the school exit door.

Being assigned a third grade I ran off two dittos for seatwork. This school had a ditto machine, paper and fluid available for teachers plus a teacher aide who ran off orders for teachers during the day as requests came in. There was also time to put a sufficient amount of interesting work on the board before the class entered.

There were 29 in the class, one having moved, and one transferred during the day. The children were primarily Spanish, some Oriental, others black or white. About six completed four assignments, many one; several turned in none. Some boys were overly mischievous but their main problem seemed to be laziness regarding seatwork. Being a substitute I did not make an issue of this. The star symbols had been displayed and were given out throughout the day as work was completed.

The school usually had "walking reading" but not on Fridays, which was this day, so the board work was read instead. A schedule on the wall indicated students went to six different rooms for reading, ranging form first to third grade levels. The school used the Holt reading materials, and much ditto work was provided for seatwork and follow-up review.

During morning recess, which was inside due to rain, a teacher aide patrolled the corridor, giving the teachers a short break, in which I had coffee and ran off an art ditto. The class played a quiet game at this time, and three pupils had been left in charge. When I returned one girl presented me with a checked record of the non-behaviors. Several names were neatly listed, with three to seven checks marked

133

after them. The girl continued talking, relating detailed descriptions of their actions. Three had been talking; two peeking (in the game of Seven-Up); Tony had said a bad word; two had run around the room; one stood up when no one had picked him; one had told a story saying another had his pencil but the pencil was in his desk. I was amazed at her detailed recall ability but did not comment on it as it was obvious she overly enjoyed reporting them.

After recess, and washroom stops there was a gym period. While they were gone, and throughout the day, I tried at various times to complete the monthly summary in pencil for the regular teacher but remained one point off all day. Meanwhile, the transfer request came in for another child, so I completed this and the cumulative record card, the office record card, the attendance record, and attendance follow-through explanation on it. These are details that can be most trying in a busy classroom. Today, with no walking reading, the noise, pressure, and usual interruptions were absent. It was a day to remember in this respect.

The teacher's attendance book was neatly done but I was unable to find a time schedule. The gym time the class told me was too early but the class scheduled at that time was on a trip so it worked out satisfactorily.

There was time to work on some of the boardwork after the gym period.

Children's lunches were served in the corridor. Pupils received the food on trays and returned to eat it in the classroom. About five brought their lunches; the others received free lunches. The menu was of macaroni and cheese, one of my favorites, so I bought a side order of it, and later gave my boiled ham and hard boiled egg to youngsters who did not eat their school lunches and were going to discard them. Sadly enough, much of the good food furnished free to school children is wasted this way.

After a short outside play period, toilet visits and water fountain stops, more work papers were finished and starred.

They reminded me of the bingo game I had promised if they did their work, so the Milton Bradley Contraction and Abbreviation Game Cards were distributed. About half of the class needed help so better readers sat by them as the game progressed. All enjoy this, and little by little the slower readers also had winning cards to report.

Art papers were happily received during the last twenty minutes but this was not enough time for many to finish them. There were a number of fine artists in this group, and papers turned in were left on the teacher's desk.

Chapter 45

Typical Teaching Day
2nd in Age Only

Remembering how difficult to find, and limited, parking spaces were near Stewart School, I arrived very early and found a spot but one quarter block distant. Regularly assigned teachers use a parking garage nearby, and there are a few metered spaces in front of the building but they require continued coin replacement throughout the day.

At 8:15 I signed in and was assigned a 2nd grade room. No work papers were up on any bulletin board; no work on any blackboard, so I looked in a few desks to find out what they could do. One paper of copied alphabet letters was all to be found. The month was October so I put easy first grade Halloween work on the front, side and back boards.

The children were happy youngsters, the usual American mixture of white, black, American Indian, Spanish; I noticed no Oriental or European. Many times I had read this was the settling area for Appalachian Whites. Twenty-eight were listed in the attendance book, two had moved, four came in late; 21 were present for the day.

To keep them quiet and orderly the desks were moved from groups to aisles, and although this made an immediate improvement, many were up and visiting others throughout the day.

Only one boy could read the list of Halloween words I held up before them, which the class then enjoyed reading several times. All of the Halloween board work was read before reading groups came up to the front to read.

It was soon obvious the group was 2nd grade in age only. Two groups read in a preprimer booklet, the other in a 1B reader. Few could tell me the sounds of the letters; one named the five vowels. The majority displayed characteristics of very immature pupils – short attention spans, need of frequent physical activity movements, constant whispering and talking, papers dropped on the floor continually. Even the printing of many indicated they were not yet experienced in producing school papers.

Before their arrival I had found a small supply of colored paper to make Halloween material and had checked the piano in the room, but as there were a few non-working keys decided not to use it.

The school had walking reading so pupils changed rooms soon after 9:00 making more of the usual noise and confusion. After seeing the box of symbol stars promised for work papers, most started to work. Only one boy was without a pencil; paper was supplied by the school.

All papers were starred for effort, the three correct ones receiving double stars. Their happiness, and apparent surprise, in receiving stars was touching.

In the early part of the morning I showed the Haunted Houses we would make so at recess time they quickly decided to remain inside to get started on this work a little earlier. Because of their apparent immaturity I decided not to wait until too late in the afternoon to present the project.

Lunch was at 11:10 and here again supervision was needed as two boys started throwing bread across the long table. Fortunately, the room was small and but two classes were eating there at the time. The lunch looked very tasty (of chicken and noodles) but I had brought my own.

Soon after we returned there was walking math for an hour so I put new work on the boards. Here again, I learned some were unable to copy simple numbers onto their papers. Three children had correct papers; most were able to copy only, having no answers, although the work was simple first-grade adding with totals to ten or less. Possibly this was the lowest reading and math group in the school; I was too busy all day to ask any other teacher about anything. It is a teacher's job to teach at the level she finds children and that kept me busy.

After math time, when the regular children returned, the art project was started. I had brought glue and scissors but was surprised they were able to cut doors and windows as well as they did. Only three needed to restart the work. Colored papers seemed to be at a minimum so I was glad so few were wasted. All were happily occupied in the project as Halloween is very important to young children. At the end of the day most wanted to take the work home so this was allowed. Three put theirs on the bulletin board for the teacher to see.

A janitor went by cleaning the corridor so he brought us an extra broom which two boys used to clean up the floor of the many scraps of paper. Somehow, this always seems a choice job at any grade level!

Only two youngsters had heard the story "Georgie" about a little friendly ghost, so I read that next. It is a catchy story and all became very quiet once the book was started. Most brought their chairs to the front as was suggested so they might enjoy the book pictures as the story was read.

There was time left for a short puppet show which they also enjoyed, a few using the puppets and talking to the class.

The boards were erased, curtains pulled and raised (old style high, double windows), chairs put up on desk tops for night cleaning, and they walked down the stairs quietly enough, proudly carrying their art work.

As I left I noticed how heavy the three satchels felt but didn't think much about it until reaching home. Once there, I realized how completely exhausted I was and how my throat hurt from trying to maintain silence throughout the day and trying to keep them in their seats. It took an hour's rest before I felt like my usual self again. Possibly I tried too hard to present the academic work to such immature children, but they were already 2nd graders – still fidgeting, talking, moving about, like beginning first graders often did.

As I rested I thought of them. One very little boy had brought up his finished writing paper to be starred as I was in the midst of the Halloween project, cutting papers and couldn't stop for him just then. The little fellow didn't bring it up again and I didn't remember it again until school was over and I was home. Another larger black boy had exclaimed, when returning from walking math, that his ball had been taken from his desk. I told him to take another child with him and go to the teacher where the child had gone but when we reached the corridor it was the time teachers had an afternoon break so I told him to wait for the teacher to return. He didn't mention it again; maybe he forgot it as I did, but I doubt it. Most likely he went after it anyway during the teacher-break period. These are experiences that often linger in a teacher's memory, sometimes forever, many of the little things she meant to do.

Classroom time seems to fly away with all the things there are to be accomplished. To me, this always seemed especially true in trying to present the many concepts of first grade work – and these "second graders" were not even advanced enough to absorb them. They had not yet settled down to be ready for regular school learning.

Chapter 46

Spanish Bi-Lingual
Haunted Houses

Lewis was a cheerful, inviting school to enter on a rainy day. The walls were off-white, with yellow lockers on one side of the corridors, orange ones on the other; floors were gray and black checkered linoleum – just the right size for the little first graders to line up on individually. Corridor bulletin boards were colorful, neat and impressive. One near the office named "Designs" made me wish to have a camera to remember it.

One of the three office clerks told me my class was a "Bilingual" one and gave me the key for the second floor room. It was painted a soft yellow, with white ceiling. Five large windows had interesting leaf art work, the leaves secured between wax papers with borders of green construction paper. Large leaf mobile artwork hung from the florescent ceiling lighting fixtures.

There were 28 pupils listed in the attendance book, two being absent. Not one child had moved by the sixth school week, indicating this was a stable neighborhood. One boy said he was age seven; two girls were five; the rest were six years of age. Some youngsters did not look Spanish, but all the parental first names in the attendance book were Spanish.

Seven pupils did not understand English, and at 9:05 a TESL (Teaching English as a Second Language) teacher came for them for a 40 minute period.

The children were all small, and very friendly. Their lockers were in the outside corridor. Inside the desks were in lateral, touching rows, which I changed to straight aisles quite soon to stop the constant soft whispering and talking.

Because it was a week before Halloween I first showed them a large Haunted House we would be making later in the day. There were many cut windows, and one door, all of which opened. On the outside were words of warning, as "Do Not Open", "Stay Out". Inside were pasted scary Halloween ghosts, witches, goblins, etc.

Before putting work on the board the class read a list of Halloween words I had brought; this was repeated several times to help more and more children learn the words. Very easy work was put on the board, and read several times by everyone before being copied. All the work was about Halloween.

Recess was at 10:15 at which time three 8th grade girls appeared to take them outside. After recess and toilet visits, another teacher came to the room for their library period. She alternated her time with stories, exercises and poems they knew and recited.

After the library period we had a few standing exercises as they seemed a little restless. Most had copied two papers and were on the third, last one. Work papers were starred with pumpkin, turkey and bunny imprints.

At noon the same three girl play leaders from 8th grade appeared. One took those going home to lunch to the outside school door; two took those having bag lunches to a first floor room to eat, then out to play until 1:00. Fifteen had been listed to receive bag lunches. As I had overlooked bringing my prepared lunch I bought a school bag for 75 cents, which consisted of a ham sandwich, fruit jello in a container, a milk carton, a banana, and a plastic spoon. I appreciated having the lunch, which tasted fine, and enjoyed eating with the children.

After lunch I looked for colored paper, large scissors and a stapler. Borrowing these, I cut outlines of haunted houses to be made. After the class returned they finished coloring a Halloween picture I had brought; the Halloween words were reviewed, the seatwork read again, and the haunted houses were started. Surprisingly enough, not one child ruined his house. This was fortunate, as the stapler did not work any longer, and there was no extra paper. One child cut a window entirely out but pasted on an outside cover to the window, which could then be opened and closed.

They were able to cut doors and windows by themselves. Many needed scissors, glue and crayons and I was glad I had carried extra supplies as found none in the room. Two-thirds had their own supplies, which was a great help. The previous year I had learned that liquid glue could be poured reasonably quickly and easily on to the tops of small, plastic cottage cheese container covers which were very light weight, and that these could be used indefinitely as the glue dried quickly and did not adhere to adjacent stacked covers. On my scissors I had placed bright red nail polish circles. Pupils' names were listed as scissors (and morning pencils) were loaned, and crossed out when returned. Primary children appreciate the use of these supplies and are quite reliable in returning them.

All were happily and busily occupied finishing their houses for some time. Completed seatwork and art papers were left for the teacher to see as was requested in the list of "Instructions to a Substitute".

The 8th grade girls came to take the children downstairs at closing which was a big help. Floor papers had been swept up and the room looked neat again.

Working with these youngsters had been fun but it had been hard work as I had been standing most of the day. Separating the desks a little had helped quiet the talking. Keeping them supplied with materials kept me very busy and throughout the afternoon questions were asked about the board words to be printed on the outer windows and door. These Halloween warnings of "Stay Out", "Go Home", "Do Not Open", etc. were reread often, each time necessitating my returning to the front board to point out the various phrases.

Several Haunted Houses looked quite neat. The children wanted to take them home and I hoped the teacher would permit it the following day. The class learned quickly and it had been a pleasure to be with them for a day.

Chapter 47

Toy Dolls are Hungry?

When Substitute Center called me to work at Ferguson Child Parent Center I felt it would be a different kind of experience.

The building seemed comparatively new; the teachers were very friendly. But the Head Teacher talked to me for five or ten minutes, and the teacher aide, who was to remain in the room, for another twenty minutes, so I was unable to read the folder of instructions handed to me.

The children waited in line in front of the building until they were called for by the teachers. All entered quietly, hung up their coats inside the room, and sat down. Roll was taken and breakfast was served, which consisted of dry cereal, milk and a portion of a banana. Only one child spilled a little milk on the table.

The class was then divided into groups of reading or math, the math given by the teacher aide. The school reading was by the Dis-tar Method, which had impressed me years earlier in a demonstration I had seen, but it was one I was not experienced in teaching.

They knew most of the sounds of the alphabet very well. Next I said words starting with these sounds, but this was meaningless to them and they could not follow through with it. There were seatwork papers on a table to be used so these were distributed. Most could print their names on their papers. The majority copied the letters well, and colored neatly, but several did not stay within the lines, and one or two scribbled the coloring paper, but they were only four years old and most were already holding pencils correctly.

Later two other classes came in. I read a story, "Georgie", about a baby ghost. Then I was sent to another room and read another Halloween Skit to the class there. While another teacher was reading the book, "Georgie", which I handed to her, I noticed a little fellow with tears running down his face. I motioned to him to come over to me and asked him why he was crying. "I want my mother," he said softly. I put him on my lap saying, "You pretend I'm your mother, and I'll pretend you're my little boy because I don't have a little boy like you." He stopped crying and later went to join others in his class as I left. When I mentioned to his teacher he had been crying because he wanted his mother she answered, "I know."

My thought went back to my first grade teaching when children were sometimes first brought into the school room, never having had kindergarten. Their daily loud, persistent yelling for the departing mother was pitiful for the child, teacher and class. In first grade there seemed so little time to learn the many concepts to be introduced that it seemed unfair to endure this long, daily, unhappy experience. Preschool and kindergartens are really great introductions to school experience for little ones.

When I returned to the room it was lunch time. The lunch was Taco and I was surprised they were able to manage putting the meat into the crisp wafer as well as they did. However, when they left the room to return home, there was quite a bit of food to clean up from the tables and the floor.

At 11:30 another group came in. They too, started with lunch. It was a smaller group of thirteen; four were absent. They were also much more quiet. While they were eating one child called out, "I got some new shoes." This started others with, "I do too" and "I got a new dress." I was glad the teacher aide had left as he did not like to hear them talking.

After lunch the procedure was the same as the morning for an hour. Then the aide left and I had the class for an hour and a half. Although they knew the sounds of the alphabet letters, they were unable to transfer this ability to other categories of learning. I tried many oral thinking activities with them without success. Not one could tell me the name of any of the words that started with the sound of the letter "b": the names of something they slept on; the name of the day they were born; a yellow fruit; a very young child, even – a toy that bounces. This, I could see, would require more time than one day for them.

Thinking questions elicited but guess answers with them. To "which is harder – pretzel or chewing gum?" they said chewing gum. "Balloon or basketball?" They said balloon. "Does a cup have a handle?" No, was their answer. "Does a doll get hungry" Even the boys thought yes. The seasons, or daily climate was unknown to them.

Quantity was also an unknown fact. To the question, "Which is more – a minute or an hour?" they said minute. "Five days or a week?" They chose the five days, but most could name the seven days. "Twelve cents or a dime?" The dime was their answer, but they could count higher than that.

A few could differentiate between kind or unkind deeds read to them.

We often stopped for physical exercises. I read the Halloween story of "Georgie", but it did not have the impact on them it has on older primary children. They enjoyed dancing to "The Polka" record and dramatized "The Three Little Kittens" song, but the enchantment of Kindergarten or first grade was missing.

At last I found something that did capture their interest. From a Fearon Teacher Aid Book, "Games, Stunts and Exercises", I read sixteen short conditioning exercises to them – all of which they enjoyed tremendously. The first one was: "Standing position. Go through the motions of climbing a ladder." The last was: "Standing position. Run in place, while swinging your arms." These were great fun for them.

At 2:25 we straightened the chairs, put crayons and pencils away, folded the papers to be taken home, and at 2:30 they left to walk to the front and meet their parents.

It had been a very difficult kind of day. All the children had been black; all clean and neatly dressed. Some little boys had worn suits with vests; most girls had hair styles that must have required hours of parting and braiding. These were the pictures I remembered and treasured. Even the mothers calling for them looked young and happy as did the children.

145

Chapter 48

Salute to Chicago

The McCutcheon Branch was a modern, one story, brick structure, having about nine rooms, plus a gymnasium; the library books were on open shelves in the wide, homey corridor. Both corridors and rooms were carpeted, giving the school an inviting, comfortable atmosphere, in addition to diminishing the noise 95%. However, throughout the day there was much running and racing about from room to room by a number of students.

The assignment was that of resource teacher and librarian, meaning I would be helping a few pupils from different classes with needed skills and taking two librarian periods of entire classes.

The first group was from a first grade room, two girls and three boys. These were children not yet ready for first grade work. One extremely noisy child came in by himself from the hall. The teacher had not been able to find him in the classroom when I called for him. He enjoyed keeping another little boy acting up as well as himself. But soon, after the board work was explained, read, and paper distributed, they were busily occupied earning stars. Five assignments were on the board. I helped one little child who looked troubled. She could not copy the question mark. I wished I had my camera to photograph her. Neatly dressed, big blue eyes, long pig tails, and sitting on her little foot. Usually I suggest feet be on the floor, but printing was such an accomplishment for her that I let her concentrate. No one finished more than one paper (I wrote two ending lines for the little girl), but each child left happily with a star paper.

The next group of four boys, first graders also, were quite naughty and noisy. They brought no pencils and had to return for them. Their sad behavior continued for fifteen minutes, talking, throwing crayons, being silly and bad, but finally they settled down and copied some board work that had been read. The Head Teacher, in charge of this Branch, brought in two pupils to be seated by me from 10:00 until 10:30 during a special program. Fortunately the four boys had settled down by then.

The program was in the gym, put on by two rooms, and was a Salute to Chicago, giving its history and present-day accomplishments. The pupils talked before microphones, which I felt was an impressive, worthwhile learning experience for them. Most had memorized their oral contributions; a few read them. Several songs of Chicago were sung. It was easy to see I had five of the school's choice behavior problems sitting by me, and as I looked around I could spot others I had had two days before when I had been called for the resource job, confirming my thoughts that most of the pupils needing special help also have behavior problems, being inattentive, not wanting to learn, but to play and disturb others.

Back in the room four third graders were next. One could read; the others could not. They were helped to read the board work, which all copied and received stars. Helping slow readers requires much time, much repetition, much listening. It can be done, but not in one day. Most of these youngsters needed to discipline themselves, and they did receive help in that respect, which was a beginning.

The next group, from 2nd grade, had one little talker, but he finally became quiet and completed two papers. Only one little girl could read. The two boys did not know the consonant sounds, which, to me, is a necessary basic reading essential. Interested parents often teach their children the names of the abc's. But it is the sound of the letters that is needed to learn to read; the names of the letters are not used until spelling is introduced later. Reading consists primarily of sounding and blending sounds of the alphabet letters. As these children could print they did some of the board copy work. And as they had trouble coming to the room and had slipped out of their room and ran here, I had them finish two minutes early and line up quietly and orderly before leaving.

The three third graders, the last group before lunch, acted up at first but soon calmed down. The work on the board was read by all and then completed by them. One did two papers and chose to do an extra sentence completion card I had brought. The best reader did two papers and then tried, "One Too Many" card, on which he was to omit one extra word from each sentence. These were catchy, requiring thinking, but fun to do.

After lunch four third-graders, all hyperactive, were waiting for me. The teacher had put them outside the room to wait. They continued to act noisy and silly for 15 minutes in the room but did do the reading – three needing help with it – and then all completed one work paper.

The last two classes were for 45 minutes library periods, the pupils to be brought to the room where I was. I went to the first room, one of third graders. This class had a good teacher, firm but loving and soft-spoken, so I did not expect to have much difficulty. I carefully lined them up, calling for the quiet ones first. Once back in the room I had them bring their chairs to sit near me in order to see the pictures of the stories read. This procedure seemed to cancel behavior problems as well as produce a more relaxed, comfortable room atmosphere.

I felt the interest, the anticipation, of the pupils as they sat looking at me. The evening before I had spent much time selecting interesting, light-weight books to bring which would hold their interest. I started with "Arty, the Smarty", a book worn nearly in pieces by use, but which proved to capture even the interest of those pretending non-interest. The next book was "Nothing to Do" which I introduced by saying it would explain what to do with a little brother or sister that always bugged them at home. Most agreed they had such a problem. For the third book I let them vote between "Georgie" and "Curious George" and was not surprised at the immediate call for George, one child asking what "curious" meant. We finished in time for a selection of used-Christmas cards, and small groups were called to make their selections, in turn, then lining up quietly to leave.

The next third grade class was one I wondered about, and it was the one for which I had spent so much time preparing. I had heard their teacher trying unsuccessfully to control them for hours, and it was difficult to know who was making more noise, the children or the teacher. I have read "the noisier the teacher, the noisier the class" and this seemed to prove the saying. I entered this room quietly, unnoticed midst all the confusion and clamor; I spoke softly, motioning for the quiet children on the list to come and line up. Somehow, quietness entered the room. The pupils then maintained a respectable line crossing the corridor. In the reading room they settled down, read the work and each completed one or two assignments.

They had brought their coats so at closing we lined up after the first bell by the nearby outside door. It was not until all were there and we had waited two minutes that I returned to the room and noted the room clock was three minutes in advance of the one in the hall, but it was too late then to return to the room. In another minute when the bell did ring there was a sudden burst of energy – and noise – and children and feet were flying and racing across the entire corridor – to the opposite door! I stood there, horrified. But it was over almost instantly and they were gone outside. As I stood there I realized their classroom was near the opposite door, across the corridor, and they were used to leaving that way with their friends. They had told me they left by this door; but we had waited too long for the bell, about three minutes. As I stood there looking at their dust and noise, the Head Teacher walked out in askanse, but the evidence was gone, thank goodness. It had sounded like a herd of buffalo charging through the building and out onto the plains. I smiled when I thought of it for days afterward.

Chapter 49

Scissors Please

The Principal at Alcott had asked me to return the previous day and as I parked the car and walked into the building I felt comfortably at ease; it was a pleasant school and an interesting 3rd grade.

Being quite early, 8:20, I asked a friendly young teacher next door where the ditto machine was. Her desk was stacked with some of the mountainous detailed paper work teachers are confronted with, much of it having to be done during classroom time, and I felt the wonderful freedom of being a substitute. In fairness, however, I must say that the reports always helped one learn to know the class better, collectively and individually, which, in turn, offered a great opportunity of helping them.

Proceeding to the ditto machine on another floor I quickly ran off two dittos on an electric machine there. One assignment contained a Halloween poem, with a number of questions about it; the other was a secret coded page of alphabet letters that, once decoded, were fun to read. In the room I filled a section of the board with arithmetic work.

Again five were absent, but different pupils from the previous day. One paid for four lunches for the remainder of the week. Five had paid; 19 were free; nine brought bag lunches.

I had brought a primary workbook for a Mexican girl who understood very little English and had her read it for me, then explained the seatwork questions; however, the questions seemed beyond her comprehension. I asked another girl to explain the work to her in Spanish, but soon she brought up two completed pages – much too fast for completion by the newcomer. The other child had helped too much, too fast. Past experience told me it would have required three to five weeks of reading and repeated questioning before understanding was sufficient to do the seatwork correctly by herself, but at least she did have something to do, and a friend to help her with it.

Ten students read together in a group in a Ginn book at level four, grade 4. These were good, reliable readers, most of them good in all aspects of learning. Four read at level 9, grade three. Eleven read at level 8, grade 2. The black boy who had not been in a book before read well with the level 9 group.

One new girl, who had been in the class but a few days, and absent the previous day, told me she had transferred from Disney School because of the noise in their "large room" where several classes were, and especially because of the "terrible" noise on the transporting bus where "everybody screamed" giving her stomach and head aches. She read for the first time in the room with level 10 and was the top reader there. She was one of the two students completing all the arithmetic work, and the only one having it 100% correct. At Disney she said she had been at level 18 but felt it too difficult and asked to be changed to level 16, which was 4th grade. (Level numbers vary with publishers.) She was a quiet child, seeming timid, and when I questioned the tears in her eyes she said she felt ill twice during the morning. I had told her at recess if she didn't feel better by noon I would contact her mother, but as I expected, before that she became interested in the work and in reading and was fine. It was later she told me of her Disney experience.

We were ready to leave at noon for lunch as knew the table space was for another class in a short time. When we returned I took the Mexican child again for reading and then Level 8. Most children were finishing their assignments; five handed in Halloween stories which I promised to send to a newspaper for publication. One boy, a smart little chap, but one who postponed competing his story for hours and needed constant reminders, never seemed interested in putting any penciled pictures on his story paper. As a last resort I finally asked another very good artist if he would do it. Suddenly the little author awakened with a start, exclaiming he would do it, which he did, and very well. Only he could have selected and drawn just the right picture highlights, which were truly delightful.

During the afternoon of the previous day, when finishing the art work and collecting scissors I had brought, one little fellow could not find the scissors he had borrowed. He maintained a girl near him had borrowed them to use. As I held a paper on which he had signed his name to receive them, I said he would have to pay 55 cents if he didn't find them. I noticed him crying in another part of the room but became busy and forgot about it. As the class was lining up to leave he quietly appeared before me at the teacher's desk and handed me 55 cents. I was so surprised I asked where he got it. "I had it in my desk", he answered, his lips quivering. I could not refuse it then, but decided to find some way to return it. During the following period I offered a 25 cent reward for anyone finding the scissors. Several students searched, without results, so I explained they must have been returned without my realizing it, whereupon he accepted the money. This had been the first time a student had seriously accepted my words of having to pay for anything, except with tears, and I was overwhelmed. My purpose had been to instill dependability and responsibility.

In the afternoon there were but thirty minutes left for the Bingo game I had promised them in the morning. We used the Milton Bradley Homonym cards and all but three were able to use them without help. This time the girls won overwhelmingly but there were many more girls than boys in the class.

It was a good group to have worked with. It left me with a feeling that children were learning in the city at a good rate.

Chapter 50

Negro National Anthem
Softly – Scream Softly

Substitute Center called very early, around 7:10, for me to go to Jenner School, adding it was for a Kindergarten Class.

At the school I said I would take any primary grade as Kindergarten did not particularly appeal to me, but this was the only opening. There were five or six lists for regular teachers to sign in on, one other sheet was for substitutes. Usually there are but one or two lists for signing in.

There was a very helpful teacher aide in the room, and for the entire day, but the surprising thing, to me, was that the pupils remained in school for the full day. The teacher aide explained there were other kindergarten classes that stayed but half a day, but this particular class was a follow-through from their Headstart Program.

Thirty children were listed in the Attendance Book; two were absent; four came in late. All were black; the school was in a black neighborhood. The teacher aide placed name tags on all desks; these had heavy cords attached to them, and the children wore them around their necks all day, which was very helpful in talking to some of them at times.

The teacher had left detailed Lesson Plan suggestions which I followed. I was surprised they were not working in workbooks as I had seen done in other well-organized kindergartens where the young children did very good work. Here they used ditto sheets, writing alphabet letters and coloring pictures of people and things whose names started with the sounds of the letters that were to be copied.

The Pledge of Allegiance was said, when all children had the correct right hand placed on their hearts. Usually two or three at this level need to be reminded to use the right hand. Following the Pledge the class immediately sang "America" with extremely loud voices, not waiting for any piano accompaniment, as is usual in most kindergartens. Next they sang another song so loudly that I could not hear the words! Two little girls even put their hands up to their ears. The teacher aide explained to me that it was the Negro National

Anthem and that the regular teacher had never taught them the words; she had put a record on and the children sang (screamed!) the words. It sounded impressive and probably was beautiful, but there was no music, just loud screaming. I wanted to ask them to repeat it softly but felt I better get on with the work.

One child knew the date and marked the calendar; the pupils discussed the weather and helped compose a short story about it to be put on the board. They told me the names of the letters for "Our Morning Story" as this was their daily custom. (I left a note to the teacher thanking her for the good time schedule and Lesson Plans, but suggested she include teaching the sounds of the letters as this would be helpful to the next primary teachers. Many kindergartens do this and knowing the letter sounds is an essential part of learning to read.)

Two worksheets, left by the regular teacher, were explained and fastened to the front board. Half of the class worked on these papers (writing two letters and coloring two pictures) while the other half came to the front of the room for reviewing numbers and colors. They knew these; the teacher had suggested finger plays but mine had disappeared so I introduced the five vowels. They learned these quickly, plus the sounds of three of them. I wished I had my record of the vowels as children learn quickly from musical educational records, but I already carry three heavy, packed satchels of school materials. These youngsters did learn quickly, and later in the day when we reviewed, several still knew the sounds of the letters that had been introduced.

After about twenty minutes the groups were changed; the teacher aide took one group; the other came to the front for specific review. This group was a little more quiet, but they, too, were able to learn the names of the vowels and the sounds of three of them.

All seatwork received star symbols of pumpkins as it was Halloween time. About five children did beautiful coloring work and received two stars on their papers. This impressed others to be more diligent with their afternoon work, when many more received double stars. In the afternoon they chose the symbols they preferred on their papers.

At toilet time the boys walked in line to the nearby washroom, took a drink from a nearby water fountain, then took pieces of folded paper towels from the teacher to dry their hands on; this gave them something to do rather than begin fighting, as well as instill proper manners. They stood much too close together in line, causing constant turmoil. I had them back up, leaving spaces in between them, but this habit requires a little reinforcement time. The time is well spent, however, as it does work well in creating orderly, quiet and peaceful lines in corridors – which was definitely not true of this rowdy class. I shuddered to think of them in two or three years unless some teacher was successful in introducing and maintaining quietness.

Lunch was early, followed by recess, so the children wore their wraps to the lunchroom, covering their nameplates. The lunch was of spaghetti so spoons and milk were distributed to the children after they carried their trays to the long tables where boys sat on one side, girls on the other. (All this had been outlined by the teacher in her Lesson Plan). After lunch the teacher aide took the class outside for a play period. She was a very good teacher aide so I suggested she go to school to become a teacher, but in her case this would have been difficult as she had ten children of her own.

After lunch the morning schedule was repeated; half the class worked on two more letters, two worksheets to write and pictures of the letters to color, while the others came to the front. This time I introduced more letters and sounds. The groups changed and the others came for review, the first group completing seatwork.

The teacher aide had a break period so we had music records of dancing to the Polka exercise instructions; dramatizing "The Three Little Kittens" record, giving everyone turns, and hearing the "Little Doggie in the Window", plus other exercises. The story of "Georgie", a little ghost, and other stories were read.

There was to be a snack time but there did not seem time for it, so apples were given to them to take home as they lined up to leave for the day, carrying all their starred papers.

One mother had brought in invitations to be distributed to many in the class, who were being invited to one of the children's home for a Halloween Party, so these were distributed before leaving.

The teacher aide and I took them to the outer door where all left happily.

They had been an unusually noisy and disruptive group. Many of the boys were always getting into trouble with others, usually boys. It was difficult to keep the classroom quiet at any time so I was really tired at the end of the day. The preschoolers of the previous week had really fascinated me, but they had been so quiet.

A quiet kindergarten class seems pleasant, but this noisy one made me glad it was the end of the week and I did not even call in to work again on Monday. They were far too disruptive. Next time I would also carry a few more catchy educational records for kindergarten classes; this might make a big difference. They needed music but had not responded to the song records I had which appealed to 3rd and 4th graders. The music sheets I carried had disappeared the previous year. There was a piano in the room but no music had been mentioned in the Lesson Plans. This was surprising as Kindergarteners and black children always so enjoy music in its many forms. To me, Kindergarten and music seem to go together.

Chapter 51

Little Helen of Troy
Did You Kiss Your Child Today?

Past experience taught me that early-arriving substitutes at LeMoyne School were given the most difficult grades, regardless of grade-level qualifications of the substitute, so I did not appear at the school until 8:30. There were cars parked in the teachers' lot, but no teachers about, and no children to be seen. The clerk in the office explained it was a "late Wednesday", meaning the children arrived later than usual and the teachers were at a monthly meeting. The assignment for the day was for a Headstart Class; the clerk also informed me there was usually a teacher aide there but the school was short one aide so I might not have one. I felt grateful for the experience I had gained the previous year in substituting in a well-organized kindergarten where good Lesson Plans were left for the substitute to follow. That particular school had used workbooks for the children, but the day's organization had made an indelible impression on my memory. Further, the previous week I had substituted in another Headstart Classroom. There had been a teacher aide there all day, plus a detailed Lesson Plan, which I had followed diligently.

The office clerk, janitor, and the incoming mothers with children, all warned me I would have a very difficult time and be worn out by the end of the day by the fighting, especially from one child, but I refused to accept this as a possibility.

By 8:50 two mothers, who were waiting in the corridor with children, told me I was to go upstairs and get the breakfast food for the children. Two heavy trays were ready, which I carried, one by one, to the room and placed in a flat desk-high refrigerator. Two mothers remained during the morning period and were a tremendous help. One got hand towels and spoons from various cabinets in the room and arranged them as placemats on the round tables for the children. One mother broke doughnuts in half and put them, with milk cartons, on the placements.

The children entered, hung up their wraps when requested, then sat down at the tables – again, when requested. I was too busy helping with all this to notice if much food was eaten, but there was but one mishap of spilled milk with this group of four-year-olds. They were nice, quiet and orderly, except for the one black boy I had been warned about. Even the lunchroom attendants told me that on the previous day he had been brought up there screaming and hitting and kicking.

There were no Lesson Plans, Time Schedule, or work sheets to be used – not even coloring sheets to be used. 24 pupils were listed in the attendance book; 2 had moved; 7 were absent. The mothers said that parents whose children had been hit by the naughty boy the previous day had said they would keep their children home. Because of all the dire forecasts about his behavior with other youngsters I watched him constantly and each time he made noise, acted up, or started toward a child, I was immediately at his side. The first time I spontaneously reached over and gave him a big hug. His reaction was surprise, a start, and then quiet behavior for a few moments. This same procedure took place repeatedly for at least 45 minutes. I had announced at 9:00 when the groups entered that he was to be my assistant and help me during the day. He tried to rebel to this thought both verbally and by stiffening physically, but I repeated it each time he demonstrated unwelcome behavior. Finally I won him over and with one hug due to naughtiness he turned and put his arms around me, kissing me for a whole minute, and not wanting to stop. Thereafter, he concentrated on following me about, sitting on my lap, or holding on to my clothes, instead of having difficulties with other children. He was a large, strong, heavy child, and had used up much of my reserve energy before the morning session was over.

Although I searched many places for paper to distribute for seatwork I could find none, so gave out school notice sheets which were blank on one side. On these I demonstrated how to draw two circles for pumpkins, putting on two eyes and mouths, one happy, one sad. On one half of the paper a circle for a turkey was drawn, with head, feathers and feet. One mother put out crayons on the tables and many children were able to draw acceptable symbols of pumpkins or turkeys for which they received bunny and pumpkin stars. I then

158

passed out colorful plastic cut-out figures of animals but was surprised to find they could not trace these without help.

Somehow I was always trying to keep up with this class instead of leading the activities. Most likely this was due to the behavior of the trying child as many times he interrupted and curtailed activities that were started. His attention span was extremely short, his abilities very limited, or nil, his cooperation zero, but at least he didn't start fighting for which I was grateful. The class was not quiet for the catchy record, "Doggie in the Window", so I changed it for "The Polka", a child's record with appropriate actions; this they liked. Each had a turn in acting out "The Three Little Kittens" record. They surprised me by clapping for each of these records.

The mothers prepared the second snack of peaches and fruit juice and children again sat at the round tables. They carried the paper towels and cups to the garbage can in the room when finished eating and then put on their coats, collected their starred papers, and waited for the arrival of their parents.

I concentrated on observing who called for the troubled boy and found it to be a frowning, angry father. One of the helping mothers, a black woman, had already informed him of his son's behavior, he said, and promised it would never happen again, adding that the teacher had always told him the child had been good. My intention had not been to complain. I inquired if the boy received loving, and kissing, at home, explaining he appeared to be starving for this in school. The father said he was often kissed at home, and left appearing very angry with the boy. He said he acted up each time he did not get his way at home.

This child, his behavior, and the father's attitude, remained with me for days. I felt there was some explanation. The mothers had told me he was an only child; my first question to the boy was to learn if he had a father. Now I was beginning to wonder if this was a mentally retarded child. He had been unable to draw a circle, or complete any coloring within a circle; his attention span was far too short – of but a minute or two; he seemed unable to play with children, but played at them; his uncontrolled, booming voice; instant reactions of physical combat – all these contributed to making his behavior very unacceptable. Usually I felt school "blue slips", examination requests for mentally retarded children, should not be

159

requested until at least second grade level, feeling the children might improve by then, but in this case, to protect other children, and also to enlist the understanding of his parents, I felt it might be a wise procedure. On the inside door of the classroom the teacher had put a very large sign asking, "Did you kiss your child today?" This made me feel she loved the children; possibly she had heard this father whipped the boy for his misbehavior and hesitated to report him.

In spite of this boy monopolizing most of my attention there was one other highlight I noted. Throughout the morning, in any activity whatever, there was a scramble amongst the little boys to be at the side of one particular little girl. This scrambling might have developed into fighting had I not been watching to prevent any such occurrence. (This might also explain some of the fighting I had been warned to expect.) Often one boy, who lost out, would come to me to report another boy; often three boys vied for her side. Once or twice the problem boy was one of them. This did not happen with any other girl, and it seemed to be between most, or all, of the boys, not just one or two. So I took a long, curious look at the four-year-old Helen of Troy with such influence. She was attractive enough, but not beautiful; the same applied to her dress, and manner; she displayed initiative, not being timid, but was quiet. I would like to have studied this more but with the one boy taking most of my time and energy this was not possible. There was certainly something very special about that little girl.

Mothers were bringing their children inside the room and standing up in the front as early as 11:45, but the two mothers who were helping and myself were too busy to even greet them. The room had to be readied for the afternoon class and the morning group dressed to leave. One of the mothers who remained during the morning had told me (when I said I didn't know what I would have done without their help) that the school expected mothers to help at least once a month or they did not want their child in the class. This surprised me, but with all the food serving it really had been helpful. However, with a teacher aide to help, it should have been managed satisfactorily; it had gone very well in another school where I had worked with a good teacher aide.

In the afternoon Headstart Classroom at LeMoyne School there were 18 present, 7 absent, a total of 25. The teacher had 20 listed on the attendance book. At the end of the day I learned one boy was supposed to be in another kindergarten class but wanted to stay in this room with his brother; the others I could not resolve, but was relieved to have an overabundance rather than be missing some students.

One mother stayed and served most of the lunch, then left; this was a tremendous help. After she left three more youngsters appeared at 12:30 but I told the boy who brought them that he would have to get their food, which he did. I was already occupied explaining the seatwork activities to the class.

One of the morning mother-helpers had told me the afternoon class would be worse than that in the morning, but I did not find this to be true. The confusion and noise of the morning class ended when they left. It must have been due to the constant interruption of the one child as everything was calm and controlled the rest of the day.

After lunch I had the group sit on the floor in front of me. I took white ditto paper from my satchel, showed them how to fold it twice, making four sections. On these I drew, with a dark crayon, four items; two pumpkins, one turkey, three ducks, and one bird, and soon thereafter drew pictures on the back also as a few pupils completed the work quite soon. On the back was a boat, a flower, a dog and a wagon.

This group seemed to be more mature, more quiet; their work was more exact. One eager little fellow, after eating lunch, and quickly completing his art paper (and that of two others) with art work comparable to that of a 2nd grader, promptly appeared before me announcing he was to go to "another school" for an afternoon project that he was "looking forward to as it was so interesting". When I said he could not leave without a note he started crying so loudly that I told him to go. I felt he was probably going to another room in the building; he seemed advanced and there was no one to ask about this. The Headstart room was isolated from any other room.

All the seatwork papers were starred and the class lined up to attend an afternoon assembly I had been notified of in the morning. As we went down the hall some of the performers were in the corridor; one of them asked, "What grade is this?" When I answered, "Pre-school", he repeated his question, so I said, "First Grade", which silenced him, although he watched quite puzzled. They were so very tiny and had been trained to walk "snake-fashion" in the corridors, having hands on the shoulders of the preceding child. It was really an impressive, lovely-to-remember, time-consuming walk, as they took such slow little steps.

Inside the Assembly Hall they sat in one and a half rows; I sat a row ahead on the end, turning to watch them. It was an upper-grade music recital, far too advanced for these little tots, but they remained quiet, looking like little toy dolls in the huge seats; some crouched on their feet; some crossed their legs, but none of this could be observed as they were so tiny in the big seats. Most had their little hands on the armrests and as these touch each other, they started little hand-touching-clapping games, but again, this could not be noticed unless facing them as I was. It was a delightful picture that I would have liked to have photographed. The part of the assembly they liked was the clapping of those present at intervals between the music presentations. And always they were smiling and happy; being in the vast area must have impressed them. As we were leaving an 8th grade teacher sent two girls to "help take them to the room" but this was no problem.

There was no fruit juice, or cookies, in the refrigerator for an afternoon snack as a lunchroom attendant in the hallway had told me; the morning mothers must have served it to the morning class. But there were nine oranges, cut in half, just enough, so I served them and all were happy. Some asked to take them home so I agreed to this as it was nearly time to leave.

At 3:00 mothers started to appear to take their children at 3:15 so I had the class again dance to the Polka record exercises and again act out "The Three Little Kittens" record. All the children stood for this, each "mother cat" having three "kittens" facing her. The children enjoyed doing this acting to the record music and words, and their actions brought smiles to the mothers' faces as they watched. I knew it would as I never tired of watching this demonstration since buying the record for a first grade class twenty years previously.

By 3:15 each child had been called for and I left for the day. Once home I was surprised to be completely exhausted as the clerk and janitor had said would happen. But it had been such a different day that I did not mind and felt I was able to handle the next pre-school class with confidence. They were like any other class – needing the same fundamentals – acceptance, orderly discipline, good seatwork, rewarding stars, and fun periods of games, exercises and music.

Chapter 52

Far Back but Art Shows
Joy of Life; Bi-Lingual

A parking place in front of Hawthorne School was not available so I drove around the block to the teachers' parking lot. One space near the front was not taken. This proved to be a great challenge to slide into but I finally succeeded. Once there, a janitor came waving me away from it, explaining that was kept free for visitors from "Downtown", so I moved to the rear of the lot.

The Principal told me to sign in for a 3rd grade "Bilingual" class, which proved to be very pleasant to work with, but some did not understand English and I was not aware of this.

Thirty pupils were listed in the attendance book; one had moved the previous day; one was absent. The teacher had left good Lesson Plans and two dittos for the class but were not noticed until later in the day as were under other papers.

When the children entered three assignments were on two of the boards, which everyone read in unison. One section was of arithmetic, ranging from first through third grade. Their printing was very good, but it was soon obvious most were unable to complete the seatwork. They only copied it, so during a morning gym period I replaced most of the material with easier beginning first grade reading work. Later I also replaced the arithmetic with easier problems.

Three groups read in the morning with me; one read with a teacher aide in the front. All three groups read in beginning pre-primer readers; the more advanced in front read from a beginning first grade reader.

This was an Open Campus School, meaning children had an hour for lunch, either eating in school (all but one had a free lunch ticket; he bought a lunch) or going home for lunch. During this time I ate my lunch at the teacher's desk and leafed through the cumulative records, noting the reading and math levels indicated for the students. Reading levels, for both third as well as second graders, was "B", meaning pre-primer – beginning first grade work. Math levels were usually C or D, first or second grade levels. Due to this, I put much easier work on the back board for them.

During the morning, when they had been busily occupied with writing the board work, and reading in groups, they had been very sweet and quiet, and I was surprised the gym teacher seemed surprised when I so informed her. She reported they were quite unruly and noisy. Later in the afternoon this noisiness did try to manifest itself often but it was not rampant, and was only in spurts, followed by quietness.

They were unable to operate the cards for the Bingo Game of first-grade reading, mainly abbreviations, so these were collected and butterfly art work was distributed. I had made samples for them to see and showed cards of colored insects, but told them I felt they were good artists and to use their own skills and color them as they liked. The results were truly beautiful, far more so than I had expected. All were colorful; some individually eye-catching with heads and faces; others included the veins; some used the sample cards and produced stunning copies. The art work seemed to reflect their joy, spontaneity and happy, loving outlook toward life. Seven or eight turned in top art work; one boy in particular did outstanding work; he was very talented in this field.

The school was having Open House the next evening so many starred papers were pinned on a large bulletin board and the impressive art work stapled to colored paper backings and left for the teacher.

One boy erased all the boards; one took charge and had students pick up papers from the floor; another collected the butterfly pictures. Other fun art work of tracing plastic cutouts had been distributed to those finishing early and these too were collected. Chairs were put up; the class lined up, and when the bell rang at 3:15 everyone left smiling.

The day had been pleasant enough, but being in a class already one and two years behind in reading saddened me. A teacher I knew there told me their teacher spoke Spanish and concentrated on teaching Spanish reading. Another Spanish teacher aide appeared in the afternoon to teach Spanish reading for a half hour, so possibly this was the explanation. They were grouped by similar reading levels so, no doubt, this was one of the lowest, and slowest English reading classes in the school.

Chapter 53

Special Kind of School
Playground Mud Changed to Award

Substitute Center had not called me for a week so I contacted Disney School as this particular school (I had heard) contacted its own substitutes. The school clerk informed me it was not necessary for me to come there to apply, but that I should call the school on the days I was available to work between 7:40 and 8:00. This surprised, and pleased, me as it was necessary to call in the previous day to register with Substitute Center.

The next day Sub Center did not call but the telephone did ring; the clerk at Disney called me. I was there in ten minutes as it was close to where I lived. There was but one parking space left in the long, long, double lines of parked cars, and I was grateful to have it.

One child, about nine, sitting outside the entrance and not wishing to enter, seemed to be enjoying one of the last autumn days. Another 6th grader, a "doorman" for the day, waiting inside, kindly showed me the way to the office, which was very much appreciated, and gave me a fine impression of the school.

A sense of calm freedom enveloped me as I walked into and through the building to sign in and I realized this was due to the openness. There were no dividing classroom walls. The vast area I observed beyond the main office seemed to have a number of groupings of furniture and teaching materials; these I assumed to be "classrooms".

My team-teacher told me my class was one of six-year-olds as she handed me an attendance book and pointed out the teacher's desk. The desk was heavily laden with teaching materials, especially a bulging 3-ring notebook, which was open to a ditto page with that day's date written on. However, the contents were such that only the teacher could understand them; this was why I seldom bothered to try to unscramble such data. But in this school I fully realized it was a day of shared time with the team teaching and I did wish it had been discernable.

There were eight reading books stacked on one side of the desk, all containing place markers and seatwork relative to the reading content. There was a vague afternoon time schedule but not one for the morning. Six reading groups were listed by name, but only a few pupils names were on but one of them. Two ditto sets of seatwork for the morning were on the desk top. I studied the teacher's manual in one large workbook until 9:00 when the youngsters entered reasonably quietly and smiling.

The team teacher had her group, and mine, sit on the carpeted floor before her and explained the morning would be a little different as their teacher was absent. 24 were listed in the attendance book; two had moved; one was tardy, one absent. There was an excellent teacher aide, who helped guide the morning activities smoothly. She later told me the times various activities took place, which was a great help.

On the small portable blackboard I wrote two assignments in case the children finished the paper seatwork the teacher had left. The morning reading period was from 9:15 until 11:00 – quite a long period. First I worked with a large group in the picture workbook relating to the sounds of five consonants. Most knew the sounds and were able to say other words beginning with the sounds being studied; one girl needed extra help. During this time the others worked in their assigned workbooks. There was a student teacher, who helped them at different tables. The large group sat on the carpeted floor. Whenever youngsters did work while sitting on the floor they used flat, solid plastic "work boards" to put their papers on to be completed. These had openings at the top so were easily carried or moved about, and easy to distribute and collect.

Next I called level 9 reading group, which resulted in but one boy. He understood the work well and was soon finished with his reading and also did the assigned work left by the teacher correctly and quickly. As he read orally I had the feeling his family background was reflected in his advanced ability; they probably had provided him with many trips and extra experiences. Later in the day the team teacher affirmed this to be true, but on another day his regular teacher told me he was advanced in some reading skills, but not all of them.

The student teacher took one group for reading and the teacher aide checked the seatwork while I took a group in Level 5.

At 10:40 there was a break for a snack consisting of cut oranges; all seemed to enjoy this. I saw none wasted.

At 11:00 the class left for a special art class in another room. During this time I put up new afternoon seatwork on the board. When asking the team teacher about math work she said they had arithmetic three times weekly, but not on this day.

About six youngsters returned as there had been a change in plans so I showed them samples of art work I had and then gave them ditto copies to do which they enjoyed and were doing very well. However the class returned before they finished so the other teacher told them to finish their art at home. Each child had individual drawers to keep seatwork papers in and the teacher told me they tried to have the children take the work home daily so it did not fill up the space.

There was music at 11:45 and the class went to a nearby room with a closed door. They sat on the floor in a large circle, two classes being together for this period. The teacher aide was there and I got a small chair from outside and remained also. They sang a Thanksgiving song they would be giving at an assembly the following week and several other songs. This music was good but the behavior of several boys remained in order only because of the discipline upheld by the teacher aide and myself.

The children all made washroom visits, then got their wraps for lunch. I walked downstairs with them. We passed a teachers' lunchroom next door, and as I had a short free period while the teacher aide took them to lunch, I ordered turkey which cost $1.00 and was very tasty. The children had the same menu, but I noted most had carried box lunches from home. The team teacher and I took the children outside for a short play period after the lunch period. She told me the play area was newly designed and had already won a fine award. It was sorely needed, she added, as the area had previously been covered with mud. There were two small spaces covered with soft sand; one had two strong, large rubber tire swings, on which four children could sit, or stand, and swing on; this was obviously the favorite sport. The other space was an interesting climbing area where most of the children spent the time as it was larger.

Following the play period there was another reading period from 1:30 until 2:00. This was started with oral thinking questions which they enjoyed, each child having two turns and nearly all were able to give correct answers. Several Mother Goose Rhymes were read, following which four were selected, written on the board and copied. Pupils chose star symbols for their completed work.

At 2:15 the room section was cleaned up, children got their coats and lined up to board the many buses waiting outside for them. I was handed a number of cards listing bus numbers and the names of children to board them, but as we neared the vehicles the youngsters had disappeared; somehow each one had entered into his or her own bus before we came to it.

Teachers returned to the school to prepare for the next day's work. I wrote the teacher a note about what had been done by the class as the class had taken all their papers home.

It had been a most pleasant, and different, experience. The inside of the school was even more inviting than the outside, but I felt it would require a number of working days in their different manner of scheduling to understand and evaluate the system and its success. Offhand, it seemed strange to me that there was such a distinct variance in reading abilities in the one group I had, one child being a fluent reader at Level 9, and producing perfect understanding seatwork, while the majority were still studying the sounds of the consonants, unable to read. Evidently homogenous grouping was not one of their aims. During my lunch hour one teacher had been talking to another quite a distance away saying she had been trying to influence someone in charge to consider regrouping the reading groups into similar ability levels, but was not having any success in her endeavor.

To me, the school, and everyone and everything in it, seemed very special. I hoped I would be asked to return there again.

Chapter 54

Disney Terminology
No Report Cards
Family Conferences

After telephoning Disney School saying I was available I had breakfast, dressed for the day, and at 8:15 the school informed me there was a vacancy for that day.

I was to work with five-year-olds in one of the pods. "Pods" meant "rooms"; "family" meant "class". A family was divided into areas of Pre-Readiness, Readiness and Language Arts, the latter being the more advanced. In Disney language my assignment was to present Language Arts to my family in their pod. Each area, I was told, had four teachers, but this may have covered the entire large room, as I was also told all the children there were the same age. I would assume it was as large as six or eight regular school rooms in size.

The quietness of the entire floor impressed me almost as much as the friendliness and pleasant attitude of the many teachers, all of whom were friendly and immediately helpful. Their attitudes seemed to include their families (pupils) so the entire atmosphere of the school appeared to be a blend of friendliness, cooperation and quietness. One teacher surprised me by sharing an art idea she had prepared for her "family", which was a Thanksgiving finger puppet to be colored and cut out. She gave me a supply of the dittos to use.

My team teacher went to get the absent teacher's Lesson Plans to show me but found there were none so I copied the time schedule from a front board. However, that schedule must have been outdated as later the team teacher verbally gave me a different schedule which they followed. It surprised me to hear her say no report cards were issued by this school. Instead, there were parental conferences. The teacher added they seemed to get the tops and the lows – no in-betweens.

When I entered the pod at 8:45 the youngsters were already there, all quietly occupied in various activities of their own choosing. The time schedule in front had listed 8:40 to 9:15 as Self Select

(Breakfast) so the children must have eaten in the lunchroom and then come to their pod for free play time. The available materials for individual, or group play, were plentiful, and the children were aware of and familiar with them, changing from one to another at times. Some were painting at easels, others crayoning pictures. Groups of three or four were seen together in plastic box-houses; other groups of four rocked happily back and forth on play-boats; some climbed in and over climbing structures; others (boys) set a table with toy dishes; some selected wooden puzzles; others formed designs with clay models.

Six of the 24 listed in the attendance book were absent. After the free period two pupils went to a TESL (Teaching English as a Second Language) class and four left for another teacher. 9:15 to 10:30 was to be a skill period so I demonstrated some art work pictures to be colored, showing them samples beforehand. Most followed the directions and outlined the objects first, then colored the items; several did very good work; all received bunny or turkey star stamps which pleased them. There was time for a story before clean-up time, so I read a favorite, "Curious George", about a little monkey. Several could not explain the meaning of "curious" beforehand. It was impressive to note how nearly all helped to put away crayons and papers and tidy up the pod when requested.

Everyone stopped at the wash rooms on the way to the lunch room, where the children in my family ate at two tables. Napkins and spoons were distributed to them; then I went to a hot service center nearby and returned with two trays of food. On the trays were stainless steel bowls containing food, family style, to be portioned out to the pupils. There was a container of mashed potatoes, some of cole slaw, and one of fillet of sole. All children received milk cartons. Many requested refills, which were obtained and given to them; a few ate three full portions of lunch items. When they finished it was my job to clear the tables, dispose of the food fragments and return the metal bowls to the service center attendants.

The entire floor had a recess period outside in the front side of the school after lunch. There were two small slides, about four feet high, and several wooden climbing blocks which were frequently used as jumping off spots. Although they were not very high, the youngsters were so very small, that I did not like to observe the jumping activities – of which the children were very proud.

When we returned inside there was another skill period with the other team teacher while I ate my lunch in the lunchroom. It was fortunate I brought a lunch as the only food left was hot homemade tomato rice soup, which was very tasty.

The entire floor was quiet when I returned; all over the room little children were lying on the carpeted floor, on their own towels, some with small coverings on them. It was Nap Time from 1:00 until 2:00. As this seemed unusually long I questioned the reason for it and was told that some of them got up at 6:00 in the morning, and that many would be riding for an hour on the bus to reach home when school was over. It took some 45 minutes to start to nap; about eight slept the entire time; some just rested; a few needed continual reminders to try to relax.

There was snack time of peanut butter and crackers and fruit juice before preparing to leave, and, of course, the usual shoe-tying, coat-buttoning and zippering to be done, both at recess and going-home times. But somehow these children seemed more mature than the usual kindergarten youngsters; most likely it was because the buses had brought them here so there was not the mother's leaving and resulting children's tears to contend with as routine in kindergarten classes in regular schools.

The school bell rang at 2:30 and all teachers walked with their families to the waiting buses. The lines were of single children; there was no bickering or quarreling; no standing lines of older brothers and sisters cutting in, or mothers and fathers waiting in the halls or on the streets. The children walked quietly to their buses and boarded them. They knew their own buses; the drivers knew the children to be on the buses.

As I returned to the building I appreciated the many new features of this school, particularly the advantages of the buses, just mentioned. They seemed to offer safety and security to the children; none of the usual fear of older children fighting or threatening them on their way to and from school. Possibly no absenteeism from lack of winter boots which a teacher often hears in regular schools.

Disney School had many different aspects of learning to offer. I felt privileged to be able to teach there and learn more of them. I had come to the school with an open mind but was very surprised with the favorable impression it had made, and was still continuing to make on my thinking. There were many advantages to consider here. I wondered how long it would take for me to make a true evaluation of this school and its programs.

Chapter 55

Sullivan Programmed Reading
Harvard – Me?
Understand the Program?

I felt hesitant to call in to Disney School as late as 8:15 but explained a new tenant had moved in below me and had been pounding nails into walls until midnight, which had kept me awake and I had not awakened earlier. The clerk hesitated a moment, then asked me to come in. I dressed hurriedly, had breakfast, and signed in at 9:00.

The assignment was for Pod 100 again, but it was with a different "family" of first graders. The teacher looked for a Lesson Plan, and not finding one, returned and wrote a time sheet for me, commenting that Mondays were different; they were easy with lots of breaks, adding that some days there were none at all.

Because of other programs during the day there could be but two short reading periods, she said, pointing out a small portable blackboard and suggesting I put work on it. I hung up my wraps and selected seatwork for the children to do which I wrote on the board. The teacher had told me I had the group that were in books. The books (I found) were Sullivan Programmed Reading Workbooks, and a teacher aide told me each pupil had an individual book to work in, which was done at the child's own rate of progress. I looked at the workbooks; they ranged from Book 2 through Book 6. The aide told me that when pupils reached the next sections the teacher handled the testing individually.

The time schedule indicated 8:30 to 9:15 to be "Self-Selected Activities" and children were occupied at 9:00 with various items of interest available in the many containers on the sides of their particular section. However, when I finished putting assignments on the board no child, or team teacher, was in sight. The time schedule listed one reading period to be from 9:15 to 9:45. I felt foolish without a group, and alone in the section. Then I remembered the team teacher had said something about it being our turn for the DIA room, which she had explained, meant diagnostic individually analyzed, and had

173

nodded toward a closed-door-room, that I had been in for a Music Period previously, so I looked there and found the families (two classes). The teacher was sitting on the piano stool, her back to the piano, facing the pupils, who were sitting in a large circle on the floor, facing her. A teacher aide and student teacher were present. Taking in a small chair, I joined them.

After taking the attendance the teacher had a boy count the girls, a girl count the boys, and another child count all those present. It seemed a good idea to have the opposite sex counting as it eliminated the problem of wondering if the child had, or had not, counted himself. A total of 36 pupils was turned in, 16 girls and 20 boys.

This was obviously Show and Tell Period. Most children volunteering had brought objects to display to the group – a number game book, a toy Baby Snoopy, a police badge, a red elephant, and an Ice Follies Program, which the teacher showed to the class. They enjoyed seeing the Clown and Sesame Street character pictures. One child mentioned she had seen a car crash on the morning bus ride; one said it was her mother's birthday that day; one volunteered he had gone to Boston. When the teacher asked when he explained, "Last summer". All had wee, little voices that were difficult to hear, as is usual with first graders; by second grade, the problem changes to subdue the voice volume. But whispering is common at all ages so soon the teacher called out sharply, "If you are talking, stand up and leave!" The period ended with a greeting song, followed by a number of other catchy numbers known to the group, all of which had finger, hand and body movements which the youngsters enjoyed.

At 10:00 they went to Choral Practise for a 40 minute period so I had some instant coffee from a container nearby and checked the workbooks.

There was an outside recess period at 10:45 which all appreciated in one of the first snows of the year, always picking the most heavily snow-laden bushes or highest drifts to pioneer under and through. Snowballing started but was quickly stopped, the teacher telling them they could make snowmen but not snowballs. Two youngsters said they were cold so were permitted to return to the pod (room).

Snack time was at 11:15 when the children received graham wafers followed at 11:20 by Social Studies, which was a short movie, again in the DIA Room, as this was sound-proof. The first movie, titled, "I Wonder", and presenting many subjects children wonder about, elicited a number of follow-up questions the pupils said they wondered about. One little girl said she wondered how the first animals started, to which the teacher said some people thought they crawled out of the water, as water had originally covered most of the earth. The next short movie was an instant hit with the children. It showed silly circles of faces about "Why I am so Happy"; then "Why I am so Angry." Unfortunately, the time was up so there was no time for follow-through offerings from the youngsters. These should have been especially interesting.

There was a short reading period from 11:50 until 12:25 in which the children took their seats in orderly fashion around four tables. The board seatwork was explained, and read in turn by the girls, then the boys, after which they copied the sentences, filling in the blanks with correct words, which were listed at the bottom. About seven completed both papers, receiving Santa and Turkey star symbols; three boys, and especially one, needed continual prodding to complete the work. The printing was very good with all but two; for the slow worker printing was obviously either a hurdle, or an unwelcome experience, as his paper was quite untidy, with many erasures, and one girl sat a great deal. Finally (when reminded) she copied the work in a tiny space on the paper very quickly, with tiny lettering. All but three finished the work before lunch time, putting their papers in individual drawers to be taken home; unfinished work was held by the teacher to be done in the afternoon.

Lunch was from 12:30 until 1:15 in the lunchroom. Many had brought lunches. Hot dogs, french fries, catsup and chocolate milk were served to the others by teacher aides and myself until one informed me it was my lunch hour.

I bought a hot drink and joined the team teacher and others in the lunchroom as I had brought my lunch. The conversation was very interesting, ranging from family backgrounds, adopted children to future college classes; one teacher had just received an acceptance notice to a university for law school (although he admitted he did not yet know what he wanted to be). He had applied to ten schools, to which another young teacher gasped as she said it cost $25 for each such request. He said the total cost was $300 as the prices varied, but felt it was a good investment. He said schools usually expected an answer by April, four months away, and that he planned to be in law school the following September. He seemed waiting for an acceptance from Harvard. All beamed at such a thought, drooling in dreamy smiles of wonder.

After lunch my group had gone to the gym for half an hour so I put afternoon seatwork on the reverse side of the blackboard for those who had finished the morning work and moved the board between the tables. Then I walked up the three flights of stairs to see the rest of the building which a teacher aide had told me housed children through 8th grade. In another school a student, who had attended Disney at 4th grade level, had told me it was very noisy in the school but I found quietness and orderliness prevalent on all floors as I walked about a little. On the upper floors the students sat in chairs instead of on the floor was about the only difference I noted except, of course, the physical size of the older students.

When my family (class) returned at 1:45 they copied the boardwork, consisting of two puzzles to be thought about and answered. One girl finished both, writing in the answers, which surprised me. The answer to the first was "milk" and drawing the item would have been sufficient, as requested. About seven asked the meaning of two or three words and I watched them try to sound them out. They knew the sounds quite well, but the two letter blends stopped a few; "children", "drink" and "white" were words they questioned. One little fellow read the entire puzzle to me but had not learned to think and reason out the answer.

All papers were starred before 2:15; chairs were put up, the board erased, and boots and coats put on. One little boy held out a sweater for me to help him put on. Feeling he was seeking unneeded help I said I had to put all my papers away first, and watched him secretly as I did so. After a surprised look he quietly slipped into the sweater by himself. Hearing another boy ask a friend for help I peeked around a stand to see a child pulling very hard, trying unsuccessfully to get one shoe into a boot. I tried to help, without success, so suggested he carry the tennis shoe, or the boot, but he persisted in trying. I went to get my coat to accompany the children to the buses and was glad to see on my return that he had accomplished the feat somehow. I had seen and felt his determination and was glad he had proved that where there is a will there is a way.

There were but five children for me to walk to buses but I found one white, leathered mitten, and then its mate on the sidewalk between the school and the waiting buses. Although I boarded each of the twelve, or more, waiting buses, and held the mittens up high, no one claimed them, so I left them on the desk where I signed in. The clerk there said that was where their whereabouts might be questioned the next day. No one seemed to know of any Lost and Found Box.

As I was checking the area for tidiness I heard loud voices of teachers in a corner space not far away. "I have not taught reading in two weeks!" Another answered, "I have not taught math in two months!" A third voice said smilingly, "I guess you just don't understand our program here!" Wondering about them, I stopped and talked to a teacher I had once worked with nearby. She told me all of the area (comparable in size to about six or eight regular classrooms) was of 6-year olds, but that those in the back had a large family (group) so had an extra teacher. These had been the three I had heard.

Chapter 56

Car Mud Bath; Have a Nice Day
Banana Leaves for Plates

As I drove from Marine Drive into the Disney School Driveway toward the parking space near Clarendon Street, I saw great chunks of dirty snow being blasted forth from the building and down into the driveway before me. There was no way to back up the incline so I moved slowly forward, hoping the shower would stop before I reached it, but it hit the car forcefully as we went through, like countless heavy thuds, spreading very dirty hunks of snow all over the car and down into the windshield open area.

Fortunately, the third parking spot was open so I parked there and wiped off the grayish hunks as the car had been washed the previous day, and if the weather turned cold it might freeze and be difficult to remove later. As I approached the entrance three school service men were working, two with a snow machine remover. I questioned where they found such dirty snow that they had showered me with as I drove in and learned they had removed it from the school playgrounds.

While I was signing in at 8:30 the clerk reminded me the teachers arrived at 8:00, and as I had been called the day before to report, I should have been there then. I had wondered about the time the evening before but was not certain about it and there had been no way to check then. Teachers' arrival time was 8:30 in other schools but it seemed the clerk had once mentioned 8:00 to me some days earlier but I was not certain – until then. I felt badly about this as she was obviously disappointed and being tardy was not a habit of mine. It did overshadow my day somewhat, but I hoped I would have another chance to prove I could arrive on time.

Again I was in Pod 100 but this time it was a different section and a different family (class) of six-year-olds (first graders). I felt very much at ease in the school as it was the fourth day working there and I was grateful for the past experiences. This time the teacher had prepared a detailed time sheet, which paved the way for a smooth, pleasant day. The time sheet proved to be a double blessing as this group was more restless, energetic and inclined to be noisier than any other I had been with in the school. Probably this explained the teacher's warning, "Please do not allow the children to become too active", which had puzzled me when first reading it. But throughout the day I was hovering over some, reminding and cautioning several to be more quiet verbally and physically; at times a few were asked to move to more isolated spots in which to do their work.

One child came in late; one was absent; 20 were present, as was true with the family of my team teacher.

The teacher had put a morning story on the board, placed word cards in a chart for sentence making, and had left arithmetic ditto sheets to be done. This, I observed, was the usual morning pattern in the entire section. A little child came to me telling me I was to underline the capitals I wanted them to start their sentences with in the work on the board. I found a smaller board on which I put additional seatwork in case they finished the work, which several did, but their next step (I found) was to ask permission to work in their workbooks, where I thought each went forward at his own pace. In this group, however, I observed a smaller progress variance which surprised me; the workbooks were Levels one, two and three. Later I found the teacher had written a note saying the students were to work on only two additional workbook pages. This may have explained the small degree of variance in their individual workbook progress. But it could have been that certain skills were being introduced and reinforced at that time. Finished papers were starred and put in home boxes.

I wondered how the children learned new reading concepts but all appeared to be following through the regular established procedures. Only one little boy came to me with papers twice, both times seeming to want social contact more than assistance. With the writing he seemed to prefer to sit and dream; the math paper he had finished, but only the first half was correct, the last half having all wrong answers, as though written without effort or interest. He admitted he did not like math much, but this may have applied to all seatwork for him, as only two lines had been finished of the first assignments.

At 10:15 we went in to the DIA (music room). The Pod Leader had asked me in the early morning if I could play the piano, to which I answered "with one hand" but explained I carried records to protect myself, to which she had relaxed, as it was my turn, she explained, to take the two families for a short period there. The record player did not work well at first, but after warming up played satisfactorily. The children were not quiet enough so I stopped the record of the "Doggie in the Window", to the disappointment of a few, and replaced it with a child's "Hokey-Pokey" record, which was a hit, as usual, as they danced to the record instructions with body movements. This was heard and acted out twice, followed by dramatizing "The Three Little Kittens" record, all having turns being mothers or kittens. A teacher aide helped keep the youngsters in order so it worked out very well, especially as the records are always well received.

Next it was time for a snack, when the children received graham wafers, as they sat around two large pieces of green oilcloth before individual paper napkins, which the teacher aide had arranged.

The time schedule indicated I was to take the pupils to the third floor to the reading laboratory at 11:00, picking them up at 11:50. I purposefully returned early to learn what they did and on entering and sitting on a nearby chair observed a very large room with seven tables, about four children at each table, all listening to a story being read by one of the two teachers there. During the reading interesting questions were asked, which stimulated the listening habits, as all appeared eager to answer the questions. The story was about animals going on a picnic. A question asked was, "Why did they want to collect banana leaves for their picnic?" Answers offered were "for fire", "forks", "spoons", "salad", "plates".

"Yes,—who said 'plates'?" asked the teacher, whereupon all eyes turned to one proud little fellow, after which all ears again listened intently wishing to be able to produce the next correct answer.

The walking up and down stairs was the only noisy experience I had noticed in the school. Not only the class I had for the day was inclined to be noisy, with feet as well as mouths, but also several other classes using the stairs simultaneously, both ahead and following us. I had cautioned the children to walk softly "like Indians" which they may have done, but with all the other noise, it seemed more fun to join in and offer their contribution. So far, this was my only mark against the school. The steps on the stairways looked to be made of cork, but they did not seem to dull the heavy-stepping noise, as cork stairs in other new schools seemed to do.

When the group returned it was a "Completion period" in which to finish morning papers, which many needed. Others made washroom visits, got drinks, or engaged in activity play of individual interest.

Lunch was at 12:30. Many carried their own lunches. Several other groups were already seated at tables and the youngsters soon took extra seats at various tables and joined in sharing the food, which was waiting, family-style, for them to eat. Several teacher aides were in charge of the lunch-hour period.

It was my lunch hour so I stopped for a drink, noticing one dish available to teachers looked like cheese soufflé. The attendants explained it was ham, cheese and broccoli soufflé which sounded just as good, or better, so I ordered it. The price of $1.70 for the dish, including the drink, surprised me, but it was well worth it as it was really delicious. Another teacher at the table where I sat was eating beef stew, which also looked appetizing; he said it cost $1.00 including the drink.

The period after lunch was supposed to be a free one for the family (class) but I offered a short oral thinking period of catchy items, which they enjoyed. Next I showed them three types of plastic cutouts with which they could make art work if they so chose, which the majority did.

After cleaning up and putting all papers away it was their gym period for 35 minutes. When I called for them the two gym teachers commented they had been hard to control throughout the period, adding this class was inclined to be overactive. I said the gym period should have been at the beginning of the day, not at the end, as I noted most seemed a little subdued at the end of the time in the gym. There had been two gymnasiums; one teacher in each room; one room had climbing materials on one side of the room. There was a wall between them, with a closed door entrance.

While my "family" was in gym class my team teacher asked me to take a black child who was evidently disturbing her as she conversed with a man. Both were sitting and talking as her class was having a free activity period. I had wondered how Disney teachers handled problem children. At first this boy objected to coming to me and also to following the instructions I gave him. I asked him to please straighten the chairs and tables to make the room tidy and said there would be a nicer job after that. The last suggestion awakened his interest so he grudgingly put the room in order, then happily erased the two boards, a choice jobs to all students.

At going-home time all seemed able to put on their wraps and boots. My assignment was to take a group of 21 to buses at still another outside school entrance. This was the third side of the school with waiting buses – about 20 I would guess, making fifty or sixty buses taking children to and from the school daily. This time we walked the entire distance to the last bus for some of the youngsters to board. There was snow on the ground and at times older children would stand holding snowballs, but each time I asked them to drop them, reminding them they could make snowmen, but not snowballs. It was a wet day and I felt the snowballs could be dangerous; fortunately, all but one dropped them. One very tall boy, looking like an 8th grader, threw a snowball toward a bus, and an answering one came from a lowered window to him, but that was all.

Returning to the room I wrote the teacher a note thanking her for the work she had prepared, packed my things, and signed out. A clerk in the second office was leaving then too so we walked out together. I commented this certainly was a nice school, that it would be hard to get used to another one after being in Disney, to which she agreed. She had been at Disney five years and had impressed me my first day in the school by welcoming me three times with a big smile and saying, "Have a nice day", when she had seen me at different locations in the building. The smiles and helpfulness of all the teachers were a part of Disney too. It was so much easier to smile when being a substitute and not carrying the heavy load of responsibility for all the children whose progress one was accountable for. Considering all the materials this particular teacher had prepared and left for me to use I felt certain she would do her best to see those in her charge made the most of their capabilities.

Chapter 57

Bi Lingual
What Would You Do?

Because there had been a four inch snowfall during the night I was up early and removed the snow and ice from my car, but as I was assigned to Blaine School, not far from my home, and accessible to bus travel, I decided to ride the bus.

This was a large school. The principal did not seem to want to assign me to a primary grade; twice I repeated that Sub Center only called me for primary grades, adding that I was a retired teacher. It seemed there had been a mix-up regarding substitutes; they wanted one that had been asked to report to another fine school. I think they had contacted her directly. Finally he had me sign in for a class "of 7-year-olds", who proved to be a very nice class. All were Spanish.

Five mothers entered with their children, obviously concerned about me. They returned two or three times advising me about this and that, finally saying that when it was 10 above zero the children were not to go outside. I told them we would remain inside. It was extremely cold in the room, a terrible current crossing whenever they opened the door. Then I noticed a tall window was open at least six inches at the top and the icy wind blowing inside. This convinced the mothers I was to be trusted and they left.

Before the students entered I had put a poem on the board about snow, followed by questions to be answered about it. This they read orally with ease before copying it. About six children answered all the reading and writing assignments correctly; the majority merely copied the work. Two sat – until later when I became aware of this when starring completed papers, after which both did some of the work. The youngsters were able to do first grade math in adding and subtracting, but only adding at second grade level.

Their continual talking was disturbing so the desks, which were arranged in twos, buddy-style, were separated to single aisles, which discouraged further conversations.

The children supplied their own papers and pencils. Six read at regular grade level in a Holt Publishing Company book, surprising for

Spanish children, I felt, as, to me, this company put out a very difficult but fine reading series with accompanying seatwork. Sadly enough, I did notice they were three quarters finished with the book, but only one-quarter into the accompanying workbook. In my opinion much of the value of the workbook was dimmed by lagging behind, but the high stack of ditto seatwork, already graded, on a nearby table indicated the children were receiving much specific help in reading skills.

The top group of six students were not fluent readers, but slowly able to read the material; I watched them sound out the words. Obviously, they had a good teacher, and had had one the previous year as well.

The second group of eight youngsters, also in the Holt series, were reading at second semester, first grade level. Two in this group were very poor readers; however, the material in both groups was especially difficult this particular day, being about art masterpieces.

The last two readers were in pre-primers and not too steady. Three children went to TESL (Teaching English as a Second Language); they were not yet ready for reading classes. Nineteen were present; eight absent, but it was an unusually cold, snowy day.

When the reading classes were finished we had group exercises and danced to the Polka exercises as well, which youngsters always enjoy invariably requesting to have the record played again. Next, stars were stamped on the completed papers.

About twenty minutes before lunch the Milton Bradley Contraction Game was introduced, but the children were not too successful using it.

At noon four went home. I walked with the others to the auditorium where they waited for a half hour to eat. Several teachers were monitoring the area. We were short two free tickets so I obtained the additional ones from a lunchroom attendant.

After lunch a Spanish teacher aide took groups for Spanish reading. I put more seatwork on the board as could not read Spanish myself. I watched them read a few minutes and it fascinated me as it looked so easy, much like French with which I was familiar. As they read I felt I would have voiced the same sounds, so decided listening to Spanish reading records would be a future hobby of mine. I could obtain such records from the library.

When the Spanish for everyone had ended I again distributed the contraction cards, this time writing the words on the board that were to be punched on the cards. More and more pupils began to have Bingo Card winners, showing they were becoming adept at the game, and learning the words. After 30 minutes of this still-slow-going I began to tire of it but their interest was growing.

Then another teacher entered who was to take them for a 45 minute period of Social Studies. After my previous experience at Disney I expected she would show a movie, as they had done for such periods, so I remained, doing other work but also listening. It was an interesting worthwhile period. Oral questions followed the movie showing.

"What would you do if you saw your best friend trying to take away a little girl's ball?" asked the teacher, to which a child answered, "Give it back." "Okay, that's pretty good," said the teacher.

Turning to another child the teacher asked, "What would you do if a girl in the room was sharing her candy with everyone except you?" "I'd be angry," answered the girl. "Why not remind her kindly about yourself? Maybe she forgot you," said the teacher.

And to a boy the teacher asked, "What would you do if a new boy came in here and he looked very lonely. What would you do?" Silence. More silence. "Would you say something to him to make him feel better?" the teacher helped, to which the boy answered, "I'd ask him to be my friend."

The Social Studies teacher was soft spoken and the class remained quiet for her. She walked quietly about saying she needed someone to help her, at which all hands, became folded, all bodies sat straight. She did retain quietness throughout the movie, the questions, and during the reading of a book later.

As I had brought two Christmas books I read, "The Little Lost Angel", and there was a short period left for some art pictures. I showed them how to put three dots on their papers, one at the top center, two at the sides about two inches from the bottom, then connect with lines, converting them to pine trees and adding trunks. Inside scribble art was drawn, then colored, each section being a different color. As expected, the children were making fascinating pictures but time did not allow them to be finished. Some took them home; others left the work to be done the following day.

Quiet boys were chosen to erase the board, others to wash them. The children then put on their wraps and lined up quietly and left the building.

It had been such a pleasant day that I called Sub Center to report for work the next day. Usually I skipped a few days as only worked a few days monthly.

Chapter 58

Calling Santa 3 Times
Be Careful Here

At Sabin School I signed in at 8:25 and was assigned a Kindergarten class. At first I was dismayed that there was no attendance book, no Lesson Plan, no time schedule, but as I had brought my own Christmas items to be used I refused to be upset. Later the teacher aide found the records in a file drawer. The room was large, and cheerful, with newly painted white ceiling, bright green walls, soft green linoleum on the floor – no carpeting.

Searching through the many cabinets I found writing and art papers to use. There were no blackboards so I wrote out two seatwork papers to use, one of letters and words, one with numbers to be done, both having relevant pictures to be copied.

At 9:00 no children were outside in the corridor and I began to wonder if I was supposed to meet them outside. It would require a few minutes to go inside and put on my winter boots and coat. But then I saw a teacher aide I knew from another school approaching with the class; she had brought them in from outside. The aide took the roll as there were so many duplicate surnames and the last names were all in Spanish; being Spanish, she could pronounce them more correctly to the class. There were 19 present, 8 absent; 4 had moved. She said there would be a different, smaller class in the afternoon. The aide remained for the entire day.

The seatwork papers were explained and put on a chart to be copied; pencils, paper and crayons were distributed. One little sharpie completed his papers so rapidly I quickly made out another number sheet for him, comparable to regular first grade, of which he did complete about 75% neatly and correctly. And knowing the aide I suggested she talk to the teacher about the possibility of having this boy considered for first grade. He was apparently a fast thinker and worker and most likely would be bored with usual kindergarten activities.

An art project was explained, samples shown, and papers and crayons given out. The children were fascinated with the work, which

187

consisted of scribble-picture art work drawn inside large tree outlines; students of all grades enjoy this activity. I had found extra large paper for them to use so it took a little extra time.

Christmas records were played while the art was done, and there was time for the Polka exercise record, which they enjoyed. Two stories – "Rudolph, the Red Nosed Reindeer" and "The Night Before Christmas" were read, and washroom visits were made before lunch. I noticed no milk was served in this school during the morning or afternoon kindergarten classes.

At 11:30 the children lined up and went to the lunchroom, being the first ones there. Spaghetti was served with lettuce salad, french bread, orange jello and milk. Sadly enough, most ate the jello and bread and drank the milk, with but a few eating the spaghetti. This saddened me until I remembered I had not eaten fresh vegetables grown in our own back yard as a child, but had chosen bread and butter and sugar instead. I had grown to be very healthy so they probably would also.

At 11:30 the children returned to the room where the parents were waiting for them.

There was a half hour break for the teacher aide and myself to have lunch.

The afternoon class came in at 12:00. Seventeen were listed on the attendance book but eleven were absent, due to the inclement weather. Three had transferred.

There was a short period of Talking Time in which four children participated, telling their experiences calling Santa on the telephone, which one child said she had done three times.

Seatwork of math and writing papers were completed as in the morning, followed by the Christmas Tree art work. Somehow these little ones seemed more advanced than the morning class, to which the teacher aide agreed. They finished all the work more rapidly also so after hearing the Christmas records and having exercises as well as dramatizing the Polka and Three Little Kittens records, they were given extra art work of tracing plastic animal forms. There were three selections for them – small animals, large ones, or tiny ones; all were very different so all took turns using all sizes.

It was very interesting to observe their tracing. Mothers had told me in a pre-kindergarten class that the pupils were not able to do the tracing unless someone held the items firmly for them. At that time I had been too busy serving lunches to notice. Here I noted the tracing was shaky with some children as the figures did slip often, but they were recognizable, and the tracing was of great value in developing their little muscles. The boys seemed to be more adept at this activity than the girls; possibly even at this tender age they had more physical strength than their opposite sex.

There was no clock in the room and the teacher aide had no watch so I was glad my watch was dependable. School was out at 2:30 and all mothers came for the children then.

The teacher aide had told me in the afternoon that the previous day two teachers in the school had been hit and knocked down as they approached the school about 8:30 in the morning, and that two more had had the same experience that very morning. Both happenings had been on the same street about the same location; both by two men. She said the men had tried unsuccessfully to take the purses. It had never been a neighborhood to walk in at night – but in the daytime at 8:30 in the morning! This was really sad to hear.

Chapter 59

Fix the Tree Now?
Rhythm Band

My assignment at Disney School was to work with 5-year-olds, but due to the icy streets and heavy, continuous snow, buses bringing in the students were arriving very late. The first bus, usually in at 8:30, appeared at 9:15. Because of this the time schedule for classes was changed accordingly. Further, while signing in I had heard an intercom message saying that all TESL and ERA Classes were to be cancelled. Later I learned that 87 of the usual 195 children in the entire pod of 5-year olds (nine groups) were present for that day.

At one time I saw a teacher counting the children. "Oh, are you taking the roll?" I asked. He nodded. Later I realized he did not have an attendance book but had merely counted the children present. I wondered if this was the way it was done with the five year olds as I had never seen anyone take roll in these groups. The one time I had been told it was my turn to take the roll with the six-year-olds a faded and worn-out list was all that was available to struggle with. There had been several names listed that the children explained were no longer in that group; all names had faint multi-colored circles before them indicating reasons unknown to me. I was told the regular teacher had taken the attendance book home to work on it.

The usual routine was a Self-Select Period, followed by Skill Time. As there were no Lesson Plans and I seemed unable to locate any specific letters or objects with which to teach skills I decided to combine colors, numbers and shapes in skill time. Meanwhile, as several children were milling about I took out several Christmas art papers that they might select, and immediately the table became crowded with children. As I drew basic outlines and displayed samples, the children went to a table for drawing papers, crayons and scissors. As the group became even larger some took the work to be completed at another table nearby.

When youngsters asked what they could do next I showed them other art work samples, which they accepted and made. Some children remained; new ones kept appearing, requesting outlines to color. Finally we made Santas on chimneys, a forever favorite at Christmas.

At 11:15 the children were taken to the washrooms, then on to the lunchroom. I was responsible for one group of eight until an 8th grader came in later. The children sat at one table which had napkins and plastic spoons waiting. I brought bowls of spaghetti, bread and salad to them and served it. They had fun pretending to be visitors from New York, and eating in an expensive restaurant. This brought forth their best manners, quietness and co-operation instead of bickering, grabbing and complaining. When the older helper came I left for my own lunch.

Returning at 12:15 I was surprised to find no children about, and inquiring was told they were in the DIA Room. Close by I saw a closed door and inside children lined the room three deep in a large circle. All had rhythm band instruments and a few at a time were playing to the piano music of a teacher. It was truly delightful to witness these babies following instructions and behaving so well with the instruments. The young instructor was really successful working with them in this field.

At 12:30 there was a movie for all the children in the Pod so all were taken to another section nearby. But the three young teachers had much trouble trying to get the filmstrips into the machine correctly so the youngsters became restless and started to be noisy. The three were busily engaged in the back so I stood up in front, doing silent arm movements and body movements. It became quiet at once, all eyes following and copying my movements for several minutes until the machine was ready. But again the strip was in incorrectly so another teacher who had come in introduced soft singing, which quieted them. The strip was again incorrect so I started saying poems with movements, and as there was still machine trouble, another teacher then taught finger exercises. At long last the strips were put in correctly. The teachers explained the filmstrips had been rolled the wrong way before putting them into the containers.

The first strip, about an alligator, was not very interesting and it was a good thing it was soon finished. The next strip about a frog was funny and held their interest. Later questions relating to social behavior were asked, which many volunteered to answer correctly.

I sat on one side of the room. All children were quiet and watching the filmstrip; a record player produced the sound. But a teacher on a far side kept talking to someone with a hat on sitting by her most of the time. One teacher aide nearby talked all period to three others and their voices were very distracting. One boy kept looking back at them so I finally suggested they whisper. No way. Their voices continued all period.

1:00 was nap time so all children returned to their groups and got their blankets to rest for an hour. A teacher aide with the group told me her job consisted of riding the bus to and from the school with the children; she started at 7:30, arrived home at 3:30. She said the school gave no report cards but that parents visited the school twice yearly to learn of the children's progress. She said the school had three Pods – Pod 110 was the beginning one; 120 next and 130 the last. Children could remain in the school from age five through age 14 (8th graders).

In the early morning I had noted one little tot walking about, closely toting a large package with her, half as large as she was. Finally she told me it was for her teacher, who was absent. And soon she requested it be opened as it was a Christmas tree. It was a beautiful blue-green, plastic tree, about three feet high, which the children helped put together, inserting the branches. As nap time was announced this little child walked toward the tree, reached up and pulled it down toward her with one hand, the other hand taking handfuls of branches from the tree.

"We'll have to put it back up now, won't we?" she piped up. Another tot was also quick to be dismantling the tree. I lifted it above their heads and took the branches, putting them aside, saying we would do it later.

As the children rested the child who had brought the tree kept fidgeting, turning, sitting up, and getting up all during the period. The teacher aide nearby said the child had been at Disney the preceding year as well and had never taken a nap. As I watched her toss and turn, and finally come to ask permission to go to the washroom, my heart ached for her. During the morning she had been constantly moving about, always talking. No doubt this child did not need this amount of rest; many adults require very limited amounts of sleep. I felt I would ask the psychologist about her when I came again. At home when I could not sleep I got up and read, washed things or cleaned the apartment. I understood why she had pulled down the tree. One teacher walking by crossly told the child to lie still; later when I questioned the teacher about the girl she said it was because she was not disciplined at home. But if the child had not been able to sleep at nap time for the past year and a half I felt there were other reasons. The long hour must have seemed endless to her, but even if I couldn't help her, she only had one more half year to endure the rest period; six-year olds did not nap in the school.

During the last fifteen minutes of the rest period napkins and cookies were put on the tables for snacks.

After the snack the youngsters began to put on their wraps for the home journey. Practically everyone needed help in putting on boots, fastening coat buttons, zipping zippers and tying scarves. Finally the twelve assigned to me to take to buses were lined up. But I noticed a little one leave for the washroom. Two teachers told us to leave as we waited, saying we were late, but I explained I had seen a little girl leave for the washroom. I told the youngsters she had worn a white coat and hat so two or three figured out the child's name. All agreed we should wait for her. Finally she returned and we left the building. As we neared the buses all seemed to hurry faster toward them although I cautioned them to be careful of the ice and snow. I walked on until all were inside; then ahead I saw two tiny ones. Reaching them I found them to be the two that had been first in line; they had hurried past their bus. Checking my list I found their bus nearby.

Returning to the pod I tidied up the floor space, put the chairs up as saw other teachers doing that. On a center table I noted some Reading Readiness Tests that were to be given the following Monday to all in the Pod.

As I had not driven, but had taken a bus that morning, I asked a teacher standing outside if she knew where the bus stop was and received my first curt reply from a teacher there. "I have no idea," she said sharply.

Others then came outside, walking down the steps as I did. Ahead I saw one open a door and walk through. I assumed she would be walking underneath on the driveway to the front area to the west where I had parked before.

"Oh, she is walking through that way," I commented.

One teacher answered, "That is our parking lot." As I walked nearer I saw cars were parked under the building. I wished I had been aware of that parking lot the day my car was given a dirty (playground) snow shower by the school engineers. The above ground rows of parking spaces were all I had been aware of then. This school had many surprises.

Chapter 60

Tiny Busettes
Mothers vs Drivers

My assignment for the day was to be with pre-school Non-Categoric (not labeled) children at Morris School. A teacher aide entered with six bright-eyed smiling youngsters – all boys. In referring to them during the day she sometimes called them EMH (emotionally mentally handicapped), adding each one had some special problem.

After the children hung up their wraps they got chairs and sat in front of me. I had copied shapes on a paper as the teacher's Lesson Plan indicated she had been working with these. One child could name all of them except the crescent which I had added; he called it a moon. The others named most of them also. Next, I said a short Christmas poem which I expected them to learn but it did not appeal to them so I introduced "There Was a Little Girl" poem, which they immediately accepted and learned.

A skill period was next. They cut and pasted white strips on red cut-out candy canes. When finished with these, four inch angels were colored and cut out to be put on their Christmas trees at home. Their cutting skills were much more advanced than their coloring abilities as most started out coloring neatly but soon became careless. However, the finished angels, once cut out, did look quite attractive.

The teacher aide took three at a time to the gym for exercises of fifteen-minute periods during the morning when the gym was not being used.

All stopped at a washroom then went to the lunchroom for a snack, where milk and tangerines were served. Each youngster opened his own milk carton, but the tangerines were new to them and some requested help in starting to peel them. Two were not hungry so let others eat their fruit.

Back in the room a child's Polka exercise record was played but they did not seem to care too much for it so I read a story, "The Night Before Christmas". Sadly enough, another teacher kept talking to the teacher aide in back of us so I soon gave up as there was no enjoyment in reading with constant talking going on. I did a few finger exercises which they enjoyed, then played "The Three Little Kittens" record. This they accepted wholeheartedly so it was played twice with two children being the mother kitten, while others acted out the story as it was played. They especially enjoyed dramatizing the soft crying of the little kittens. Seeing a picture of Rudolph, the Red-Nosed Reindeer, on a record, they asked to hear that one so it was played, followed by "The Night Before Christmas". I showed the book pictures of the story as the record was being played.

It was time for the morning class to go home so they put on their wraps, two asking for help with their zippers, one with coat buttons. No one wore boots as the weather had turned much warmer. As they stood in line the teacher aide passed out surprises to them as their weekly awards. These were small plastic colored soldiers, each child selecting one to take home. She later told me these were purchased with personal money for the children.

I walked outside to the busses with them. There were four busettes (small busses) waiting. I looked inside, explaining I had never seen such small busses. They were miniature copies of large busses, having but four small double seats on each side. The teacher aide said they held a maximum of 19 children but they looked much smaller to me.

The aide and I returned to the room straightening it and prepared for the afternoon class. We also ate lunch before the next group was to arrive.

The aide informed me there were five classrooms of these children in the school, explaining they came here from all over the city. I learned there was much absenteeism for various reasons, and particularly due to parental problems. The aide told me that some teacher aides rode on the busettes with the children to and from the school.

As we waited outside for the afternoon class one bus had arrived and I helped the driver clean the bus windows, which seemed to be nearly as dirty on the inside as the outside. But after waiting some time we learned that no children had come for the afternoon class in our room. The teacher aide reported this to the office and I was assigned to test children for reading progress tests who had been absent when the tests had been given.

The students were all Spanish, about ten years of age, and each one did very well on the tests; two had perfect scores; one but two errors.

While I was grading the results the adjustment teacher had a meeting in the room with the bus drivers. It seemed the parents were often complaining the drivers did not pick up their children, to which the drivers maintained this was an old complaint, usually from the same families, and that they were the ones who did not have their children ready. One driver said he could not hold a bus and three squad cars for one child who was still inside getting ready. Others said the children went out to play and did not remain near their homes. It was usually the same old excuses, they related, but that day one had been different. "The door was stuck". Mothers argued the busses did not come on time; the drivers said there were traffic lights, pedestrians and weather hazards to contend with, making it impossible to arrive at a definite minute. Because of these, they insisted, individual children's names could not be listed to be picked up at a certain moment; this was theory that did not work out in practise. All agreed the parents were not dependable in having the children ready.

The adjustment teacher said one mother had called that morning saying they waited and waited, to which the driver answered there was no problem; the child lived only two blocks away.

One driver was asked about a certain child's behavior on the bus. The driver said the child jumped and cried a lot. He was told that if he could not handle him that he was not to pick him up.

The adjustment teacher asked about the teachers, wondering if the same one or two kept them waiting. To this the drivers agreed. Some were wonderful ones but too slow. They added it was difficult to keep the busses too long at the school as when they sat waiting for 15 minutes they were then that much longer off their scheduled runs.

The drivers complained that sometimes the parents were not home when they delivered the children, saying the parents insisted the children were to be returned to the school at such times. But the adjustment teacher objected strenuously to this, explaining they could not do so; the insurance did not cover them during such time. (I gathered the youngsters were to be delivered to a police station in such instances.)

Helen Marie Prahl

As I sat grading the tests and hearing these problems, which did not affect my life, I was reminded that regardless of one's occupation, there always seemed to be problems to be ironed out, and one's personal harmony seemed to depend on overcoming them. Classroom confrontations between children were usually quickly solved by private corridor talks, followed by apologies and sheepish handshakes. Sometimes more time was required to soften some child's animosity, but apologizing was a habit I really tried to instill, feeling it paved the way to more harmonious lives.

Chapter 61

Class Rules & Punishments

Driving west from the lake on Diversey to Schneider School was a mistake as I did not find Hoyne Avenue and had to cross an elevated construction, several blocks too far west, then try to find the school on numerous one-way streets, all this taking an extra fifteen minutes, so that I signed in at 8:45. Three substitutes had already been assigned rooms; my work for the day was to teach remedial classes in various classrooms.

Teaching reading, and especially remedial reading, was always particularly interesting to me, but one needs specific materials for this, suited to the pupils' needs, all of which were home. It would be impossible to carry such supplies about as there is such an abundance that can be used. A teacher of remedial reading first finds the weaknesses of her students, then introduces specific materials to strengthen them, using much reinforcement.

A Daily Program outline, obtained from the office, indicated the classes were of 45-minute duration, and from the room numbers the grades appeared to be from 7th down through 3rd.

The teacher's desk was sandwiched in the corner of a hallway cloakroom, and as one little latecomer had much trouble trying to make his coat remain on a hook I went to help him, commenting it looked like a warm coat. "Hi," he said, "You know what? When I was five – then I was six – my mother bought that." His warm smile and friendliness made me feel glad to be there.

The first group of four, ages 12 and 13, were very poor readers, reading at 2nd and 3rd grade levels. We reviewed five reading skills, letter blends, ten used the Milton Bradley Contraction and Abbreviation cards. I showed them how they could make charts to study and improve their reading at home.

The next group of eight, ages 11 and 12, were not bad readers, being but a year or year and a half behind their grade expectancy levels. They were alert, quick to respond, good thinkers. There was time to use the Bradley card game on Homonyms as well as the one on Abbreviations and Contractions. Being impressed by their interest, their teacher came back to learn what materials were being introduced, saying she had class money to purchase items. Learning there were four such games available in teachers' stores, she said she would buy them.

At 10:35 I was listed to relieve an upper grade teacher for 15 minutes. Noise from the room carried out into the corridor, making it sound like a disaster area, and inside it looked like one. Several students' chairs and desks were seemingly isolated somewhat, placed by blackboards, near the entrance, on both sides and in front of the teacher's desk; two were outside in the corridor! Talking was rampant, loud laughing constant, chairs and desks were every-which way, legs were crossed, feet out in aisles. Although the students looked likeable, I was glad my time there was for only the fifteen minute period. As the teacher, a young man, left, he commented smiling, "No one is to leave the room."

Surprisingly, I had fun with them, joining in their conversation, as they were not interested in gym exercise games, or any games. I watched the two door exits and managed to keep everyone inside, although there was much walking about by several pupils. When the teacher returned he commented I was to return at 1:00, which clouded the rest of my day, and I was constantly planning to bring special material to capture and hold their interest at that time.

The next group of six were 6th graders, eleven and twelve years of age. As they quietly completed sentence skill cards I supplied, there was sudden, constant noise from the ceiling, which surprised me as this had appeared to be the top floor. The children explained it was the gym, adding they wished they were up there. They said the rest of their class had gone to a typing class.

Their room was very neat, and the most attractive, inviting and interesting one I had ever been in. Seatwork was neatly written on 2½ blackboards. The walls were of cheerful colors; white ceiling, pea-green walls, marble oilcloth on the floor. Very neat educational skill charts, on orange backgrounds, appeared on all wall spaces. I knew from the board work and chart printing that their teacher was one of the best as her interest, and ability, were reflected in everything there.

A chart of (12) *Class Rules* and corresponding (12) *Punishments* so intrigued me that I quickly copied them in shorthand. The teacher later explained these had been formed by the class officers. The teacher was neat, attractive and soft spoken. The punishment rule number corresponded to the rule number – so, if a student ran about in the room (Rule #1) then he was asked to hold two dictionaries for 15 minutes (Punishment #1). During the reading period the students said that punishment rules were enforced by the class officers daily, admitting that nearly everyone was punished at one time or another.

CLASS RULES

1. No running in the room.
2. No chewing gum.
3. No fighting.
4. No teasing.
5. No one does any one else's work without permission.
6. No getting out of your seat without permission.
7. No doing lines for fun.
8. No reading corner class work is copied.
9. No eating in the room.
10. No leaning on your chair.
11. No swearing.
12. No trespassing.

PUNISHMENTS

1. Hold two dictionaries on each hand for 15 minutes. (As I read this rule aloud one girl in the group commented, "that's hard!" I asked, "Does anyone have to do the punishments in here?" She nodded, adding, "me – mostly everybody."
2. Fine 5 cents.
3. No reading corner for one week.
4. 150 lines: "I will not tease others".
5. Lose your job for one week.
6. Fireplug exercise. (I asked what this was. "It is standing on this table." "Doing what?" I asked. "You are down, facing the floor. You raise up on your arms; you raise one foot at a time up and out and down. It's hard."

7. Do five times as many lines.
8. Legs and hands up (on knees) for 10 minutes.
9. Fine – 10 cents.
10. Frog stand for 10 minutes.
11. Coatroom. Possible conference with Principal.
12. Sit on hands. Do work after school.

The group enjoyed both Bradley card games after completing the skill cards; they were quiet, disciplined, orderly – as expected after reading the rules on the chart! We also tried out many oral thinking activities, which I asked their advice about using with the problem room I was to return to at 1:00. Although they enjoyed all the work, no one was confident any of it would be acceptable to the 7th and 8th graders.

After lunch at 1:00 I entered the room of 7th and 8th graders and it was obvious (as I expected) they had not been given any work assignment by the teacher. It was possible to keep some of the noise down for possibly five minutes, long enough to read a list of modern-day work definitions by a college professor, but the class behavior was too impossible to distribute any Bradley card games or introduce oral ones. Not being gifted musically all I could do was wait for the 15 minute break to end. But the expected fifteen long minutes dragged on into twenty and twenty-five. Finally, in utter disgust I picked up my satchels, opened the door, and as the "teacher" entered I left.

When I entered the next room a 4th grade, the class was very unruly. A Spanish teacher was at the teacher's desk. When I asked them to be quiet a Spanish boy in back near me started laughing so loudly that I stood by him, saying I expected his apology. When he hesitated the teacher in front called him by name, telling him to apologize, which he did. After that there was no more trouble and the entire room became quiet. Later I noticed a different teacher in front so the one there must have been relieving the regular one when I entered. Probably they had been giving her a difficult time.

Five students came back for help in reading skills. We used Cards I and II, abbreviations and homonyms, as well as upper grade city and alphabet games.

The last group of students were from nine to twelve years of age. The teacher was black, soft spoken, and was having a most difficult time as about four black pupils were very disrespectful and taking advantage of her. They kept talking back and forth across the room, even though she repeatedly asked them to be quiet; they rose and walked across the room without permission; they laughed loudly without stopping. It was obvious she liked them, and her job, but was not a good disciplinarian. After several minutes I could not stand it any more and spoke up telling them they had a good teacher, and they should respect her. I spoke firmly, calmly, and faced the trouble-makers.

The noise stopped immediately and we were able to have the reading without further difficulty. One of the behavior problems came to the reading group, as I had expected. Children with behavior problems usually have reading problems, but I have many times seen the behavior difficulties fade away when reading skills were mastered. As the boy approached I pointed to a seat beside me in which he remained quiet. This was a lower grade so we used only the contraction and abbreviation cards. They were slow readers but finally managed to start winning in the game contests.

I felt sorry for their teacher, she was young but already looked tired. Not being able to maintain order was going to make teaching a very difficult life for her. I thought of two acquaintances of mine who had dropped out of teaching simply because they were unable to maintain discipline. As I thought of them I felt this teacher might be happier in some other type of work as well.

Teaching is hard enough for one able to maintain discipline. It is not an easy profession. But teaching is work that proves to be deeply rewarding to those who devote much time and effort to seeing their pupils show progress.

Chapter 62

Reading Ahead
Math Behind

It was Monday and bitter cold, one degree below zero, a day I really felt like remaining in bed for another hour or two. But I had called Substitute Center the Friday before so rose, dressed, had breakfast, and waited for their call. Before Christmas their calls had come in around 7:30, or before, but this day in January there was no call by 8:00. I had skipped a day of work the previous week because a pet was ill, so really wanted to work this day. Finally, at 8:00 I called Disney, and they called me to work by 8:10. As I was leaving at 8:25 the telephone was ringing, no doubt from the Central Agency.

I drove to Disney School on Marine Drive and on entering noted closely the underground car parking entrances. There were three entrance doors, all closed, so I continued on to the outside parking area. Fortunately, the third space was vacant; probably someone living nearby had used it and had just left.

After signing in for a group of 6-year olds the assignment was changed to an upper floor of 9-year-olds. This was fine with me as I had been with the six year groups so often that I had been considering asking to be changed to another level. But as I left I noticed the substitute taking the other group was going to the far side where I had never taught, but had heard those three teachers talking about their school experiences twice, and had been hoping I might be sent there to learn more about that group firsthand.

On arriving at the 2nd floor receiving desk I was ushered, for the first time, to the regular teacher's "desk", which was in a section among about twelve other desks, sort of a faculty section. There was a name on the desk – and an Attendance Record! This was a relief to see. I glanced at it before removing my coat, noting it was merely a list of names, but with proper pages to note absences, which had been done in pencil. It was not a regulation attendance book as used in other public schools. Later I was busy putting seatwork up for the students and handed the record to a student teacher to take the attendance so did not see the book again.

There was but one small portable blackboard to use, about four by five feet, which was not nearly enough to list work I had brought, so I took large pages of construction paper on which I wrote more work with a Flowmaster Marking Pen. There were three other substitutes in the same section that day so it took the teacher in charge much extra time to show all of us the proper desks, where to put coats, where the groups of children were, etc. so I did not arrive at the teaching area until a little after nine o'clock. The students were ready and waiting, some in chairs before desks, others sitting on the carpeted floor.

Sensing their restlessness, I turned, and decided on another procedure. The teacher in charge had commented they were capable of 5th grade work, so I told them I had heard they were able to do higher grade work and suggested they become secretaries and write a letter I would dictate. The new idea appealed to them, but it was so totally new that the procedure was soon an obvious failure. I saw but one paper that appeared like letter format, neatly written. Others wilted along the way; most had great trouble even starting, although I showed them on a sample, just where to start writing the school address at the right top section, as well as where to write the name of the company we were writing to on the left side. The dictating was painfully slow, and repeated over and over by requests. Still many sat. Somehow the short letter was finished, and I wrote it on the board so they could correct their work. But as they looked like they had suffered a traumatic experience I did not pursue the matter, or check any papers.

The noise on the entire floor area, the first I had noted at the school, had seemed to be a constant one, like a dull toothache; then there was a bell ringing sound, which the children said meant they were too noisy. This was repeated twice during the morning, the head teacher then informing them they were too noisy both times. A short quietness followed the ringing, after which a somewhat more subdued noisiness continued most of the day. The noise seemed to come from one group in the center of the room, then joined by others.

The children said they read from books, but when I chose one child and asked those who read with her to come to the back section to read, they said they had finished reading their reader and the new ones had not yet arrived. I said I wanted to hear them read so had them get the book they had finished and each read a section. They were reading at Level 17 in a Scott Foresman book; Levels 16 to 18 are fifth grade readers. One child was a very good oral reader, one good, one satisfactory, and two were quite weak in ability to sound out and read the names of characters in the book. The majority of students, the second group, were at Level 16, and also without a book; they had gone to read with the student teacher, who had them work in their workbook, as did the group who had come to me; they enjoyed doing this.

During the last half of the period we used the Contraction and Abbreviation and the Homonym Bingo cards, which were well received, as usual. Being good readers they soon mastered the Homonym cards so more time was spent on the Abbreviation ones which seemed a little more obscure to a few, although this game is actually for first and second graders.

The next period was one of math and most students left for another section, new students appearing. It was soon apparent they were unable to do 3d grade work so I showed them how to add and carry and to borrow, which is usually introduced and mastered in second or third grade. Only one boy and one girl were able to understand and follow through with this; I had the feeling when these students came that they did not represent a high level in math.

Next I dictated numbers, asking them to write them. "One hundred dollars and one cent" was the first, which not one could write correctly. Easier ones followed. I wanted to concentrate on place value, using the decimal. If there had been a larger blackboard to use it would have been easier for them. This board was a difficult one to use as it was crumpled in many sections and not clearly viewed because of this. By the end of the period a few were able to write easy amounts correctly, but they needed much help in arithmetic. Much solid and repeated help. Most classes, from 2nd grade up, can master writing dictated amounts in 20 or 30 minutes, but this group seemed to have no solid foundation in math. However, with a large blackboard much more might have been presented and accomplished. I hope I might be sent to this group again.

The teacher's lunch period followed the arithmetic so I left for lunch. Teacher aides took the children to the lunchroom. I had inadvertently left without my lunch so had ravioli. There was no more coffee, as usual, so I had home-made soup, which was always especially good there. I ate with another substitute who had taught a year in a suburb and was delighted with Disney, being there for the first time.

1:30 was listed as a Social Studies period and the children from the entire area, probably three or four classes, were seated on the floor before the screen. The noise and restlessness grew but no teacher, except myself, was there. At 1:45 a teacher came. She turned the lights off; a second teacher appeared, and a third, later I learned some students had gone to another place for a science period. The filmstrip shown was on Ethnic Studies, "The Peoples of America", and the teacher introduced it well saying the teachers had talked about the subject and decided this one best conveyed the social background and ethnic groups in Chicago. She took many good notes as the strip was being shown and later held their attention with her questions involving the characteristics and differences of the many groups. The variances in foods, clothing and games were especially interesting to the students.

At closing time I noted one boy wanted to rush through the lines so he and I became rear guards, which I explained entailed great responsibility in keeping students quiet and in proper formation.

It was still bitter cold outside, and as the others entered their buses, I learned his bus was the one most distant, which he finally dashed off to when all the others had boarded buses.

Returning to the school I collected my things, erased the board and signed out. A student teacher was leaving so I drove her to a bus nearby. She said she was to spend part of her practise-teaching time at Disney and part in a traditional school. She asked which I preferred and I said Disney was different, but I preferred having my own classroom. I did not tell her that the present day trend of having walking reading classes even changes that concept. At my last school I had heard a first-grade teacher comment she felt she was "losing her class" with the walking reading. I agreed with her.

In first grade a teacher teaches all aspects of learning all day and needs her students with her to reinforce the various concepts throughout the day; this is not possible when they leave to go to other rooms, and the teacher does not get to know their strengths and weaknesses this way. However, in upper grades, the advantage of walking reading does become more apparent.

I cherished the many memories gained through teaching primary grades for a number of years; but I also remembered the remedial reading classes with six-graders and how pleased they and I were when they made progress after their interest was captured. Teaching is interesting, and satisfying, at any level.

Chapter 63

Put Your Best Foot Forward

At 7:30 Substitute Center called, telling me to report to Stewart School. The school did not supply parking space for teachers, but I found a quarter-space by a No Parking sign on a side street. Three quarters of the car was in the restricted area but parking spaces were at such a premium in the area that I left it there.

After signing in at 8:35 I was assigned to a Kindergarten Class, the only primary grade left on the sheet. Four substitutes had signed in ahead of me; two spaces were still open, probably for higher grades.

Although Kindergarten never especially appealed to me, I was no longer apprehensive about it as through experience had learned that the very young children need the same basic materials as older ones – work skill assignments in the three R's, art, physical activities and music. If time permits games are fine – both oral and physical.

An Attendance Book was on top of the desk, but no Time Schedule, no ditto work sheets to be done. But I had learned to carry my own samples of seatwork for all levels so this was promptly handled by clipping sample worksheets to be copied to the top of a painting easel.

It was a bitter cold day, below zero, so many youngsters were absent. 32 names were listed in the Attendance Book; 6 had left, one transferred in; 16 were absent, leaving 11 present for the morning class. When taking roll it was noticed that three tiny tots were not listed; they were supposed to be in another room, most likely a pre-kindergarten class, as they were taken away by a student helper from the office.

As the children copied the seatwork papers I took one child at a time and copied the outline of one foot, cut it out and had the child decorate the outline. After putting their names on them the footprints were put on a front bulletin board, headed "Put Your Best Foot Forward".

This activity was followed by coloring large butterfly outlines I had drawn. When all papers were completed, and starred, music and

209

story records were listened to. They enjoyed the child's record of exercises, "The Polka", and acting out "The Three Little Kittens".

Two youngsters took a note to the office inquiring the time they had lunch and the arrival time of the afternoon class. They told me they received milk in the morning, but the lunchroom attendant said they had never sent milk to the room. The children agreed they ate lunch, then returned to the room for their wraps and work papers to take home, but at 11:40 I had them wear their wraps and take the seatwork with them, which turned out to be the correct procedure. Another teacher was waiting for them in the lunchroom; she told me she took charge of them and sent them home after having lunch, adding it was my lunch time.

Returning to the room I ate the lunch I had brought and was ready for the next group at 12:00. Again 32 were listed in the Attendance Book and six had already left. Twelve were absent for the day, leaving 14 present.

These children appeared to be much larger than the ones in the morning class so I felt they would be capable of more advanced work, but their work was the same as that of the earlier ones. Conversation started about the time of the year so calendar events were discussed. They knew the name of the month, day, date, but could not tell me the date of the last day of the month, which was then pointed out on the large wall calendar. They could name the days of the week, and tell the number of week days, but did not know the names of the months so I produced a catchy record naming them. After this was played twice most of them could join in and sing the words which named the twelve months. Past experience had taught me that most children remembered these names, even a year later, after having heard the record but twice.

The morning procedure was followed – seatwork, footprints, art work, exercises and records. They especially enjoyed learning a poem, named, "There Was a Little Girl" and acting out the "Three Little Kittens" records.

Chapter 64

Good 4th Grade Class
3:30 Ghost Area

The call from Substitute center came at 7:20 and I left at 8:00 for Bell School, but the heavily falling snow on top of thick ice caused extremely slow driving so it was not until 8:30 that I signed in the school and was assigned a fourth grade class, one without handicaps, as is common in this school.

As the students entered before I finished the board assignments I had two students collect, and handle the milk money and tickets, which was a great help. 37 had been listed in the attendance book; two had left; three were absent, a very good record for such a day.

It seemed to be a good class, but one that liked to talk continually amongst themselves, so I turned from the board, deciding to dictate a letter. Their frowning, sour faces toward this decision surprised me, but I continued with it. Progress appeared to be extremely slow with the majority. I noted many restarted several times; some merely sat, and there was the sound of disgusted crumpling of papers, followed by plain sitting and glaring. I walked about noting the work after it was finished, and it was obvious this was above their level. Only about three or four had been able to formulate a proper business letter, although I had told them where to write the headings, body and ending. I then wrote the letter correctly as it should have been for them to correct themselves, but the math period started before I finished this and students left and others entered.

In introducing the arithmetic period I dictated short problems which very few were able to relax and listen to so few gave answers. Little by little more became attentive and there were more answers given correctly. Next I gave catchy problems which they enjoyed and ended up by solving as well. Some book work was completed; then I dictated amounts for them to write. As I had anticipated, those weak in English work were shining examples in math, alert and eager to give answers. In but a few tries most in the class were writing correct amounts given them. Each time I wrote the correct amount after dictating it. I had also seen stacks of math papers on the absent teacher's desk and knew they were well advanced in this field. The entire group was happy and smiling by the end of the period.

Because they were so disappointed at being kept inside at recess time I decided to have interesting activities. Apparently they enjoyed the games offered, but each seemed dull to me until I introduced the Kangaroo Hop and Threading the Needle. Both became hits and I quickly picked six, then eight, assistants, who learned to do both and had fun helping others in the short time.

There were three reading groups, but all read from the same book, at Level "J" which was 4th grade level. Two had finished the book; the majority were two-thirds finished, and the third group was one-third into the book. The oral reading seemed satisfactory so each read a short paragraph. I started silent reading for answers to questions I formulated. This seemed new to them, but few teachers have much time to devote to this type of reading. Several from each group learned to answer correctly in but a short time.

At one time, during silent reading, the Assistant Principal stepped in, asking how things were going. When I commented it was a good class, adding that I knew it was when they entered, he seemed surprised, and later in the corridor at noon another teacher offered me her sympathy, saying she had had the class a few days earlier and "it was the worst class she had ever had". They had not been a problem to me at all. Possibly it was because I had said I did not like talking but said if they remained quiet we would have Bingo Games in the afternoon, but that noisy students would not receive cards to play. They agreed it was a fair arrangement, and with a few reminders, the class remained a good one during the entire day.

As we lined up for lunch I learned the lunch tickets had already been distributed to those who had taken the money, which was appreciated. Ten had paid 40 cents for their lunches – a rich class in my experience, as usually it was free tickets for the majority, or entire classes. Here two paid 20 cents; two were free; the others went home as it was an Open Campus, having an hour for lunch, the school closing at 3:15.

I took my lunch and ate in a small room where lunch was served to teachers. The green asparagus looked so good I asked for a side order of it, but learned it was all cooked to order. I had been told of this when I signed in at 8:30 but had brought my lunch and not considered it then. So I took coffee and ate what I had brought, plus two cookies from the counter.

There were six tables of teachers there, with about eight teachers at each table. I left early and in passing the library saw another group sitting at a long table there. As I stood looking they invited me to join but I did not. It was a nice feeling to be invited though as I had been thinking what a refined, quiet and interesting group they appeared to be. I continued walking to the main office, where one of the clerks told me they had 85 teachers in the school – more than in some high schools, she said.

After I returned to the room a group of boys, about 30, came and sat on the corridor floor outside, which was carpeted. Although their noise did not bother me too much, I thought they might enjoy some music so I had one of the boys get a phonograph I saw in the room, place it on a desk, and plug it into an outlet inside the door. I think they enjoyed the music as much as I did until the bell rang for afternoon.

The afternoon started out in finding and offering solutions to personal problems they discussed, which appeared beneficial and interesting to everyone. It started when one small boy asked permission to go to another room to report another boy who persisted in causing him trouble. After the talks he didn't ask to go again so he, too, must have found a better solution.

The Contraction and Abbreviation Bingo Cards were distributed, followed by the Homonym Cards, which held their attention as they always do, offering as much learning values as they do in enjoyment in playing and winning.

Throughout the day I had been receiving written notes from students as this had been suggested to stop the constant raising of hands to talk about this and that. As three had been for washroom visits we went as a class. The girls' toilet was at one end of the long, long corridor; the boys was at the other end. In the morning I had accompanied the boys, but in the afternoon, as no one was in sight, I stood outside the door, watching both directions.

During this time a teacher stepped outside, but I did not notice she had left a child out there when she went back inside as he had remained sitting on a chair close outside the classroom door, so not visible unless close to the door. Suddenly I saw fighting which in

213

seconds turned into a very hard physical combat fight. I could hear the solid hits far down the hall. By the time I reached them there had been many such. Obviously, a room problem had been put outside; both had called each other unacceptable names and the fight had quickly started. I insisted they apologize in turn, then shake hands, but inwardly felt very guilty I had not been there. However, I later reasoned, had I allowed two boys to go by themselves the same thing could have occurred, and with even more serious results. The child from the room had extremely red marks on his face, which remained for some time. Neither cried or seemed hurt. They had seemed evenly matched, and probably enjoyed the episode when recalling it later. The other teacher was wrong as she had closed the door with the boy out of her seeing or hearing range. I knew I would never again permit boys to travel that distance alone.

Returning, I offered another compromise to the class. Several subjects for composition writing were offered as stimulants. They were to select a subject, and when it was turned in they could select an art project, samples of which were shown to them. It took a little time for them to get themselves started on this, but finally all finished and received the art papers, most of which were but started when the closing bell rang, so they were given the choice of completing them in school the next day or at home. A few completed ones were left on the teacher's desk.

When I signed out at 3:20 no one was in the office, the Principal's office, the halls, or classrooms. It was ghostlike, strange. I walked on outside. No child, no teacher was in sight. As I stood looking about the deserted area I knew, without a doubt at all, that I too would be leaving at 3:15 the next time I taught here. Then I, too, got out of sight.

Chapter 65

1st Grade Work in Kindergarten

Although I was up early, dressed and ready to go when the call came from Substitute Center, when I went outside the weather was so dark, snowy and windy that I walked to take the bus instead of drive. Brennemann School was easily accessible by bus and the car was covered with four inches of snow.

The room for the day was a morning Kindergarten and afternoon Pre-School class. All the children were Spanish, some speaking English and there was a teacher aide for the day.

There were twenty present in the morning, only four absent; one had moved. It was an alert class, who did very good seatwork of printing and art work. Being so capable, they were also inclined to be talkative, requiring several reminders to be more quiet, which the teacher aide said was a problem with the regular teacher as well.

The class was in an individual mobile but the floor was not carpeted. Fortunately there were sufficient tiny chairs for all to sit on, and a number of long tables for seatwork.

When the papers were completed they were starred; then there were exercises which they enjoyed. Music records were next. "I'm a Little Teapot" was accepted half-heartedly; the "Polka" even less; only one youngster asked to have it repeated, which was a surprise. But "The Three Little Kittens" was a hit and each child enjoyed acting out the song, being either a little kitten or a mother kitten.

Only one child admitted to having heard the story of "Curious George" so that was read. All were very quiet, listening intently, but I wondered how many understood all the words. However, the book did have interesting explanatory pictures. A few poems were read, one learned, and a few fingerplays introduced. Last were oral thinking questions which all seemed to enjoy but few would try to answer.

The teacher aide was Spanish, who also spoke English fluently. She said the regular teacher was English, also fluent in Spanish. She said there were days of English and days when only Spanish was spoken in the room. The teacher aide said they had little, or no art work, adding they did work papers all of the time. During the lunch break time between classes I looked at the stacks of ditto seatwork. They were being given first grade assignments, which explained their quick learning abilities.

21 were listed for the afternoon class; two had left, but only nine were present. They were very quiet and orderly, and did very good work for being pre-schoolers. They were able to copy the letters and numbers and to color within lines in the art work. While the morning class did not receive food, these youngsters were given graham wafers and jello during the afternoon. Later there were inside games for recess and music records.

These little ones enjoyed "The Polka" as well as "The Three Little Kittens". They heard the same story, poems and fingerplays as did the morning class.

At closing time coats were zippered up, scarfs tied about their necks and hoods pulled down. Carrying starred papers they left with happy smiles, as did the teacher and aide.

Chapter 66

Musical Chairs

Substitute Center had not telephoned by 8:30 so I called and asked if there had been a shortage of jobs. I was told that was true and that all the placements had been filled although I had been ready to leave at 7:30 I was still sleepy so returned to bed. At 9:00 the telephone rang. There was a vacancy for first grade at a large school; but within five minutes another call informed me it was filled. The operator asked me to wait a moment; checking again she found a Kindergarten opening on the southwest side. I told her it would be fine if they had a parking area. She checked and advised one was available.

At 9:45 I signed in at the Miller Child Parent Center. A young black teacher was giving the children a gym class in the room; the teacher aide told me she had just arrived. The gym teacher was helping the youngsters walk down a narrow five-inch board for about five feet. Some were afraid to try; the first child moved too rapidly and slipped off, but enjoyed the effort and was willing to try again.

I took working materials from my satchels to use and put them on a bulletin space nearby and wrote two alphabet letters on a chalkboard. Papers were obtained to be used, and pencils taken from my satchels as there was not a supply in the room.

Following the gym period the teacher aide said refreshments were to be served so I helped with this. The youngsters were very well behaved. Twenty-two were listed in the attendance book; six had been changed to other classes, or had moved one had enrolled the previous week; four were absent, leaving thirteen present. It was a snowy, blowing, wintery day so in comparison with other schools this attendance was very impressive, making me feel the parents were truly involved and interested.

Lunch consisted of fillet of sole, mashed potatoes, salad, milk and apples for dessert. The aide prepared most of it. We both helped them cut the fish into small pieces, a few saving us the trouble by quietly picking it up and eating it. The fish was not greasy, or drippy, and as there were no knives, it was difficult for the little tots to separate it into bits wiih the plastic forks. However, when I showed them how to turn the fork cornerwise down into it, and then out and up, they were able to do the same. Only one child asked for a refill and she was given another portion; the majority ate most of the free lunches served to them in the schools.

After lunch I showed them how to hold a pencil and how to make the letter "O" across a top line of their paper. Most were able to do this. The "h" was more difficult but most wrote it somehow. Then they wrote "Oh" three times and drew a face being surprised, as this is taught as a surprise word. For faster learners there were two lines on the reverse side of the paper on which the digits "1" and "2" were written, and two snowmen drawn at the bottom. Three boys completed the two papers. All in the class received stars on the papers to take home.

One by one they took turns going to the toilet in the room. It was time to begin putting winter wraps and boots on so as a few were being helped by the teacher aide I played a few children's records, which they acted out. They liked "The Three Little Kittens" best.

Parents started coming to take their children at 11:45 but continued arriving until 12:30. Meanwhile other parents were bringing in even smaller ones for the afternoon Pre-School Class. Four arrived by 12:00; eventually there were ten present for the afternoon, one being a tiny new enrollee that very day.

At 12:00 another teacher brought in the hot food I was to serve so I quickly prepared that for the few present, placing two extra paper plates with food at a table. These were soon taken by new arrivals so two new ones were prepared; this was repeated until the ten had arrived, the last two coming in at 1:00. Most of the youngsters seemed to come by twos, with their cousins. As with the morning class these little pre-schoolers learned to cut the fish into small bites by watching me do so. The little new enrollee just sat so I fed him bite after bite. He was tiny as a doll and dressed like one too.

The teacher aide had had to leave at noon and had warned me the afternoon would be difficult, although there would be less children, saying that dressing them for departure time would be especially trying. Knowing this helped as I was alert to snatch early-coming mothers to help dress the others, which they did, so there was no trouble this way.

218

After lunch the gym teacher came and took five to another room. They did especially well for such tiny tots, holding the pencils correctly and making respectable "O"s. A few managed the surprised faces as well.

The work papers were starred and I showed them how I colored a large butterfly, of which I had prepared several ditto outlines. One or two could be future artists, but most merely made little marks all over the page. One little girl pressed the red crayon so hard into her paper that it looked like thick, dried paint. She used all the crayon too, much of it covering her little hands and nearly all her fingers. I suggested she try to wash it off while I moved the paper to another table.

The tiny boy who had just enrolled quickly adjusted to the group. At first he had cried, but as he had brought a toy truck I asked him questions about it and he soon forgot about the tears. Furthermore, two other children spotted the toy and tried to play with it all afternoon. At times he let them, but watched closely, and soon afterwards claimed it. He was pleased with the crayon picture and made many small colored marks on his paper, in groups.

Another little girl spent much time on her paper, but all she had done was make an interesting face on the butterfly. I was too busy to check on her work again as the others returned from the gym class. I was busy showing them how to color the outline and use the crayons.

The morning class had lined up for home without their papers and as I did not know them by name I had not reminded them of them. So when the afternoon group finished the work I folded the starred papers and asked if they would put the work into their coat pockets. Each one surprised me by happily agreeing and then promptly doing so. I had expected to have trouble finding their wraps for them. Instead, each one went directly to his or her own coat.

There was time for a few children's records which they enjoyed. Then we played the game, Musical Chairs, a few times. This was new to them, and as much fun for me as for them. The little ones put aside (taken to another group of chairs to sit when they were without chairs) stood and had their own little musical chairs game as the record was played! A few thought they were to return to their own chairs when the music stopped, but no one cried, or remained angry. And two or three were catching on to how to stay close to the chairs by the time we had played it a few times. Even those who were taken to the 2nd group appeared to enjoy watching the others play as the game continued.

Next I made a circle of chairs and asked them to bring out their wraps and put them on the chairs saying I would help them, one at a time. This worked out very well, because as I said previously, I invited the first few adults who appeared to help. Two cousins had long boots and complete snow outfits (head to toe, one piece), and an older sister, who had come to take a tot home, and was helping one of them, had so much trouble she was completely restarting. When I came to the cousin with the same snowsuit, I went next door and asked the teacher there which to start with – the boots or the snowsuit. She said the snowsuit; the boots went on last. But a mother appeared then who helped with that job and did it very quickly and easily.

One little girl was left waiting. No one came for her by 2:35 so I took her to the office. The clerk said the teacher aide usually stayed until 3:00 and the parent probably knew this. The little girl did not cry, for which I was grateful. Had the weather not been so trying outside I would have waited with her, but I was in an unfamiliar location and driving on an icy expressway on such a dark, snowy day was not inviting. By the time I reached home the school had closed as no one answered the telephone. I decided to send the child a valentine for her good behavior and my inability to wait with her.

But it had been a beautiful day. Previously I had dreaded being with Kindergarten and Pre-School children. Now I appreciated them as much as other primary youngsters. They were wonderful. I had heard that black primary children were especially endearing and now I agreed. They really captured one's heart. Such beautiful qualities – quietness, sweetness, friendliness, receptivity, joy, it had been a pleasure, and a privilege, to be with them.

Chapter 67

True Teaching Possible

Substitute Center called me at 8:20 for a teaching job at Rogers School on the far northwest side. I called the school saying I would be late and asked them if there was a primary grade available. The clerk said the only opening she was aware of was for the library, and this was the job I had for the day.

The neighborhood was a residential one with an abundance of space; there was not the high density of population as I was accustomed to around most schools. The majority of homes were of brick and two stories high; a short distance away were some brick apartments of about three to five stories, nothing higher. The school was adjacent to a public park so there was a great deal of vacant ground with trees and tennis court space.

On the desk in the library was a time schedule which indicated the first period that day was one for Preparation, followed by a reading period; however, no reading level, or grade, was listed. I collected writing paper, chalk and a chalkboard to be used and wrote a short letter on the board for seatwork.

The Reading Class surprised me. I had expected first or second graders. All were boys. One tall 8th grader entered, followed by three others from 5th, 6th, and 7th grades; there were five 4th graders. On the desk were reading books and ditto seatwork that could be used, but I introduced the Milton Bradley cards of Contractions and Abbreviations, followed by the Homonym cards. The 8th grader did not seem to enjoy these so I told him he could make acrostic word games, and suggested five words to be used. The others enjoyed the games and the time seemed to fly by.

After recess an entire 6th grade class entered so I decided to dictate a letter to them. First, I told them that I did not expect them to be able to do well with this work as no other class in the city to whom I had dictated such material had turned in good papers. They seemed to think they were capable, and I was aware this was a choice neighborhood, where parents would most likely be interested in the welfare, behavior and progress of their children, but I still doubted there would be a perfect paper. It surprised me to note the many students who chose to SIT when I began to dictate. In about six minutes their teacher happened to return and I quickly informed her of this, whereupon everyone began writing.

They were to put the school's name and address on the top right side but as some said they did not know the address I dictated that too. Observing some did not know the format of a letter I told them to write the name and address of the company to whom we were writing on the left side. I also warned them that many students had misspelled "Gentlemen" in letters I had seen. The long, involved, one-sentence letter with an additional "Thank you" was finally finished. Then I wrote it on the chalkboard for them to correct their work. About half the class handed their papers to me; six of them were good, the two best having but three errors. One had spelled "truly" with an "e"; one wrote "Il." for "Ill." and "advice" for "advise". One had no comma between the cities and states in the headings; neither had written the date, or separated and centered the last two words, "Thank you". But these were the top letters I had received in the city in the year and a half I had been substituting. They were pleased to hear this and asked me to tell their teacher. I forgot so later mailed the letters to her with a short note.

The next class was one of 5th and 6th graders. I read a long list of definitions for "Vocabulary of Youth Today" which most, especially the boys, enjoyed tremendously. Next there was an oral alphabet game of cities and countries which they were very alert in playing, selecting interesting locations and reasons for being there. Three did not behave well and were asked to write an essay entitled, "How to Behave in the Library". Later I noted one had written a page of, "I will be quite in the librey", but at least he was busily occupied and stopped interrupting the activities.

This was an Open Campus School, having an hour lunch period, so the school re-opened at 1:00, and closed at 3:15. I went to the teachers' lunch room for a short time; the teachers were friendly, quiet and refined.

After lunch a delightful second grade class entered so the Bradley Contraction and Abbreviation Game was perfect for them. They were very sweet, smart, and more quiet than noisy. The last half of the period was spent playing "Oral Fun with Words" games.

Unfortunately, although they were evenly divided sex-wise, the boys won 10 to 5.

5th graders entered next. I used two sheets of abbreviations I had collected of commonly missed words; they, too, missed many of them, although they were really pretty good. Their interest, and alert attitudes were impressive. They enjoyed the Bradley Homonym Card Game. Again, the boys won, this time 21 to 5. They were evenly divided, 14 boys and 14 girls.

All day I had been dreading the last class, which I thought was one of 8th graders, but it turned out to be one of 7th and 8th, all really nice students. They quickly mastered the abbreviations, enjoyed the oral word games and the alphabet game of cities and countries, in which they responded with fascinating answers. The last half of the period was for doing their own work, as they requested, using dictionaries in the room. Several girls chose to work on other word games and acrostics. They were a fine group of individuals, not at all the rowdy, undisciplined ones I had encountered in other schools at that grade level.

At noon I had been in the office and overheard a male teacher calling a parent to report that a student had not turned in required seatwork. As I drove home later I wondered if the teachers in the school appreciated the family backing they enjoyed, and the class of children they were privileged to teach. This was a school where true teaching could be done with little, or no, time wasted on maintaining discipline. It was a pleasure to know there were such schools in Chicago, and a blessing to have been in one of them for a day.

Chapter 68

Scored 2nd on Reading Scores
Not Good Secretaries

Substitute Center called at 7:30 and I left at 8:00 for a school not far away, but with the one-way streets, it was a most difficult one to reach. By the time I found Lincoln School, and even more difficult – a parking place, it was 8:30 and I signed in at 8:35. There was but one vacancy left – a 6th grade. (At noon I learned there was another substitute in second grade that day – probably the room I was called for!)

The words of the Assistant Principal and another teacher rang in my ears as I walked up to the third floor. "They are a good class". I hoped I agreed at the end of the day.

A minute after I entered two teachers came in. As I removed my boots they were reading to me the time schedule left by the regular teacher which was on top of his desk. The note was clear, concise, a great help, but I wondered why they were reading it to me.

As the teachers left the class entered. They looked pleasant and intelligent; later they told me they had scored second on the city reading scores the previous year. 28 were listed in the attendance book; 2 had left; 2 enrolled; four were absent.

There had been no time to put work on the board, and as the first period listed on the teacher's time schedule was for English I decided to dictate a business letter to them. They looked at me in surprise, as classes always do when this is suggested. I stopped and explained to them I had been doing this in 6th grade classes for over a year and had yet to receive a perfect paper, adding the previous day there had been two with but three errors. The immediate superior attitude in some was apparent; others donned the usual nonchalant non-caring guise until I mentioned I expected to leave the papers for their teacher. This prompted several to produce paper and search for pencils.

As I dictated the smiles disappeared quickly; there were the usual continued requests for repetitions of each few words; many restarted at different times. The letter was short, one sentence, plus a "Thank you", but it was a long sentence, requiring proper spelling and punctuation. Finally, when everyone had finished writing it the bell rang for the next class and many students left. At lunch a man teacher told me the first class I had was a very noisy one, adding he had them for the last period and really dreaded that time. I had felt they were giving me the usual "Substitute treatment". I knew the loud noise, almost yelling, would not have been heard had an assigned teacher been there.

I could have given them their usual workbook assignment as the teacher had recommended but I felt a change would be welcome, and interesting, for them.

As the bell rang most of the students left, with noise, yelling and much gusto.

I looked at the time schedule; the next period was marked for reading. "Work in stories. Class knows what to do" the note said. I sat quietly watching them enter. Inwardly I was boiling. I decided not to introduce any more interesting activities. I would not raise my voice; I refused to let them upset me. They sat looking at me questioningly, and seemed surprised when I quietly read what the teacher had written. They had heard the former pupils' comments in the hall and were probably waiting for me to say, or do, something that they, too, might pounce upon and have the same fun. I sat quietly watching them, grading the letters of the former period. When a student talked, or rose to walk, I motioned with my hand to be quiet, or sit. One, who returned late, and noisily, and who had been in the former class, was asked to write an essay on Classroom Behavior before recess. This also seemed to dampen any misbehavior of others present. The period was quiet – and dull – throughout.

At recess time there was an announcement over the intercom saying it was an "indoor-outdoor recess". While this was meaningless to me it seemed understood by the students, who rose and left. I asked one student if I was to accompany them down the stairs and she said it was not necessary, so I remained in the room and finished grading the letters written by the first class. Their work was neat, with a few exceptions, but there was no perfect paper. The best ones had five, six and seven errors. Not one had written the date (which I had purposefully omitted).

Nearly everyone had put a comma after "Gentlemen", two writing "dear Gentleman" several misspelled words, especially "address", "distributor" and "Yours truly", but the majority were written neatly, with reasonable letter format. They were the best letters I had seen from a class as a whole. Had there been time for the letter to be written on the board for them to see, and absorb, I felt many would have been able to write one perfectly another time.

During the recess period a teacher brought in two girls telling me that if students remained in the building the teacher was to stay with them. These two girls had been out in the hall making noises, and faces, during the recess period and I had gone to the door and told them to leave. I didn't know where they had gone, but each was asked to apologize to both of us and then go outside. They did put on their boots and wraps then. I think the students who wanted to remain inside went to the auditorium, or gym.

A gym period followed recess and the pupils did not return to the room until 11:20. During the gym period I went to the girls' washroom. Of the six stalls, no door would close as all had been jarred so that the alignment was off and closing was impossible. One door was completely removed. I was surprised in their neighborhood, but the noisiness I had encountered with the 6th grade and the behavior of the two girls staying in the halls at recess, I was not too surprised.

11:20 to 11:55 was listed as a Homeroom Study Period. The students entered quietly. They looked like they had had a complete workout in gym. After they were seated I held up the program saying it was a home study period. It was so quiet one could have heard a pin drop.

One of the girls who had been reported at recess by the other teacher had entered talking flippantly and walking past her desk, talking to someone. I asked her to come up in front, asked her name, wrote it down, explaining she was being reported for her recess behavior. I then asked her to write an essay on Classroom Behavior. She returned to her seat, put her head down, and kept it there the entire period. At noon I asked everyone except this child to line up for lunch, and after they left I returned to her. There were tears in her eyes. She said she was not an only child. I told her to stop crying and to go to lunch.

At noon I joined some teachers at their table; they were pleasant and friendly. As it was near the end of the semester the talk turned to the progress of students and the vast amount of paper work facing teachers at this time. As I returned to the room I felt relieved to be a substitute. Regular teachers had mountainous records to complete. However, I used to enjoy it. Delving deeply into specific areas gives a teacher a deeper insight into a child.

Math was after lunch and I started by dictating large amounts of money; the class was adept at this, understanding place value very well. Several mathematical puzzles were read, which they enjoyed and worked out. The students participated, offering ones they knew. It was a good period, enjoyed by everyone, and also a quiet and orderly time.

Following this was a Social Studies Period but they insisted they had done this assignment. I introduced an alphabet city game in which they were to state a city and say what they were to do there, the experience starting by corresponding with the letter of the city. It was a fun thinking exercise for those who participated. I really wanted them to write the answers but they voted to do it orally.

The last period was one for art. I had brought a new art ditto and wondered how it would turn out as the scene had been copied from a black and white picture that had impressed me in one of the schools. The students seemed to enjoy it. That evening, at home, I studied ones they had given me and made other samples to show.

After the class left at closing time I left the stack of dictated letters they had written – poor ones for pupils known to be such fine readers!

Chapter 69

Men's Beauty Parlor
Good Class

At Greeley School I was assigned to a 5/6 grade class. The room was cozy and warm with one usable front blackboard, the back one covered with maps and charts. Desks were arranged in an interesting way, six long horizontal rows, facing each other, but with about four feet between them.

The front board was covered with work before the class arrived, consisting of a poem with ten questions, a thinking word game to complete the alphabetical lists of cities to write. Many used a huge globe for this.

At 9:00 the students entered smiling. The girls came in first and hung up their wraps, boys waiting in a line inside the room until the girls took their seats. This was really impressive to see. However, the boys remained in the coatroom so long I finally looked in. Six or seven were still brushing and combing their hair. It looked like a beauty parlor – and their hair styles did too; all looked especially neat and interested in their appearance.

Attendance was taken first. 50 were listed in the book; 15 had been marked out in red; 30 were present; 5 absent. One boy came in at noon, having been to a dentist.

The seatwork was explained and reading was started. There were three reading groups. Five students were in the first group, three absent. They read at Level "H" (third grade) had soft voices, but read the material quite well. It was impressive that I could hear every soft voice as there was no noise in the room. None at all. It was really unbelievable. This had to be a really super teacher.

The next group of 14 were half finished with a 5th grade book. One was a fast reader, the others slower but able to read. The material was unusually difficult, being questions about pronouns and required much concentration to answer.

Eleven students came to the third reading group; they were reading at Level "K" (6th grade). The oral reading in this group was fine; three read rapidly; all understood and could answer questions relative to the material.

One boy finished the work while the last group was reading so I suggested he write a poem, story, make a drawing, etc. and I would send it to a newspaper. He wrote a very sweet story about a pigeon that he had rescued after being hit by a car; he had kept the bird, mended its wing, named it, and said the bird did not want to leave him.

I could not believe how quiet the class was and asked a student if the teacher was soft-spoken. He said she was not, but she did have a wonderfully behaved class and one that read well too.

Because they had been so quiet I let them have art after the reading as they said the library period was during the last period when I usually had art. I had already promised to have English Bingo Games in the afternoon.

Lunch time was 12:25 and when signing in I had been told to be sure they kept their lunch time as the school had a tight lunch schedule. We left the room at 12:20 but met another third grade class downstairs that the students said had time ahead of us so we let them pass. Occasionally the girls peeked inside the lunchroom doors but informed us the table were still occupied. It seemed they were waiting for their assigned places to become available. I looked into the room. It was so tiny! There were but 12 lunchroom tables there, room for only three or four classes. A teacher inside saw me looking in and had those seated in our seats hurry and leave.

The class took their trays to their tables and I sat with them. I had brought my own lunch. "They give good lunches – pizza, chicken, hot dogs," said the boy next to me. Others agreed. What a pleasure to hear complimentary words about the school lunches. The food that day was hamburgers on a bun, cole slaw, fruit salad and milk. For years I had seen children toss out their lunches, often without even sampling them. It was a pleasure to witness the healthy and polite atmosphere here. A growing boy across from me inquired among the students until he found a girl who would give him her sandwich! I was used to observing begging and deals made for cookies only. In 10 minutes another teacher was asking the group to leave so everyone swallowed last bites and stood.

229

The girls were sent upstairs to the washroom and I went with the boys to one in the basement. As we walked back upstairs one boy commented he could hardly wait to be in their new school. There was to be a new one ready for them soon.

Returning from lunch there were oral thinking contests, math dictation, in which they were quite good, and letter writing dictation.

The Milton Bradley Abbreviation and Contraction and Homonym bingo cards were used until Library Time, one side of the room competing against the other.

One boy remained to straighten things and wash the board when the class left. I collected my work, then studied the cumulative record cards of the class. The results were of the previous year, so bringing the reading scores up to date a year would result in 14 being at 6th grade, 14 at fifth and 11 at fourth grade. In math the scores were much better with 25 at 6th grade, two at fifth and two at fourth.

These had been conscientious students; when I wrote the proper letter format on the board that had been dictated nearly everyone was busy copying it, or correcting his paper, which was in contrast to many classes' disdain toward correcting their work. These students actually wanted to improve. It was the best class I had ever been in.

Chapter 70

Korean Class
Too Many Teachers

At 8:10 I signed in at Greeley School. The Assistant Principal did not reveal the grade level when I asked, but mumbled they were Korean. (There were four Korean students in the class.) She asked me to remain the rest of the week.

In the room I put 3rd and 4th grade work on the first two boards. Noticing one boy peeking in at 8:40 I had him remain and take the chairs down. He told me it was a 5th and 6th grade class! So I added higher level work on two more sections.

The school must have made many changes in the first of the school year as of the 65 students listed in the Attendance Book 30 had been crossed out in red ink, making it very difficult to take attendance. 30 were present, 4 absent, one expelled the class said. All received free lunches.

No math had been put on the front board so I asked one boy to write some computation problems. Several students objected to what he put there so a girl wrote material on an adjoining board. Students were told to select and complete either section.

At 9:05 eight third graders appeared for a reading class. They brought me their workbooks saying they were to have a word test, which was given them. Most had 100 on it, one girl having but one error, but one boy had six. They said they had finished reading the book. All were reading at about mid-year first grade level.

At 9:45 the class said they had gym and it was also the end of the period for the third graders so they left. I took the students to the gym. The gym teacher said after their period they would have a basketball contest with another grade.

I found five of the group remained in the regular room so later I had them go over the blend chart a number of times. All were able to blend the first row except the one little fellow who had the six errors on the word test. He was not yet ready to settle down and learn much of anything. His time was spent being silly, laughing and talking every minute of the day. He appeared Spanish, but said he had been born in Chicago.

Right after the class returned from gym at 11:00 an Urban Gateways Special Teacher (an artist and resident) appeared. "I have never heard this noise," she said. "If there is any trouble I will walk out." I explained they had just won a basketball game.

"Okay. But calm down now," she said. "There is someone in charge of taking care of the markers."

"I am in charge!" called out a child.

"You don't call out. You know that," the teacher said.

White paper and colored marking pens were passed out to students. They had changed their seats into groups. (This looked interesting but invited constant talking.)

The teacher wrote on the blackboard, "Repeated Patterns. Use Organic Shapes". She drew two samples on the board, then told them to fold their paper into four squares and make the shapes. They were to select the best shape and repeat that on another paper, then color the final paper, repeating the colors of the first shape.

There was much conversation among the children. They got up and walked around, calling out constantly. The art progressed well but the noise and disorder grew as well.

At 11:15 I told the students who had finished their work to give it to the teacher, tidy up their desks and line up for lunch. The school had a very small lunchroom, large enough for only four classes to eat at one time, so it was necessary to maintain a tight schedule. At 11:20 we left for the lunchroom.

Returning from lunch we made up four rules for classroom behavior. The four rules had corresponding punishment procedures. Rule #1 was No talking; #2 No walking around the room; #3 No pencil tapping and #4 No falling off chairs. Punishment Rules for disobeying were #1, Stand with hands UP 5 minutes; #2 Stand holding two dictionaries in each hand 5 minutes! #3 and #4, Sit in an invisible chair 5 minutes.

The rules were no longer written than three had broken the first and two more the second. Punishments followed as outlined, but the atmosphere did not appear to change much.

Those who had not finished the art work went to one large round table in the back to do so. This was not too good an idea as the talking there was continuous. Contraction and Abbreviation cards were distributed but in two minutes another teacher appeared to take a good number of the class for reading again in the back of the cloakroom. The Bingo game started but several were so noisy they did not receive cards to play for some time. The class enjoyed the game and we then changed to the Homonym cards for awhile.

No one had done any math work so I stopped the games and introduced oral math thinking games, then word concentration game contests. During this time the group was quiet and interested. But when the reading class in the cloakroom was over and those students returned the usual turmoil was again prevalent.

The class looked surprised when I asked two pupils to erase all the boards. I knew I would not return to the room again with all the noise. Report cards were distributed and I went down the stairs with them.

As I walked to the office I realized the Assistant Principal had not visited the class that day to see how things were going as she had the day before. She had misrepresented the class to me, both in grade level as well as behavior. As I signed out she asked me if I would be returning and I answered, "No, I'm sorry," and left.

I was sorry about the noise, about the way things had been misrepresented, but most of all I was sorry I would not be helping those children in first grade books. I had wanted to show them how to use the bland chart to sound out unknown words. It might have speeded up their reading tremendously. A few of them had been noisy, but all had been very interested in taking their reading test that day and I had really wanted to help them.

That evening in retrospect I realized the children had been over-stimulated by extra curricular activities all day and I had never had an opportunity to instill quietness. After the reading group read there had been a gym period, followed by a gym basketball contest that they had won. Following this another teacher had appeared, a special art teacher, who worked with them until lunch time. After lunch another reading teacher had come in and taught in the cloakroom. There had been continual changes for them all day. Unfortunately, it had been a hectic day for all of us. Everyone wanted to help but "too many cooks spoil the broth".

Chapter 71

Grade Level Readers
Gym Class Interesting

Substitute Center called me to go to LeMoyne School at 7:30 so I went back to bed for a half hour. I did not want to arrive at that school until after 8:30 as the Assistant Principal assigned the difficult higher grades to the first-appearing substitutes, regardless of what level they were trained to teach; it had happened to me twice.

I signed in at 8:35, was the first substitute, but was assigned to a "first grade" – which I learned from the pupils (and their reading) was a second grade – by a newly appointed Principal.

22 students were present, 8 absent. Three paid for their lunches; two paid half the amount; 4 went home; 13 received free tickets. I felt the neighborhood must be improving economically as I did not recall having anyone pay before.

There was another surprise. The pupils could read! I had had upper grades previously where many had been behavior problems, and reading at very low levels, far below their expected achievement levels. This class was quiet, could read, and quietly did the seatwork. There were three reading groups two of which read from the same 2nd grade book in different sections. Two little fellows in front read in a "Rhymes and Tales" book that they knew by heart.

I starred the seatwork during the lunch hour. The school was one with a free hour at noon, closing at 3:15.

After lunch the Milton Bradley Contraction and Abbreviation cards were explained and distributed. I had wondered if some of the youngsters would be able to read the words and play the game but all seemed to be able to play. I sat in front watching the two little fellows in 1B reading books, and helped them in the beginning, but they found many of the words, and one even had a turn of winning a game. He looked like he would burst a button off his little vest when he stood and called out his winning words! Many had winning turns, instead of just a few with lucky cards, and this was more enjoyable to everyone.

The gym period was next and I entered the gym with them and watched. Some youngsters were more adept at physical exercises than others; I noted that two who were tops in the academic work were somewhat awkward here, and vice versa – other were shining lights in the gym pursuits but had difficulty in the classroom. This is why I used to like teaching a first grade class where the teacher kept the class all day, for throughout the various enterprises a teacher could get a whole, rounded picture of the children, collectively and individually.

Part of the class went to nets and tossed bean bags over to partners on the opposite side. Several had butterfingers at first, but with a little practise became adept at catching.

Next the gym teacher said that when a beanbag, or volleyball, which some used, was dropped, or bounced, those two partners were to sit and watch the others. One boy, excellent with all the exercises, had a partner who was also good, but in his last exercise he dropped the ball. The other boy could hardly accept this. He fumed, stomped, turned about, then started tossing the ball again, but other students, sitting, called out he must stop.

Even more interesting, to me, was the action, and reactions between two girls. A black child had been very gymnastic and caught the beanbags every time, whereas her Oriental partner (a top classroom student) dropped it nearly every time at first. But now, for the first time, in the last exercise, the black girl dropped the beanbag – and the Oriental child had great difficulty accepting this! I had been very impressed with the patience and understanding of the black girl throughout the game, and suddenly the picture changed completely. The Oriental girl looked ready to explode; she was completely frustrated, and it took some time for her to become normal again.

Back in the room there was time for a short art period which everyone enjoyed. I marveled at the quietness when they started the project. I had shown good examples of finished pictures beforehand and they had chosen dittos to color. Some had their own crayons; the teacher had enough extra ones to be used. (I had taken a supply as had expected any room in this school to be in dire need of any supplies.) Seven had signed up to borrow pencils from me in the morning, but all had been returned in the afternoon except one.

Some did very good art work, but of course none were as good as some samples I carried done by 6th graders, so I left the finished ones for the teacher. Some were left in their desks to complete the next day.

Boards were erased, and washed, and window blinds pulled down as the room was in the basement. All chairs were put up so the janitor could sweep more easily, and they lined up quietly. In fact, they had been quiet all day – until but a few feet from the exit door when they suddenly made a dash for the outside, at which time there were wild cries, loud and shrill, from nearly everyone! I was glad it was a basement room and no other class, or teacher, was close by. But I had to smile. Going home has a special appeal to everyone.

Chapter 72

Circus

The call came at 8:20 so I called Patrick Henry School saying I'd arrive before 9:00 but had just been called for 2nd grade. The neighborhood was a residential one of many homes, primarily of wood, some of brick and stone; there were a few two, three and four-story brick apartment buildings. The school was a very large, old one with an extra-large playground. The librarian explained the playground was used by the Park District Program when school was not in session and on weekends and summertimes. Three small, one-story, one-room, sturdy units on the ground evidently housed the needed equipment.

On entering the classroom I noticed the board was so chalky that the two helpers present were asked to please find pails and wash it. It was still wet as the class entered so a contest was suggested to see who could list the most words starting with "br", not using books, or dictionaries. Two desks were sandwiched next to the teachers, indicating behavior problems, but the most difficult problem child proved to be a handsome, taller boy in the back of the room. Fortunately, all three of them captured my heart so their trouble-attempts did not bother me. I later noticed none of these three participated in any group activities of games and dancing; as I expected, they chose to save their efforts for personal endeavors later, and they merely watched others enjoying themselves in group activities.

The class promptly informed me that their gym period was at 11:00. I used this as a leading incentive, knowing all youngsters love gym periods. As I put work on the board it was explained that two papers were to be completed as passes to leave for the gym class. Eventually everyone became busy. As pupils paid for and handled their own lunch monies this did not require time, and after attendance was marked, reading groups were called to the front. About twelve were in the second grade, second semester reading book, eight in a first grade reader, and five were in pre-primers; four were absent.

They knew the letter sounds, but few blends. Only one girl completed all the work and was given extra thinking card-work to do.

Feeling the chap sitting closest to me could be a champion dissenter, and learning he was interested in math, I told him he could grade those papers if he did his work and stayed in his chair. Remaining seated was difficult for him, but he tried, keeping his eyes on the math board. Unfortunately, no one was able to do the 2nd grade math, which surprised me. Obviously the concept of carrying in addition had not been presented to them. I had listed first and second grade adding and subtraction but no one could borrow either, so my friend did not get to grade any papers. However, if they had copied the work and done the easy computation, I let them select the symbol they preferred to "star" their work. I had brought a box of seven symbol outlines, and a red inked pad to use. Most selected a fat little bunny; some chose a flag, or a Santa entering a chimney. A few took Lincoln, Washington, a Jack-o-Lantern, or a big star. It seemed great fun to select their own symbol, which seemed to stir a somewhat greater effort to try for another paper for another choice. Without these, I felt little or no effort would have been put forth; this class did not appear at all energetic – except for the one little worker.

During indoor recess we had fun exercises and one child passed out cookies as it was her birthday, and we sang the conventional song which pleased her.

At 11:00 all but four were ready for gym, but I could not bear to retain the four very long as felt every child should have the gym period so let them go after just a few waiting minutes of doing work papers.

After lunch the oral thinking questions were introduced but not one was able to catch on and answer them. Next the Milton Bradley Bingo game of Contractions and Abbreviations was explained and distributed. They did not seem capable of this either but when 7th grade boys entered at 2:15 with movies the older boys were really surprised when the class voted to continue with the games and not have movies. They looked like they were not hearing correctly and wanted to stay and see what the games were. There were a few winners in the Bingo games but it went very slowly. I had the slow readers sit with their cards with better readers to help them. The interest was there, but much more basic training with contractions and abbreviations was needed for them. Because of this it was fortunate that we had been invited to another 2nd grade room to see their circus at 2:50.

I had not disclosed this beforehand as was not certain we would have time to go, but the class lined up in somewhat orderly fashion, and went down the steps to the other room. A very large red and white "CIRCUS" sign on the door-window welcomed us in.

Once inside, I was overwhelmed by the many things going on simultaneously – the continual motion, everyplace. Movement; action. Entertainment. Things going on; things to do. "Do anything you want", the teacher was saying. "If you want to write on the board, there is the chalk". Several boys were happily writing on the board. "I've never seen anything like this!" I exclaimed, to which she sighed, "Yours is the last class. I think I can stand just this one more!" She was young, attractive and healthy looking.

In the center of the room was a high, rotating podium, holding a three-foot Panda. Across the room an area was covered with heavy gym mats, on which young girls in gym suits repeatedly performed cartwheels. Nearby, at a refreshment stand, popcorn, cookies and soft drinks were handed out in tiny paper nut cups as youngsters sauntered happily by. Many large, stuffed circus animals to be seen and played with waited on another side. And the big excitement – the hit of the Circus – was a "free ride" on one of the two red wagons!

Having been asked in advance to select two children for the free ride, these had been lined up for the big event. Two red wagons followed one another from a starting point around through the cloak room, where a dark curtain had been fastened, and lights flashed on and off constantly, red and black. Room helpers of higher grades and 2nd graders happily pushed and pulled the wagons. One turn around found two lines of eager youngsters hoping for a chance to ride. It was really wonderful to see their eager anticipation, and the fun the "pushers" and "pullers" were having as well. During the delightful melee I rounded up most of the class and think everyone managed to get on one of the wagons. Smaller children were put in side by side, larger ones alone.

The clock indicated our ten minutes were up, and somehow the children were collected and returned to their home room, which was put in order, boards erased, papers picked up, and everyone lined up and walked down the stairs, again reasonably quietly.

It had been an interesting, exciting day. Frankly, I had not been at all interested in visiting the Circus, but what an impressive experience I would have missed had we not accepted the invitation! It was a wonderful memory to review over and over again. The disappointment in those eyes at hearing they could not have free rides, and then the lighting up in them when they were later rounded up to wait hopefully in line. And, of course, it had been the behavior-problems who had felt and expressed their hurt, dismay, and then joy and excitement the most! Always.

On the way out I stopped to again thank the teacher who had given the Circus and mentioned I had a calliope record, used when I too had had a Circus in a first grade class. When hearing hers was about worn out I silently decided to bring her the one I no longer needed; here it would be in good hands. Just seeing the work papers up in her room showed she was a good teacher; the bulletin boards were alive, inviting; not faded, tired and dull like in the room I had just left. Yes, walls usually mirrored the atmosphere of any room; and the progress as well.

Chapter 73

Reading Fine
Printing Zero

I signed in at 8:35 for a first grade class at Ravenswood School and put work on the board for the children when they entered. 33 were listed in the attendance book; seven had moved; two came in late; not one was absent!

There were three reading groups, the first group of eleven being at Level 5 (1B) in a Ginn Company book. All were good readers. The second group of ten were just starting the same book; they read two stories and were good readers also. The third group of five were Spanish, reading in pre-primers at Level 2, but they could read at this level.

As I had anticipated from seeing many stacks of ditto seatwork piled up in the room, the pupils were extremely weak in their printing. In fact, they did not know how to copy a 4-line poem, but made it continue, as one continuous sentence. Five youngsters copied all assignments like that – one word following another over the entire paper, not even leaving spaces between the words. Obviously they had had little, or no writing papers to do.

I had shown the students the box of stars, explaining they would receive a star for each completed assignment. The work was easy enough, but the writing from quite a number was not acceptable. As three had completed the work, but in unreadable fashion, they were asked to redo some of it; the second time it was neatly done.

In the third reading group was a little Spanish girl that the children told me just sat all day, doing nothing. She did spend time crying, which they said she often did, but eventually she also read with her group and did the writing and art work. I knew she could read and do the work and she knew I knew; it was a silent, mental thing between the two of us. We accepted each other and quietly respected each other's knowing. She had already done workbook pages beyond those assigned, and all were done correctly. In art work she surpassed any other child in the room. She chose the most difficult of the cut-out lettering to be done and refused to change her selection, so I helped at the end of the period as time was disappearing.

During the morning and afternoon upper-grade students came to take the children to the washrooms; this was very helpful as the toilets were far apart.

This was an Open Campus School, having an hour lunch period, so some students went home; some brought lunches; some received lunch cards with their names written on.

I ate in a small restaurant nearby, then returned, starred work papers, and ran off art dittos for the afternoon.

When the class returned they told me they had a library period, and as I had carried two filmstrips I had been wanting to use the librarian let me show and read them. The strips were especially good ones and the class really enjoyed them.

Later two stories were read, "Curious George", and "Jack in the Beanstalk"; then art work was presented. Three sets of small, plastic art object outlines were placed on front tables for them to select and trace. Each child took two at a time, then exchanged them for two others. This was good exercise for their small muscles, as well as fun to do.

Twenty minutes before closing I started to put things away, but one quiet child came up crying. It took some time to understand his problem as his voice was so soft. It seemed he had lost his gym shoes! I could not understand anything else. I offered a reward for anyone finding the shoes, and finally a little girl did find them, so things ended happily. She received a money folder in which to insert dimes.

When the bell rang the children had their coats and boots on but my school items were not assembled. After dismissing them I returned to gather and pack my things which took 15 minutes. It had been a joy to teach first grade, but now in substituting I decided to plan things differently. There would be continued board work, both morning and afternoon as they needed the writing exercise, but the art period would be shorter, followed by an earlier clean-up time which would provide a more enjoyable day for everyone.

Chapter 74

Oral Game – One Little Sharpie

At Greeley School I was given a second grade class. Entering the room I covered four sections of the board with seatwork. A Spanish mother entered. She looked surprised and upset. I smiled, but we could not understand each other and she left. I wondered if she was disturbed to see a substitute or if it was her inability to speak English.

The class entered noisily, each child contributing his or her share. The adjoining cloak room seemed a fine meeting spot, and a noise center, so I stood there until the pupils entered the room.

Soon everyone was seated. I explained if they were quiet there would be word games, records and valentine-making in the afternoon. Everyone agreed to this and they were reasonably quiet with continual reminders.

26 were present, 4 absent. Milk was sent for. All received free lunches.

Board seatwork was read but I noticed several could not read it so on another two boards I put easy poems to be copied.

Reading was started. Seven children came to read in the first top group. They were reading in the middle of a 1B reader. Two stories were read. Four pages of the corresponding workbook were graded.

Twelve were in the 2nd group. They were finishing the last story in a Pre-Primer and had already finished their workbooks so did the board work. The third group of eight were in a Pre-Primer and had finished their workbook. The last group of four read in a Pre-Primer but had no workbooks as yet.

Every child read with the eagerness and interest of a first grader – as, indeed, they were in reading abilities, even though they were ages seven and up, and in their second semester of second grade.

Apparently writing (printing) was not stressed in the room as this was done carelessly on nearly every paper. But stars were given for the effort put forth. Early in the morning, while walking about between reading periods I had noticed answers were not being put on the papers, so I wrote them correctly on the board.

When reading the seatwork, which asked the name of their school, city, country and President, no one had been able to name their country, and only one could name the President. Later these, too, were written in their proper places on the board to be copied correctly. But most did have the pages in the workbooks done correctly. The workbooks were at their reading level. Most of the board work was at 2nd grade level as I had understood the room to be at that level.

Several requests were made to visit the washrooms during the morning. But one boy did not bother to ask. Just before lunch he pointed out to me he had already "gone" at his seat! I wondered if it had been an accident or intentional as he mentioned repeatedly he would go get the janitor. I did not answer him as felt we could speak to him after lunch when we passed his office, which we did and he came up at once with a big mop. No one else noticed what had happened.

The desk of one little boy was beside that of the teacher, indicating he needed special watching, and it was soon obvious his special problem was constant loud talking and trying to attract attention to himself. The boy had an abundance of charisma and outside such a busy classroom could have been a heart stealer, but in the room he sat doing practically nothing – until he realized without producing a minimum of two papers he would not be able to make a valentine, whereupon he promptly sat and did the work!

There was no Time Schedule in the room so as the class lined up for the washrooms I stopped in the office nearby and asked the time of our lunchroom period. It was 11:30 so there was just time for the children to visit the washrooms and then return and check their seatwork. When the papers were checked it was found several had done NO paperwork, but, as usual, while I checked, and stamped the papers of those finished, practically everyone who had SAT was busily occupied completing the required two papers.

As we sat eating lunch the girls told me the class often received stars for being a very quiet class. The lunchroom was VERY SMALL – large enough for only three or four rooms to eat at one time. There seemed barely enough time to eat. I noticed four boys had not finished their lunches when an aide came over telling them to stand and leave. In fact, I had only a hard boiled egg, banana and milk, and had not had time to drink the milk! I wished I had checked the time we sat down, but maybe we entered a little late. I remembered we did not have to wait to enter the room. Evidently it was wise to appear here early.

After lunch I pinned up Valentine poems and sample valentines to be made. The poems were read, paper and cardboard hearts distributed, and while they copied the one of their choice I cut paper for the second valentines and wrote their messages on the board.

As the class wrote the second ones I prepared the third project. Fortunately, about six youngsters were able to cut hearts from folded strips of paper, so after cutting a supply for themselves they helped others. It was a time consuming, but fun, endeavor, and a needed one for strengthening smaller muscles, and the finished projects were well worth it.

The Assistant Principal entered and asked if a certain boy had been present in the morning. I replied he had, that he had gone to a Speech Class at 11:05. It seemed he had left the school about that time, which was not a new occurrence. In about a half hour his mother, the one who had come in so agitated at 9:00, came in with the boy and the grandmother. I put my arms around him and said I wondered how anybody could skip school when we were going to make valentines. He took his seat but did not seem too interested, and 15 minutes before closing I noticed he had left his half-finished one on a desk top.

The teacher had a sufficient supply of crayons to be used but was short of glue. Fortunately, pupils shared what they had brought and there was barely enough. Only six scissors were found in the supply box; I had brought six so they managed with these. The papers to be used were ones I had brought.

One little boy could not find his scissors in his desk so I tried to help. No wonder. His desk was completely stuffed with seatwork papers he had not taken home. They were pushed in so tightly I could barely get my fingers inside. All were put in the wastebasket. Inside were duplicate workbooks and reading books, which were given to those without them.

At 1:50 a teacher aide entered and before she could say I was to take a break I saw we needed her! She helped and I helped cut the needed tiny hearts to be pasted on their work, and with her help everyone caught up.

At 2:20 there were a few minutes for oral thinking games. The lowest level ones were used, which were just right for this class, who thoroughly enjoyed them. Interestingly enough, one little fellow who had made very messy valentines, was the shining light of the class in this area and he loved it. He beamed as he quickly answered for the boys each time, and I said he was a little sharpie.

There was something especially lovable about these youngsters. They were alive, interested and eager, and these were inspiring qualities. Indeed, in this respect they seemed like first graders, but they were older, so already a year behind in their schooling. Some of them were beginning to mature, and maybe a few would be able to catch up. I hoped so.

Chapter 75

Fireman Visit
Time Plates on Wall

At McCutcheon Branch School I was assigned a 2nd grade class and was able to put sufficient seatwork on the board before the children entered.

24 pupils were present, three absent. Four paid for lunches; the rest received free tickets.

The board work was read and explained, but a visiting Fireman was to talk to them at 9:30 so we went to another room to hear him. He explained he worked for the Fire Prevention Department in Chicago, who tried to prevent fires.

Each child was given a free coloring-reading booklet, which contained interesting, worthwhile reading and figures to be colored. He discussed points of interest on each page, most of which was very impressive to the pupils. How to leave a burning room was explained, which he said was important because most children die from smoke inhalation in such instances. He explained they were to put a sheet by the door, if it felt hot, to keep the smoke out, and to open a window. They were to be the firemen in their homes and check worn electric plugs and cords. They were to learn two ways to leave their homes and to practise such fire drills at home with their families.

Returning to the room the class said they were not to have reading because of the visit, but I had it anyway. As the school had "walking reading" they went to other rooms to get their books. But I did not take them ahead; instead they reread one or two stories. It did not seem fair to go ahead of their regular classmates.

The children were a mixture of Oriental, Black and white. The Oriental (Korean and Vietnamese) were by far the best students. Ages in the room ranged from seven to nine.

The top reader was an Oriental girl, who said she read alone in her walking reading room. She was reading at F-G Level (2-3). All students above the Pre-Primers knew their reading levels.

Nine children were at E-F level (second grade) and all read well. Three were Koreans; two from Viet Nam.

Five youngsters read in a 1B, first grade book, but they could read in it.

The others read in various Pre-Primer booklets, not yet able to read in hard cover books. But they, too were capable of reading in the soft cover ones.

One little fellow, always smiling, was unable to read, so I made out some word cards for him. When asking him what words he wanted to learn to read he quickly said, "One, two, three," etc. up to ten. I printed the words and wrote the numbers on the back, telling him he could teach himself the words. On other cards were written, "Oh, mother, father, look, baby, boy, see." These were put in an envelope for him with his name on the outside.

The first board assignment had been a letter to a company requesting a free game booklet. Most were able to copy this in a reasonable manner; many wrote their home address, which I had suggested; others copied that of the school and their room number. A copy of the booklet was displayed, one any young child would enjoy having.

At 11:15 while having a small group reading I heard one boy exclaim, "Boy, I am tired!" He got up and moved back to his own desk. I wanted to stop and have exercises but I felt I should finish all the reading groups first. However, they came up so slowly that it was noon before all had read.

There was time to star the seatwork before lunch so this was done. Stars were given for each section copied, two for work that was answered, rather than just copied. One boy and one girl received eight stars each, the highest numbers, but each child did some work.

The room itself was carpeted, inviting quietness, but the pupils were not noisy; it was one of the most quiet rooms I had been in in some time. Second grade, I was beginning to feel certain, was a pleasant one for a substitute to have. They were capable of doing seatwork, or reading, and usually being quiet as well.

At noon the children put on their coats and boots but I intended to remain in the room. Quite soon they informed me I was to go with them. Then I learned they ate in McCutcheon School, about a block and a half distant, so I quickly prepared to accompany them.

It was necessary to cross two streets, but there was a School Patrol lady to help cross Sheridan Road, as well as a traffic light.

After lunch the class was supposed to have a gym period but the teacher was absent. I asked if I could take them in and this was satisfactory. The children did not seem to want to do exercises so I obtained basket balls to use and various games were played with these which all enjoyed. There was no net to do the games I had seen done by a gym teacher, but the games were fine.

Returning to the room I checked the letters to be sent to the company for the games booklet, having some add their last names, or their address, etc. As I glanced at the clock I was amazed to see it was 2:00! The afternoon had flown by.

The students colored pictures in their fireman booklets while I put my things away and then oral thinking games were played. They enjoyed these, as youngsters always seemed to do. And the scores between the girls and boys were about even; both groups had quick thinkers.

At different times throughout the day children had pointed out to me the times listed on a time chart their teacher had made of paper plates. This was both attractive, and functional, as the youngsters often correctly read to me the designated times, to the minute. The first clock, with hands pointing to 9:00 had words beneath it reading "School Starts". Others were, "Reading" 9:15; "Recess" 10:30, "Lunch" 12:25; "Library" 1:45; "Gym" 1:00 and "Go Home" 2:30.

At 2:25 all put their chairs up, picked up papers on the floor, and lined up to leave. When the bell rang one boy ran about the center lobby of the school a little, but most left quietly through a side door close by.

It had been one of the most pleasant days I had had in some time. Even the bus came along quickly and there was no need to transfer. As I got off I noted there were four 151 buses in a row and I thought how nice it would have been to have seen one of them during the 20-minute wait that morning.

Chapter 76

Honey Be Good

I left early, at 7:30 for Waters School. The Sheridan-Wilson bus driver told me no bus went 2500 west on Lawrence, the location of the school. He said I could transfer to a Montrose or Wilson bus, but added he went to Lawrence "if he had time". I remained on his bus, rode to Lawrence and Campbell and walked about two blocks to the school.

After signing in at 8:30 I was assigned a 3rd-4th grade class. As I completed putting seatwork on three blackboards the Principal entered and talked a few moments. She was very pleasant. I recognized her from a picture on a central bulletin board I had seen near the office. I was pleased, and surprised, that she stopped in as this had been so unusual in my experience. The short visit really started the day off with a pleasant, friendly tone.

The students entered at 9:00 and roll was taken. 26 were present, one absent. Two received free lunches; the others went home or had brought lunches. This was an Open Campus School, having a lunch hour from 12:00 until 1:00, closing at 3:15.

Walking reading classes started at 9:05, when some children left and others came in. Nine were in the first reading group; all were at level "H" (3A); all read fast orally. However, at the end of the reading only one Oriental Indian boy could answer the few questions I had jotted down during their readings. He had been born in Chicago.

The next reading group consisted of 17 pupils. All were at "G" level (3B). There was but one rapid reader here; the others read moderately slowly and the bell rang before any understanding questions could be given.

At 10:15 a warm, friendly voice spoke over the inter-com system. The Principal told the students they would have inside recess. There were a few disappointed sighs, but it was very cold outside. Two monitors entered, but the class did not want to play the usual games presented by them. I introduced "Threading the Needle", a challenging physical body-twisting exercise, which about eight were able to perform. Next a travel game was played that everyone enjoyed. One child started traveling as a frog; he hopped to another child's seat, and told him to travel as a mosquito, etc. All ages enjoy this game as older students change the animal names to conform to their more mature levels. I once witnessed a 6th grade class turn this into a fascinating, innovative game. Ever since I have wished I had jotted down some of their unusual ideas, but much of their success was due to the acting ability of some students. I can still see one boy enjoying his role as a monkey and scratching gleefully.

After recess oral thinking games were introduced but the class was not alert enough to be able to answer these, so contraction, abbreviation, homonym and math bingo games were played. I had seen stacks of multiplication dittos so knew they were good in math and had made up a game from a ditto worksheet assignment.

During the lunch hour I went to the gym to get milk as the water in the drinking fountains was unusually warm. It was surprising to see only bag lunches and milk being offered; there was no lunchroom; no hot lunches. Students sat on benches at long tables, or in groups on the floor.

As I had noted each floor corridor had a ditto machine, plus a container of fluid, on a table available for teachers' use, I returned upstairs and prepared art dittos to use in the afternoon.

When the children returned at 1:00 I found practically no seatwork had been done, so everyone completed that next. I graded papers as they finished and were put into a receiving box.

At one time so many washroom requests were made that everyone stopped and visited the restrooms. The boys' toilet was nearby but the girls far away down the hall, so I stood in the center watching both. But the boys returned to the room instead of lining up as they left the washroom, and soon a boy came to me saying one boy in the room had hit another boy on the head and they were fighting. This was most surprising as the children had seemed so nice and so quiet, but I felt it was serious and hurried back. Although one boy had been seen to hit the other, he emphatically denied it. I asked them to step out in the hall as the culprit was becoming so excited. In the corridor I asked if they would like to be friends and was pleased at their prompt acceptance of this. Both quickly shook hands, smiled, and re-entered the classroom. The situation had quickly dissipated into nothingness.

There had been a minor talking problem with one girl throughout the day and several times I had asked her to be quiet. Finally in the late afternoon her loud voice became very disturbing as I graded the piled-up papers so I moved her desk away from the others by the entrance. She refused to move to it, remaining and continuing talking, which, in turn, caused four others around her to join in constant laughing. I motioned to one boy on another side of the room to come to me, and out in the hall I asked him if his teacher had trouble with this girl. He said she did, and that the girl often refused to conform to the teacher's request. The next time the child started talking I went next door and had the Assistant Principal talk to her outside the room. He was a soft-spoken individual, and soon the child returned. Her desk was moved back and she remained quiet – doing nothing but glare defiantly. For days the first word of the Assistant Principal's message to the child rang in my ears – "Honey, would you step out here a moment?" Why hadn't I invited her outside to talk, and why had I allowed her to upset me? The child needed help to melt her stubborn resistance and I had contributed to her problem. Although I apologized several times during the rest of the day, she remained aloof and glaring.

While the class had been doing the seatwork I had been occupied grading and starring papers that had been turned in. Strangely enough, I did not seem able to catch up and the stack grew higher and higher. I wished I had not had the bingo games in the morning but had had the class finish the work and leave the papers on their desks at noon as usual. Finally, when I did finish and was returning the papers it became apparent the morning reading class had put their work at the bottom of the basket. I had been grading seatwork of two classes! I also later realized that had made it very difficult for me to cope with the constant talking of the girl in the afternoon.

There remained but little time for record music and art work. Three ditto outlines were offered and the students selected one of their choice.

At closing some students asked about homework and I suggested spelling but only about one third seemed pleased. My next offering was to write a short essay about their school, or Chicago. Again, little acceptance. Finally I suggested they make up some bingo games for math and explain them to their teacher. This idea was gladly accepted so all left happily.

As I signed out several teachers were leaving and I asked if anyone was driving to Broadway or Sheridan. One was and I had a ride all the way home as the teacher lived two blocks from me. On the way he said the Principal was very friendly and interested in her work, adding she stopped into the various rooms two or three times monthly. He agreed that both the Principal and Assistant Principal were pleasant and helpful, adding both were well liked. He added the Assistant Principal had formerly been a student in the school.

Chapter 77

Holt Books Read at Home
I will lern to not tok

At 8:30 I signed in at Budlong School and was assigned a 2nd grade class. Five assignments were written on the board before the students entered.

33 names were listed in the attendance book; only 2 had left in six months, indicating a stable neighborhood, and only 1 pupil was absent.

Before oral reading groups were started I learned it was a 3rd grade, but there was too much work on the boards to be changed, so I told them they could complete any two of the assignments there, and then write a story, or draw art work, to be sent to a newspaper for publication. About 12 students submitted stories, of which five were acceptable to be submitted to the paper.

The top reading group, of 9 students, read first; all read at "G" level (3A) in a Holt book. My interest was considerably dimmed when I learned it was their practise to read the stories beforehand at home; then in school the teacher asked questions concerning them. Their oral reading was so-so, rather slow, and quite unimpressive; they did not use workbooks. I saw stacks of ditto seatwork on a table. All this surprised me as I had expected superior reading and seatwork from students in this neighborhood.

During the reading there was suddenly terrific noise from an adjoining room, the door between us sounding like it would be broken down at any moment. It sounded like we were behind pinballs of a bowling alley lane. The class explained there was a gym class next door. The noise sounded great fun – for those on the other side! But it was not constant and did not bother us too much. Not nearly as much as the noise INSIDE the classroom. The talking was so constant that I had the readers move their chairs from the back to the front of the room so I could see who did the talking. This didn't help too much though and it continued throughout the day.

The next reading group, of ten students, were also at "G" level in the same book. All were slow readers; many pointed to each word as they read. I suggested they keep one finger on the center of the line to retain their place in reading, but reminded them that pointing to each word was indicative of first-grade reading. They did not have workbooks to use.

The third reading group, of 8 students, read at "D" level (1A), also in a Holt book. With one exception, these were extremely slow readers. One said he was unable to read and explained, "They didn't teach me to read in the school I came from." "And where was that?" I asked, expecting to hear of some faraway place. His reply, "Brennemann" really startled me. I had several friends teaching there, so pursued the matter. "What was your teacher's name?" He did not remember. "What room were you in?" Again, no recall. "Why did you move?" He did not know. I let the subject rest as it is usual for non-readers to blame their former schools for their problem. A little later I had a student borrow a first grade book and had the boy read in it. But he was right. He could not read a 1A book.

Because half, or more, of the class were to leave at 1:00 for a Greek bilingual program, the Milton Bradley Contraction and Abbreviation cards were used before lunch time. These were really good review for the class and they enjoyed the games as well.

The school had an hour lunch period so I ate in the basement with the school clerk where there was a snack and drink machine.

After lunch the students remaining wrote stories and had art work until the others returned at 2:30, at which time we had oral thinking contests.

Two students had persisted in talking throughout the day and eventually been asked to write an essay on Classroom Behavior. Later when they handed their papers to me I was busy checking the newspaper stories and merely observed they had simply written a list of single sentences on their papers. I realized they did not understand what an essay was, but it was not until that evening at home I was fully aware of their needs. One boy had written one page of, "I must be quite". The other had covered both sides of his paper with 56 lines, reading, "will lern to not tok."

Chapter 78

Mobile Unit

Funston School was 3600 west so I left at 8:00 to arrive early enough to be assigned a primary grade. At 8:40 I was the first substitute to sign in, three lining up behind me. There were about eight or ten vacancies to be filled for the day. My room was a first grade in a mobile. Mobiles are self-contained units (having toilets and drinking fountains) located near the regular school. This school had 13 such units, meaning the school enrollment was outgrowing the regular school, which was a large, old, three-story one. Mobiles are the size of one regular classroom.

The mobile was well heated with blackboard space on one wall. The room was filled with ditto work completed by the youngsters, but having been a secretary for a number of years before entering the teaching profession, and encountering such an incredible amount of illegible writing of adults, I have always felt teachers should provide a great amount of writing for the children, and insist that it be *legible*. So I covered the blackboard with seatwork to be done.

The youngsters were mostly white, a few Spanish, a few black; they were average, or above, but quite noisy. The seating, movable chairs, was attractive, but the closeness may have contributed to the constant talking, which kept me busy all day trying to stop.

Every child in the class could read, and with assurance. There were but two reading groups, one child reading in both, which showed the teacher was alert to one's progress. After silent and oral reading they worked in their workbooks, which were graded during the day. About three pupils were weak in understanding the written work but three others were better in the written assignments than in oral reading.

Arithmetic was also put on the board. They were astonished at this, being accustomed to putting answers on dittos. Two did not know how to put the figures beneath each other; two did not draw the lines, and one wrote them horizontally, probably as in the ditto papers. But only one little girl did not know how to subtract at all. I drew little circles for the numbers and let her cross out the number to be subtracted. She then saw how to do it very quickly.

After lunch we had oral fun-thinking questions, learned a friendship poem; copies were made from poems on the board, and everyone read two more stories and did two more workbook pages which were graded. Two youngsters searched for a record player, finally returning with one from the office; then we had art work while listening to Hans Christian Andersen Stories, and then to songs. Their art work was really impressive, but only about three finished before it was time to go home. The bulletin board work looked like it could use some new work so I suggested they complete the work the next day after showing it to the teacher. I left her a note saying she had done a good job teaching them to read.

Having taught first grade for years, it has always had a special place in my heart, but the constant noise in this one dulled a good impression to carry away.

As they had finished most of the board work, that part was erased, but the easy poems were left for the next day, just in case the teacher might want to have them copied. The entire class was being tested the next day, so she may have appreciated some easy work for them before the testing.

Chapter 79

Relaxed, Friendly Class

Peterson School's Second Grade Class was a teacher's dream – no discipline problems, so it was a day that did not drain one's energies.

"Another one today! What is this!" piped one little fellow as I greeted the class. "Are you a professional?" queried another smiling up to me.

Surprisingly enough 13 students were starting Ginn readers at level 6 (1A); another 18 read at Level 7 (2B). Although this was a "Walking reading" class students said they were 2nd and 3rd graders, so even in this so-called privileged neighborhood some students were starting their education at slow paces – already a year behind expected achievement levels.

There were LD (Learning Disabilities) classes, Greek classes, a Musical Instruments Class, and one for advanced readers who read in Junior Grade Books.

It was also surprising to find these 2nd graders did not seem to be alert thinkers. It was necessary to use low level word game material for them. Usually after a few examples 2nd graders quickly enjoy such oral competition at their own grade levels.

Another surprise occurred at closing time. As the class was lining up I commented, "Oh my! The talkers will have to give me a kiss!" But as I bent down instead of giggling and sudden complete silence I heard voices. "I was talking", "Me too", "I was talking too." I stood up smiling and facing a beaming class. It was a memorable moment. For them and for me.

A quiet, happy order was prevalent in this school where both students and teachers were relaxed, friendly and smiling.

Chapter 80

Oh – My Nail!

Substitute Center had not called by 8:00 so I undressed and went back to bed. But at 8:10 the telephone rang and I was up and at Hawthorne School by 8:30.

The assignment was for a First Grade room, but my experience at this school had been the children were very, very slow so I put easy, beginning reading work on the board. This proved to be right as they were still in Pre-Primer booklets.

32 were listed in the attendance book; 7 had moved; 3 were absent; 22 were present. One-third were 7 years of age, the others 6. Two children paid the regular lunch price, one paid half price, thirteen received free lunches.

The board work was read, and explained, and papers were passed out. Four children needed pencils; they wrote their names on a list and returned them at closing time.

The top reading group of three children had already finished the booklet, "A Duck is a Duck", so I had them re-read the last story, as felt their regular teacher should put them into new books. Each youngster could read the words in the Pre-Primer.

The next group of six were part-way through the same booklet. They, too, could read the words but were a little slower in remembering them. It was obvious they had been taught to remember the words and not to sound them out.

The principal came in and said I was on recess duty so I went outside with the class. About four other classes came out then too, and three other teacher aides were there. At one time I noticed a boy going through the school gate, leaving the school grounds, and starting down the street. I called to him and he returned. A girl standing near the school entrance said he was her brother, so I told her to tell her mother about his action at recess.

When we returned to the room I read a story, "Curious George", which everyone listened to quietly. It is a story all young children enjoy and one that holds them spellbound, possibly because it is about a monkey and has good actions pictures.

The work sheets were given stars and then two more reading groups were taken. The third group of ten read in the same booklet as the others. They were quite slow, so after a child read a section, I had the entire group re-read it in unison.

The last group of three were just starting the book. They were so immature that it was difficult for them to keep watching the reading unless they were the readers.

The remaining seatwork was starred before lunch, and the children put on their coats. A few went home; the others went to the basement to eat lunch in the school.

I ate my lunch in the room and then went outside to see if I could get my car out of the ice. In the morning I had not been able to find the parking lot and had left it ice-bound on the street in some deep grooves. Three boys from the school agreed to push me out for a substantial fee, but I was relieved to be free, and I then drove into the school lot.

Returning to the room, two easy poems were put on the front board to be copied. But when the class returned a Spanish teacher said she took eight for a Bilingual Spanish class for 90 minutes.

The others read another story in their booklets and copied the poems. In the morning I had seen a record player and as the class had various art work they heard a Hans Christian Andersen story record and music records.

The Bilingual children did not return until 3:00 but they had time to color a ditto sheet of spring birds in a nest.

One little fellow finished all the seatwork in the morning and afternoon also. Most did one or two papers in the morning as I checked before they had recess. And it was while I checked that at least one required paper was completed. Some had been sitting the time away as the oral reading groups had read.

At the end of the day as I was leaving the building the Assistant Principal was in the hall. I asked him if the school had some advanced classes, explaining any class I had had in the school had been unusually slow, and I had found some schools grouped their faster students together. He hesitated, then said there were a few faster ones in the classes.

He asked me how the class had been and I said, "Fine, but very slow." He then inquired if I had had trouble with one boy. I said I had not and he was surprised at this, so I added that type of child had a special appeal to me and we usually got along.

The child he referred to had been a black boy, a real scowler. On entering he had taken a seat, put his elbow on the desk, hand on his head, and sat frowning and scowling. When given papers to pass to his row he did so but returned one – his own. The class explained he always sat, that he didn't like to do any seatwork. "Oh," I said, "Then he doesn't like recess, or art, or games. Because only those who do the work will have the fun times too." He continued to sit glaring.

Later he continued playing with a tiny metal car, tapping it on the desk until I took it. (It was placed with two other such little cars in the desk drawer.) He resisted fiercely at this, and as I did manage to get it, I cried out, "Oh, you broke my nail!"

Something about this got through his icy reserve. I could feel it. Maybe it was my voice, its tone, or the hurt I felt. I flipped the nail back but it was in a really bad way. Finally I taped mystic tape across it for protection until I reached home and could cut it off.

This happened just before recess. The boy could not be left alone in the room so I had him put his coat on with the others. But outside I insisted he not play, but remain near me. I could feel his inner rebellion to this and finally asked him if I let him play if he would do the work when he came in. He quickly agreed and left at once. After recess he did good writing work, very good art work and caused no more trouble.

Fortunately for me, primary children with behavior problems have usually appealed to me. They present a challenge, sort of a game and I enjoy trying to find a way to win them over. I feel that basically such children want to conform but put on an outer façade of pretense, which even they like to have pierced and fade away. Once this occurs they usually do very good work; their resistance power has been converted to working power.

Chapter 81

½ Bunny Star
Teacher My Pants Are Falling Down

The call for Coonley School came at 8:00 so I called the school to learn if there was a parking lot available. I was told teachers could park on the school playground, but I found an acceptable spot in front of the school. As I entered several young boys were playing out in front and using quite vulgar language. As two started to fight I commented, "Boys, you should not fight here." One little chap quickly retorted, "We can fight here if we want to!" But the older girl monitors by the entrance door reaffirmed my warning to them as I went on inside, and the combat ceased.

I was assigned a First Grade class and no other vacancies were listed for the large school. The room seemed large and airy. The walls were painted cream and yellow; windows were on two sides. Desks were parallel, desk tops adjacent to one another, in four rows. 33 children were listed; two had moved; two were absent.

Five assignments were put on the boards before the children came in, and the teacher had left four worksheets to be done, plus reading tests to be given to one group.

At 9:00 the class entered, and from then until closing there was constant commotion. Coats were hung up in an adjoining cloakroom. Before the work was explained a mother entered with a child, a note in her hand. She asked me to tell the little girl to go to a friend's house at school closing time. I said, "Can't you tell her?" The mother said she could, but the child was so little, she might forget. I said I would try to remember, but with 30 children in the room, I might forget too, which I did (without meaning to.)

Soon another mother entered with a boy, saying he was sick but she was leaving him in school! She put her hand on his forehead saying he had a fever, but added she had to go to work. I looked at the boy. He said he was okay. I told her I thought he would be all right. (He sat all day doing no work, which I discovered much later.) His desk was next to the teacher's, signifying he needed special watching for some reason, or extra help.

I explained the board work next, having the class read it, thinking they could do it as the roll was taken. Papers were passed out, but seven children needed pencils. Their names were listed, and pencils were given them, which were returned at closing with one exception, as usual.

Lunch money was collected next and I was very surprised to see such a long line forming for this. I was in the middle of writing the nine individual names of those paying, and the amounts, when a student entered with monthly school call for membership, so I had to stop, have the children sit down, and take attendance. Usually, I took it first but these children appeared so restless I thought it would be better to get them occupied as soon as possible; I also felt a few would come in late, and it would save time to wait a few minutes for roll taking. Many of the class were very immature, not listening to instructions, so it took extra time to take the roll. They were to raise their hand, say, "Here", and look at me. Only about one-fifth did this. So, often it was necessary to stop, repeat the instructions, and wait for children to face me and answer the roll, putting their hands up. Otherwise it was very difficult for a substitute to take roll correctly.

33 were listed in the book; 2 had moved; 2 were absent. Two were "at the dentist", which I noted in pencil as felt the dentist was in the school, as he was. There was not one black child in the class, which surprised me. In retrospect, I didn't recall seeing Spanish or Oriental children either. The youngsters were white, very immature, restless, and talkative.

Again the children lined up to pay for lunch tickets. This time an urgent message came over the intercom. The Principal said a certain report HAD to be in the office by 2:00 that day – that she was taking the summary of all such reports to the District Office the next day. I quickly went next door and asked a teacher what I should do. She said I could not possibly make out such a report and not to worry about it. (I felt the regular teacher had probably remained home to finish the report.)

For the third time students lined up to pay for lunch tickets. Nine paid the daily price; one paid $2.00 for the rest of the week; two had paid paper money the day before; one child paid 15 cents for milk. Six said they received free tickets. I did not list their names. 18 tickets were ordered and $5.95, with an explanatory note, was sent to the lunchroom. In ten minutes an attendant from the lunchroom was back saying she did not understand the order. This surprised me, as it was obviously self-explanatory. She was puzzled by the $2.00 and the note regarding two who had paid the day before. She talked to them, learned they had paid; she took the daily change from the $2.00 and left the remainder in the office. She also wrote down the names of the six who were to receive free lunches. (In distributing the tickets at noon I found one little girl who had paid had come up and was listed to receive a free lunch on the list from the attendant in the lunchroom! This group was really immature.)

Because I did not know the students the former details took extra time and it was 10:00 before the reading groups were started. The teacher had left a very good time schedule and also four sets of ditto seatwork to be used; we used three of them. The low reading group was to be given the final part of a reading test so they were called to a center table. But as we started another teacher entered saying it was time for toilet visits.

I took the girls from two rooms to a washroom in the basement. The other teacher took the boys in another direction.

When we returned from the washrooms two playleaders entered to take the class for games. At first I said we were too busy, but then I looked at the class. After all, they were only first graders and recess is so important to all children. I introduced "Thread the Needle", an exercise which several could do, and next the playleaders played "Simon Says". The leaders were a little slow at this so I took over. Soon all but five in the class were sitting; they were then announced to be winners.

The tests were restarted, but there was so much copying that I immediately separated the group so this was impossible. Giving the tests was very slow going because of their undependability. It was difficult for them to keep the correct places, even the right pages. At one time one little tot was crying. She said she "couldn't do it". I told her I would continue with the test and then repeat all of it for those who needed more time. This was done and several seemed to profit thereby. The little girl was then at ease and I noted she was marking the correct answers the second time. At last we were finished. I suspected a few boys marked anything just to finish, but one boy took his time and the ones I observed had been done correctly on his test form. Previous test pages had not been graded, so I left an explanatory note for the teacher, telling her the students had been separated to avoid copying and that one section had been re-read as they had been confused.

At 11:15 the first reading group of five pupils was called to read. They came with a soft-cover booklet and a workbook, "A Magic Afternoon" by Harcourt Brace, which they were halfway into. The children read two workbook pages, by turns, and read one story in the book, taking turns. To me, they seemed very poor readers, needing help on most of the words.

The next group of seven pupils read in "A Happy Morning", an easier book than the one of the top group. They were able to read the book correctly, but were unable to think to do the workbooks. Evidently this was why they did them together in groups.

The third group, some of whom had been tested that morning, said they had just finished reading their Pre-Primer, but I wanted to hear them and had them find the booklets. They did so and came for reading. Twelve were in this group. They were happy, carefree, and several were unable to stay on the correct reading pages for the few minutes we were reading before lunch. I was surprised to find that six were able to read the booklets; however five missed far too many words. The book was a red one and I forgot to jot down the name of it.

It was 12:00 so those whose names I had listed received their lunch tickets. However, four children lined up for free tickets who had not stood to be counted previously, either by me, or by the lunchroom attendant who had come up and written down the names of those to receive free tickets. I had one extra ticket obtained from the girl who managed to be listed as paying and also receiving a free ticket, so this was given to one youngster. The situation was reported when we reached the lunchroom, and the three children received only cookies and milk.

I was really surprised. The school had prepared ONLY enough lunches for those that had been ordered. I was so glad the lunchroom attendant had come to check the order. The four had not come to either of us for tickets. We were late in arriving at the spot to eat, so other teachers, and myself, continually reminded the children to eat fast. But they just sat anyway. Dreaming.

Helen Marie Prahl

The lunch was in a foil container, similar to TV dinners, and consisted of a hamburger patty to be put between sliced buns, corn and French fries, plus milk. It was a lunch that could not be eaten rapidly, but the children did not seem to even try. Finally, we had to line up and three boys had eaten but a few bites of their sandwiches. Several children had shared their lunches with the three little girls and I took them enough french fries and corn to feed them sufficiently. But one of these little girls was not ready to leave when the class had to be lined up. She stood in front of the huge discard container trying to eat her two cookies! A teacher standing there said no one was permitted to take food from the basement room.

Several boys and girls were asking to go to the washrooms so I took them after we returned to the room. I learned we had to return to the basement for this purpose, both for the boys and the girls. Once back upstairs, the other teacher came in, reminding me it was my turn to take the boys to the washroom, so everyone had to return downstairs again!

When we returned I starred seatwork papers; a few had been started before lunch. Now all were completed. One star was given for work copied from the board; two stars for work that was answered – of which there were a very few. I felt several were able to put the answers down but as this procedure was so different for them, they merely copied the work. They were used to the ditto seatwork, and many more had that done correctly, but I was suspicious many had been copied and took time to have each child read one section to me if his paper was correct. One girl received 14 stars; two had 12; five had 10. A few had but ONE. One little fellow had only done half of one assignment, so he was given but half of the bunny star – the back end of the bunny. He had sat all the time. He spent the remainder of the day trying to match up his half of the bunny star on his paper with the front half of it that appeared on his desk top.

Good sample colored pictures of three ditto pictures were shown and discussed, then the children chose the picture they wanted to color. Ten did not have crayons, and those of the teacher were gone, so I let them borrow a new box of 16 I had brought. They were returned in many small pieces, but at least I had a happy memory to carry away of the ten using them at a back table, instead of sitting

266

with downcast faces or walking about borrowing from others and talking even more.

The children who received ten or more stars got to do another art project as well; then it was time to get ready to leave.

As I expected, it took a good ten minutes to get them to pick up papers from the floor, and put their chairs up, take their homework assignment papers home that the teacher had designated, and line up. I had started getting my things ready some time earlier.

It was surprising to hear six or seven boys come to me for help in closing their jacket zippers. "Teacher, will you zip me?" they asked. Each time I called out for someone to help and each time four or five offered their assistance. Above the din I heard one child repeat, "Teacher, my pants are falling!" I looked down, and sure enough, this little one was holding up the sides with both hands. I put down all my things and buttoned him up. Others were clamoring for help to find their homework assignment pages. "Teacher, I can't find the work to take home!" But they were ones who had sat all day without doing much work. Once home I thought I should have helped all the children find the math pages to be done at home. There just weren't enough minutes in the day to accomplish all the miscellaneous duties required in teaching first graders, especially those so much less mature. True, the teacher had not had it repeated on her time schedule, but I felt they so needed extra help in reading.

As I walked out of the building a neighboring teacher asked me how I had liked the day. I said I didn't know. They had been noisy and very immature. She said she had had the class early in the year and said it was known as one of the worst in the school. I did not question why. They were little first graders, most of them extremely immature. I told her at least I had not been bored and could endure anything but that. Once home, I had a happy memory of them. The art work had been left for their teacher but I think most students took home their papers with stars on. I had seen them clutching them as they walked down the stairs. Suddenly, I realized I was so tired I hurt all over. I had to lie down and rest for two hours.

Chapter 82

Complete Math Paper for Gym Pass

When Substitute Center called me to report to Hawthorne School I thought it would be nice to have a third or fourth grade as the classes I had had there had always been so far behind grade achievement expectancies. When I signed in I was given a 3rd-4th grade.

The room was neat and airy. The ceiling, back and one side wall were painted white, the front a deep rose-red. Windows covered one side; blackboards were on the front and back, coat hooks were opposite the windows.

The teacher had the most beautifully-kept attendance book I had ever seen. It had tiny, but legible printing, all done in capitals, and the left side of the book contained weekly time schedules, exquisitely done, and a great help to a substitute. One problem a substitute frequently encounters is working without a time schedule.

26 were present, 3 absent. The school had Open Campus, having an hour lunch hour, and closing at 3:15. One student paid for a lunch ticket; 25 received free ones; 6 went home for lunch.

The teacher had left math work to be put on the board, to which I added three other assignments.

At 9:15 Walking Reading started and nearly everyone left, new students coming in.

The reading class of 22 that entered read at Level 11 – "J" (4th) and all were good oral readers. All read at the same level, from the same book, at the same time, taking turns. The material was very interesting, about dinosaurs, and each student had three turns. When the oral reading was completed there were questions to be answered as seatwork, which they said was usually assigned as homework. As the one-hour period was half over I told them they could complete the questions then if they so chose. Some preferred to do the work at home and did the board work. They said they usually played games for the remainder of the period but I did not accept this. Some wrote compositions on "Chicago" which I suggested.

Recess followed the reading period and I walked to the basement lunchroom for cookies and a hot drink, and brought up the milk orders for the class.

A half hour remained after recess prior to their gym period so I announced a completed math paper would serve as a pass to leave for the gym. This was followed by numerous groans and noisy remonstrations but I remained firm and everyone got busy. All papers were handed in within the half hour time.

I went to the gym with them. The teacher was a young black female, assured and competent. The class was noisy and she said, "Someone will be sitting in my office doing some work – the first one I call will do this!" Her voice was firm and the noise ceased.

The first exercise was "Jumping Jacks". They jumped in place, counting aloud until they reached 45, while the teacher silently took roll.

The next exercise was to "Fall and Drill". The children dropped to all fours, put one foot out at a time, then rose; this was repeated four times.

Next, the teacher divided the class in half. Part of the students went to the back of the room and sat on two mats by some ceiling rings. The other half remained in the front of the gym and played Volley Ball over a net. I went to the back and watched the ring exercises where two students used rings on mats.

1st exercise: Child grasped ring, took three running steps and swung back and forth five times each.

2nd exercise: Child put both feet into the rings; put knees through the rings; took knees and feet out and with hands holding rings pushed body over backward, landing feet-first onto the mat below. They were adept at this so had learned previously.

3rd exercise: Child took a small hop; put feet through rings; pulled body up; sat on rings; slid out.

The group in front was using much energy, but not effectively so I finally went up in front. However, although I made suggestions in how to hold the wrists to return the ball, only one or two listened and the time continued to pass ineffectively, the balls flying every-which way and bouncing on the floor each time after crossing the net. I started keeping score with my fingers, which brought a slight improvement but not much. Many students had already dropped out and sat waiting for their turns with the rings.

Soon the groups changed places and I returned to watch the ring exercises again.

The lunch hour followed the gym time so everyone lined up and went either home or to the basement for lunch. I learned I was on lunch duty so patrolled the lunchroom for half an hour.

Although I had brought my lunch, fried chicken was being served and it smelled so inviting I tried to order some but was told I had to do so at 9:00 in the morning. But that was all right as I had planned to have broiled chicken that evening at home.

The students had returned when I came back to the classroom so I distributed art work to occupy them while I graded the math work. They looked so alive, so alert, that I had expected excellent seatwork from them. It was surprising, to me, to find the two best papers had two errors each from the ten computation problems; other papers had more, some having eight mistakes. I wondered why the teacher offered problems this difficult, even though the work was only straight adding and subtraction.

The Milton Bradley Homonym Bingo Card game was introduced next, which they enjoyed. This was followed by the Contraction and Abbreviation card game. This they were familiar with as the game was in their room on a game table. Next there were oral thinking contests. Everyone enjoyed these and they were alert to answer them quickly.

Two girls had been quite difficult, refusing to be quiet or respectful. At noon I asked the Assistant Principal to stop and talk to one. But as he did not appear later I took one girl to a different room nearby, where the teacher agreed to keep her for the afternoon. She returned at closing time, quiet and shamefaced. The room atmosphere was much improved once she was removed.

It had been a welcome change to have a higher level in the school, but primary teaching was what I really preferred to do most of the time, and as I left I was pleased to agree to return the following day for a second grade class.

Chapter 83

Read Only 4 Pages
Good Teacher; Good Class

At 8:15 I signed in at Hawthorne School for a 2nd grade. I had brought much material for a very slow first grade level as this is what I usually had found second graders to be in the school. But I was in for a very great surprise. The teacher had left a bountiful supply of seatwork for the three reading groups, and her instructions were the best I have ever seen.

First, a morning story was put on the board, plus a seatwork assignment from "Spice". Two short poems were written for slow students to copy. (This was my only addition.) An assignment from the teacher's manual was written on the black board for the top reading group. All students were to receive a full page of math addition work to be done – 30 problems! This surprised me. The problems were not easy ones. However, most of the students handled the page by merely writing whatever numbers came to mind, at least after a few lines of working on it. Later I wished I had told them to fold the paper into thirds, doing but one-third that day. Even the students good in math had five and six errors.

The class entered smiling. One little fellow came to me asking, "Teacher, do you have the Lincoln and Washington stars?" They remembered me from the previous year!

There were 25 listed in the attendance book; three were absent. Four paid the regular price for lunch tickets; one paid half price. Fifteen received free tickets. Sixteen received milk.

The top reading group of seven pupils read at Level 7 (2B) in a Ginn book, "The Dog Next Door". All were good readers. Three workbook pages were to be done which they said they knew how to do. In addition they had nine other assignments, which most completed.

The next reading group of four pupils was at Level 6 (1A). They were half way into the book. As one child was reading I called, "Next." "I'm not finished!" she said, looking up surprised. "Oh, do you read the entire page?" I asked. She answered they did and as there were but four in the group each read an entire page. My reason for changing readers was to keep all eyes on the reading done by others.

They read only four pages and closed their books. When I suggested they start another story I was confronted with many objections. "Oh, no!" "That's too hard!" I asked if they read but four pages each day, which they said was the procedure. They had started in the middle of a story and had not been interested in reading it again from the beginning. Each insisted, "we have read that part". We turned to the workbook pages, which they said they were able to do. They had seven other assignments to do.

Eleven children were in the third group, reading at Level 5 (1B) in a Ginn Book, "May I Come In". All could read except one little Chinese boy, who seemed unable to read any of the words. Later in the afternoon another teacher stopped to take him for help in a special class. There was no ditto for this group to do, but two pages in their workbook were assigned. They were far behind in the workbook but this group was very immature. I was glad the poems were on the board for I felt they would like to copy them, which they did do.

The class said recess was at 10:00; this was verified by a neighboring teacher. All stopped work, put on their coats and waited by the downstairs outer door for the bell to ring. But two school monitors came along and informed us recess was ten minutes later this day because it was a "late day" so everyone had to return to the room and sit down for another ten minutes.

During recess I went to the lunchroom and had cookies and a glass of milk. On the way back I was told there would be an Air Raid Drill so the children, who had just returned, put their coats on again. They lined up inside as the bells rang; then everyone walked out of the school grounds until the clear bell was sounded. An older boy, standing nearby, was shivering as he had no coat on or sweater, so I wrapped part of my coat around him. He had not been in his classroom when the bells rang. When the clear bell rang I suggested he hurry back inside which he did.

After the air raid drill we ordered milk for the class but received a note saying it was too late.

During the lunch hour I had Chop Suey and learned from the lunchroom manager they did not send milk after recess to rooms as then the children would not eat their lunches. This was a good idea which I agreed with, but I asked if we might have the milk in the afternoon. This was agreeable with her and I knew the class would be pleased as they had been quite disappointed in the morning. After lunch several children brought items to the front of the room for Show and Tell. There was a huge "Things To Do" book, a tiny bingo game, two dolls and opera glasses. All students were very interested in these personal items. Show and Tell was obviously a very special time to them.

At 1:25 the milk was sent for. Everyone was surprised and happy about this.

At noon I had intended to grade seatwork but had visited with teachers and all afternoon I was deluged with completed work from workbooks, ditto pages and blackboard assignments. As the students turned in their papers they selected art work to do. At 3:00 I gave up the grading as felt the class had behaved very well and deserved more personal attention. Most of the work had been graded except the workbooks from two groups. (I returned at 8:00 the next morning and completed grading as had been asked to return again for another class.)

There were oral thinking games which they enjoyed and were alert enough to answer quickly and correctly. This class had really matured from the previous year when I had had them. They were now quiet students who could read, print, and think. It was truly wonderful to see such improvement. I left a note congratulating the teacher.

Chapter 84

Happy Class; Happy Teacher

At Hawthorne School I was assigned a Kindergarten Class. There were 22 present, 3 absent.

The children sat quietly in a large circle until the roll was taken and the seatwork assignment explained. The teacher had left two ditto papers to be done. One was to circle two pictures which were alike on a row, and to cross out those that were different; the other was a math paper. The children were to circle the correct number of flowers in each section, then color the flowers.

On the board I added two writing assignments, one of letters and words, and one of numbers to be written. Another math paper was added as well. The numbers 7, 8, 9 and 10 were written on quarters of a math paper, and triangles, squares, rectangles and circles drawn in each section, the amount corresponding with the number written there.

When the five papers were completed they were starred, and stapled together, and the child received an art paper to color.

The group finished about the same time so the next period was spent hearing records. They enjoyed a child's Polka record, acted out "The Three Little Kittens", played a Musical Chairs game, and became trains when hearing train record music.

At 11:00 they put on their coats and went to the lunchroom. The lunch was ham and cheese sandwiches, fruit salad, french fries and milk.

After lunch they visited the washrooms, then returned to the room for an hour's rest period. Small mats were put on the floor and another kindergarten class joined them for this period.

It was my lunch time so a teacher aide took the class for the rest period. I had ordered the regular lunch so ate with the teachers. It was surprising to hear two teachers admit they hated teaching as I had always found it very satisfying work. Later at home I realized I, too, had been very restless at their age and may have felt the same way had I taught then. Instead, I had traveled for a few years when out of college, and later worked as a secretary for a few years before entering the teaching profession. The restlessness had left by that time and I found it a great privilege to be working with young children and seeing them progress.

At 12:50 I returned and the same procedure of the morning class was repeated with the afternoon youngsters. They had been in the school in the morning in another kindergarten; the classes were now exchanged.

Roll was taken, seatwork explained and done. There was a little difference in that three art projects were put on different tables so the children took turns working with each of them. The projects consisted of medium small plastic art symbols that were copied with pencil, then colored. All were very different so everyone liked working with the different items, in turn. It was pleasing to have all the items returned – after a little searching by most of the class. A story was read, and oral games played until closing time.

Kindergarten is a pleasant class to have if one has enough challenging material to keep them occupied. If the children are happy, a teacher is happy. This had been an enjoyable day for all of us.

Chapter 85

Well Organized Plans
Gym Exercises

At Nettelhorst I was assigned a Kindergarten Class. The Assistant Principal wished me a nice day, and every teacher with whom I came in contact was very nice. One even came in to see if things were going all right.

Two children came in at 8:30; two more at 8:45. The others entered at 9:00. 23 were present, 2 absent. One little fellow was very helpful in getting items we needed so I told him he was my new assistant. He beamed. "I am from Puerto Rico, and I know what everybody says in English!" he said proudly.

The teacher was exceptionally well organized with the teaching procedures. She had left a good time schedule for morning and afternoon classes, as well as a number of ditto seatwork sheets to be done by the children.

The class was studying sounds of the letters "N", "J" and "K" so after the roll was taken the children remained sitting in a circle and each child gave a word that started with the sound of "N", then the "J" and last the "K". The teacher had left two sheets of ditto work for the class to complete. The children voted to sit in chairs at tables to do the seatwork. Pencils and papers were distributed and the work explained, but the class completed them together. One picture on each line was to be crossed out if it did not have a picture of the correct starting sound. Most of the children could do the work correctly.

The next paper contained items that went together, like a camera and a picture, glasses and a book. The children named the items, then drew the lines to connect the proper pictures. The third paper contained sets of items. The pupils counted the number in each circle and wrote it beneath. The concept to be learned was the most and the least, so pictures of these two were colored, the third picture being crossed out.

For arithmetic the teacher had arithmetic paper divided into four parts, a number – 7, 8, 9, or 10 – being written on each section. The children then drew 7 triangles on one section, 8 squares on another, 9 circles on one, and 10 rectangles on the other.

At 10:00 two third graders came to take the class to the washrooms, and then return for games. I had a hot drink and some cake in a room for teachers.

However, when I returned to the room, in just a few minutes, the class was not there. Earlier I had noted they had gym after recess and had asked one child if I took them for the gym class or if there was a gym teacher. "No, you get a break and two other ladies take us," he had replied. I reasoned he had referred to the third graders so I walked up to the gym.

The class was sitting quietly in four diagonal rows facing a teacher. She was giving instructions on how to use the new mats and ceiling rings. Four children, one from each row, came forward to use the rings, in turns, doing the following:

First exercise: Stand under the ring. Hold the rings; lean forward, feet on the floor. Lean backward on the heels. Feet on the mat, lean right and circle around. No bending the arms.

2nd exercise: Hold one ring in each hand. Pull the body up to the chin, count 1-2-3. (One little girl was unable to hold the ring. She looked up at it and gave it a little slap. She tried again but was unable to remain holding her body up.)

3rd exercise: Hold the rings and bend the knees up. Arms must be straight; bend the knees only. Hold 1-2-3.

4th exercise: Hold a ring in each hand. Take three running steps; put knees up; swing forward and back four times. Put feet down. Stop the rings.

Watching them I could well understand why youngsters look forward to the gym periods. It had even been fun to watch them.

After gym it was time for milk and cookies. One child put down orange papers for placemats; each child received two small cookies and a milk carton. Records were played and dramatized. This was the first time one little tot smiled. She had been crying for her mother most of the morning. They enjoyed, "I'm a Little Teapot", "The Polka" and "The Three Little Kittens".

Pencils and crayons were put away and papers folded. All put on their coats; a few asked for help with buttons, zippers and tying shoe laces. One mother entered; she said most mothers waited outside; she added some youngsters went home by themselves. I watched and saw quite a number run home alone.

In the afternoon class there were 21 present; 4 were absent. They were a little less mature than the others, but not much. The seatwork was similar to the morning.

In the afternoon class there was time to hear a story, "Curious George", and to color large butterflies. Several here did exceptionally fine coloring papers.

It had been a most pleasant day, due to the fine training and organization of their teacher. This was a kindergarten class that children would enjoy and not be bored as basic learning concepts were offered. The youngsters learned to think, to reason, to follow directions, and to be orderly in putting materials away, as well as the usual social behavior graces. I had been in only two other kindergarten classes as well planned as this one.

Chapter 86

Distar Reading Books
Field House

At Budlong School I was assigned a 2nd grade. All the board space, on two walls, was covered with assignments, and from the instructions in the Plan Book, it sounded like the work was for this day. I felt no teacher would put that much work on boards for a substitute, so I had three pupils enter a few minutes early to look and see if they had done it, which they had.

As it was 9:00 by then I quickly erased most of the work and put up seatwork that I always carry. The teacher had left one English book open and had designated the board work to be used so I copied that for them to do also.

34 students were listed in the attendance book; 4 had left; 3 were absent. Three received free lunch tickets; others brought lunches or went home at noon as the school had an hour for lunch, closing at 3:15.

There were four reading groups, all reading in Distar reading books. The first group of seven read from Storybook I, which looked like 1B reading. They read three stories, each having three turns; their reading was very slow.

As they read I looked about the room at the class. It was the most handsome one I had ever seen, and they were very quiet also. Each child quietly did the work on the board, with a minimum of quiet whispering at times.

Five youngsters read in the next reading group. They were in Storybook 2 of the Distar series and all read smoothly.

The third group of six children read the Storybook 2 also but were farther along in the book. They had fun reading and all laughed at the story; these were good readers.

Group IV had six pupils; they read in Storybook 3 and were faster, smooth, oral readers. Each one read orally very well. The stories in the book held the interest of the children. They were clever and interesting – different.

At recess time two upper-grade students appeared to take the class to washrooms, I went to the basement to have a hot drink and look for a ditto machine. I thought they had hot consomé but there was only coffee, which was mostly hot water. I didn't mind as long as it was hot.

After recess we played the Bradley Contraction and Abbreviation Bingo game as the class told me they went to the Field House in the afternoon for the last period. This was verified by the office. It took a little while for them to catch on to play the bingo cards but then the boys did quite well. They won 33 to the girls' score of five. But after half an hour of the game playing I had them complete the seatwork. I walked about starring some papers before the noon hour.

At noon I ate in the basement room and then waited my turn to use the ditto machine so this took most of the noon period and the papers were not graded as I had planned.

At 1:00 roll was retaken and one absentee came in for the afternoon. All papers were given stars. The majority of children had completed nearly all of the assignments.

Music records were played and they enjoyed playing Musical Chairs even though chairs were not removed. The children moved about the entire room. This way everyone had more fun at all times instead of being removed from the game. They skipped and danced about as the music played. They could not foresee when the record would stop as I had brought a Musical Chairs' Record. Next, a child's exercise Polka record was played, followed by singing music for a short time.

Art papers were passed out and there were several good little artists in the room. By the time they finished the art it was time to go to the Field House, a building on the school grounds. I asked one child what they did there and she said they played bingo and other games; that in the summer they played outside.

The children said sometimes someone came for them to take them and otherwise they went alone. I had been asked by the Assistant Principal to cover another 4th grade room during the time they were gone, but I did not like to have them leaving alone to go to the other building. I watched from a 3rd stairway window, and the children were running all over the grounds, this way and that. In fact, I felt from the way they ran there was trouble on a side I could not see. I remained watching.

Surely enough, a teacher from the Fieldhouse came from that building over toward where the largest group of children had gathered below. I went back to the office as felt something had happened. It had. I was glad I had sent for a written note saying they should go to the Fieldhouse alone. One boy had hit a girl, a new child to the class from Yugoslavia, and she was crying. I had him apologize, but the girl was thoroughly shaken. Nonetheless, she chose to return with the class instead of come with me.

I went to the 4th grade room and they were just as fine and quiet a class as that of the 2nd grade. They enjoyed the Bradley Homonym Bingo game I took. Here there was a close tie, with the girls winning 26 to 25.

When I returned to the regular 2nd grade room I learned the boy had again hit the new child on the return trip. There had even been a teacher there then. It really was too bad as others told me he threatened to hit her after school also. I talked to him but was not sure I accomplished much. He was the only black boy in the class.

Only 14 minutes were left so we had oral thinking contests. Here the girls won constantly; the boys couldn't seem to catch on to play this game in time. The girls won 18 to 5.

This had been another pleasant day. Second grade is really a pleasure for a substitute to teach. The children are quiet and teachable and so sweet. They were so pleased with all the star papers they carried home as well.

Chapter 87

Embroidery Work for Boys

After my alarm rang I fell asleep again and did not wake up until Substitute Center called; I did not arrive at McPherson School until 8:30. Five substitutes had signed in ahead of me; one arrived behind me, but she had been there before and knew the people in the office. She was sent to a TESL class (with their good wishes and comments that she would have a teacher aide all day, and a student would show her the way there). I quietly waited my fate and was assigned to a 6th grade elementary class as all primary openings had been assigned. One office clerk said there was just one 8th grade left to cover, so considering this, I felt I was fortunate to have any other elementary level.

The class turned out to be a good one, academically and behavior-wise. The reading levels were "J" (4th), "K" (5th) and "L" (6th). 32 were listed in the attendance book; one was absent – "in Mexico" the class said.

The teacher had left a Time Schedule, so detailed and self-explanatory, that I wrote it on the board. This eliminated numerous comments about what should be done. However, I felt the students could do the work faster than the time she had specified so later I put two assignments on another board which soon proved to be right.

The time tables, spelling words and sentences were done in the morning before recess. At recess time the class lined up, then informed me their teacher went outside with them so I put on my coat and accompanied them. After recess they worked on the seatwork until Library Hour at 10:30, and while they were gone I graded some of the papers.

They returned noisily from the library, commenting the teacher waited for me to call for them. This I should have done but somehow it had not occurred to me. They had gone alone and so I did not think about calling for them. Because of the continued noisiness of two boys I took them to other rooms and left them there as the teachers said I could do. They were really not too bad, but several warnings had not been effective and I felt if I did not stop them somehow the class atmosphere might steadily become intolerable.

A Science period was to follow the library one but the teacher had not left the correct page for the material, so I decided to dictate a business letter. This, or course, was a great surprise to the class. I explained I had been doing this when I was sent to upper grades and that I had never received a perfect paper. Because of my past experience I dictated the letter through, slowly, one time, explaining I would repeat it again, which was done. As in other classes, many asked for continued repetitions as the dictation proceeded, but I said I would continue the letter and dictate it again when finished. The letter was repeated slowly six times. A few papers were handed in fairly early, but some students were still trying to get started when it was time to leave for lunch. (Had I not warned them I intended to leave the work for the teacher, I doubt many would have struggled through, or even started, the experience.) The majority of papers were in by lunch time.

At noon I drove home to obtain the Milton Bradley Bingo Games for older classes. One was on Synonyms and Antonyms and the other on Prefixes and Suffixes. Returning, I ate my lunch in the Teachers' Lounge with other teachers.

The students returned at 1:00 and one of the first was a boy who had been put in another room. (Both boys had been told to return to the other rooms in the afternoon.) He said he had talked to his mother and she had said he was wrong, that he should apologize, which he did. (I had told him I planned to call his father that evening – NOT his mother.) His behavior was improved, but obviously he was not well trained in disciplining himself to remain quiet.

A few students had completed all the assignments so they were given art work sheets to be colored as their papers were turned in. When the majority of papers were in the Bingo Games were started. I started out calling the words, but tried out different students for this job until one was found with a voice loud and clear enough to be heard. Of course, all the trouble-makers volunteered for this job (and most likely they would have been very good at it) but I felt the well-behaved students should be rewarded and kept trying until a capable one was found. The class liked the games, especially when I started a contest between the boys and the girls. Fortunately, it remained close at all times.

A little later I changed to the Homonym Game as that one seemed a little more fun; the class agreed they liked it the best also. These games offer enjoyment to students, plus having much learning value. There was a little trouble on the score-keeping so a boy was assigned to record the girls' points and a girl kept those of the boys.

Meanwhile I graded the dictated letters. Their papers surprised and disappointed me. I had felt I might receive some really good work but this was not so. One boy had but four errors, but the mistakes rose rapidly to nine and higher, mostly in the twenties and even much higher. It was sad as so many did not know (probably had forgotten) anything of letter format. Teachers usually present this yearly from 2nd or 3rd grade on up.

In dictating I had said to use their school name and address as their address. The letter was to a company in Gary, Indiana. Many started with the Gary name and address at the right, top. Only two had a date. A few merely wrote what I said (or tried to) word for word across their lined papers from border to border. A great many spelled "gentlemen" as "gentelmen"; there were several other variations, the most unusual being "genearol". In fact, their spelling as a group was unbelievably sad throughout the letter. Some even misspelled the name of their school. "Yours truly" varied from "Yours turely", to "Truly" to "Truelly" to "Trully" and "Yous Turely". About five wrote "to" and "From" on their headings. One girl skipped most of the pain and merely wrote "To" and "From" and her name.

After lunch, before the Bingo Games were started, the boy who liked to talk so much, asked, "Teacher, what do we do when we finish?" I asked if he had finished the seatwork. (They had been told to bring it up and exchange it for an art paper to color, which several had done.) His expected, "no", caused me to answer him with words that kept him quiet for some time. I explained that intelligent individuals never had to ask anyone what to do; they always found something of interest. I added we didn't live in a dull world, and people who were bored were not using the intelligence they had. I said it was a good thought for them to remember as long as they lived because it would be true that long.

Throughout the day some students, particularly about seven boys, chose to work on embroidery work when their required papers had been completed. They did this during the Bingo games, which surprised, and impressed me. Their teacher had offered them an interest that blessed both the student and the teacher. Most of these boys were inclined to be flippant and talkative without a special interest as this one. I didn't notice any girls choosing this activity, only the boys.

The teacher had left math homework to be copied onto the board which I did and the students copied it before leaving at closing time.

The boards were erased, papers picked up and chairs put on desk tops. The class left quietly as I went down the stairs with them.

As I walked along the street a girl from the class asked if I would be returning the next day. I said I didn't know but added I was more at ease in primary grades as had been trained to teach at primary levels. I added she was in a good class. She nodded but added there were some trouble makers. I agreed, but assured her they were not nearly as severe as in other schools. It really had been a good class.

The only trouble was the amount of papers to be graded. I had let the students see their errors on the dictation and had written the letter correctly on the board at noon. Their letters, plus a letter from me, was left with their teacher. But there had been no time to look at the other seatwork they had done of what I had put on the boards so I had taken that work home. That evening I found the seatwork had been done correctly and would have been great fun to have had read orally had there been time.

I could appreciate some advantages, and disadvantages of teaching upper grade classes. One advantage was that during the Bingo game it had been possible to have a student call the words to the class. But, even so, there had not been time to grade all the day's seatwork before closing, resulting in a disadvantage to teaching elementary and upper grades. In primary classes I had always managed to grade five or six seatwork papers during the day so they could be taken home the same day. However, one primary paper was like but one paragraph of a two-page elementary paper; there was just no comparison.

Chapter 88

Messy Attendance Book
Good Art Work

Because I had missed a primary assignment at a school the previous day by arriving ten minutes after another substitute, this day I had set my alarm for 7:00 and was ready and waiting for the call when it came from Substitute Center at 7:40.

It was for a school I did not like to go to, but when I hesitated I was told it was for a third grade room. My objection to going to Audubon was because I had once been given a 6th and 7th grade class of severe discipline problems instead of the primary grade I had been sent there for. Many months later, after two other experiences there I had reported to Substitute Center I did not care to teach there any more.

As I signed in at 8:20 four vacancies were being listed by the clerk. She gave me the last one on the list, a third grade class. Walking into the room I saw there was an abundance of board space – three long boards, and all covered with chalk assignments! But I was early enough to clean them. Looking around I found a small pail of clean water and a sponge. Before I removed my coat or boots I washed all the boards, giving them time to dry by the time I was ready to put work there.

35 were listed in the attendance book; 2 had left, their names having been inked out completely by a black flowmaster pen so they were unreadable. The book was one of the messiest I have ever seen; it was unbelievable. Taking roll I discovered one boy's name was even written backwards, his first name being first, instead of last. Later during the day I learned the teacher in the room had had a first grade class the previous year. I had taught in her room then; it was one of the reasons I did not want to return to the school. The attendance book had been unreadable, many names listed in soft, tiny pencil writing, the room so messy, the children so undisciplined. Attendance books are permanent records of children and can be highly influential in law cases. I wondered why this condition was allowed to persist.

The class entered reasonably quietly. One recognized me as having been their teacher the previous year in second grade. I had had a feeling this might be the same class as I drove over. It had been such a wonderful day then – no discipline problems and the class had done perfect work, quickly and quietly.

In the room the desks were shoved together in a very sloppy, disheveled fashion, giving one a downcast feeling on entering. As soon as everyone was seated I moved the desks into orderly straight rows with aisles between which looked neat, and I felt would induce a more quiet atmosphere.

Only two girls were absent, others promptly reporting they were "playing hooky" as they had been in the school, and noting there was a substitute teacher, had left. It occurred to me to report this but another teacher told me the truant officer had been in the school the previous day, so I handled it in a different way. When the class went home at noon I told them to tell the girls' mothers, which they did, and both girls were brought in by one mother at 1:30 in the afternoon.

Six students paid 40 cents for their lunch; one had a reduced amount; 16 received free tickets; two brought their lunch; the others went home as it was an Open Campus school, closing at 3:15.

Before the class returned I had written a poem on the board to be copied and ten questions about it to be answered, plus two additional fun word game assignments, and a board of math work. This, I felt, should keep them busy during the morning, and, if necessary, I could change the boards for afternoon work.

After the work was read and explained I called the various groups to read in the back of the room. The first group was the second reading group in the room, a group of eight; they were slow, hesitant readers, who were reading in their second book of the school year. The next group was one of twelve; they were good, fast readers, in their third book of the year. The third group was of five slow students, one a Spanish boy, who seemed conscientious but had trouble keeping up with the faster readers. He needed much oral help with the language. One boy read so much faster that I wondered why he was in this group; he said the teacher was planning to change him to another one. Four Spanish children left early in the morning for a Spanish class where they told me they had Spanish reading and math. I asked if they had any English reading and they said no.

287

The class was far different from the previous year. There were other children present now, but that was not the reason. In reading they no longer knew basic reading skill rules, and when I reminded them of them, they had forgotten how to listen. Now reading seemed only reading words orally. Silent reading for questions was a forgotten art; the previous year they had excelled at this, the same as knowing the important necessary skill rules. No more. It really was sad as they were still very alert and smart. The quietness of the previous year was gone as well.

Several rose to talk often; there were frequent requests to go to washrooms. The politeness; the charm; the receptiveness of the previous year were no longer there. But it had been the same way in the room of this teacher with first graders the year before. The six-year olds had been continually getting up and walking around. The atmosphere in a room can usually be attributed to the teacher.

The class had told me they had a gym class the last period and I had promised them we would have Homonym Bingo Card Games in the afternoon, plus an art period. I remembered the good art they had done so decided to introduce that while I checked and starred their morning work. This would leave a short period for the game and then the gym time. It worked out very well this way; there were many more top artists this year. One child had a five by eight foot mural on a back wall he had made, which was really very interesting. Another had made a beautiful chalk picture, which had been framed and was on a wall.

Some students completed their art faster than others; some chose to do a different one as well; others chose to play the Homonym Game, so in front was a group enjoying Bingo, which grew during the hour to the majority.

The gym teacher decided to have the gym class outside so the children wore their boots and coats.

I straightened the desks again, washed all the boards, and put up a few of their art work papers on a small bulletin board. The pictures seemed to brighten the room. I was glad I had brought paper so I could run off ditto work while they were gone.

A student helper came in at closing time. He was so surprised, and pleased, with the room, exclaiming it looked "so roomy". He was sure the teacher would like it; I hoped so.

Chapter 89

Change the Channel

At 9:00 I signed in at Carpenter School as Substitute Center had not called me until 8:30. Children were entering and about five or ten minutes later I heard someone call down on the inter-com that one class was without a teacher and the children were wondering what they should do. The clerk in the office had told me when I signed in that the Pre-School vacancy for which I had been called was filled. Four other substitutes had signed in ahead of me on the sheet and there were four other sheets for regular teachers to sign in on, so this was one of the larger schools in the city.

The Principal took me to a room where there were but three children. I asked if it was an EMH class (Emotionally Mentally Handicapped) and he said it was not, so I assumed it was one with emotional problems, formerly called Social Adjustment, then ERA (Early Remedial Approach). The Principal took the girl, age 11, with him when he left, leaving me with two students. She was made errand girl for the office.

One boy, black, was 10 years of age; he was very quiet; the other child was white, age 7, and a constant talker, or singer. They told me another boy usually arrived an hour late but he remained absent for the day. Later I learned the late-comer and the girl, who had been taken to the office, often engaged in physical combat, following quick reactions to one another.

The 7-year old did a little reading at 2nd grade level, but stopped and did not want to do other work; the other boy read a few pages at 4th grade level. Both started working on puzzles on various desk tops.

I showed them samples of colored Easter Eggs students had done which impressed them and both boys started coloring ditto sheets. A few weeks earlier one little artist had made a very beautiful large colored egg on a sheet of construction paper, which she let me have. This so impressed the older black child that he made a similar picture on a card, with a greeting, for his sister's birthday, which was on Easter, a few days away. He spent much time on this, was very careful of it, and was rightfully pleased with his work. I put it inside a

289

larger folder paper to carry home. It far surpassed any other art work he did during the rest of the day.

At recess time the older girl returned from the office, saying it was fun to be down there and go on errands different places for them. However, she became interested in the art work the boys were making and remained in the room the rest of the day. She later admitted it had been dull sitting in the office.

When the bell rang for recess the boys put on their coats and went outside with some playleaders who waited on the first floor for the students. The girl showed me where the lunchroom was and I invited her to join me for cake and milk.

The teacher had left a note to watch that the older children did not "pick on" the younger boy. It seemed to me, however, that the little one was constantly taking advantage of the older children. Throughout the day they continued to alternate their interests between art work and working on puzzles, and the younger boy was continually reported for slipping over to their puzzles and working on them, which always annoyed the other children. The little boy seemed to feel justified in doing this, and when they became angry he went to a side wall, slid under some desks there and cried, then pouted, for some time. This was repeated many times throughout the day. Often he remained there crying for five or ten minutes. Otherwise, he was either talking, singing softly, or whistling. Often, I slipped up behind him and "changed the channel". This stopped him each time for awhile.

Their lunch period was at 1:00. We went to the lunchroom in the basement but the two older children hurried ahead when returning and I sent a note with the little fellow that they were not in the room. Later I hard a slight noise and it developed the girl had put herself in the small coat closet and the boy had slid behind a back paper wall chart. On the inter-com I informed the office the children were present. I did not appreciate her squeezing onto my new coat in the coat locker but realized hiding has always been great fun for children.

Aside from the Easter Egg art work I had brought five other types of plastic cut-out art objects to be traced, so everyone was occupied with one or another all afternoon. In addition they made flying birds to hang in the room and take home and the girl made birds, bunnies and eggs to put inside the classroom window.

At one time in the afternoon the little boy had done something and the older girl reacted instantly by slapping him in the face, but I was standing there and as fast as it happened the girl apologized and she and I both encircled him in our arms. Fortunately, this time he did not cry, but accepted the apology and the incident was forgotten.

A teacher can usually sense disaster, and at one time when I was making art samples to be used, I felt the girl was up to something and walked over to where she was. I was right. As I opened the cabinet door which she had just closed, I saw she had completely covered the inside of it with black marks from a charcoal stick-pencil she had found in a box. Her hands were as black as the box; her eyes full of glee. She was then asked to clean it up, which she did with tissue papers.

Late in the afternoon the Principal stopped by to see how things were going. I was glad to be able to give him a good report. It was then I learned there might have been difficulties had the absent boy been present.

The children had been likeable but teaching this type of child had never appealed to me for a regular assignment and I had carefully avoided taking any required subjects for it when attending college. Two of my teacher friends had taught such classes and enjoyed them for a few years, but even they changed to other classes. There were seldom over five or six students in such classes. This was due to the background behavior of the children and their explosive, unpredictable behavior.

It had been a different kind of day. I had watched them very closely every minute as felt I was treading on miniature time bombs, ready to explode at any time. Fortunately, because of the small membership, the relaxed atmosphere, and the abundance of art materials and waiting puzzles, there had been no major catastrophe, but one such day was sufficient for me to remember.

Chapter 90

Show & Tell a Hit

Arriving at Hawthorne School at 8:25 I noticed there were five vacancies; I was assigned to a Kindergarten Class.

The teacher must not have anticipated being absent. There were many ditto sheets stacked in neat piles to be used, but she seemed to be so organized that I decided to use my own ideas for seatwork and not interrupt her follow-through papers. The room was one of the neatest I had ever seen; her desk was NOT covered with the usual papers – there was not even one; the cabinets were a wonder. All were unbelievably neat and orderly.

24 students were present in the morning class, 1 being absent. After the roll was taken the children sat at chairs beside tables arranged in one long row. Crayons were in baskets on the tables. Primary pencils were in a cabinet nearby.

The children were shown a seatwork paper consisting of numbers written on the first line from "1" to "6", which was repeated on six lines. After the digits were written the children were to circle "1" on the first line, "2" on the second, etc. and "6" on the sixth line. Following this one picture symbol was to be drawn on the first line, two on the second, etc. I had made an Easter Basket on the first, two bunnies on the second, etc. and ended with six Easter eggs. The children were well trained and ALL were able to follow directions and completed the paper.

On the reverse side capital letters were written. "S" was on the first line, followed by a line of "e"s; on the third line was "t" and the fourth had "h". The next two lines said, "see the" and the children drew two bunnies and Easter eggs.

Next a math paper was done. They folded a paper two times and in the corners wrote the numbers "7", "8", "9", and "10". In each section symbols were written; the quantity depending on the number so specified there. This was done quickly by the class.

The next project was to make an Easter Card to take home. First small yellow folded pieces of paper were distributed. The pupils were to draw an egg so that the top of it rested on the fold, and in cutting, the egg was not to be separated from the fold. Those who cut their eggs apart pasted them on without the fold. On the outside of the fold was written "Hello", and on the inside "I love you". The cut-out egg was pasted in the center of the outer card; other Easter eggs were drawn beside it in crayon. On the inside of the card they wrote, "Easter is here"; their names were put on the back.

Beautiful Easter pictures from two Ideals Magazines were shown and stories and poems read. The children loved both the pictures and the stories and poems. Six pages of sample colored Easter Eggs, done by other classes, were shown. Then ditto pages of egg outlines were given to the children to color.

They were busy until 11:00. One little fellow said, "Teacher, is this the last work paper?" When I said it was he sighed and added, "Boy! Am I tired!" I wondered if I had given them too much seatwork to do. But they looked so energetic and happy being occupied. Years previously I had taught first grade across from a Kindergarten class and mothers of the children in the Kindergarten used to tell me how bored the youngsters were there. The time was spent singing and playing with room toys, and the children longed to be in first grade and be challenged with interesting seatwork.

At 11:10 a teacher came for the bilingual children. They went to lunch and then to another kindergarten for the afternoon session. Seven children remained in the room. One little fellow said, "Teacher, where is our milk?" I took them down to the lunchroom and obtained six milk; one had brought his lunch and milk. The one child ate his lunch with me in the room; then he joined the others in playing with clay. At 11:50 one little boy said, "Teacher. When the next bell rings we leave." I said, "Thank you," but marveled that these little tots could be so observant in knowing the clock time. At noon they left.

I found a ditto machine near the Teachers' Lounge and ran off some ditto work during the rest of my lunch hour.

At 1:00 the afternoon class came in. 19 were present, two absent. They were less mature than the morning children. The same work was presented and they were able to do it in their own fashion. However, the work was rounded off to make it easier after I noted they were less able to complete it as readily.

Helen Marie Prahl

At 2:30 the work was finished and the children sat in a large circle. One had an item for Show and Tell so several others remembered they, too, had brought special things to show the class.

There was a tiny racing car, then a large book about a Cookie Thief. The child who brought this was a good talker; he turned all the pages in the book, one by one, explaining the story to the class, which they enjoyed. It was a comic book, but one they really liked, especially when displayed by a child with such talent. The children clapped enthusiastically when he finished.

Other items were hair barrettes, a fire engine, a tiny hand-made leather purse, and a Keymonica. This was another hit with the class. It was a musical instrument that the child blew into, pressing keys, so the tones were different when the buttons were changed. It had been brought inside a plastic bag and the class waited very quietly, with great interest, as the boy reached inside to get the instrument. The bag was so large it took him two or more minutes so the interest grew more intense as he tried to get it out of the bag. They clapped long for this one when he finished also.

There was time for a short rolling ball game before putting on coats to leave. Several came for help in fastening coats.

The children in this room had been well trained; after each activity a child had quietly taken a container and collected the pencils, and later the scissors, paper and paste. One even passed around a wastebasket. When the children left the room was as neat as when they entered that morning. Those children were receiving excellent training in good habits as well as progress in readiness educational skills.

Chapter 91

Easter Party for
Hard of Hearing

At Bell School I was assigned to an intermediate class in the Hard-of-Hearing Division. The regular teacher was present also; it seems there are usually two teachers in these classes. She was soft-spoken and quiet in all her actions with the class.

There were eleven students, ages 11 to 13; five were girls. The room was of average size; the desks varied from small to large; there was a television, a radio and a sink with running water. Easter Baskets, painted with brightly colored designs, lined the window sills; all had paper handles stapled on.

The students had invited a pre-school class to visit their room that morning for an Easter Egg Hunt, so they were busily occupied for some time hiding items about in the room. They hid colored hard-boiled eggs, tiny boxes of candy, wrapped candies, chocolate eggs, chocolate bunnies, and brightly colored hard candy Easter Eggs.

Next they practised standing in two rows and sang, "Here Comes Peter Cottontail". The teacher had written out the words, with the syllables counted, on two charts, and she pointed to the numbered syllables as they "sang". Their singing was primarily by hand and arm signs.

The teacher said, "When the little children come you have to be in line and act big. Do you understand?" They signaled and grunted they did.

Soon 13 little ones entered. The older students stood in front of the room, facing the back; the babies sat on the carpeted floor facing the students. The little ones were hard-of-hearing too. Some wore earphones; some did not.

Three of the older children were dressed as bunnies from neck to toes; two were in white; one wore a new pink fuzzy sleep-suit. All had tall cream-and-pink bunny ears, painted on whiskers and pink noses and cotton floppy tails. I had pinned on the ears and tails and painted on the whiskers and pink noses. The older children sang their Easter song, then leaned down and shook hands with the babies and gave each one an Easter Basket. (The baskets I had admired on the window sills had been made for these primary children. The teacher said the students had colored seven dozen eggs!)

Each older child took the hand of a little one to help search for hidden eggs about the room. This was really delightful to watch, and it was impossible to see which group was having more fun. All eyes were beaming with joy and excitement. One teacher took Polaroid pictures which quickly reflected the interest of the groups. The regular teacher was surprised at the good behavior of one black boy; he was taking care of a tiny beautiful black girl in such a fine way; she said he was usually a continual behavior problem. The little one kept trying to eat some of her candy and he was kept busy stopping her. The children had been told to save their treats to eat after the lunch period. When the Easter Hunt was over the older students took the hands of their little charges and escorted them back to their rooms.

On their return to the room the teacher had the pupils put the desks and chairs back into place; they had been pushed back to the sides of the room. Then on the board she wrote a story of their Easter Party for the little ones. The students helped with ideas for the story. The teacher was very patient with those who interrupted. She smiled often and was very soft spoken.

At noon the children ate in the school lunchroom. The teacher went to an outside restaurant. I joined a friend in the teachers' lunch room.

After lunch the students brought their chairs to the front of the room and sat in chairs facing the blackboard where the teacher had written the story in cursive writing. The teacher stopped. She stood still. Then she motioned and talked with her hands, saying softly, "I am waiting for quiet."

The teacher finished writing the story of the morning experience. She then read it to them orally and with hand sign-language. The children had turns reading the story. The teacher watched and corrected their sign-reading, commenting, "good – Fair – Perfect – Do it again for me – Good – I don't understand you. Start again – Do it again – Good – No, one sentence. Do it again – Very good – Excellent."

Turning to one child she said, "Now you can read from here to here." Different children had turns. The teacher continued her remarks. "You don't know that word. It is 'noticed.' Good – *Down town?* We went *down town* with the baskets? We went *down stairs!*" Most were good readers. She turned to the one poor reader, "You have not paid attention. I will have to tell your mother." The boy made hand signs to a friend. The teacher replied, "You can move if you want to."

The class returned their chairs to the desks and copied the work on the board. When finished they helped get ready for the Easter Party.

The teacher had them move their desks back "so they would have room to dance". One boy kept signaling the teacher. "If we have time maybe we will watch you dance," she told him.

The teacher walked about between the desks putting a tiny, fuzzy, colored Easter chick on each desk. All had paper cups on in which Hawaiian Punch was served. Small colored paper plates were passed out as the children from another hard-of-hearing class entered and sat in five rows. Those in the last row became increasingly impatient and worried as children in the first rows were going to the front table and selecting candies and eggs but there was more than enough to fill all the plates. I think both the teacher and the students brought treats for the party, but this occasion had cost the teacher a tidy sum.

Radio music was played and later there was dancing. Turns were taken. One girl danced; two danced together; one boy pantomimed like a clown, much to the delight of the class. An older student, just passing by, stopped in and was invited to dance; he had such rhythm that he seemed to BE music. He made everyone there feel like dancing.

When he left the teacher danced with the students; she demonstrated how to take two steps, then one, on each foot. Then students hooked hands on the shoulders of the one ahead and danced in a line, following the steps of the teacher. It was very sweet to see. She really loved her work and was perfectly at ease with this age group.

The pre-schoolers returned to thank the class for the morning Easter Hunt. Their teacher had made an experience chart to read on which she had attached the Polaroid pictures she had taken. When they left the teacher danced with different students, showing them how to dance.

Meanwhile, I collected and washed plastic glasses, discarded paper plates and egg shells, picked up paper bags from the floor, etc.

At 2:50 the teacher had the class finish cleaning up and get ready to go home. I went down the stairs with them and out to their busses. There were ten busses waiting on the street. All the children left with their eyes glowing with the happiness of the day.

I climbed the three flights of stairs again to tell the teacher she had done a fine job with them; that they were a good, quiet group. She said they had made much progress, adding they had been quite a "rough" group in the Fall, adding there was much improvement yet to be made.

I felt she was an excellent model for them and had done much to create the good behavior I had seen. She was one of the most quiet, loving and effective teachers I had ever seen. It had really been a humbling experience to witness her manner with the children.

Chapter 92

Melting Pot

The first graders at Stone School represented a melting pot of nationalities, five being from Russia, three from Iran, two from Mexico and one each from Iraq, India, Israel, Burma, Bulgaria and Syria.

It was impressive, and most unusual, to note that not one child had moved during the seven school months. And in the classroom not one requested a pencil, crayons or scissors.

The entire back blackboard was covered with cardboard bulletin materials and the front one with miscellaneous hanging charts, all of which were removed for the day's assignments. Desk papers indicated dittos and workbooks were used. A few children completed reputable printing work but the majority were in need of much daily practise.

There were four reading groups using Houghton Mifflin books. Eight were in a First Primer, the others in first and third level preprimers. Two in the bottom level could not read at all and did not know any letter sounds. All others read well orally but only two completed the easy board seatwork; others merely copied it without circling correct answers.

Noise was prevalent in this school. No hall monitors were obvious and students were often heard rambling about and playing noisily in the corridors.

Chapter 93

Sharing Time a Hit

The Lesson Plans for this day at Alcott School (third grade) were so good, and so much seatwork had been put on the board, that I decided to follow the teacher's suggestions. However, it seemed to me the class would be through with much of the work sooner than was outlined, so I put four poems on the back board. At 8:30 another teacher had told me it was "a good class – but very vocal", so the poems were all on quietness. (Later when the class was seated and the poems were read, quietness did prevail for a while in the morning.)

26 were present; five absent. Two paid the regular lunch price; one paid half price; 16 received free lunches. Each child had a card with lunch data on to carry to receive lunch.

One girl reported she was to leave at 11:30 to take a preschool child home. I wrote a note to the office to have this affirmed. Returning, the child said the Assistant Principal wanted to talk to her again at 11:00, at which time she left.

There were four math problems on the board; two were of computation; two were problem situations to be solved. The boy who finished first, and correctly, graded those of the other students. He reported many were incomplete and that they had not thought out the problems correctly so had not used proper methods in solving them. At 9:25 the remaining papers were collected and students went to the board to work out, and explain, the work there.

While the children did a math book assignment, the page of which was listed on the board, I called a group to come for reading. There were seven in this group, who read at Level 8 (2A). They were slow readers and did not seem to know the basic reading skills with which to unlock unknown words, Moreover, they appeared unaware of the importance of the skills, and I explained two essential ones to seeming unlistening ears.

Toilet visits and recess followed the reading group. I went to the school lunchroom.

A "Free Reading period" of 15 minutes was listed on the teacher's schedule following recess. It sounded interesting as she had written

"Everyone reads. No one may listen to the record player or work in groups today, but may help themselves to a book." I skipped this period as wanted to hear the other reading group. Two or three pupils later asked about the period, so it must have been a welcomed one; it had sounded inviting.

The next reading group of 19 students read at Level 10 (3A) and all were good, fast readers, most of whom read with expression as well. One boy had not come to read, which I learned later, but had continued doing his seatwork. However, he was the one who had graded the early morning papers, and was an unusually verbal child; he had written a very good composition for me at an earlier time, so I felt he was a good reader.

During the morning I was determined to keep pace in grading the seatwork as it was brought up. I had quickly jotted down the math answers from the teacher's manual, and by noon I had finished grading and marking those papers.

All lined up for lunch at 11:55 as there was a tight schedule in this school. As we were going down the stairs the girl who had left at 11:00 to take the preschool child home reappeared. Everyone had to wait while I returned up the steps, unlocked the door, and let her hang up her coat and get her lunch ticket.

A Science Period was to follow lunch, but I substituted using the Homonym Game, followed by the Contraction and Abbreviation one. One of the top readers took over, once I showed her how. Meanwhile I graded the stack of reading and spelling assignments that had been turned in.

After lunch a boy had gone to the board and printed "Sharing Time" with two activities to take place. A girl's name was listed and two boys' names were written, indicating they would give "A Play". The time was limited; three minutes for one individual; five for two. These were offered after the Homonym, Contraction and Abbreviation games. The girl had been a sitter during the day, turning in no seatwork, so I wondered what she had to offer now; unfortunately, she talked in too much detail, nullifying interest at the outset. And the boys had not rehearsed their "play" sufficiently. Obviously, it was the idea of one, who had probably not been definite about what the other child was to do, so the second one soon dropped out. This did not stop the other "actor", who seemed to delight being in the limelight and took the place of both actors, quickly changing places. His comedy acting was interest-holding, but the plot lacked substance. I told him he had talent and was a good entertainer and suggested he check library books on clown acting and pantomime.

At 2:00 the art papers were distributed and a beautiful silence enveloped the room. It had been noisy all day – like bubbling mud pots in Yellowstone Park erupting periodically here and there throughout the day.

By the time the closing bell rang about half had not finished the art. Some were very good artists and the papers that had been turned in were left for the teacher.

A homework assignment had been left on the board by their teacher so everyone left promptly and happily.

Chapter 94

UNICEF Class

At 8:00 I signed in an Brennemann School and was assigned a First Grade class.

This was a very mobile neighborhood; in September there had been 33 students in the room, but nine had moved within 6 months; six were "A" (first enrollments in a Chicago School). 28 children were presently enrolled.

The class appeared to be so Cosmopolitan that I asked what countries they were from. Five were from the Philippines; three from Korea; two from Jamaica; one from Laos; one from Yugoslavia; six from Tennessee and ten from Chicago. Seven were black students. They looked like a happy, healthy group of youngsters.

Two paid for their lunch tickets; one paid half price; 19 received free tickets. An intercom message came at 9:03 reminding it was time to say the Pledge of Allegiance; after this a patriotic song was sung.

"Walking Reading" followed the morning exercises. The teacher had left three ditto seatwork pages to be done and I had written two assignments on the board. There were three reading groups. Seven read in a Holt preprimer at Level 5; eleven read in another preprimer at Level Six, and eleven others read in a reader at Level 7. All were capable of reading at their levels. Each group read two stories, the students taking turns reading orally.

A recess period followed the reading classes and the children went outside to play. Returning, they finished the seatwork, so I put up two more assignments on the boards. The papers were graded, and returned, before lunch. (First grade work can be handled quickly.)

Hot lunches were brought on rolling serving equipment to the corridor. The children carried their lunches (ravioli) on trays to the classroom and ate the food there. In this school the library was used as a lunchroom by the intermediate grades.

After lunch there was a period for Show and Tell but no one had brought special items to show. Several students came to the front to talk of trips they had taken or of personal experiences.

Helen Marie Prahl

Two short science movies, one about frogs, one of horses, were seen after lunch. Both were especially interesting.

There was another period in the afternoon of "Walking Reading" which pleased me. This was the only school I had been substituting in that offered afternoon reading classes. When teaching regularly I had always repeated reading classes in afternoons and had been very surprised to find no schools doing this. Additional seatwork was put on the boards which the youngsters completed.

Following this there were music records. They enjoyed a child's exercise record of "The Polka", dramatized "The Three Little Kittens" record and heard a story, "Alfred", about a small boy and a dog.

Throughout the day there were exercise periods while they completed the seatwork. All the students did beautiful printing on their papers. When all the papers were finished the children were given an art picture to color; there were a few good artists, but the majority did not do good coloring which was a surprise. Samples had been shown before the papers were given out; possibly some details on the work should have been pointed out and suggestions made.

It had been surprising to me to see the children continue doing the many seatwork papers they did throughout the day. At times I wondered if too much was being expected of them, but without the work they started to become noisy and talkative, whereas if I continued erasing completed work and putting new work on the board they remained quiet and occupied.

A teacher had warned me in the morning that the clocks in the school were not working properly and throughout the day we learned of the recess and lunch periods by observing other children in the halls. (My watch had stopped running the previous week!) Most of the students were busily coloring their pictures at closing time as well, when someone called out, "Everyone is going home!" I looked in the adjoining room, and surely enough, everyone had gone. The children put their chairs up, picked up several papers on the floor, and left.

It had been very pleasant being with the younger children again. The secret seemed to be to keep them busy working as otherwise they did appear to be a talkative group. But there is something very special about first-graders; they really slip into one's heart. This had been a class of smiling, happy faces, and so Cosmopolitan that they reminded me of a joyous UNICEF Christmas Card.

304

Chapter 95

Identification Please

Arriving at Morris School at 8:05 I was assigned a third grade. For the first time I was asked for my Identification Card. The card gave my name, Social Security Number, and clearly indicated I was certified to teach Kindergarten-Primary classes. Observance of this, I felt, should certainly stop some schools from assigning teachers qualified to teach elementary grades to primary ones; and vice versa, as they had been doing. That had not been fair to the teacher, or to the children. I hoped the card-checking procedure would be followed daily.

The school was quite new, and the former old one had been demolished. The room I was in was neat and attractively decorated with charts, mostly pertaining to behavior habits in the room. A chart on the inside of the entrance door read, "1. We raise our hand and do not talk. 2. We respect others. 3. We are silent in the halls. 4. Our lines are straight. 5. We control ourselves." However, this must have impressed me more than the children. Much of my time was spent reminding them to be quiet during the day – inside the room, in the halls, even in their gym period.

The teacher's desk was neat and orderly. There was a fat folder consisting of completed homework papers, and another extra-fat one marked "For the Substitute"; this contained a Time Schedule for which I was grateful, plus an abundance of dittos for reading seatwork. A student teacher, who entered when I did, had told me she remained in the room all day, that there was "Walking Reading", and that I had a low reading class at that time.

A fast look into the Homework Folder indicated first and second grade levels of work, and leafing through the cumulative records cards revealed the room varied from first and second to third and fourth grade in abilities. There was only one blackboard (a brown one) so I wrote ten assignments, ranging from easy first grade to fourth. I was more comfortable using work with which I was familiar and felt confident the amount of work would keep all levels occupied.

The class was comparatively small, 20 being present, 1 absent. Most were Spanish, and constant talking seemed to be part of the classroom climate. No doubt this was due to the modern grouping of desks, but I did not take time to rearrange them. Time seemed to be at a premium all day. One child paid for his lunch; 19 received free tickets.

Walking Reading started at 9:10 and most of the class left. The board work was explained to the newcomers and oral reading was started. I took the lower group at Ginn Level 5 (1B) beginning First Grade. Seven were in this group; they were three-quarters through the Ginn primer book and their reading was sound; each had a number of turns and two long stories were read. Two children were next, also at Level 5, they were extremely slow and hesitant readers, about one-third into the book. Their foundation was very weak; they did not know all the sounds of the letters, and knew no blending skills; both were Spanish. All the children had paid attention and watched the reading places in their books. The two youngsters were seven years of age and seemed to learn quickly. When one continued to stumble on the work "then" I wrote a list of seven "th" words, then "wh" words, and after going over these but twice, then folding the paper to cover the beginning "th" and "wh", both children were able to read all the words quickly and correctly.

The student teacher took the other group of twelve, who read at Level 6 (1A, First Grade, second semester). They were fluent readers, at ease with the material, and could answer understanding questions.

After reading there were toilet visits, then outside recess.

For the next 45-minute period I was to take a science class in another room; that teacher came to teach a social studies lesson. A teacher aide brought a record player and filmstrip machine on a rolling stand, but the class in the other room said they had heard the filmstrip, so I used my own oral thinking material questions. This held their attention throughout the period because it was new to them, because of a contest between the girls and boys, and because all students enjoy challenging thinking questions. In fact, it was a tie when their teacher returned and they kept asking for more questions – but the tie continued, and I had to leave to take the other class to lunch.

Thirty minutes were delegated to lunch and toilet visits again, after which there was to be a math period. But as the other class had so enjoyed the Oral Thinking Contests, they were repeated again. This class also liked them but they were not as alert and fast to play as the other room, so the material was changed to a little lower level.

A gym period of 40 minutes was next and the majority changed to shorts and gym shoes. Four students did not have this equipment so sat apart from the class doing paper work. The student teacher, and I, remained to observe the gym exercises. It surprised me that they talked constantly, not seeming to pay respectful attention to the many instructions, and three or four times I finally reminded them to be Q U I E T. Each time the gym teacher thanked me; he also had repeatedly asked them to be silent. But each child seemed to enjoy the various exercises, even though some were not very adept at doing them at first.

When they entered they did running exercises about the entire gym until the teacher took the roll by observation. Next there was jumping; feet were together, then apart; hands were clapped above the heads. Then the feet remained together; arms were swung laterally. This was done fifty times while the teacher got out some mats for tumbling.

For the tumbling the children were to bend before the mat; roll over, keeping the knees close to the chest. Hands were to be kept out and up as they came up. As they bent they were to be on their toes and push!

Next, the tumbling exercise was preceded by running steps. They had several turns trying this; a few were relaxed and did it easily; several had extra turns and individual help each time, sometimes ending up performing satisfactorily.

The final tumbling exercise was a running, jumping-rolling, standing feat. A mat was rolled across the beginning of the practise mat. (This one worried me each time a child started to perform; it looked difficult and hazardous but I was completely inexperienced in gym work.) Many youngsters fumbled this one, which did not surprise me. It looked very hard to do, but no child seemed worried or concerned. They all wanted to go on and on with the gymnastics.

Returning to the room we passed a water fountain and after observing the gym exercises I understood why children always asked permission to get drinks of water after gym classes. Everyone got a drink and the girls went to the washroom to put on their regular clothes; the boys changed in the classroom.

The math period was next; oral dictated amounts were new to them and most needed this review. The time was short so I started with easy amounts to make it easier and progressed at an even keel to the more intricate ones.

There was time for the art dittos and it was immediately apparent everyone appreciated this. There was sudden complete silence until the papers were completed; they seemed starved for art work. It was nearing closing time and I did not have time to walk about observing their work so at times asked them to hold up their papers. It seemed everyone was doing top art work; I was so impressed, and surprised, that I asked for an explanation. They said they had had another teacher the first part of the school year who had taught them to appreciate and do good art work, as well as music, but he had been sent to another school. It was obvious he had taught them to outline first, to color completely, and deeply, and to do the work conscientiously. No one had hurried, or scribbled, or been careless. Many had not finished when it was closing time so they were told to complete the work the next day.

About ten minutes before closing the city test results of the previous year in reading and math were brought in; these were on one large sheet, and easy to absorb quickly. The top score was 5.3 (fifth grade, third month). One was at third grade; seven were in the second year range; six were in the first year scoring. Six had no scores listed. These results were comparative to the levels listed on the cumulative record cards I had seen.

The boy who had the top score of 5.3 sat at a desk beside the teacher. While he had caused me no trouble I told him his score showed he was smart enough to control his behavior and that anyone entering the room could see he was a problem because of his desk location. I suggested he concentrate on improving his behavior and said he might then be put in a higher grade if he turned in good seatwork. He seemed to accept this, and if he followed through it could be a blessing to both himself and future teachers.

As I signed out I told the Principal, who was standing nearby, that I had had an interesting class. She invited me to return the next day, but when I learned it was for a sixth grade I replied I was not at ease with any class above fourth as I had been trained, and was experienced, in teaching the primary levels – Kindergarten through third grades. On returning home I called Substitute Center to register for work the next day.

Chapter 96

Gerbil Book

Although I arrived at Alcott School at 8:05 no teacher had called in to advise the clerk there would be a vacancy, so I waited until 8:30 before calling Substitute Center to find out who would be absent. Finally I called and learned the name of the absent teacher, it was for a $2^{nd}/3^{rd}$ grade class.

Seatwork was on the board when the class entered. 36 were present; 1 was absent. One boy collected the lunch money and obtained the paid and free lunch tickets from the lunchroom. However, when he returned another boy suddenly realized he had not brought up his money, so both returned to the lunchroom.

On entering the room I had been surprised, and pleased, to find it was the one for which I had brought a gerbil book. Previously when I had taught in the school I had visited this class and had noted their interest in the class gerbil. I had promised to bring them a book about gerbils I had sent for which had been written by a 4th grade boy, and published. The day was started by reading the booklet, which everyone especially appreciated as it was so clearly at their age and interest level.

Reading classes were started. Seven were reading at Level 9 (3B) in a Ginn book. These were good readers. One girl was a little careless, missing two words. She said "sweeter" for "sweater" and "flowered" for "forward" but corrected the word when questioned.

Five read at Level 8 (2A). They were one-third into the book. It was deeply impressive to hear the improvement of a child from Ghana, Africa. A few months earlier when I had been in the room she had been unable to read the material; now she was completely at ease with both reading and speaking.

Seven were at Level 7 (2B). There were two very good oral readers here. I asked the others why; they reported these two did not do the required workbook assignments, but said one was now changing his habits and nearly caught up and the teacher was considering putting him in another group. Four in this group were very slow readers. One boy was unable to read the material. He missed most of the words; however, he seldom watched the book when others read. I suggested someone help him a little in the afternoon when their seatwork was finished. The girl sitting next to him suddenly became his "teacher-helper". She pointed out each word as he or others read. At first she did not wait for him to think and sound out the words when he read, but she quickly learned to do this so became his helper for the afternoon period. She requested easier seatwork, which was provided, and graded the work he did.

The class ate lunch in the school lunchroom. Returning to the room I noted a boy was passing out papers and asked what he was doing. He replied they were writing papers (cursive) and said they were supposed to do them daily "even if there was a substitute".

Suddenly loud bells rang for a fire drill. It was really wonderful to walk outside into such beautiful summer weather in the month of March!

Returning to the room the board seatwork was done orally and children were called up to do the math adding and subtracting as they were just learning to work with fractions. Several quickly became adept at this. Next, I dictated financial amounts to be written. This was a new experience to them and at first no one seemed able to write the correct amounts. But with their good background they soon learned to list the amounts by keeping them in a vertical row with the decimals directly beneath each other and again several were soon doing this correctly.

Art work was distributed which this class always enjoyed, and there were about five minutes left later for oral thinking contests.

They said they did not have homework assignments on weekends, and everyone left with happy faces when the final bell rang.

Chapter 97

Bare Room

At Andersen School I walked into the barest second grade room I had ever seen. Later I learned it had been vandalized nine times in the past six months, possibly because it was the last room at the end of the long building. The only items to be seen were desks, chairs, and an empty bookcase. Chalkboards covered two walls, cabinets another, and windows the fourth. Window ledges were completely bare, as were the windows – there were no shades at all. The room was bare, dismal, uninviting.

The children lined up in the corridor and were asked to hang their coats in the hall lockers there before entering the room. Once seated, those sitting in the bright sun were informed they might move to empty desks, which they did.

After the morning Pledge and Patriotic Song the class sang a cheery "Good Morning to You" song which was very pleasant; it brought smiles to everyone.

Two of the 29 listed children were absent. The pupils appeared to be primarily Spanish, then Blacks, and a few whites.

Seatwork on the boards was explained. The teacher had left good sample work to be copied on the multiple board space, but there was no chalk to be found; fortunately, I had brought a supply, and an entire stick was used writing the many assignments as no workbook was being used. The class had just completed a phonic book so relied completely on board assignments.

There were six reading groups and it was very difficult to make much headway in reading. Although in their second grade of school, the class was just starting to do first grade work; they were already two years behind in their academic education. One boy (8 years of age) read in a Harper Rowe book at Level 8. One little fellow tried to "read" in a Level 4 preprimer, but it was meaningless to him. He obviously relied on memory of the sentences he had heard read; few words were read correctly by him, and he seemed to have no knowledge of the sounds of any letters.

The majority of the class were at various pages in a Level 7 Harper Rowe book and were able to read at their designated places in the first year, first semester book. Most of this group knew the letter sounds but were not able to blend them, or to cut words into syllables to sound them out. They relied entirely on word sight reading, and waited to be told any new words.

The clock was not working and my watch had stopped the previous week. Late in the morning it was a welcome relief to have a pleasant young teacher aide appear and ask if I wanted to take a "five-minute" break. The "five minutes" surprised me as in other schools it was for ten or fifteen minutes, but I was grateful for the five. In fact, in other schools I seldom took the breaks; here I was already exhausted. The children had been constant talkers, up and out of their seats, talking with loud voices, never listening to instructions.

I hurried down a LONG corridor of two buildings and went down the stairs to a basement lunchroom for coffee. A break was never more welcome.

Lunch was at 11:20. One boy had paid 40 cents; all others received free lunches. They talked continually and very loudly and I kept trying to quiet them. (Two days later I realized this partly explained how the time disappeared daily; I was continually busy keeping them quiet.)

Everyone stopped for washroom visits on the way back to the room.

It was to be their recess time but there had not been time for two reading groups so they danced to a Polka Record and had room exercises, then returned to the reading groups. Others worked on the assigned seatwork.

There was NOTHING in the room for anyone to do when the work was finished. Not a single thing. No books. No games. Nothing.

At 1:30 an intercom message from the office invited us to hear an Assembly Program, so we quickly lined up and left. The program (given by a 4th grade) was delightful, music with lots of dancing and body movements that kept the primary-age audience interested. But to me time was of primary essence and not knowing in advance of this invitation, I was concerned because the day's seatwork had not been graded.

When we returned at 2:05 the children seemed overstimulated, restless and noisy. It was difficult to keep them in their seats as I walked about checking and grading the work. Then I heard a loud bell, but as there were three more sets of papers to grade I told the children to remain seated until I finished grading the work, then they could hurry and get ready when the last bell rang.

Suddenly a clerk appeared in the doorway, calling out that we were to LEAVE QUICKLY! She said that was the LAST BELL. I had been so occupied I had not heard a previous one. Everyone jumped up, put chairs up, picked up the papers on the floor, and left.

At 2:50 when I signed out I was told the class must put on their coats when the first bell rings and line up; they were to be ready to leave when the 2nd one was sounded.

I went home, collected 30 small children's books, six boxes of crayons, a stapler, scissors, and packed them to take the next day as I had said I would return.

Chapter 98

Lunch Disaster
Leave by First Bell

After signing in at Andersen at 8:00 for the second day for a Second Grade Class (doing first grade work) I filled both the front and back boards with work to be done as I knew they had no workbooks. Next, I checked the attendance records for their absence and tardy days and recorded these on the report cards.

When the children entered I changed the seats from groups to straight rows to stop the talking. Again, only two were absent, a different two.

The previous six reading groups were cut into four groups. One boy read alone at Level 8 in a Harper Rowe book; one child was at Level 4; the others were in two groups, both reading at Level 7 in different sections of the same Primer; one group was starting the book; the other was half finished reading it.

The board seatwork was explained and the children were told they could take a book, or a game (educational word cards) after three papers were completed.

The room was far more inviting with several good art pictures up on the walls of work they had done the previous day, plus the bright books and games on a table to be used. There was something special about these children; they made you feel they really needed you.

The three reading groups had finished before lunchtime at 11:20. In the lunchroom the class went in line to get lunch trays of food. I went to an adjoining room for coffee and fruit. When I returned I saw two rows of the classes were sitting together, facing each other at the long lunch tables. A few sat at another table. I decided to sit facing the few, knowing they were apt to cause problems.

The Principal came over and asked where my class was. I said they were in back of me, but I had decided to face the problem-children that I had lined up last. He told me to sit with the class and face the two rows, which, of course, I did. This soon prevented me from seeing what happened when one of the boys behind me put food on the head of another sitting by him. I was so disgusted when I saw all the food on the boy's head that I sent the other boy to the Principal, who was standing nearby. I felt if he didn't want me to watch them then *he* should have.

I had brought a small clock to help keep on schedule (the teacher had left a fine time outline.) But in the afternoon a teacher aide appeared saying it was their library time. This was on the schedule for the next day, but the teacher rechecked and said the time had been changed. I had wanted to distribute more art work to be done for the walls but let her read to them. However, when she later distributed art papers to be colored by numbered sections and the children started for the new crayons I had brought I said the crayons were for special wall pictures only. By the time she left there was not enough time to do any more art work for the walls.

I put the answers on the boards to the work there and again demonstrated how to do the math work of carrying in adding and borrowing in subtraction. Boards were then erased.

One little girl asked to go to the washroom. But I had to refuse. An intercom message at 1:00 had said no children were to have the keys and go unlock the washroom doors. I knew the child had to go. So did I. But I had been told in no uncertain terms the previous day to have the class OUT on time. Stopping to go and unlock the toilets and let children go then (all would quickly say they had to go when one went) would have made us late again. I was really sorry as I knew she had to go. As we were lining up others reported she "went" in the room. I answered sharply, "She couldn't help it! It's not her fault", and the class left. As she passed me when leaving for the outer door I told her how sorry I was. I felt I was about to have the same experience any minute.

After they left I quickly went to the washroom, returned, packed all my things (leaving 25 small books for them) and left. There had been no parking lot, no clocks, no library books, no blinds, no workbooks, no gym for first-graders, no movie period, no chalk, no break except the one for five minutes. The teachers even took the primary classes outside to recess and returned to teaching. Other schools had teacher aides relieve teachers who were on outside recess duty; otherwise, teachers took turns watching the rooms. This school seemed to be unaware of the Teacher Union Rules; it was like moving the clock back twenty years.

It had been an experience I did not want to repeat, so in signing out I told them I would not be back.

Chapter 99

9 Stars for Me

At Audubon I was assigned a 2nd grade, one in which most of the children read at 2nd grade level. It was a class of good, quiet children.

There were blackboards on two walls, so I erased some writing and covered the boards with assignments. (Later I learned the teacher had put up work to be done.) But I wrote smaller and had much more there; furthermore, I preferred to use my own work as I was familiar with it and could grade it more easily.

23 were present, 3 absent. Four paid the regular lunch price; three paid half price; nine had free tickets; 7 went home to eat.

The yearly City Reading and Math Testing of students was being finished in other rooms and several students left and returned for this several times during the day.

A number of students completed the seatwork assignments before lunch and were given individual sentence cards to be done.

The first reading group of seven students read in a Ginn Book at Level 6 (1A), first grade, second semester, and all were good, solid readers. The next group of eight read at Level 8 (2A), second grade, second semester, as did the last group of eight, who were in the same book but half way into the book. Both groups read with ease and understanding. The last group read after recess.

At recess I went outside with the children. My station on the playground was near a street where at times children ran outside the fence and played on the sidewalk. Two boys were in the street playing with a ball when I first arrived, so I remained standing at the open gate to watch throughout the period and was kept busy as many youngsters tried to slip through. Suddenly several children ran past me. I tried to stop them but they were followed by more and more. Looking up I saw that all the children on the playground were running toward me, out through the gate, and around the fence corner, into the front entrance to the school.

At 11:00 the seatwork papers were graded and starred. The teacher had left a very good time schedule which was very helpful. Art work was given out to be done as the papers were being checked.

At noon the children went home or to the lunchroom. I had noticed my sample art papers had been left in a school I had been in the previous day so I drove back and got them. There was barely enough time left to eat my lunch in the teachers' room when I returned as traffic had been very slow due to streets being repaired.

At 1:00 the class was to have a music period but the Assistant Principal felt he should wait until more students were present as many had again been called for the testing program. Those remaining enjoyed the Milton Bradley Contraction and Abbreviation Bingo Card Game. The boys were winning but at 2:00 in a class vote recess won over Bingo by one vote so I went outside with them again.

After recess the record player was still in the room so records were played and different art work was presented. This class had a number of good artists and it surprised me that the teacher did not have some of their art work on the bulletin boards.

The record player was returned to the office, papers picked up from the floor, and everyone was in line to leave when the closing bell rang. As the children left one little boy said, "I hope you have a nice day tomorrow," indicating he had enjoyed the day as much as I had.

This boy had received nine star symbols in the morning on his papers and I had heard him exclaim then, "My folks will think I'm getting smart. I never took this many stars home before." And he was smart too. He was the only child who had all his math problems done correctly. Obviously the class had recently learned to add and carry, but most stumbled on the last subtraction figures involving borrowing. They received stars anyway as most had but one or two wrong.

It had been a pleasure to work with such a well-behaved class, and their good academic progress would not have been possible without it.

Chapter 100

Crayon Game

Arriving early at Burley School I found a parking place in front of the school. But once inside I had to wait about twenty minutes as no teacher had called the clerk to say she would be absent.

The third grade room to which I was eventually assigned was unusually neat, cheerful and inviting in contrast to the very old building. The traditional fastened-down chairs contributed to the neatness in their orderliness. The plaster on the ceiling and back wall was cracking and pealing, probably from leaking, but the bright pictures on the bulletin boards, plus a huge mural of the Chicago outline on Lake Michigan, blended together to offer a most pleasant atmosphere. The old building even had an air circulating system that felt like it was air conditioned. The top of the teacher's desk was neat and orderly even though it held a good supply of books and manuals.

Although I was late getting to the room it was a late Wednesday when pupils came in at 9:15 so there was time for covering the two large blackboards with work to be done.

The teacher had left a good time schedule and work materials for the students to use, plus writing paper and construction paper for art, plus many emergency activities to be used.

Nineteen children were present, seven absent. Four paid the regular lunch fee; two paid half; thirteen received free tickets.

Eight students read at Level G (3B) in an American Publishing Company book; all were good readers. As we started the reading there was suddenly a loud BANG on the ceiling which the children did not seem to notice. They said the school gym was above them.

Seven children read at Level E (2B) in a book by the same publisher. These children were not too secure in their reading. One was far superior to the others and when questioned did not know why he was not with the advanced group. (He did turn in all the seatwork and was not a behavior problem that day, but there must have been an explanation.)

319

The class stopped for toilet visits then went to recess. I stopped in the school lunchroom but the counter and shelves were completely bare, so I got only coffee and then went outside with the children.

After recess the third reading group of three children read in a 1A Banks book. Sadly enough, the first story was too difficult for them, but they could read the following one, so it must have been the material. I looked closely at the two stories and the second did seem to have many easier words. I checked their knowledge of sounds of the letters and each child knew them. Later in the day I was able to have some dittos prepared for the class and gave these children copies of a list of blends to study, which I told them would improve their reading considerably. The three were conscientious, and very humble about their reading; two were Spanish; one was from India.

At noon I ate with a few teachers in the Teachers' Lounge and was surprised to hear them all say what a terrible room I was in. I explained inside the room the class had been fine, but they did have trouble remaining orderly outside of it, either in the halls or going down the stairs. One teacher said she had had a terrible time at recess because of them. I had not seen any teacher out there when I had gone outside, but the playground did cover a large area. I had even questioned some children about not seeing any teacher there; they explained that teachers came out when the bell rang for coming inside. However, I learned long ago not to rely on the words of children – they can be most unpredictable and unreliable.

After lunch another boy appeared; he explained he attended a different school in the morning. When I asked why he said he went to a class there to learn to discipline himself. I had him bring up his reader and saw at once he was far ahead of the others. It looked like a fifth grade book and he read it easily. He said the Principal planned to put him in another grade soon as he had now learned to control himself.

Seatwork papers were checked, and stamped with stars; then the Bradley Contraction and Abbreviation Bingo Game was started. The class was not too quiet in the afternoon and it was necessary to continually remind them about this.

Art papers were given out; all seemed starved for this area but only a handful had crayons. As the seats were fastened down I took the few packages of crayons from the teacher's desk to a long table in the back and put the only five moveable chairs there where five at a time could do art work. Others shared a few packages in a corner section and the rest borrowed from friends. Many of the students produced superior art pictures, as good as the samples I had first shown them, but one child told me the teacher "did not seem to care about their art". This surprised me as she did have such colorful bulletin boards. (She used magazine pictures and miscellaneous art objects.) Their work was so impressive I asked to keep a couple sheets and gave those children additional ones to remake later. The work was left for the teacher to see and I felt she must have been pleased with some of them.

The teacher had left two homework assignments which were put on the board; both were in books and I noticed that most students took their spelling and math books home as they left.

Once home, I realized I was completely exhausted and had to lie down and rest for an hour; I even fell asleep which was most unusual. Keeping the class quiet in the afternoon had been quite an ordeal; it had been necessary to continually remind them to remain seated and be quiet. At closing one little fellow had shown me a big pocketful of crayons he had picked from the floor of ones being thrown. He had formerly been reprimanded for being the instigator of this activity which had been reported twice and I thought it had been stopped. They really acted fast when I was not looking directly at them.

But the class had been quite a loveable group. I left a note to their teacher saying just that. The note was beside the pile of broken crayons that had been brought up as the bell was ringing!

Chapter 101

Wall Clock OK Just Three
Hours Slow

There had been no call from Substitute Center by 8:00 so I reasoned there would be none, as had occurred the previous day. At 8:15 I walked to a mailbox a block distant to mail some letters. Once home again, I changed to "at home" clothes and started to type a number of seatwork papers I had prepared.

At 8:45 the telephone rang, informing me I was being sent to Budlong School for a third grade class. I called the school, saying I would arrive as quickly as possible but would be a little late as had just received the call from Sub Center. I signed in at the school at 9:20.

It was a good school; a good class. Everyone was working quietly when I entered the room. A teacher was in the room; she had taken the roll; two students were absent. I glanced at the attendance book; only three pupils had moved in eight months. In many schools this number, and more, moved weekly.

The regular teacher had the class well organized and the students were following the usual procedure. They wrote their own personal "morning stories", followed by writing the spelling words ten times each. They explained the morning stories could be individual, pertaining to the weather, their thoughts, what they had done the previous day, or evening, etc. In her Plan Book for the week the teacher had noted a number of creative ideas, the first being, "Things that Make Me Happy", "Happy Thoughts, "Spring Thoughts", which I read aloud and a few wrote of these during the day.

The room clock was not working; but one smart boy in the room shared his discovery with me; he explained the clock was running, but was exactly three hours slow! This was a great help in knowing when to get ready for recess and lunch periods as my watch had recently stopped running.

I distributed a ditto fun page to do of finding three-letter words on a large wheel, while I wrote seatwork on the boards, as felt more work was necessary to keep them occupied during the reading periods.

This was the first third grade class I had been in that did not have dictionaries; usually there had been supplies for entire classes, as learning to use these books was part of the third grade curriculum.

I was especially glad I had brought the new seatwork and put that on the board. One assignment necessitated selecting one of three words to complete the sentences, each word containing four or five syllables. I did wonder if they could read such long words, but they read the words in the first sentence easily, and most papers were later done correctly. The other paper was one of deductive reasoning, and here again, the seatwork was done correctly.

There were four reading groups. The first group of nine students read in a Houghton Mifflin book; this was a third grade book, but it was surprising to me to learn that no child was aware of his reading level. I looked at the cumulative record cards, which indicated those in this group had been at Level "F" (2A) the previous year, so they were probably at Level "G" (3A) presently. Three were rapid readers; seven were slower; all were able to answer questions about the reading with understanding.

Nine students also read in the second group; they read a third grade book by the American Book Company. This group read more slowly, but more evenly, and also understood the material.

Five students were in a Ginn company 2B reader, which surprised me. With no discipline problems, I wondered why these children were behind in reading. One child was a good, fast reader; the others were quite slow.

Not a child whispered, moved about, or talked! Absolutely no discipline problems! This was like being in a different world! As quiet as in one's own living room. It was a pleasure to be in such a school – an oasis to remember when engaged in a room of constant turmoil. Here a teacher could really teach, without interruptions.

But no child in the room had a workbook of any kind and this was another surprise. So many reading skills to be covered. How could they all be presented properly without one, especially at third grade level, with 1½ year's variance in the reading levels?

At recess I was on duty on the playground with the children. It was a very large area with much space for playing. As with most schools, much equipment remained but in skeleton form. The swings had been removed, or tied together, the high, metal poles still held

323

climbing steps, but only two round rings remained to perform with. At distant points there were two slides, and one spot still had a flat, round merry-go-round.

Popular sports were ball throwing and running. Seeing a number of young boys piling up on top of one another I went in their direction. They said they were "playing" but I explained it did not look safe, and sure enough, within minutes one boy did not get up after another rough-and-tumble episode. After this the group dispersed. The little chap at the bottom had already had several stitches across his head (which another boy pointed out to me), but he insisted he "liked to fight", and enjoyed these encounters.

After recess and toilet visits the fourth group of but three boys read in a 2B Banks Company reader in which they were three-quarters finished. These boys had been asked to sit close to my desk early after my arrival because of their inattentiveness and inclinations to whispering and just sitting. Of those in the class, these were the most immature, still wanting to play, not yet ready to settle down. After reading but one story it was lunch time so I told them we could read again in the afternoon and try to get them closer to the end of the book, so they might finish it by the end of the week. This pleased them and each paid close attention during the readings.

Four students had lunch tickets to eat in school; the others went home. I had brought my lunch and ate with teachers in a basement room, after which I ran off ditto art work for the class to do in the afternoon.

After lunch the last group read several stories, leaving just enough so they could complete the book by the end of the week. They could read the material but were very weak in a number of reading skills. I suggested to one boy he really needed outside help to catch up and another child, living near him, offered to help him sometimes as the one in need had no one at home who spoke the language. The child did have a library card so I explained he could ask the librarian for a book at his reading level.

Many students in the room were unusually slow in completing their seatwork papers so those finishing were allowed to take art papers to color. It was wonderful to see that each pupil had his, or her, own crayons. This was a surprising change. In many rooms only two or three students have crayons, and sometimes the teacher's supplies are very meager. What a contrast in big city neighborhoods!

At one time one boy was softly whispering to another. I had him come up in front and sit on my lap, explaining if he acted like a baby, he would have to be treated as one. The class smirked a little, but continued quietly with their work. The boy felt foolish and soon said he could keep quiet and do his work, which he did.

An oral math period in which financial amounts were dictated, then written on the board, seemed to benefit everyone. At first no one seemed to have the correct amounts, but as they watched the correct figures appear on the board, they quickly caught on. I had told them several times to keep the amounts in an orderly, vertical column with the decimal points directly under each other as this would make it easier to write, and to understand the amounts.

Not enough time remained to use the Bradley Contraction and Abbreviation and Homonym cards, which I was sure all would have benefited from, so I opened my oral thinking folder. The period quickly became a contest between the boys and girls, which added to the fun, but thinking contests appeal to all grade levels. At first the group was slow in reacting with correct answers, but as time went on more and more children began to contribute answers until most in the class were able to answer before the end of the period. And the contest ended in a near-tie as well.

It had been a harmonious, relaxed, different, kind of teaching experience, and as the children left the room I wished them a happy evening. One boy returned the greeting "to you also", then stopped, saying, "But we're supposed to say that to you. I hope you have a nice evening." It was truly gratifying to have been with such a polite, wholesome group of students.

Chapter 102

Concert Class; Good Class;
Bicycle Rules

At Blaine School I was assigned a 5th grade class. I had remonstrated unsuccessfully to the grade level, saying I was a primary teacher. The Principal and the two clerks in the office tried to reassure me it was a very good class and I would have no trouble. They did not understand that this age level did not appeal to me.

The attendance book indicated 39 had been enrolled when school started in the Fall, but now, eight months later, eleven had left, indicating a transient neighborhood.

The teacher had written a time schedule on the board, with assignments for the entire day, which was the best I had ever seen. It was really practical as we used it and covered many subjects. Most schedules left by teachers leave far too much time for students to complete the assignments; this, however was a tight schedule and one we did not completely fulfill.

Everyone was present at 9:00. But half the class left for a Concert Class. I thought they would return at 10:00 or 11:00 but I did not see them again until 1:00. I inquired about the special class and learned there was a fee of $1.35 to enroll in it in the Fall. I think this covered their attendance at Concerts during the year. Some of the students played musical instruments in the class, but playing them was not a necessary requirement, as others joined simply for music appreciation, and further study.

The students did their work quietly, after one or two reminders that they were 5th graders, and followed the subjects, and book pages listed on the board. The class was working in a Scott, Foresman Skill Workbook, which their teacher told them was an 8th grade book. No level was designated on the book, but it certainly was one for upper grades. One pupil said the teacher did not have an answer book but figured out the answers herself, so I did also. (Later I found a Teacher's Manual.) She had put the work on the board so I felt I should grade it.

To me it was boring sitting waiting for them to complete the work, so at recess I was glad to leave and go to the lunchroom for coffee. It was a damp, cold day outside and the coffee was good and hot. On the steps I met the Principal, who asked me how the room was. I told him fine, but again said I was trained for primary teaching. This he did not accept. I explained an 8th grade teacher would not be at ease in a 1st grade room, and I was more comfortable in a primary room. However, anyone would have been fine in the class I was in that day. The Principal knew what a good class it was. Principals are usually aware of the abilities, attitudes and behavior habits of the classes in their schools. They have the job of assigning students to classes every year, as well as teachers to those classes.

After recess I graded the workbook seatwork, which had been done on writing papers, not in the workbooks. (Teachers have learned to save the workbooks to be re-used.) During this time a few questions were asked by students and each time talking erupted throughout the mobile; usually it died down, but one time, after a few minutes of continued loud talking, I politely requested them to be quiet two or three times. As the talking still continued, I said loudly and clearly, "I *insist!*" It became quiet immediately and remained so for a while.

Grading the math work took much more time and the papers piled up ahead of me. Later I learned the teacher simply marked the incorrect ones, whereas I had been writing the correct answers and encircling the incorrect digits in their answers.

All the assignments were long ones; the sentence-completion work had been of two assignments; the math covered two pages of work they turned in. (This teacher was really driving them, and I felt at least part of the good reputation here was due to her hard work. She left no time for sitting or talking.) Of course, a teacher also needs good material to work with. These students were nice; they were sweet, and all seemed to have the abilities necessary to do the work.

Finally the math papers were all corrected. Then I learned the procedure was that the students were to correct those marked wrong and turn them back in, so I was still busy for some time with the checking.

At 11:33 I mentioned it was time for the Oral Spelling that was listed on the board for 11:30. Several children said it was too late, as

327

others had already started writing their words. (The second part of the assignment was to write each word at least 25 times.) But I said we would do as the teacher had written. I then said the words, mixing them up, which they at first objected to, but I continued to mix them. The next step was for the students to take turns in spelling the words orally. The class enjoyed this.

Four students had paid the regular fee for lunch tickets; one had paid half the fee; these went to the school lunchroom; most of the students went home or had brought their lunches. I drove home to get two Bradley Bingo games for upper grades but later found we did not have time for them.

At 1:15 another teacher entered for a Guidance Period. The subject was about bicycles and she was a good (and a quiet) teacher. She spoke softly, but held their attention, and quickly noticed anyone not following the orders she gave. The teacher reviewed, and discussed bicycle rules for about five minutes; then she said, "Start." The students then wrote for several minutes. At 1:30 the teacher called, "Stop!" Children were then called on to act out what they had written; and the class guessed the bicycle rule being demonstrated. Everyone seemed to enjoy this. At times the teacher walked about, stopped and wrote on a paper. Later I heard her say as she stopped again, "If I see pencil writing you will be disqualified," so that was most likely what was happening. If students had written fourteen or more rules she read their papers orally.

Next she read certain rules, asking them to think of their own bikes and wonder if their bicycles could pass the test rules she read. Last, she talked of the first bicycles invented and showed book pictures, later discussing the differences between the first and the modern bicycles.

When the teacher left the students took their English books from their desks. I read the explanatory pages for the lessons to be done and then the students wrote the required sentences in the two exercises. One subject was on using quotation marks; the other was using the exclamation mark. A total of 25 sentences were to be done from the two chapters. When I commented it was quite a lot the class said they usually had 35 sentences to do.

About fifteen or twenty minutes before lunch some students had completed their work and had been given sheets of ditto art work, so now when they finished they worked on this. The students who had been in the Concert Class in the morning soon noticed this and asked for copies to do also. The teacher had listed a period for Science, but I let them all have copies of the art pages. It was interesting to see them work so conscientiously in this field. I had shown them good samples I had collected from other classes and they were apparently determined to outdo any pictures I had. And they almost did that, but another sixth grader had given me my favorite, a Luna Moth, a few weeks before. Nearly everyone had their own art colors to use, either very large boxes of crayons, brightly colored art pencils, or colored brush pens. And they did their work diligently and beautifully. They had worked so hard all day that when they gave me a paper I asked if they wanted another one, letting them select a new subject if they so desired. Most of them took another paper to do.

It had been a different kind of day – satisfactory and different – but I still preferred to be with a primary class. To me, teaching primary children is a very satisfying experience.

Chapter 103

Taffy Apple Day
One Bad Apple Present

At 8:10 when I signed in at Hawthorne School I noticed another substitute had signed in ahead of me – for the first time in months; she had signed in at 8:10 also. I stopped and ran off a supply of art ditto work before going to the room.

I thought it was a good class I had had before so filled the boards with two levels of work as the grades were second and third. I was glad I had made up new seatwork on the past weekend and had lots of good, new material.

At 9:00 the students came in, a little noisily. First, the lunch money was taken. Two paid full price; three had half-rate prices. Five received free lunches; the others went home. It was Taffy Apple Day and five students lined up with money to pay for their apples, the individual amounts varying with the number of apples ordered from one to five. There was a total of ten apples ordered and $2.50 collected. I had listed the names of the students, with the number of apples ordered, and the amount of money paid.

In a few minutes a girl entered with a large box containing taffy apples. She said, "I am supposed to take the money and go." The teacher had left a large envelope on the desk, the outside saying, "Taffy Apple Money". We opened the envelope and found 50 cents. I laughed and handed her the money, reaching for the box of apples. But she took the box and left. A man returned and figured out the lists of the regular teacher and the one I made. Then he left the box of apples. I checked the number against the list I had and it balanced so everyone was happy.

The class told me they had a gym period at 9:00. I looked on the time schedule on the board and saw it was listed for 9:10. Next I asked who received milk and had those children line up; there were 14 and it was gym time so did not write down the names. (Later another boy said he, too, received milk, so I passed out small paper cups, and three other boys sat by him, sharing and smiling. It looked like they were having a party.) Next two students were sent for the

330

milk. I had learned that in this school the milk had to be obtained early, before recess, or it was not sent. As expected, the pupils said to send for it after recess, but I had learned not to wait.

The class was taken to the gym, but I returned to make sure the two students returned with the milk. They had, and it was in the room. While the children had gym I ran off a few more ditto sheets to be used. (I had learned to carry my own white paper for this purpose.) I wanted to watch their gym period exercises but the time disappeared too quickly. Before running off the dittos I had stepped in the gym and asked one boy to stop for me when the period was over and he did so just as I was finishing the work.

We stopped for everyone to get drinks, then returned to the room. A teacher aide stopped in and I had her take the fast reading group for reading; I took the second group. The top group (I later had them read for me also) of eight were in a 2A Ginn book. They had had workbooks, which were up-to-date with the oral reading stories, but there were no rapid readers; all read slowly and one child had several errors.

The second reading group, also of eight children, were in a 2B Ginn book. Many here read with expression; all but two were fast readers; one boy missed but two words. This group seemed to be on a sound, secure footing. They, too, were up-to-date with the workbook.

The third group read in a 1A Ginn book and were nearly finished with the book, which greatly inspired them. They read the book well and had finished their workbook.

Six heavy assignments were on the two boards; some students completed all the work during the morning; a few boys just sat out the time.

During the lunch hour I graded the work that was left on the desk-tops and after lunch it was decided those who had finished would start the art work. To receive an art paper it was necessary to complete three of the assignments. This activated a few sitters to start doing some work, especially when sample art pages were shown.

Only four students (those who had finished the work) had their own crayons. I learned there was a supply for the room and found quite a number of unboxed crayons in a drawer. These were put on a tray that had been covered with a large piece of paper. Then two children sorted the crayons, putting five assorted colors into paper cups on paper plates.

The class voted to play the Homonym Bingo Game so the time was divided between this and the art work. For a change, the girls won far ahead of the boys, although they were even in number.

The last 25 minutes were given to the art work. Each child chose a sheet and took crayons. There were a few very good papers. It was sweet to see several brought to the desk that said, "To my teacher, Miss _____" (the regular teacher).

The boards were erased, chairs put on desk tops, papers picked up, and as they lined up several students asked if I would return the next day. Just then the clerk called over the inter-com and asked if I would return the next day. I asked what grade it would be for and when told a third-fourth grade I agreed to return.

Once home, however, I found I was completely exhausted. The class had several unruly children who caused continual disturbances throughout the morning. One boy was particularly troublesome, and one of the worst behavior problems I had ever encountered in my entire teaching career. He made a continual nuisance of himself almost every minute. His mother was a teacher aide in the school, and a very likeable person, of whom I was very fond. I had seen her talking to him in the room that morning and learned then that he was her son. Three different times during the morning I referred him to her and she took him at times for short periods, but his trying attitude and impossible behavior had continued.

Shortly before the lunch hour when he was again acting up just before, and during, a reading session, I jotted down some of his actions to show his mother. He had bitten into a girl's Taffy Apple, raised his foot and put it against the back of a girl's blouse in reading, torn up a child's seatwork paper, talked without stopping several times; walked about the room; in reading his book had not even been open for some time (later he read rapidly and well); when I called him three times to get his lunch ticket he did not come, but remained at his seat; when I asked the free lunchers to stand for tickets he stood too (he had paid for his lunch). The list could go on and on; this covered but one ten-minute period.

At noon I walked toward his mother who was sitting on a chair near an entrance, but she appeared so upset when seeing the list she waved it away, saying she did not want to see the paper then, and as she was obviously expecting another child quite soon, I did not want to bother her further about him. But somehow, she did affect a change in the boy. In the afternoon he tried to behave and did so. Two other substitutes in the school had come to me and told me the mother did not accept misconduct reports about her son; they said she did not believe them, and refused to face reality. The mother and I had always been good friends and I was sorry about the experience with the boy, and was relieved she had changed his attitude at noon.

Once home I had to rest for two hours before fixing dinner, and remained worn out all evening. Had I realized this at the school I would not have agreed to work the following day. I was up until midnight getting seatwork ready for the higher grades as had not typed up such material the previous week.

Chapter 104

Noisy Class

Because Substitute Center called late, after 8:00 plus the traffic being unusually slow, and my not knowing the best directions to take, I did not arrive at Beidler School until 9:00.

The grade assignment was for a Kindergarten Class and when I entered the room the children were seated in chairs, arranged in a double semi-circle.

Twenty-four pupils were present, four being absent; there were seven girls and seventeen boys in the class, but the constant, unrestrained, loud talking made it sound like a hundred were present. They seemed utterly oblivious to any instructions given and unimpressed with warnings, to I had to isolate a few to make even a slight impression on the group; even this lasted but a few minutes. A teacher aide was present, who told me (when asked) that the regular teacher was "not very good in managing the children".

The teacher aide got paper, pencils and crayons to be used while I took the roll.

I demonstrated the proper way to hold a pencil and how to copy the letters and words on the board, starting at the top and moving in a forward motion – not writing from the bottom up and backwards, as one or two usually start out in Kindergarten.

Eventually two writing papers and a math paper were finished and all were starred with bunnies, pumpkins and Santa star symbols.

The next project was to draw, and color, a butterfly. Usually I made the outlines in the early morning but had arrived here too late so I slowly showed them how to make a round head first, next two antenna, then a long body, and finally the two wings. It was fun to watch their individual progress, and interpretation, in this endeavor.

The art work captured their attention and interest and each child was busy. Many pictures resembled beetles, or insects from Mars, but art is individual and beauty in the eye of the beholder; each little artist here was very proud of the work being done. There were one or two outstanding artists, who were asked to hold up their papers to the class, but this only caused many others to quickly come up to show theirs also.

Several asked to go to the washroom so we lined up. The toilets were nearby so I let the boys enter in a group, but immediately the noise became so powerful that I went in with them and waited a couple seconds until it quieted down. The girls went to another room and everyone got a drink and returned to the room.

The children's Polka Record was played; this had special exercises designated to be followed, and is a favorite with youngsters, so it was not surprising to hear requests to have it replayed. Next, the "Three Little Kittens" was acted out by everyone; then each three "kittens" had a "mother kitten" and the record was played again.

There were ten minutes left so Oral Thinking Games were read. They were good at this until we came to one game naming opposites. This concept was unknown to them. After several samples, with repetitions, a few children were beginning to answer "hot" when "cold" was given and "over" for "under", but the time was up for the morning and the regular game could not be introduced.

I went to the lunchroom with them and ate my lunch there. I noticed two children from other rooms toss out their lunch food, but the kindergarteners ate it with relish, as did I. The menu was ravioli and I ordered it instead of eating my regular lunch.

The afternoon group was much more mature, and quiet, than the morning class, and it was easier to work with them.

Three seatwork papers were finished before another teacher came in, explaining she was the librarian. She read them a story and had them recite poems she had taught them.

When she left the art work was done, followed by the Oral Thinking Games in which these youngsters were very alert and quickly responded in learning to give the names of opposites so more advanced games could be played.

As I left the clerk asked if I'd like to return the next day, but when I learned it would be for the same Kindergarten Class I said the morning class was too noisy and undisciplined, so I called Substitute Center to register for another school.

Chapter 105

Slowest Class Ever

Avondale School was located in an area surrounded with small homes and trees, so I expected orderly, quiet students. When I signed in at 8:20 I was pleased to be assigned to a 3rd grade class as I had recently made new seatwork for that level and had been looking forward to using it.

I was to work in a mobile classroom and my intuition strongly warned me the children could not do regular third grade work so I searched about the room for work done by the students. None was on the bulletin boards, but I finally found some ditto sheets crammed into small desks and was astonished to see it was work with beginning sounds, indicating first grade work.

On the boards I put easy 2B seatwork and was ready for them when the bell rang at 9:00. Although I stood smiling as they entered it was surprising to note their quick acceptance of me. Usually several students react with dismay to the appearance of a substitute teacher, but these youngsters seemed happy and remained smiling.

24 were present, 2 absent. It was a noisy class and a difficult one to keep quiet. In taking the roll I explained to them that legal cases could be greatly influenced by school attendance book records, even 20 years in the future, and this helped maintain quietness during the roll taking.

The board work was explained and papers were passed out by two girls, who apparently had that job assignment. Only one boy needed a pencil.

Ten students said they received free lunch tickets so I had them write their names on a list; the others went home or brought lunches as this school had a free lunch hour and closed at 3:15. Later in the morning lunch tickets were brought to the mobile, the number needed having been reported by the two boys in the room, and one of the girls present distributed them as this was her regular assignment. It was a good feeling to be relieved of the usual lunch collecting and recording duties – non-teaching responsibilities which sometimes became confusing and time-consuming.

The top group was called to read first, and I was really amazed. Their reading book was a first grade book in which they were only to page 35. Ten were in this group; they could read the words but were weak on "wh" words and also with contractions.

Eleven read in a third Preprimer and only two of these had workbooks; they explained the others did not bring money to pay for them. The two were up-to-date with the workbooks according to the stories in the book and the group was nearly finished with the booklet, having but six more stories to read. However there was another Preprimer to be read before starting the first grade reader and but six weeks remained in the school year.

Four children read in a second Preprimer, and although they were half way into this their reading was very weak; these were Spanish children.

During my lunch hour I checked through the cumulative record cards. Only one child was listed at Level D (1A) reading in February of the same year, and interestingly enough she was the one that had already attended seven schools! Later in the day I spoke to her, asking if her father's job necessitated the frequent moving. She said it was because of the actions of her two older brothers. There were eight children, she explained, and her mother was busy with the two little ones and unable to keep track of the older boys. The mother had been married twice and the second man had left the family, but he did bring them money. The information saddened me and I was sorry I had mentioned the moving, but such insights do bring understanding. Teachers are used to broken homes, working mothers, children with keys hung about their necks. I had seen two such enter the mobile.

The record cards, and the attendance book, revealed there had been many changes in this class during the mid-year of the school. In February those achieving above 1B level had been moved on, and the entire class had become one which read at beginning first grade level. Even their math levels were low; only seven of the group had above "B" level, which surprised me. Often children with low reading levels score much higher in arithmetic.

Their noisiness, mentioned earlier, was constant. It explained, to some extent, the low achievement levels, as no teacher can do much teaching under such circumstances. Their greatest difficulties seemed to be immaturity; they still wanted to play and laugh and talk. Half of the class were Spanish and learning a new language was an extra problem for them. It was the end of the school year; next Fall they would be in fourth grade and be starting first grade work – three years behind in school.

At noon I ate my lunch in the teachers' lounge and asked if I had an unusually slow class. About five teachers were there, having classes ranging from 2nd to 8th. They seemed to be in agreement that classes in this school were quite slow ones. One teacher volunteered that she had had a class once recently that was at regular grade level; her eyes sparkled with remembrance at the fine things she could accomplish with them in 8th grade.

During the morning recess period I had added some easy 1B work on a standing, movable board, and at noon I erased more board work and replaced it with easier seatwork.

At noon I walked to a nearby grocery store and bought a box of cookies. It had been some time since I had brought treats and it was a nice feeling to be doing it again.

In the afternoon the slower groups read again; then it was library time so we walked to the regular building and up to the third floor. I waited as they selected books they wanted to take out as I wanted to search for two books myself. Fortunately two students chose the two books I wanted to see so this worked out well for all of us. I was happy to see the books, and they were doubly pleased with their books when I pointed out they had taken very special ones.

The last period was spent doing art and most of the children had their own crayons. After sample pictures were shown they did very good work, and it was put up on a blank wall of the mobile where they said a mural painting they had done had been.

The telephone in the mobile rang; the clerk asked if I would like to return the next day. But two days of noisy classes had worn me out and I told her I had other plans.

Returning to the teacher's desk I sat down and looked at the brightly colored pictures across the wall; they seemed to brighten the entire room and my spirits as well. I hoped the teacher would feel the same way about them.

I hoped that during the summer the students would grow into maturity and settle down by Fall so they could start to make regular progress in school. This is possible with older students; I have seen it happen.

Chapter 106

New School
Lost Coat

As I drove past Greeley School it seemed a little too quiet, I wondered why no one – not a thing was moving around the neighborhood. Something was different. I parked across from the entrance and walked to the door. A sign said, "Go to the new school, 822 Sheridan Road". I felt foolish. I should have remembered the school might have moved by this time. This spot was eerie now. Ghostlike.

A teacher ahead of me got the last parking space on the new school lot so I parked on a street nearby. I didn't mind as at least I was within the proximity of people.

Inside the school I was assigned to a third grade room. The clerk said the school had been open about a month; she handed me a new set of keys, pointing out a small "elevator key" I might want "to take advantage of". How thoughtful of someone to offer this surprising convenience for school personnel, I thought, as I placed my heavy briefcase and leather bag inside the elevator and rode to the top floor.

After hanging up my coat I looked about for seatwork to see what the students could do, but none was on the two new bulletin boards which displayed welcome signs, so I looked at the cumulative record cards. The cards indicated the students had been at first and second grade levels in February, a few months earlier, so I covered the front, and only, board with those two levels of work.

As I was nearly finished with this a mother, and child, entered the room. Learning the boy had not found his coat the previous day I suggested the mother wait a couple minutes until the children came in. Past experience had taught me that usually someone recalls what had happened in such situations.

The class entered noisily and happily. It took five minutes to get them quiet enough to ask about the boy's coat. Several children offered their personal remembrances. "It was on the floor"; "Joey was kicking it around"; "The twins had it at closing time". The two twin brothers arrived late, but insisted they had been fooling when they pretended to be taking it.

Finally another student raised his hand. He said the boy had taken his jacket (not coat) to a reading class on the first floor and had hung it up, adding it was still there. The mother and boy went to that room, later returning with the jacket.

After the roll was taken (28 present, 3 absent), the class said they had gym from 9:00 until 9:40. There was no time schedule to be found and it was already 9:30 so the girls who had gym clothing quickly changed in the coat section, which was a partially separated division, while the boys changed in the classroom.

In the corridor the noise continued so I frequently stopped moving toward the stairs and reminded them it was their gym time they were wasting. I refused to escort a noisy class through the school halls or down the steps.

When we finally arrived at the gym the teacher had left, probably assuming the class would not appear that late, but he came in very soon. I told him they were late because they were so noisy; he reminded them they had been noisy in the gym class the previous week.

The gym teacher explained new procedures for entering and leaving the gym and presented a ten-point grading system (including wearing proper gym attire), to be started the following week.

Then, as no class was programmed to follow their period, which was over, he let them remain longer for racing games. The group was divided into four squads, each having two relay runners, who were posted at quarter and half-way points on their racing courses, to whom wooden sticks were to be handed and carried forward by the new runners. It was fun to watch and quickly evident that the Squad closest to me had not listened for proper instructions. Although fast runners, they were constantly forgetting to hand over the stick to the team runner, so no scores were made, but everyone seemed to enjoy the activity anyway.

After the gym period we stopped for the milk order and gave the attendant the number of students to eat lunch that day. The class returned up the three flights, stopped for washroom visits and drinks, and again changed their clothes inside the room.

A teacher of a bilingual class stopped to take five children for a Spanish class. I told her one of them had been quite disruptive and she reprimanded him in Spanish so severely that he started to cry. This so impressed me I told her I better learn Spanish. The children had reported to me this boy had been swearing at me in Spanish, but as long as I did not understand him it did not bother me. (I even thought it was funny.) The bilingual teacher told me the regular teacher had been absent the previous day also, and said the class had been uncontrolled and boisterous all day.

The board work was explained again but there were continual questions about it as few bothered to listen. Hands were up continually. When, at long last, it became quiet I looked up at the clock; it was 10:40.

Another hand was raised. "Teacher, where do you get the answers to those?" The child had pointed to the easiest 1B work on the board, which had been read, and explained, three times. "In your head!" I answered, pointing to his head.

I finished putting up the last 2A seatwork on the board, but soon two girls had finished all of it, and correctly. I then saw another small, movable board and filled it with 3A work that required deeper thinking. A few students took this board in stride and finished it after lunch.

Not finding a time schedule, I had sent a child to the office earlier to learn the lunch time, which was 11:55. At 11:50 the children told me it was lunch time, but I assured them the office had informed me it was 11:55.

At 11:55 we walked down the stairs to the lunchroom. It was cozy, like a restaurant, with booths, tables and dividers. As the attendant came by I commented how nice it was there. All the children were seated and eating quietly. She smiled, looked around, and said, "Yesterday they were all over the place!"

I soon learned the class had been right. In but ten minutes another attendant said our time was up. Evidently the 11:55 meant eating time, not starting out time. The menu had been fried chicken, spinach, gingerbread and milk – not a lunch eaten quickly, but we had to leave. As I stood to leave I saw one little fellow trying to push a good-sized portion of gingerbread into his little mouth. I was surprised that a new school provided such a tiny lunchroom; there was room for only four classes inside at one time.

Back upstairs oral reading groups were started. One handsome, arrogant black boy, who had been causing trouble all morning, started acting up again. I marched him out of the room in a huff. I had talked to him in the hall that morning as saw the home key hanging around his neck and felt he needed special attention, but talking had been useless, as he had continued to be up and out of his seat all day, shrugging his shoulders each time I admonished him. A black teacher was going by in the hall with a class, and when I explained he had been told to behave 20 times she took him with her to her room. At closing time she sent another child for his coat.

Within ten minutes the office called over the intercom, asking if another boy was present. (This boy had been the worst offender in the room since entering that morning.) The office asked if he had brought his father, or a note signed from his father, and when learning he had done neither, informed me he should not have been in the room, so he was told to take his coat and go to the office. This took care of the two worst offenders, but there were many eager to take their places.

There were three distinct reading levels in the room, but the abilities of the children surprised me as they did far better than I had expected. Twelve students were in the top group, reading a Harcourt Brace Level 8 book, at Level G (3A), and each child was a solid, confident reader. They had barely started this book and were to page 26. Each one had two turns, and each paid attention to the oral reading; each knew the place when called to read. They had workbooks that were up-to-date, but the current pages did not relate to the stories read so I had them continue with the board assignments.

The next group of eight were at Level E (2B) in a book by the same publisher. They could read, but were slow and hesitant, and did not understand what they read very well. Most were Spanish. They were nearly finished with the book.

The third group of eight were at Level D (1A) and many here were noise-makers, which was to be expected. They were starting the book that day. All of these were Spanish students. Some were inattentive, not yet ready for serious school progress.

Soon after the reading one small Spanish boy left his seat and came to talk to someone near my desk. He, too, had been a noisy, flippant child throughout the day. Turning about, I picked him up and plopped him into a tall metal wastebasket, which covered him nearly to his shoulders. I was surprised he remained there, but as he stayed quiet it seemed a good spot. When two janitors entered and looked at the wastebasket and its content, I told them to empty the basket, that we didn't need him in the room. They came to fix a pencil sharpener, which someone else had already fixed.

It was surprising to have one of the two best readers in the room be a continual problem. One was a girl, a good, and clever thinker, who did her best to outmaneuver me all day. I overlooked much of her misbehavior because of her seatwork ability but finally asked her to write an essay on Classroom Behavior. She sat a long time, then handed me a paper on which she had repeated those two words in two long columns. I explained it was not an essay and asked her to think, then to write four ways to behave in a school room. Later she handed me a second paper on which she had written three columns of "I will be Have". I gave up and accepted the paper without comment.

I had wanted to have Bingo Contraction, Abbreviation and Homonym contest games, but it was already 1:45. I had laughed when the class said it was recess time at 1:30 but now I felt they should have a pleasant period, so a vote was taken between art or bingo and the art work won.

Samples were shown and children lined up to receive papers. They were given choices of two ditto sheets. The Spanish bilingual teacher had loaned us sixteen boxes of crayons to use so these were distributed as none were found in the room and only three students had their own. The work they did was colorful and impressive. At closing time the crayons were collected and sent to the teacher on the first floor, but as the class was leaving the two small students returned, out of breath, with the crayons, saying the bilingual teacher had left and her door was locked.

The art work and crayons, with an explanatory note, were left on the teacher's desk. I visioned many in the class clamoring to return the crayons the next day. However, as I passed the room the following day I noted all were seated and quiet; their regular teacher had them well in hand.

Chapter 107

Audio Reading Machine a Hit

It was surprising to be called by Substitute Center at 7:00 as the calls had been coming at 7:40, 8:00, or later. The call was for Hamilton School and parking was a surprising problem because the street-cleaners had blocked off half of the area. After driving around the large block three times I signed in and asked if I could park in back of the building; eventually quite a number of teachers parked there also.

The day's assignment was for a third-fourth grade class, which proved to be a quiet one, with abilities to do work at their grade levels.

Only three of the twenty-nine students were absent. Seven paid the regular price for lunch tickets; nine received free ones; the others brought lunches or went home as the school had Open Campus, with an hour off at noon, closing at 3:15.

Walking Reading classes started at 9:10, when all but two pupils in the room left and students reading at Level "E" (2B) entered. The regular teacher had left instructions that this level would come to the room so I had work on the board for them to do. There were twenty students so I took ten at a time in the Harcourt Brace book they all used. Only one student was a poor reader; he was a very tall boy, a constant talker, inattentive, and unable to read many first grade words, being especially weak on "th" and "wh" words.

After the two groups had read I listed the "th" and "wh" words on the board, and had the students read them; next I erased all the "th" and "wh" letters and again the students read the words. This is a special help for first graders to learn such words, and I watched this boy as the exercise was done. It had been put on the board especially for him, but he paid no attention at all, but continued writing a seatwork paper. He was a 12-year old boy, unable to do first grade work. He still wanted to laugh, play, and talk instead.

At 10:10 the regular class returned to the room; they worked on the board assignments until recess time at 10:30, at which time they lined up and went quietly down the steps. I had overlooked bringing my lunch so went to the lunchroom and learned I could order one there, which I did.

After recess the class had a library period; as I waited to return with them I noted they were enjoying an audio-visual filmstrip about a whale.

The class stopped for washroom visits on the return to the room; lunch tickets were distributed, and everyone left for lunch.

After the noon hour the students completed math work I had put on the board. I graded work-papers of the morning that had been finished.

There were two children in the room, both Spanish, who were unable to do third and fourth grade work so I gave them first-grade work cards to copy and correct; this they were able to do. In the afternoon they took turns listening to records on a Borg Warner No. 90 Audio Unit machine. The machine supplied earphones, reading and math records, and visual picture frames with reading. The two students understood how to operate the machine and enjoyed using it. Once seated before it, they were to press the correct button relating to the picture and reading sentence being shown; if this was done correctly a new picture and relative reading material appeared, but if not, the same material remained on the screen. The pictures were in color. I watched for a while, and the children had learned to press the correct button about 85% of the time. The machine was a real treasure and several students soon stood watching it being used, but after a few minutes of viewing they were asked to sit down. The unit was far too expensive to be tampered with.

As papers were turned in the students selected art papers to color, and as some had many colored art pens and pencils to work with, some very good work was turned in.

Afternoon recess period came during this time but the class voted to remain in the room and complete the art work and then to have Homonym Bingo Games. They were very good at learning to operate the cards and there was a close game contest between the boys and the girls. The boys won by one point but there were about ten minutes left so Oral Thinking Games were presented in which the girls won by one point.

This had been a good class; they seemed to enjoy completing the seatwork as well as participating in art and game activities, so it had been pleasant to work with them.

Chapter 108

Lots of Materials
Popsicle

Finding Lincoln School was a problem because of the little one-way streets, but there was a parking spot across from the school which balanced the time I had spent looking for the location, and I signed in at 8:30 for a third grade.

No class work was displayed on the bulletin boards so I searched for the cumulative record cards; these indicated many in the room had been at 2B level when the year started in September. I put 3B work on two bulletin boards requiring thinking for completion answers.

The students entered at 9:00; they seemed quiet and looked capable of doing the work. Children in three rows said they were at third grade; two were at second, but they read some of the work to me so I felt they too could do it. Only two of the 30 students were absent. Three paid the regular lunch fee; eight said they had paid for the week on Monday; one received a free lunch ticket; others brought lunches or went home to eat as this school had Open Campus, offering a lunch hour and closing at 3:15.

Walking Reading Classes started at 9:15 and all but four in the class left. Seventeen of the newcomers read in the first reading group in a Houghton-Mifflin book, named "Fiesta". All were good readers. A play was read in which role parts were assigned; the pupils were alert to read without being reminded, as usually happens in play reading. The "parts" were changed after half the students had turns, and this was repeated twice, everyone having two turns.

Twelve students were in the second reading group. They read in a Ginn Level 10 (3A) book. There were two weak readers in this group, one boy and one girl. The girl paid little attention when the others read. Again, each child had two reading turns.

Following the oral reading I graded the seatwork papers but there were too many to complete before the period ended so the papers were returned, and the class read the work on the board. Only one child had 100.

From 10:45 until 11:15 there was a half hour work period. Three students were brought in from a second grade as their teacher was absent. The Principal had been their teacher during part of the morning, but now another teacher was dividing a group of students from that room. She explained they were not to come to me in the afternoon. The work was explained to them, and I continued to grade completed seatwork papers.

At noon I ate my lunch in the room, graded papers, and put up more work to be done. The room had neat, cheerful two-foot curtains covering two-fifths of the high windows. The opposite wall of the room had supply cabinets. The upper four-cabinet doors were covered with long strips of Manila paper on which were colorful flowers made by the children. Under each flower was a child's name. The board headings said, "We Are Good Spellers." This was one of the most attractive room bulletin boards I had ever seen.

Another front bulletin board near the entrance displayed magazine and postcard pictures of New York City.

A table in the back of the room contained a bonanza of interesting items for students to use – a globe, memory games, metric flash cards, math multiplication cubes, four miscellaneous math games, fish, birds, states and planet cards, etc.

A bookstand nearby had two shelves of books and two of boxes of games, puzzles, chess, checkers, jig saw, Chinese Checkers, two boxes of play money, etc. There were more interesting activities in this room than I had ever seen! There seemed to be enough for three or four rooms.

The noon hour was drawing to a close. There was barely enough time to put another seatwork assignment on the board.

At 1:00 the class returned to the room. Among them was one boy holding a Popsicle in his hand.

Boy: "Teacher, what should I do with this?"
Teacher: "Why are you bringing it in here?"
Boy: "May I take it to the lunch room?"
Teacher: "They will be closed."

I became busy with the many other students who were entering and presenting questions. Afternoon roll was taken and the class changed again for Walking Math. At 1:30 another boy was sitting at the desk of the boy who had had the popsickle. The new child said,

"Teacher, something smells here." I looked by his desk where the students were pointing.

Obviously the former student had left the popsickle in his desk and it was melting and dripping through the desk onto the floor. The children could find no paper towels, or Kleenex tissues, in the room, so I took some from my purse and cleaned the floor. More was dripping from the desk, so I pulled the desk aside and dumped the contents onto the floor. It looked like an accumulation of quite some time. A child was sent to the boy's washroom for more paper towels to clean the desk but returned saying there were none there, so a girl got some from the girl's washroom.

When the boy returned who had brought in the popsickle I questioned him further. He explained he had bought it from a street vendor by the school.

Teacher: "Why didn't you eat it outside?"
Boy: "The bell rang."
Teacher: "Why didn't you eat it outside?"
Boy: "I would be locked out."
Teacher: "You mean they lock the door?"
Boy: "Yes."
Teacher: "You can ring the bell."
Boy: "I can't reach it."

It seemed from the children's conversation that the regular teacher permitted them to go to the lunchroom to eat such food, but I had not understood this. I had thought he wanted his Popsicle kept for him in their freezer. He appeared upset from the experience for some time – until we started the art and bingo activities.

At 2:20 a student stepped inside the room, saying, "Bus!", whereupon one boy got his coat and left. The others explained this was the regular procedure for students who used the bus.

In the morning when I passed a neighboring room I had noticed several dioramas stacked, Pueblo fashion, on top of a piano, and at recess I went inside to examine them more closely. One of them really fascinated me and I borrowed it at noon to show to the class.

It was of a bathroom scene, constructed in a three-sided shoe box. Tiny latticed windows opened at the back of the room onto bars (made of toothpicks); the toilet seat was made of paper, with a cotton cover on top of a cut-out doily covering. The tiny wash basin was of a match-box base, turned up and held by a solitary toothpick. Two rugs, made of tiny doily centers, decorated the floor, one in front of the toilet, one by the wash basin.   On the wall was a tiny picture inside a doily frame, one pen-drawn clock, and one wee magazine dog picture.   One single thread held another tiny cupped doily center, representing an electric light, the thread (cord) hanging in the breeze. The front side of the box was covered with white thread sewed across it like a spider web, attached to which were two small, black rubber spiders.

When the Bradley Homonym Bingo Game was played the girls started out ahead, but the boys caught up and passed them in scoring.

The day ended quietly, as it had been all day. Boards were washed, chairs put up, papers picked up, and the students went down the steps like little ladies and gentlemen, not running and shouting.

As I signed out I told the Principal I had had a good class. Another teacher commented, "This is a good school," to which I agreed.

Chapter 109

Like College Exams

The telephone rang at 7:00, requesting me to report to Coonley School. After answering it I returned to bed as was very sleepy and was not sure I cared to go to this school after a terrible class I had had – one I wanted to forget and did not write about. After resting another half hour I felt there were good classes in the school, and I might be sent to one, which proved to be true.

I was assigned a First and Second Grade Class and before they entered one board was covered with 2A seatwork. At 9:00 the roll was taken (five absent; 23 present) and lunch money was collected. Nine paid the regular fee; two paid half; four received free tickets.

Board seatwork was explained, and additional work was put on another board for the first graders.

The class was quiet, orderly, and able to do the seatwork. A few first graders came to inquire what a few words were ("shoe, kite, meat").

After recess there was a library period, during which I added math work on the board for the two levels.

The teacher had excellent, interesting, neat and functional Lesson Plan Books – one for each grade level. Preparing such Plan Books required double time of her. Both the preparatory books, and the attitude and behavior of the class, reflected the interest and work of the teacher.

Lunch was at 11:30 so tickets were distributed and the class was downstairs in line at that time. In this school the pupils received hot lunches, TV style, that were prepared in advance. Cookies and milk were available as well.

After lunch Group I read from Harcourt Brace books at Level 7, 2A (2-2). Six students were in this group and all read easily with understanding; their workbooks were up-to-date, and graded.

Next, seven first-graders read in Level 5 (1-2) books. They read two stories satisfactorily and their workbooks were up-to-date also.

351

Only four children were in the third group. They read at Level 4 (1-1) and were finishing the book, having but one story to read. Three were rapid readers but one needed much help; he missed many words.

Two Mexican children read from the first preprimer booklet; they read three stories. One was a new arrival and was hesitant with some words. Both children were quiet and well-behaved in the room.

As the students selected and worked on artwork papers I went about the room, grading the seatwork on their desks. Many received many stars on papers to take home. The work had required thinking and was not too easy. Some students hurried through the work, putting down incorrect answers quickly, but the majority had tried to produce good papers. This especially pleased me as I had spent three days of the Spring Vacation period remaking seatwork assignments and was interested in presenting the new work. I had explained to them the work was similar in style to high school and college entrance examinations and such testing would be easier for them if they were familiar with the style of questioning.

There was a short period left for the Contraction and Abbreviation Milton Bradley Bingo Card Games. The two Mexican boys had been asked to erase the boards, and when they finished I gave them cards also. One sat near my desk so I watched his card, helping him. After the game had been played about six times he began to recognize about six of the words and press them by himself. He had not seen such words in the first preprimer; it proved the value of these cards, which offer fun in learning through competition, review and physical manipulating the words on the cards. There are 43 words used; 22 contractions; 21 abbreviations. The boys started out winning at first, but later the girls caught up and ended winning by two points.

It had been most refreshing to be with such a fine class – one eager to learn, quiet, well-behaved and capable of producing good work. I felt part of the credit was due to the work of their teacher. They were a credit to each other.

Chapter 110

Sweetie Pie

Signing in at 8:25 at Coonley School, I commented to the clerk I was a "trusting sub", whereupon she smiled and offered me a "good" first grade class. My memories of Coonley were mixed and I wondered about the "goodness". Previous experience with a little first or second grader flashed before me; that little fellow was following so well in his fifth-grade brother's footsteps that he caused unbelievable school problems, both in and out of the room.

This class, however, was one a teacher dreams of, well behaved, and with great academic potential. Noisy, yes, but their love and interest in school activities far outshone the talkativeness.

Although my search through closets, drawers and desks for writing paper was in vain, to my surprise I found a live, little parakeet in a small cage! The seed and base-paper needed cleaning so after the children started to work I changed the water, blew out and replenished the seed, and changed the paper. It was surprising to find a tropical bird left overnight in a school room, and I hoped it would not be left there for the coming 4-day Thanksgiving holiday. Throughout the day the little bird cheerfully joined in the children's chatter with bird talk; it had a lovely tone. The children said it didn't "talk" yet.

Remembering a former experience in the school when three or four little ones did NOT receive a lunch, but only had milk and cookies, I took special care in recording all lunch details. Two paid half price; seven brought lunches; eighteen paid the full price. Had I not written down the names for each category there would have been difficulties again as six-year-olds don't always remember whether or not they paid at 9:00 for food to be eaten at noon. As it was, one little girl brought up a sandwich she found in her desk, which no one claimed. One boy was absent so someone suggested it was his.

Seatwork had been put on the boards before they entered, so after the roll was taken and lunch money collected assignments were read. For writing paper they drew lines on arithmetic or plain white paper.

There were three reading groups, all reading at the same place in the same book, and as they had just completed one booklet, all were being tested, so I followed that procedure and two more test pages were completed and graded. I wanted to hear their oral reading so each group took turns. Two or three needed special help in the last small group, but the entire class was obviously a top group.

In the afternoon, following more reading and math, animal travel games, finger plays, exercise games, and art were enjoyed. The art work was colorful so several papers were put up on the walls.

At 2:20 everyone cleaned up desks; two erased the board, and wraps were put on. At 2:25 they lined up in front of the outer door until the bell rang.

I returned to the room to get my things and turned the lights on. I saw the little parakeet in the back, so pulled the shades down to retain as much heat as possible; then I walked back to talk to "Sweetie Pie" as the children said it was called. Throughout the day the little bird had seemed friendly and not afraid of me, but now it turned its head away as I knelt beside it. I wondered if it was because the lights had been turned off and it had been left in the dark, or whether it dreaded the long dark, cold nights, so I left one line of lights on, hoping the heat would be helpful. I knew the janitor would turn them off when the room was cleaned. I wondered if the bird was left alone weekends too.

I marveled at this teacher's trust in the good health of her little pet. I too had a parakeet, but it never liked cold weather so from early Fall until summer each night I carried the cage to the kitchen where the gas stove pilot lights gave it the continual warmth it seemed to need. The apartment living room was too cold for it. A school room! Never! Her bird was of a stronger caliber. It looked like a young bird and so tiny.

As I signed out the clerk invited me to return the next day, but on learning it would be for a fifth grade I declined. I was a primary substitute teacher and preferred to go home with a sore throat (from continually reminding first graders to be quiet) than to leave with a behavior headache from an upper grade.

In later weeks I learned the parakeet survived the holidays and the teacher had taken it home.

Chapter 111

Cockroach Present

At Blaine School the clerk assigned me to a "First or Second Grade", but the children said they were Second and Third Graders. Again I was blessed with a class of good pupils.

Eight assignments were on the board when they entered, but lots of envelopes, containing class picture money, were turned in, and were to be collected that day. This took a great deal of time to record properly as various amounts were paid, the envelopes stating one amount, but the cost had evidently been increased so another amount was supposed to be paid. This was in addition to the regular morning collections. Many Oriental children were listed, with unusual names so it was necessary to refer to the attendance book to be certain which were the last names. At last two lists were finished, one to be turned in to the photographer, and one left for the teacher.

Twenty-seven were listed on the attendance book; only one child was absent. Eight paid the regular lunch price; four paid half price; three brought lunches; eleven received free tickets.

Library was to be at 9:00 but we arrived at 9:30 due to the many collections, plus the class talking and interrupting. The Library was in the main building so the children left their coats on to leave the Annex and then walk up three flights of stairs. When asked to be quiet and walk quietly they did so. But once in the Library the Librarian had to remind them three times to be quiet.

Those who returned books were allowed to get new ones. Others had to wait until the following week. The Librarian suggested they take the books home and read them, adding that the next week they would tell the others about the stories. She displayed a very attractive diorama of Bambi which a child had made for Open House a few weeks previously. Book reference cards, completed by the children, were collected. Three minutes were left of the period.

"Who remembers the poem we had last week?" asked the Librarian. Several youngsters recalled things to relate and there were a number of questions, followed by hands raised to answer them. Pupils then put their coats on and lined up to return to the classroom.

There were three reading groups, all reading in Holt Publishing Company books. The top group of twelve pupils were finishing a Level 9 book, "People Need People", a first-semester, second grade book.

Four were in the next group, one being absent. They were reading in a Level 8 book, "A Time for Friends", a first grade reader. The children said they, and all others in the room, took their books home for reading, and none of the Holt seatwork was used. Two of this group left for reading in another room. They said they were Korean and also went to another room in the afternoon for Korean reading.

The children in Levels 8 and 9 read well, but they were reading at first and second grade levels, not at the second and third grades, which they said they were in.

Group III consisted of eight children, reading at Level 7, in a book, "A Place for Me". They were three-quarters into this book, a first semester, first grade book. All were much slower oral readers; one could not read all of the words.

Some papers were starred before lunch, which was at 12:30 in the main building. In the lunch line one little boy told me he had brought a quarter to school but another had taken it. I asked the other child for the money; he said it was his. And he had bought cookies with it. I divided them between the two.

After lunch and washroom visits I called the two to the teacher's desk and wrote down their names for reporting the incident to their teacher. I asked one, "Are you sure you didn't lose your quarter?" He nodded, adding. "Yes." Then, "I loosed it. And he took it."

I gave up and finished the note to the teacher. One boy could look me squarely in the eye, saying he had brought the money; the other could not, but I left the matter for the teacher to handle.

After the groups read again the remaining seatwork papers were starred, a Christmas story was read, and art work papers were passed out. Most children had their own crayons and their art work was very colorful.

About this time a girl's voice cried out, "There's a cockroach in my desk!" Everyone seemed horrified until I answered, "I'm sorry. I saw it this morning on the floor but I didn't feel like stepping on it". (I thought it would leave; it never occurred to me it would crawl up a desk.) I told the class, "In Japan they are sold as pets." Again, all were aghast but I explained there were so many people living there, and such little space, that there was no room for larger pets. Very tiny cages were sold for these insects.

I told the girl to get it out of her desk but this seemed difficult, so I walked back and dumped the contents on the floor. The insect clung to the inner top of the desk until shaken out, whereupon it raced across the floor. I finally captured it in a paper cup but screamed (to the delight of the boys) when it crossed my hand. At last it was put in the cup and held there by an envelope across the top, and one boy offered to dispose of it in the boys' toilet.

Only a few stragglers were left outside as I left the building fifteen minutes after closing. I noticed two were from the room I had been in, one the boy who had gleefully offered to dispose of the cockroach. He kept edging closer to me so I frequently turned around as he had been throwing snowballs at the building as I opened the doors. The ground was very icy and slippery, but when he threw a snowball past me I stopped, returned, and reported his actions to another teacher who was then leaving also. It was the first time a snowball had ever been directed at me and I was glad the other teacher appeared at the propitious moment. She said she would report the incident to the teacher. Otherwise, it had been a most pleasant day.

Chapter 112

Distar Method

There was a teacher in the room when I arrived at Goudy School. She explained we did team teaching until 10:30, at which time I would go to another first-grade room for one and one-half hours, and in the afternoon I would be told what rooms to teach in. It was surprising to have her smoking openly in the room, leaving a used ashtray openly on the top of her desk and filling the room with cigaret smoke.

A blackboard covered the front wall, one section of which had seatwork, so I asked her if I could add more work. She said she had just written the work there and would add one more assignment, which she did. Seatwork, she added, was graded and sent home daily. This pleased me as work, especially for primary students, seems meaningful to them only in the immediate present.

The teacher showed me the corner, partitioned off by a movable screen, where I would teach the Distar Reading System. Although I had never used this I had once seen a demonstration and felt it was a very good one. I studied the teacher's manual thoroughly before the children appeared, and it did not seem as difficult as I had anticipated.

After the pledge and patriotic song, the girls were counted. They said their number as the teacher pointed to each one; next were the boys; then the entire group. One child wrote the final figures on the blackboard for the current date. The roll was then taken.

Next the "h" sound was presented to the entire class by the teacher, and reinforced for ten minutes, after which the board assignments were explained.

When eight children came to me for reading I learned they were several days in advance of the lesson indicated on the records but the studying had prepared me and the routine seemed very similar. The children were helpful and we covered all the outlined suggestions. The pupils not only knew the vowel and consonant sounds but were able to blend sounds and substitute and add letters to make words from root words; this surprised me as it was but their fourth month in first grade. I was even more impressed with this method.

One boy could not find his workbook so I wrote a short Christmas poem for him to copy. It was then I learned he did not know how to read, so I changed the work to "Have a Merry Christmas". I told the teacher how smart and eager the pupils were and said when they were given reading books they would make rapid progress. She was pleased to hear this, adding that when their teacher felt they were ready for reading the students would then come to her.

In the next first grade room I had two youngsters in the first reading group who were at Level 8 in "All Kinds of Places to Go", a Holt, Rinehart & Winston book. Both were quiet students who read confidently, with understanding; both were also able to spell and complete the workbook pages.

The next group of seven were at Level 3 in the Holt series, "Rhymes and Tales". This group was extremely immature and it was difficult to keep their attention on the books or the reading. Two short stories were read, taking turns. Three or four other groups were reading in the room with various instructors, and while there was noise it did not seem to bother us or other groups. However, due to their immaturity these children fidgeted, paid little attention, quarreled, stood up, dropped books, etc. making it difficult to complete the reading.

Lunch was at 11:30 and I ate with the class. The children obtained trays of food that was served from a movable hot food conveyor in the corridor and returned to their seats to eat. As they sat eating the room was suddenly enveloped in a beautiful quietness. The usual loud noise and turmoil was done for ten or fifteen minutes.

During this time two of the poorest readers (and most immature) came over to me. Their teacher was eating nearby and when I commented privately to her about their inability she had them read from a list of words pinned on a chart nearby. They read much better individually from the list than when reading from the books with their group.

I was to stay with this entire class for one hour so introduced thinking oral games while they finished eating. But even the lowest level was too difficult for them so I showed samples of art work they were to do, drawing samples on the board as to how they were to make the outlines. Several here did outstanding work and there were a number of the opposite extreme, who did not listen to instructions.

When the art work was finished I read a Christmas story, "The Night Before Christmas", which is always very impressive to first graders, always inviting complete quiet at the mention of Santa Claus.

My next, and last hour was to return to the first grade room where I had started. The teacher had had to leave for an emergency, one she had told me might occur. This class also did Christmas art work and heard the holiday story.

Chairs were put on desks, wraps obtained from lockers, home papers distributed, and all left quietly, supposedly from one door, but after we turned a corner few remained in line. Others quietly (I hoped) had left from other exits close by. As the streets were covered with ice I felt it best for them to have chosen an exit nearest their homes. I saw no children in the long hallway as I returned to sign out.

Chapter 113

My Shoes?

It was 10 degrees outside, and icy under the snow, so although I was called at 7:30 to report to Jahn School, thirty minutes were spent waiting for a Belmont Bus. At 8:30 as I signed in other teachers were relating their parking problems, and related worries, so I was glad I had taken the bus. The school did not have a parking lot.

The teacher had left plenty of seatwork for the class of first graders, but I used my own as was used to it and could grade it more quickly.

A mother stayed and offered to collect the lunch and milk money; this was a great help as the school had been closed the previous day due to a snowstorm. The mother, and a lunchroom worker, had problems collecting, listing and returning coins for the previous day. I was fortunate to be free of this time-consuming work. The mother collected, recorded, went to the lunchroom and returned the overpayments to the children. 32 pupils were listed in the attendance book, three having left, but ten were absent, probably due to the weather, leaving but 19 present.

Board seatwork, put on before the class entered, was explained and read, and papers were passed out.

There were four reading groups which, due to gym and Assembly practise, took most of the day to complete. The entire school used the MacMillan Reading Series and these youngsters were in the Pre-primers, the first three groups reading in "Things You See". Nine were in the first group, five in the second, four in the third. All read three stories; all groups were at the same page in the booklets, but the first group were more solid readers. The second group were slower but good readers.

When the inside recess bells sounded we had fun exercises and activity games.

Gym class was scheduled for 10:45 so only part of the second reading group was completed. Many students had brought gym attire so they changed in the room. Nearly all had gym shoes, but, if not, they removed their boots inside the gym and wore socks.

First, the girls hopped around in a large circle on one foot, then on the other. The boys then ran around the same circle. The class was then divided into four groups; each sat at the base of a huge ladder. After directions were given the children took turns climbing, then descending the long ladders.

Next the gym teacher carefully explained how to climb, and descend, using the underside of the ladders, monkey-like fashion. Most did this easily, but one child, taller and heavier than most, had difficulty, as did one small child, so the teacher held their backs as they climbed. After climbing five or six steps they let themselves drop down to the mat below.

The following ladder exercise sounded very difficult but the majority were able to do it. This, too, was an under-the-ladder exercise. Children were to grasp hold of a ladder step, pull themselves up, raise their chins above their hands to between the steps (as though peering over), hold until the teacher called, "One-two-three, jump", then let go and drop as she added "rest". This was fun for the participants as well as those watching and waiting turns.

The last endeavor was a backward somersault. They sat on a low ledge, let their bodies slide through onto the mat, pulled their feet through above them, then made a backward somersault. Each had two turns as the teacher called, "Sit on the chair; fall in; roll away."

After this each child had a choice of doing any of the exercises twice – climbing (on top or under the ladder), "picture window", or "falling in the chair". Most chose the simple climbing on top, or underside, of the ladder.

The second reading group had not finished reading two pages but it was time to prepare for lunch when we returned so everyone put their wraps on and lined up. Some brought lunches; some ate in the lunchroom (tickets were distributed); others went home as this school had a lunch hour and closed at 3:15.

At noon I learned from another teacher that this was an average class. She had the slow group and said they were very, very slow. After I ate my lunch I walked about the room noting the many fine items for the children to use for play and reinforcement in all areas of learning. But the youngsters started returning before I could absorb all the material and equipment available. Later all I specifically recalled were the piano and the record player, which was unlocked, and on a table.

After the roll was again taken the second group finished their reading.

At 1:30 another teacher appeared saying it was Assembly Practise time, so everyone lined up and left for the assembly where they practiced singing Christmas Carols with another class.

When they returned four children read in the third reading group. These could read, two needing a little help with the sounds, but the other two were very slow.

Two pupils were in the last group, reading in "A Magic Box". They read three stories and seemed to be able to read the material easily enough, but another child in the room told me these two had not passed the test in order to progress to the next book.

It had taken until 2:00 to complete all the reading groups but there had been gym and Assembly practise. The minute we finally finished one little child asked to go to the washroom so all lined up. Usually when one goes others keep requesting to go too.

Papers were then starred. One boy had completed nine assignments, all correctly. Three had SAT dreaming. Children who received two stars for completed work received art papers to do (after samples were shown) so most youngsters got busy and quickly finished enough work to receive the two stars.

About ten did impressive art work to leave for the teacher. These were given duplicate papers to redo the work at home.

Homework was distributed (and art papers also given to the sitters to complete at home). Wraps were put on, chairs placed on top of the desks, and all lined up and left quietly.

Teachers had been especially friendly and helpful at this school. Throughout the day I received smiles and was offered help if needed. When signing out the keyboard was gone so another teacher showed me where to put the key. As I walked toward the outer door another teacher asked where I lived, saying she would have been happy to offer me a ride; however she was not driving my way.

The children had been quiet, interested, and well-behaved; a mother had helped with non-teaching collections; the teachers and principal were pleasant and friendly; the school clerk had given me paper for the art work. I thought how fortunate these teachers were to be working in such a friendly and cooperative atmosphere. It almost made me wish to be working full time again.

After but three minutes of waiting my bus was visibly approaching when suddenly a little boy appeared in front of me, asking if I had been teaching in the first grade room. When I nodded he said his little sister had left her shoes and papers in the room. I looked around and recognized the child, who was wearing shoes.

"The door is not locked," I explained. "The janitor will lock it later. You can go back if you want to, but I have to be home by 4:00." At this the father got out of the car and glared at me angrily for a complete two minutes. Finally he got back in the car, telling the boy to forget the shoes.

As I boarded the bus I wondered why he had not parked the car and accompanied his children inside instead of apparently feeling it was my duty to walk back the half block over the heavy ice to the school, carrying my two heavy satchels. I was sorry about her shoes, but later felt they may have been gym shoes, which would surely be safe in the school during the zero weather weekend.

Chapter 114

Fire

On Mondays I was usually called by 7:00 but received no call by 7:50 so called in to Substitute Center. I was told that I didn't travel so far as some substitutes so would have to wait until being called. Then she told me to report to Waters School.

At 8:00 I left but did not arrive at the school until 9:00 as had to ride three different buses and the last one (Lawrence) required a 30 minute wait. Once there it was necessary to walk back three blocks over the icy, slippery sidewalks.

There were three vacancies in the school; one substitute had been assigned to one; I was sent to a second grade room.

The class was already in their seats, talking merrily. Roll was taken, ten being absent; 22 present. One child paid for a lunch; one received a free ticket, so those two went for the tickets.

As the talking persisted I showed them pictures of the art work the QUIET children would do in the afternoon. This helped a little, but two boys had difficulty remaining quiet. Their desks had already been located apart from that of the class and one required continual reminding to be quiet throughout the day.

Six students were in the first reading group; they read at Level 5 in "Together We Go", a Harcourt Brace book. They were half way into the book and did satisfactory reading; only one was a little slow.

The next group of six had finished the Level 5 book but were waiting to be tested before proceeding. Each took turns re-reading the last story in the book, and all were good readers.

Nine were in the next group, reading "A World of Surprises". They were half way finished with the book and said they read one story daily. They said they had silent reading first, but as all but two had taken the books home I felt silent reading and questioning would have been pointless inasmuch as the majority already knew the story. They were good readers but one could not sound out the word, "made". I wrote it on the board, then crossed out the "e" at the end, explaining the rule that in most one-syllable words with an "e" at the end, the "e" is silent. But the "e", I added, had a job to do; it signified that the vowel preceding it sounded like its name. The child knew the long sound of the "a" so could then read the word.

This same reading skill had to be explained, and demonstrated on the board, for the second reading group also, where "Drake" was an unknown word. While this is a first grade reading skill, it is often necessarily repeated and reviewed in higher grades.

As the group was finishing the story reading fire alarm bells started ringing loudly so all quickly put on coats and lined up. I hurried for the attendance book to carry outside. It was 30 degrees that day and some children near us were without coats and visibly shaking. One wore a very thin sweater so I called her to me and wrapped my coat around her as she stood close. It was many minutes before she stopped shaking. It seemed those without coats had been in a different room, probably for special help, when the alarm rang.

Unfortunately for them, all were outside a very long time. Four fire trucks came. Eventually it seemed there must have been a fire. A few policemen did enter the building but only a few small objects were carried in. At noon I learned there had been a fire on the third floor – in the teachers' room. It seemed a can of ditto liquid had exploded, and also that an oven there had been leaking for some time but not repaired. I learned the damage had been done by upper grade students, who were being questioned by the school.

When we returned from the fire drill some bells continued to clang so I reasoned an air raid was in process. We huddled against a wall for some time until a clear signal was given. However, the clanging outside our door continued. The bells were stuck.

It was seven minutes until twelve so I had them put their wraps on for lunch as it would have been impossible to have reading with the loud clanging. During the lunch hour the bells were fixed.

After lunch, when the students returned, they wanted to talk about the school fire. One reported that two girls had died; another that two were overcome with smoke in the teachers' room. I told them the facts that had been told me.

After roll was taken one little fellow came to me saying his foot hurt. I had him remove his shoes and socks. There was nothing wrong with his foot, but the two pairs of socks were dripping wet. "You really had fun in the snow, didn't you!" I said. He nodded, beaming. I told him to wring out the socks and leave them off until he went home. (I remembered how I had worried about the wet feet of my entire class during my first year of teaching.)

While the group was reading a messenger brought in a note requesting a list of the equipment in the room. I told him the teacher was absent and suggested he return for it the next day. But my intuition warned me he would be back, as he was, with another boy. I had hastily looked about and listed six audio visual equipment aids which surprised me, as the majority of schoolrooms have but one, or none. This one had a large TV, two phonographs, a Language Master, Radio, Film Machine, and one Earphone. I handed the list to the boys and asked them to search for the model and serial numbers, which they found without too much difficulty. I copied them for the regular teacher.

The Bingo Contraction and Abbreviation Card Game was introduced. This was quite slow-going but little by little a few learned to push in the correct words and gained winning cards, the boys finally winning by but one point.

There were indoor exercise games at recess, toilet visits and after papers were starred, art work was distributed. Two students had completed all the seatwork with correct answers; many turned in excellent art papers.

A few in the class remained talkative all day, but it had been an alive class.

When signing out I was horrified to see the school key rings had slipped off the clip to which I had fastened it on to my purse. I returned and checked in the room and searched outside where we had gone during the fire alarm. No keys. I felt dreadful but told the Principal I must have dropped them in the snow. He reacted calmly saying a child would probably return them. His kind attitude deeply impressed me.

Once home I checked one of my satchels for something – and found the keys! They had dropped off in the room. The next morning I called the school saying I would return them within two days, which I did.

Chapter 115

Teacher's Mistake?

As I entered the Second Grade room at Ravenswood School I saw there were only two small sections of a blackboard to be used for seatwork. The rest of the front board, as well as the entire back one, and the pull-down board sections covering the coat hooks for the children – all were completely pasted over with papers.

Fortunately for me another teacher brought in a small portable blackboard which I used for math. Also fortunately, I carried two short poems that were copied on large construction paper; these were pinned on a wall. Three assignments were put on the small space and later in the afternoon one was erased and replaced; two others were crowded below those on the board.

Roll was taken; two were absent, 29 present. One paid for lunch; two received free tickets.

Reading was divided into four groups, the childrens' desks being grouped together according to their reading abilities. This made it easy for the teacher to go from one group to another during the reading period. However, the children said walking reading was to start the next day.

Six children in Group I were reading in a Ginn Book, "The Dog Next Door", Level 7, a 2B book. They were solid readers and half way into the book.

The eight pupils in Group II were at Level 5, reading "May I Come In?" All were good readers but were already a year behind. When I commented they read the book well they said they had already read it in first grade the previous year. "Teacher must have made a mistake," explained one little fellow.

Seven children in Group III read at Level 6, in "Seven is Magic", a 1A book. All read well except one little boy from the Phillippines, who seemed afraid to attack works until shown how to divide them into syllables, then sound them out. He seemed to grasp this quickly, as well as to note little known words in an unknown word, and finished the page without more difficulty.

At recess time four seventh grade students appeared to take the children to the washrooms and then supervise the class for room games.

After recess the eight pupils in Reading Group IV read from "Helicopters and Gingerbread", Level 4. They were part way into this book. Five did fine reading; two seldom knew the place; one was unable to read at all. This child was extremely immature, never knowing the place, and during the morning had written but two words of several assignments.

A librarian entered with a record player and filmstrip machine. It was their library period. She played a Christmas record about a child who learns that Christmas is a time to give presents as well as receive them; that to find happiness we have to give it to others.

During the few minutes left before lunch some of the seatwork papers were checked and starred.

After lunch the rest of the seatwork was checked. The printing was quite sad and it was obvious that only one morning story was written daily, the remaining seatwork being ditto papers. Two children could do the second grade math; seven completed all the seatwork correctly.

One girl had brought a new "Frosty" Christmas record so we borrowed a record player and enjoyed this as art work was done. As samples had been shown and carefully discussed, there were many fine pictures turned in later.

The teacher had left a book to be read, "The Valiant Tailor", (47 pages!) warning she would be asking questions about it the next day. I read quite rapidly but barely finished by closing time, 25 minutes later, and my voice was getting more raw by the minute. The story did seem to hold their attention, but I would have liked to discuss it a bit, to explain and reinforce parts of it, but there was no more time.

We were barely ready to leave when the final bell sounded but all chairs were up and the janitress was putting the shades down.

I signed out and went to wait – and wait – and wait for the bus. On nice days I was sent to closer schools, with parking lots, but in snowy, icy weather I traveled to more distant schools, with no parking areas. This I was used to, so I was grateful for the buses I had to wait for.

Chapter 116

Stairway Yelling

At Coonley School I was assigned a First and Second Grade class. On entering I saw that while large blackboards covered two sides of the room the teacher had pasted school items over all of the front board except one little space. Also, one foot of the entire bottom of the remaining side board was also covered with pasted items. There was nothing to do but use small printing, and close together. Apparently little writing was done here.

29 were present; two were absent. Thirteen paid the regular lunch fee; eleven received free lunches; five said they brought lunches. I wrote down the names of those to receive lunch tickets, relieved that the collections and recordings balanced with those present. In one immature class here I had once ended up at lunch time with four pupils without tickets; after this experience individual names were written down to avoid noon difficulties.

When I asked the 2nd graders to raise their hands only two did so. One boy was not certain, so I checked his cumulative record card. It did say, "P8", indicating his second year in school, but his reading and math levels were both "C", either pre-primer or first grade level. The record card indicated this boy had already attended THREE other schools! My heart ached for him as he was starting out a year behind in his beginning school years.

Group I had ten children. Two came from another room. An 8th grade Korean girl brought a 2nd grade workbook down to be corrected; she remained and did two additional pages. While the workbook assignments were done correctly, and she could read them to me, she could not understand other questions I asked her, like, "How long have you been in U.S.?" or "Were you here last year?"

The group used the Harcourt Brace Reading Series and all brought books and workbooks. They were in the second Pre-primer, "A Happy Morning", about two-thirds into the booklet. Another 6th grade boy, from Korea, joined the group for reading. This group could read fairly well. One story was read daily, they said, and two workbook pages were completed. These were done and graded.

Group II had nine students. They were in the same reading booklet, but just starting in them. Their reading was slow, hesitant, and many needed much help.

Group III consisted of one student, reading "Sun and Shade", a first grade primer. She was to page 29 and was a good little reader, fast and confident; she missed no words, but said "mudder" for "mother".

Group IV also had but one child, a girl just starting to read, "Sun and Shade". She was quite weak in all areas of reading, seeming to be unfamiliar with beginning sounds, or basic words.

At lunch time when I called names to distribute paid-for and free tickets an extra child came for a free ticket!

"But you raised your hand when I asked who brought lunches!" I exclaimed, horrified, for I knew that in this school lunches were prepared ONLY for the number requested. I told him I was sorry but I knew from past experience there was NO WAY to obtain a lunch for him. And I knew that in the future I would also have to have those bringing lunches to stand by my desk so I could write their names also.

We proceeded to the lunchroom, each child holding a ticket but once there I could not find the child without a lunch, or a ticket. All seemed to have lunch trays. At the tables, as I continued to try to find him, another child said that he had remained in the classroom! In a few minutes he volunteered to go get him. Meanwhile two students did not care to eat their food, so I saved these trays for him. One was a rolled beef sandwich, one a sloppy Joe. He sat staring at the food for some time; then slowly ate a few bites. It looked good to me.

When we returned to the room I realized it was a very immature class. Only two pupils had completed three writing papers. Three had written but two words. Few papers were legible. It was obvious little or no writing was being done in the room. I showed them the star symbols they would receive for completed assignments and more time was given for the work.

Outside we heard the upper grade classes as they left the lunchroom and went to the stairs. The noise was unbelievable – lots of calling out and loud yelling. This continued for over ten minutes. One quiet little boy came to me saying he thought he was "going to throw up". I suggested he sit in the back of the room and play with a toy. After about 15 minutes he said he felt better. The noise had somewhat subsided.

The children had second turns reading, made washroom visits, colored art papers, and heard two Christmas stories. Their Christmas tree outlines were so wobbly, and small, that I turned their papers over and drew larger ones. I had brought paper to be used when learning I was to come to this school but was surprised to find most of the children did have crayons. The majority did not know how to make "scribble outlines" so I quickly made them, but the finished, colored pictures were quite lovely.

The class was to visit the Museum of Science & Industry the next day and all but one had brought the required money and signed trip slips.

All put their chairs up and lined up after coats and boots were on, then walked down the steps in orderly fashion. I hoped several mothers, or helpers, would be helping on their trip the next day.

Chapter 117

Access to Excellence

It was a day in the 40's, without too much ice on the streets, so I was sent to Hawthorne, a nearby school that had a parking lot.

The assignment, their only vacancy that day, was to a class in the Access to Excellence Program. This, I had read, was a new program, completely voluntary, where students chose the schools they wanted to attend.

The class consisted of children 9, 10, and 11 from 4th, 5th and 6th grades. During the day I checked the cumulative record cards, which indicated the majority were at reading levels "G" and "H" (3d) at the beginning of the school year in September, four months earlier, a few being at "C", "D" and "E" levels. Eleven had been in one school, five in two, two in three, and one child had already attended four schools.

24 were listed in the attendance book; four had left; two were absent, leaving 18 present. Two paid half price for lunch tickets; the others received free lunches.

Thirteen pupils read in Reading Group I, a Ginn Company book, "A Lizard to Start With", Level 10, Grade 3. Most were good readers, but two or three had difficulty. The class said the regular procedure was for them to read silently at their desks and complete the seatwork requested in the reading books, but when a vote was taken all voted to read orally up in front. Besides, I wanted to hear them read. Each brought a chair to the front of the room.

The two who were weak readers needed review in sounding out unknown words; they especially needed help with one-syllable words ending with "e". Sample words were put on the board (cap, cape, cop, cope, cut, cute, etc.) with the explanation that usually one-syllable words ending in "e" had a silent "e" but the "e" signified the preceding vowel sounded like its name. This seemed helpful to them, as one admitted he then remembered that rule, and both did figure out other words.

Group II consisted of four students reading in "How It Is Nowadays", a Ginn book, Level 8, (2A). They were to page 18, just starting the book. Three were solid readers; one needed help with the same reading skill as the two from the previous group. All in the room had been asked to listen as the reading skill was put on the board, and explained, but obviously this child had not paid attention, so the work was repeated.

Group III had but two students who read from "A Dog Next Door", a Level 7 Ginn book, (2B). They were to page 8; both pupils had been very talkative in the room. One read rapidly. As he had done little, or no, work all morning I had checked his cumulative record card and noted he had been in a very good school for the previous four years; the other boy had been in four schools, a new one each year. I had asked him about the constant moving at recess. He said his parents were divorced, that he had lived with one, but was not with the other one. He could not read six to seven words on a page, so the book was much too difficult for him. He never paid attention when the other boy read, or when explanations were put on the board. Although nine years of age he was extremely immature.

When the class went to lunch I was on lunch duty just outside the entrance to the lunchroom. Another teacher was in the hall keeping students quiet; my duty was to send in a few at a time to obtain their lunch trays. To me this seemed an excellent plan as there was reasonable quiet both in the hall and in the lunchroom, where two more teachers walked about observing behavior and voices. Pizza was being served, a favorite with children, so not too many trays of food were discarded.

After lunch the students had math, English and spelling work, all of which were graded.

Art papers were distributed during the last thirty minutes but only one paper was impressive – and that had been done in pencil instead of crayons, as suggested. It had been done by the boy who moved yearly and never seemed to listen.

It had been a strange experience from the beginning to the end of the day. The teacher had left a good time schedule and an abundance of ditto seatwork, which I had decided to use, but when the class appeared they claimed that had already done six of the eight sheets. This was probably true as even those who requested math sheets looked quite disappointed when receiving the sheets.

Because of this I used my own work. Several fun, thinking assignments were put on the board. But this group seemed to be more interested in talking and just sitting than in completing much work.

By the last period I had expected to see some good art papers but here again I was disappointed. The children were likeable but far from self-disciplined, lacking in good work habits, only interested in constant talking. It had been a different kind of experience, and a disappointing one.

Chapter 118

Two Teacher Desks
Gym Hoops

At Hamilton School I was sent to a first grade room. Here again most of the blackboard space on three sides of the room was covered over with either art work or school items. As only two sections were available on one wall, I cut down the printing size of the board assignments and managed to put up enough work to keep them occupied, especially as I carried two assignments printed on large construction paper. During the morning one paper fell and it was difficult to find a pin.

Although the teacher had two huge desks, both were covered, on top, as well as inside, with this and that, utterly disorganized. I soon gave up searching and found two pins in my purse to use.

There was a time schedule and attendance book. 27 were listed in the book; 4 had moved; one was absent; 22 were present. Five paid the regular lunch fee; seven received free tickets; four had brought lunches; six went home at noon to eat.

When entering the room the youngsters gathered in front of me most of the time. "Teacher, we have gym", was one announcement. I sent a note to the office to learn the gym time. Two children were sent to get the lunch tickets.

The board seatwork was read. One little one was standing in front of me. "Teacher, I got…" in a wee voice.

Teacher, "Yes?"

Child, "I got this," pulling at the sleeve of his sweater.

Teacher, "You have a new sweater?"

Child, (beaming) "Yes." Immediately three others were on their feet to come up in front, so I quickly announced we would have Show & Tell Time later.

Twelve were in the first reading group. They were reading in the 4th Preprimer, "Just for Fun" in the Harper Row series, near the end of the book, which they finished in the afternoon reading. Some missed a few words but most were good readers, knowing the consonant sounds. When they did not know a word they were asked the letter sounds and then requested to blend the consonants and vowels; most were able to do this, and they seemed to enjoy trying this technique.

One boy, who was unable to read any of the words, was asked why he did not have a booklet.

"Because."

"Because, why?" persisted the teacher.

"Because my mother put it away someplace." He was never paying attention, so never knew the reading place.

All read two lines, and had two turns, but as it was their gym time and several pages remained to be read, they returned to their seats and prepared for the gym period. The majority had gym attire.

The gymnasium was on the third floor. Three teachers were decorating a Christmas tree on the stage for the program the following day. The decorations looked like store items but had been made by students.

The gym teacher had the children lie on the floor, then sit up, then touch their toes, as he counted "1 –2 – 3"; "1 – 2 – 3."

Next, they turned over and were on their stomachs, reaching for their feet as he counted, "One – two;" "one – two."

A walking exercise around the gym was next. "Hands on hips; hands up;" called the teacher. "Start skipping – now walking." At times his call of "Freeze!" stopped all action. There were jumping, sliding, running and walking times.

The class was divided into two lines and were given large hoops to roll across the room and back. These plastic hoops were nearly as tall as the youngsters and it was fun to watch the exercise. As it was a speed contest those waiting turns yelled with excitement and hopped up and down with glee, cheering their sides. Few were able to keep the hoops in an upright position, or in straight lines, but wandered all over the place, the hoops spending much of the time falling flat on the floor. At times they slipped away, causing the children to run after them. Some seemed unable to roll them so they bounced the hoops a few steps; others picked them up and carried them; one little girl threw hers in disgust at her inability to control it. It was very interesting to observe their actions and reactions. Some pushed the hoops; some pulled them. Some held them from the inside, some from the outside.

A shuffling exercise with the hoops was next, keeping the feet inside the hoops, causing the hoops to move forward across the room. This appeared a little easier for most to do. Usually once they got the feet rhythm going they made progress, but soon most stepped ahead, and outside of the hoop, and stumbled. (It looked to me that had they fastened their eyes on the goal instead of their feet this exercise would have been more easily mastered.) Even slow walking caused them to walk outside the hoops, leaving them behind. Some children went fast, some slow; all were fun to watch. Those wearing gym shoes, or socks, had an easier and more successful time than those shuffling in heavy boots.

Running with the hoops was the next contest. Here the greatest difficulty was exchanging the hoops with the next contestant. One little girl gave up and tossed hers at the next child. One boy had trouble keeping his pants on; they were too large and kept starting to fall. The children looked so very cute running with the large hoops that I wished I had a movie camera. Some grasped the front of the hoops; some held the backs. Often they were dropped. There was much healthy noise.

At the end of the gym period the instructor had them stand by squads, then line up by the door.

Returning to the room we stopped for washroom visits, changed clothes again in the room, and went outside to recess. It was my turn to be on morning recess duty, which I usually enjoy, but much of the ground was covered with hard, bumpy ice so walking over it was not at all easy. Of course, this did not bother the pupils. They ran, raced, slid, fell, and fought, on it, but instead of hurrying to the culprits I sent nearby messengers. There were no mishaps but to me it was a relief to be inside on solid footing.

After recess some children said I had not collected the milk money so I asked how much was to be collected.

"Six cents, or a dime," was a quick answer.

"If you have six cents, line up," I said. "I have no change." Four brought me the six cents but in two minutes the money was returned from the lunchroom, the children reporting, "No milk. It's too late."

"Those who paid, come and get your money," brought no response. "Okay. I will keep it." Still no response. I had to call the four individual names I had written down.

Reading Group I finally finished their reading. This left but one story in their Preprimer to be read which was done in the afternoon reading.

Group II consisted of three children reading in "City Days, City Ways", the Harper & Row third Preprimer. They were somewhat over half way into the booklet.

Group III were in the second Preprimer, "Outdoors and In", on page 19, the booklet having 70 pages. Four were in this group. One girl had so much difficulty in reading that when an older sister came in to talk to her I suggested she help as the little one really needed special assistance.

After the morning recess the papers had been checked for star giving as while the groups read the teacher had noted much sitting and day dreaming instead of working. Very little work had been done, but after the Santa stars had been given, most youngsters began at once to do one or two assignments.

Group IV read in "Janet and Mark", the first Preprimer. Three Oriental children were here at the beginning of the book, and only one seemed able to read.

Returning from lunch the children again congregated about the teacher's desk.

"Teacher, I hurt my finger."

"Teacher, she was hit with a snowball." (This child's face was red from being hit!)

"Teacher, I saw Santa Claus!"

First graders can easily steal hearts, and school time, unless one is on guard. The child who had been hit was sent to another room with a very verbal student to identify the boy who had thrown the snowball, but after caps and coats had been removed, finding the thrower proved difficult. The girl's face soon appeared normal again.

Papers were again checked. Many received one Santa star; three children also received a bunny and a big star for doing three assignments.

Reading groups had second turns; then the seatwork was again checked. One little boy (the one unable to read) seemed unable to copy from the board, so I printed, "Oh see Santa" for him on a sheet of paper, repeating the words on three lines. This he could reproduce a little more legibly, but printing did not seem to be much of a practised skill in the room. Only three children had reputable writing papers and printing was an extremely slow-going process for them. Seven came to borrow pencils to use.

Their art work was surprisingly good. Samples had been shown and they chose the type to make. Nearly everyone had crayons. The majority chose to leave their pictures for the teacher to see.

At 3:10 the room was put in order; wraps put on, and all left quietly.

There had been soft talking most of the day, but it had been a nice class to have been with.

Chapter 119

Top Class
Top Teacher

As I approached LeMoyne School a very little girl was standing outside the entrance. It was two degrees below zero and a good half hour before 9:00 so I told her to come in and stay with me. A guard sitting near the door asked if the child was with me as we went inside, but I said she was and we continued to the office.

There were twelve vacancies listed on the sheet – and no other substitute had arrived! I walked outside to the hall and waited awhile, but when the new principal entered I returned inside. The clerks and principal talked about the vacancies and then (having twice reminded them I was a substitute for primary grades) I was assigned to a first grade.

As I walked outside and asked the little girl to help me find the room number I then learned she was in the class I was to teach. The children appeared before any work was put on the boards, but this was fortunate as I learned from them that this was a Second Grade, not First. However, to be certain I checked their cumulative record cards, which indicated the children were in their second year of school. As all appeared to be alert and mature I chose 2A seatwork, which they were able to complete. 34 names were in the attendance book; six had left; 14 were absent; 14 were present.

As I walked past a very tall wastebasket the odor I had smelled as I entered the room again almost overwhelmed me – a mixture like sour smoke, very powerful! I put the container out in the hall and later in the day a teacher aide informed the engineer about it. When he came over and smelled the contents he, too, moved away quickly and said the janitor must have forgotten to empty it.

Board work assignments were explained and reading was started. Four students in Group I read in "Special Happenings", Page 110, a Holt Rinehart Book, Level 12 – a Grade 3-2 book! They were beautiful readers and read as rapidly as grown-ups.

Group II, also four students, were to page 102 in "Way of the World", Level 10 Grade 2-2. These were also good readers, a little slower than those in the first group, but still fast readers. A few students kept telling one boy the words. I folded a paper for him to keep the place, but it was small and he dropped it. I felt it was bothering him to have the others prompting him and he was finally a little sharp with one. He then told me his glasses were broken. When his long page of reading was finished he sighed with relief. The glasses had been broken three days previously. When he had a second turn I held a pencil below the lines and he read fine, without difficulty. No one needed to help him.

Four students read in Group III in "People Need People", page 242, Level 9, Grade 2-1, at their expected grade level. They were also good readers and read fast enough, although a little more slowly than the previous group. One little girl here liked to correct the other readers occasionally, or supply the words before they read them. But when it was her turn to read she read several words incorrectly. This group finished the last story in the book.

Because of the zero weather there was inside recess and the children were glad. We went to the washrooms and a teacher aide, passing by, took the boys. I noted this school had developed an admirable idea. Toilet paper, on rolls, was hung on the corridor wall OUTSIDE the washroom. (Students sometimes have tendencies to throw such paper around the toilet rooms, and also to stuff the toilets with it.)

Reading pantomine guessing games were acted out during recess, followed by "Simon Says". But I quickly noted the majority were very alert in the last game so most became instant winners.

Only two students were below level in Group IV, "A Time for Friends", Page 22, Level 8, Grade 1-2. One girl was unable to read one word, "come", but before I could help her figure it out the other child said the word. She also stumbled on "anything" and "what". Before this only one child had missed any words, or needed help. This was one of the best – or, more likely, the best reading class I had ever been with in primary grades.

After lunch seatwork was graded. A few students had completed the work and had correct papers except for Second Grade Math. No one was able to complete the subtraction computation with borrowing, even though it had been carefully explained that morning. This skill takes a little time to master.

The class was very quick to understand the Milton Bradley Contraction and Abbreviation game and thoroughly enjoyed it. The day was finished by drawing modernized outlines of flowers and coloring them, a new experiment, which proved to be interesting and successful even though there were no previous samples to be shown.

Working with such a fine class of students was a distinct pleasure. They were quiet and well behaved as well as top readers. Their teacher had done amazingly well with them in reading. In June of the previous year the majority had been marked to start reading in the fall at "E" level, 2nd grade. Obviously, this teacher had had solid review and kept progressing as but four months later the top group had gained one year, the next group one-half year. The children had workbooks which were also up-to-date, and the teacher's desk was covered with piles of ditto work to be done. A filmstrip machine, and record player were in a cabinet, but the usual extra teaching aids were not apparent. Evidently here was an individual that got top results without them. I wanted to meet her the next time I was in the school. She had to be a very special person.

Chapter 120

Personal Reading Cards
Graded Daily

Although I started at 7:45 and lived reasonably near the school, it took one hour to arrive at Hamilton School. The weather was zero and I had to wait for 20 minutes on Sheridan for ANY bus, and again on Addison for 25 minutes. Fortunately, there were buildings at both locations in which to stand and wait.

Once on an Addison Bus, the young bus driver told me he had attended the school, adding "it was a good school". He was right. After the noisy classes I had had the previous week, this school – and class – were like being in a different world.

As I signed in I saw there had been three vacancies but two substitutes had been assigned; the other vacancy specified "music". But the clerk must have received a late call as she came over and wrote a name, telling me to take a 2nd grade class.

Some work was on the board when the students entered, but all were quiet as I wrote another assignment. Of the 29 listed names in the attendance book one had left; one was tardy; four were absent, leaving 24 present. Six paid the full luncheon price; ten received free tickets; seven went home; one brought lunch.

Nearly all left the room for the "walking reading" period and it was surprising to see that only eleven were in the group to read. They entered and sat quietly in a circle; not one talked. Each had turns reading an entire page in "It Happened This Way", a Harper Rowe book. They were just starting the book and each had three turns. The pupils had individual cards to receive reading grades for each day, which they carried with them. The reading abilities varied from excellent to fair. The poorest ones did not watch the book as others read; this is a usual characteristic of poorer readers.

At indoor recess time two upper grade children came to take the regular class to the washrooms. Later they had a blackboard reading (phonics) game contest in which the pupils supplied the needed consonants to complete pictures. It was an educational fun game which both the class and those in charge enjoyed.

Reading Group I were finishing their 2nd grade book. Eleven were in this group; they also brought cards to record their daily oral reading grades. These were able to read with average 2nd grade abilities.

After lunch the math and English board work was explained, and Reading Group II (the same ones that read first in the morning) read again in a different book, "Sidewalks", a Singer-Random House Book, first grade. These were very slow readers and it was a very good plan for the teacher to have a second reading time for them. It showed she was interested in their progress.

After reading the seatwork was starred and at recess the same two upper grade students took the class to washrooms, followed by playing the reading blackboard games again.

A few students did top art work; most were only fair. The entire class had remained quiet all day. The students said they had a quiet teacher who liked it quiet, and all agreed that they too, preferred a quiet room.

Chapter 121

Belmont Bus No More!

No call was received from Substitute Center until 8:10. It was icy and cold outside so I called the school to inform them I would be late; then I asked what grade I would have. Learning it would be 3rd grade I took four ditto seatwork sheets to be done plus a higher level of art work.

I decided to travel by elevated and fortunately did not have to wait for a train, which was waiting at the station. Because of this I arrived at Waters School as the students were entering at 9:00.

After taking the roll – 3 absent, 25 present – the students were given word contests to do while I put two assignments on the board. They listed as many words as they could that started with "br", and then wrote lists of action words. One boy had 32 "br" words; two others wrote 30 action words.

As this school had an hour off for lunch only three students had free lunch tickets; the others either went home or brought lunches.

Two thinking assignments were on the board; the four ditto assignments were placed on small numbered chairs in front of the board to be completed in consecutive order after the board work was done.

Pupils remained in the room for reading and math and although I was glad I had brought a math ditto, when I saw the double addition problems on the board the teacher had left I felt the ditto was too easy for them.

Evidently it was a homogeneous reading room as all read in the same book, at the same place, near the beginning, so I had half read at a time. They were at Level 9 in a Harcourt Brace book, "Ring Around the World", a third grade, second semester book.

Most were good readers; a few were a little slow; one or two Oriental boys did not seem to understand some words, but they read well. Three were unable to explain their oral readings, but it was an unusually difficult chapter.

Two 6th graders came to take the class for games at recess so I got coffee. However the games I had introduced looked like such fun that

I returned to watch. Unfortunately the enthusiasm for the "Let's Travel" game had soon evaporated and they were playing "Eraser Chase" on my return.

Several students had done most of the seatwork before lunch so I was kept busy trying to catch up grading all the papers. My intention was to have those finishing first help grade papers, but only the last assignment was one they could have helped with, and that one I did easily and quickly. However, I was occupied throughout my lunch hour and on into the afternoon grading their work.

Most of the seatwork was good. There were some 100's and some sad ones. It was surprising to see two papers of very good thinking on the two written assignments. It was even more surprising to see no perfect math paper. The work covered a variety of arithmetic from 2nd through 3rd grade levels. The majority missed the easy short division, which was later explained.

Only ten minutes were left for the Milton Bradley Homonym Game, which the girls won five times.

Art papers had been distributed earlier as I continued to grade work. These results were very, very fine.

It had been a pleasant day as the class had been quiet and well behaved. When I complimented them on their behavior I was told the class "problem" was absent.

Returning home I just missed the elevated train but appreciated sitting and waiting as the hours of concentrated paper-grading had been a little trying. When the train came and proceeded to my home station, I then STOOD and waited 45 minutes for a Belmont bus before starting to walk. And as I continued the mountain climbing over high, narrow, snow-piled "sidewalks" and down into slushy, slippery footsteps of deep slush I felt I would never again waste energy standing and waiting for this late-late Belmont Bus. As I slowly and carefully trudged my way home for what seemed 100 blocks not one bus passed by.

Chapter 122

Father Comes for Homework

The call to teach at Chappell came at 7:15. As this was a new school to me I called CTA to make certain I traveled the correct route. I was told to take a Ravenswood "A" train but experience had taught me that the "A" train did not stop at Belmont so when a Belmont Bus came, which was going far west, I remained on it until Western Avenue, where a northbound bus was coming, enabling me to sign in the school at 8:30.

The teachers' parking lot, I noted, had been partially cleared of snow. However, I hesitated to drive in winter on icy streets, and parking could always be a problem if the school did not have a lot.

On entering the building one was greeted by a very attractive bulletin board in the front hall of ice skating figures, and the school atmosphere was pleasant and friendly. Teachers passing in the corridors were smiling, and during the day the Principal came by and shook hands with me.

The 2/3d grade class to which I was assigned was quiet and well-behaved.

As I was finishing one board assignment a father entered for homework for his child who was ill that day.

Library Hour was listed as 9:00 to 9:40 so after taking roll (30 present; 5 absent) I took them to the library and returned to complete the board assignments.

As I came back with the class a female entered, informing me I had a new child from the previous day. When I asked for the enrollment form she said it would be brought in later. I jotted a note to the teacher about this, adding there was no new child present. Usually enrollment forms are brought to rooms with new students, as the forms contain necessary information to be recorded.

We had barely started to read when Play Leaders appeared saying the children had washroom visits before recess.

After recess, during the reading, a second new child was brought in, who was just enrolling.

The first group of students read a Harcourt Brace, Level F book, "Going Places, Seeing People", which is a 2nd grade, 2nd semester reader.

The second group read a Scott Foresman Company book, "More Friends, Old and New", also a 2nd grade, 2nd semester book, at the same level.

The third group also read a Scott Foresman book, "More Fun with Our Friends", a first semester, second grade book.

Wanting to show them the location of the story background I brought a huge globe to the front of the room and after pointing out a specific location asked them the names of the various continents, oceans and seas. Surprisingly enough, only one boy, a German newcomer, could name Lake Michigan, so we reviewed a short geography lesson which all seemed to enjoy – and benefit from.

At noon I ate in the Teachers' Lounge and learned another substitute was assigned to a 7/8th grade class and was having a very trying time with them. I was grateful to have arrived early to obtain a primary class.

After lunch all groups read again. Another teacher came and took five students, but by the time the three groups had read they returned and I had them read. At first they objected, insisting they did not read in their home room. But I wanted to hear them so they joined me, sitting up in front.

They were an intriguing group – five youngsters from five different countries, Syria, Greece, Italy, Germany and France. I held up a 1B first grade book but it seemed too low a level so I produced a 1A, first grade, second semester book, which seemed about right. They read orally in unison. The "th" and "wh" words appeared to be a problem and as there were two or three of these on each page, we stopped and I printed these on the board in two columns. (the, then, them, there, their, they, this, that, than, those, these and what, when, where, which, who, why). After they read them twice I erased the "th" from the first list and had them read the list pretending the letters were there. This alerts children to the differences in the sounds of the letters. After saying the words twice the "th" was rewritten and they seemed much more familiar with the words, as usually happens. The same drill was repeated with the "wh" words.

The class voted to skip afternoon recess as time was disappearing fast. As the upper-graders took them to washrooms I starred the completed seatwork papers. After the students finished playing reading-blackboard games with the Play Leaders (a regular, very good exercise) everyone read the board assignments together and answers were marked on the board so those who had not finished could then do so and correct their own papers.

Art samples were shown to which there was no reaction, which surprised me, but later I saw many were also doing top level work in this category.

The entire class had remained quiet all day. The students said they had a quiet teacher who liked it quiet, and they agreed that they, too, preferred a quiet room.

The teachers had been so pleasant, smiling and helpful. At closing time one offered to drive me to Sheridan and Lawrence, which was a great help.

It had been a very pleasant school to have been in.

Chapter 123

Chicago Snowbound

The Broadway Bus Driver did not know where Kemper Street was, and I got off the bus one long block before Fullerton. Walking down side streets trying to find Lincoln School was difficult. Hardened snow and ice were piled high on both sides with but narrow paths made by earlier pioneers along the unshoveled streets. Cars came along the streets so it did not appear wise to proceed that way. Walking along, up and down and around, on the icy snow paths I soon realized I had confused the location of Lincoln School with Alcott, a little further north.

Occasionally other people came along the streets who offered directions until I finally reached the school. Had I remained on the bus until Fullerton it would have been easy to find.

Although I signed in at 8:05 the absent teacher had not yet telephoned to inform the school of her absence so I waited. Meanwhile, an art banner, displayed on a wall, was so interesting that I spent the time copying it. The banner consisted of multiple small squares of designs and childlike pictures, all in soft pastel colors.

The classroom was cheerful and inviting with short, bright yellow curtains along the ledges of high windows covering one side of the room. Childrens' art work was on a long mural on the back wall.

No classwork was on any of the bulletin boards so I had searched in a few desks to learn their ability levels but found no work. Much of the blackboard space was covered with posters and charts, so I used small second-grade printing and was able to get four assignments on the front board. When the children entered they were able to read the first grade work I had put on the board.

28 pupils had been listed in the Attendance Book, four had left; one was absent, leaving 23 present. Four paid the regular lunch fee; one paid for two days. Five paid for milk, one for two days. Six said they received free lunches, but after I sent for the five milk orders the lunchroom attendant inquired if white or chocolate was desired.

This time nearly all of the students present rose, saying they received milk! It seemed six had paid for milk on Monday (four days earlier) and eight received free milk – although but six were to have free lunches. I gave up trying to understand all this and wrote down the names in the various categories, first having them stand in different sections of the room to avoid duplicate listings. By this time four had left for a dance class but others reported their names, saying that one (the only one in the room) was to have white milk. When the milk arrived later this little child chose to have chocolate milk that day like everyone else! Figuring out the milk order and listing the names after trying to hear their tiny voices had taken 20 minutes, after which one alert little fellow said they had Library at 9:30.

A note was sent to the librarian, who affirmed their time. The children took pencils to record books taken from the library, and returned books selected previously. When I later came for the class I saw the librarian was reading a storybook to them about Curious George, a little monkey.

While the class was in the library I read several of the school stories of "The Great Snow Storm" in Chicago on a large bulletin board in the hall, several of which were especially interesting. One boy related how he had jumped off a porch into a snowdrift – and soon found himself covered to his neck! A lady coming along the street helped him out. After one student spent an hour helping his cousin shovel snow from his car on the street they found it was the wrong car! One pupil spent time feeding wild birds; another used his new skis to get about.

The children read from an Open Court Company workbook and then completed a multiple choice exercise as the teacher read questions from the Teachers Manual. Later I asked a neighboring teacher if this was an advanced class and learned the school did not group by abilities. She said both first grade classes would finish reading the first hard cover 1A book before summer vacation, but as they were but half finished with the workbook and said they did but two sections weekly, I wondered how this would be possible in the remaining four months.

During the lunch hour I noted the abundance of equipment in the room – a piano, record player, opaque projector, SRA Laboratory Box, three cabinets of books, four long tables, one round one, two painting easels, two pocket charts – and a child's chess table with two matching chairs. Books and games were in abundance. The small portable tape recorder on the teacher's desk made me feel this must be a school that did not experience the usual school break-ins.

After lunch the students completed the seatwork assignments. As these were starred they proceeded to IRA work, which they checked themselves and put in their individual folders prepared by the teacher.

The last period was of art projects. Many youngsters had good supplies of crayons and felt tipped pens in various colors which helped them produce fine papers.

Boards were erased and washed, chairs placed on desks, coats and hats put on and as the last bell sounded they left quietly through a nearby door.

Chapter 124

Monitor Hall System

Awakening at 8:00 I realized my alarm had not rung. After informing Substitute Center of this I was told they would call me back, which they did, sending me to Swift School.

A bus marked "Devon" came, which I let pass as elevated travel is faster, but the Belmont 77 did not appear. I waited and waited. Finally, I arrived at the school at 8:50 and was assigned to a third grade class.

I was also told I was on Playground Duty from 9:00 to 9:05. It seems most teachers don't like this duty but I had always enjoyed observing the many children outside, their behavior and experiences. This day was cold, the ground being covered with hardened snow, plus a number of icy patches. One very tiny girl was busy running after three boys, but when they caught her the fun stopped and she cried. Most such playground experiences are quickly handled and forgotten by youngsters so I had learned to let the children work them out. One's intuition, or a student, warns of more serious situations.

It was encouraging to hear a fellow teacher comment, "You have a nice class", as I entered the building.

Seven stacks of ditto seatwork were piled on the teacher's desk, but remembering the difficult time I had had recently with trying to grade all the papers of a third grade, I decided to use my own seatwork assignments, which were thinking questions, requiring the students to complete blackboard work with handwritten answers.

A neighboring teacher entered, informing me I could obtain any ditto papers from the office in ten minutes, which was nice to hear; most schools take hours, or days to accomplish this; most let the teachers run off their own ditto work, hoping the machines will hold up.

The class was VERY talkative, so I started a word contest – with prizes – to get them interested. However, by the time I had put the work on the board the talking had not diminished. The seating in cozy groups encouraged this, and I felt it would take too long to change to straight rows, so I decided to start the day with art work.

394

The decision was a good one. The students were really impressed with the samples shown, but then I discovered I had but ONE kind to be done, not TWO. I took the second master ditto and sent it to the office with a note. Much, much later in the day (not ten minutes) a girl came showing me the faint copy, but I assured her we would be able to use it as it was art work, not seatwork.

To capture their interest in the board assignments I explained the work was like high school and college exams. I had devoted much time to searching and selecting challenging assignments for various grade levels, which I carried about daily.

I explained it would be impossible for me to grade all the papers that day so those who finished first would help grade seatwork papers. This resulted in a few rushing through the work, but they had far too many errors to have the privilege of grading work of more reputable workers. At last one student had three perfect papers so she helped grade.

The room clock was wrong, but fortunately one student had a watch. He informed us of recess and lunch times.

All received free bag lunches (bologna sandwiches, jello, apple, and milk) and as there were two absentees, two extra lunches were shared. There had not been time to check the lunch list as the inquirer had appeared when I entered with the class before taking roll or putting up assignments, so I had given him the number of a list on the desk.

In the afternoon there were oral reading groups. The two groups read in Holt readers at third grade level and the majority were good, fast readers, each group having two slower ones. The stories were longer so each student read two or three times.

Most had their own crayons; there was but one package in the teacher's desk. Most took their seatwork and artwork home. I explained that teachers were seldom interested in work assigned by substitutes.

The room had a very commendable corridor monitoring system. Front and rear guards kept track of any (the slightest) hall or washroom misbehaviors, and when returning to the room recorded such on a very large chart list of the students, deducting points for misbehavior. I had another student oversee this who understood the program to ensure fairness as I felt with the teacher absent the monitors might be too severe, or take advantage. I had noticed a few students attempting to defend their behavior.

A student informed me the school had silent reading during the last twenty minutes so we had thinking word game contests. All became interested quickly; all were eager, alert. One black boy, who had been a problem all day, and had done but one board assignment, now became a shining light, as did one girl. Little by little others caught on. It was a good, fast, challenging, thinking game.

An upper grade student came to take the class down the stairs at closing. Several were slow to get in line but all the chairs were put up and the room was in fine order. The 7th grader waited patiently, commenting they "were always slow". Then the class left in an orderly fashion, going down the stairs quietly. This really impressed me as the students were physically much larger than average groups of their age, and all had been very vocal throughout the day. I thought of the thunderous stomping and yelling of upper grade classes I had heard using stairways in other schools and realized this class would have been completely unmanageable without the room behavior chart and the school escort at dismissal time.

It had been a good day but the talking and paper grading had taken its toll and I went to bed early. I had noticed many tired looking teachers that day; they really worked hard in that school.

Chapter 125

Excellent Teacher Plans
and Records

It was a pleasure to sit at the desk of a neat teacher like one teaching first grade at Brennemann School. The desk top was free of any material but that to be used that day; there were understandable Lesson Plans, three sets of dittos to be used, a Time Schedule, and Teacher Manuals opened to the pages to be used. In addition, two assignments were on the board, dated for the current day.

Being aware this school had Walking Reading, even in the first grade classes, I added several more assignments on the board to keep fast workers occupied.

The teacher had prepared a chart-name list of the lunch money to be collected (weekly and daily) which eliminated much confusion. Three paid the regular weekly lunch fee; four paid the daily reduced price; four paid the reduced weekly fee; eleven received free lunches. One child reported his mother would bring his money later, which she did at 10:30, after the records were handed in! One little boy paid fifty cents "that he owed". 24 pupils were present, 4 absent.

Walking Reading Classes started at 9:25 and three children became noisy and quite unruly, continually disrupting the class, but as it was the day following a weekend on which I had necessarily rested more than usual, these behaviors did not bother me. It seemed nice to be with such young children again, and eventually the problems did complete some of the expected work.

All the board assignments were read by the children, after which I showed several star symbol awards that would be placed on completed work. To get them started I stamped a few bunny symbols on a few papers. This proved effective and most then proceeded to copy the work.

It was soon apparent the majority were unable to select the correct fill-in words for the board work so these were written in the blanks. This was, indeed, a low-level, first grade but many produced fine writing papers. The group was not yet ready to start soft cover reading books.

I called about eight children to the front, who had completed one page of work. I quickly wrote the alphabet letters for which they were able to give the correct sounds. Next, I printed the seven week days, which they sounded out. As they learned these reasonably quickly and could say them when mixed up, I printed the names of the twelve months. Well grounded in knowing the beginning sounds they were able to sound these out also, with a little help and review. Three small groups, in turn, repeated this procedure.

Youngsters brought up papers as soon as completed to receive stars and this continued throughout the entire day. They were allowed to select the star symbols they preferred of the eight available for the twelve very short board assignments.

There was indoor recess due to the wet playground and a neighboring teacher watched the class while I had a short break. With such restless, talkative, mobile youngsters this was a welcome help.

Walking reading was over and after recess the regular room students copied the board assignments.

11:30 was their lunch time and students quietly lined up; to get their hot food on trays brought to the corridor by the lunchroom workers. The lunch was hot dogs on buns, mashed potatoes, milk and halved apples. Several did not care for their milk, or apples, so these were shared with others who wanted them. Even so, four milk cartons were returned. Later I wondered if chocolate would have been preferred, if offered.

In the afternoon there were Walking Reading Classes again so after they entered I wrote two short poems on the board which were read, copied and illustrated as small groups came to the front to review the day and month names again. Periodically fun exercises were enjoyed as children so little seem to need such diversions, and they obviously did enjoy them, settling down afterwards to do the seatwork.

The last period was spent doing art papers. Most pupils had their own crayons and the five who did not sat at tables put together and used two cigar boxes filled with crayons belonging to the teacher. Many produced really fine art pictures. Samples of some pictures had been shown but not of all the outlines as many children finished papers so quickly that I offered other selections to keep them occupied. It was surprising to see such fine art work done by these immature youngsters, which was apparent in their restlessness, talkativeness and continual movement, as well as delayed readiness in ability to start formal reading.

But energy and eagerness they had in abundance and many would be able to go forward easily the next year with the solid foundation of sounds they were receiving. The majority appeared to be from non-English speaking families, Spanish, Oriental, but this language problem would be overcome soon by this fresh, healthy, eager generation.

Chapter 126

My Turn Please

At Blaine School I was assigned to a Kindergarten Class. It was nearing Easter so I changed the regular seatwork accordingly. Three sets of Easter sentences were printed with a Flowmaster Pen and pinned in front of three tables. Below them were math symbols to be copied and counted.

17 children were present.

Gym was scheduled for the first period so after they changed to proper shoes we went to the large gymnasium. Two Kindergarten classes took gym together. The first exercise was one of walking fast, then "Freeze"; walking fast – "Freeze"; skipping – "Freeze"; running – "Freeze".

Next the children sat in rows. The teacher explained, and demonstrated, how to bounce the ball against the wall four times, then each child was to give the ball to the next individual. It was fun to watch as they were so little, so cute.

Teacher: "Did you have a turn?" Child nodded.

Teacher: "Did you have a turn?" Another nod.

Teacher: "Who was first?"

Child: "Me."

Teacher: "Has everyone had a turn now?"

Class: "Yes".

As the gym teacher started putting the balls away several hands went up. "I did not have a turn!" "I did not have a turn!" The teacher returned and gave them turns.

A game was next. The teacher explained how it was to be played. One child was to throw a large rubber ball at the children running about and those hit by the ball were to be out of the game temporarily. However, the first child with the ball ran holding the ball and touched other playmates, but those touched remained running. Few had listened, or understood, the rules of tossing the ball. Everyone just kept running and enjoying life!

After three youngsters had had turns with the ball the class was huffing and puffing so the teacher called for a short rest period; all sat two or three minutes before resuming the game with added zest and screaming.

Roll was taken again after gym to mark the late-comers whom a mother had brought to the gym. But there were four more children present than on the book this time. Finally they admitted they were from another room, but in the kindergarten for the first period.

Pupils were seated at three long tables. Pencils, crayons and paste were put on the tables. The seatwork was pointed out, read and explained; writing paper was distributed.

This was a good class, well trained and quiet. The majority also did fine writing papers. All received Bunny Stars on completed work. After three papers were finished two art papers were done – one large Easter Egg and one fuzzy pink bunny.

Pictures from two Ideal Easter Books were shown and two stories were read.

Last, two records with exercises were played.

Children quietly got their wraps and lined up to go home. Very few asked for help with zippers, boots or snow jackets.

The afternoon class of 25 seemed physically larger, and were very noisy throughout the entire time. There was a mixture of good, and sad work; two were unable to print letters; three did not stay within outlines when coloring.

Whereas being with the morning class had been a real joy, the afternoon was very trying and closing time was welcomed with relief. However, I did feel that a regular teacher would become attached to this group, understand them, and a more harmonious atmosphere would be maintained.

Chapter 127

Fridays ESEA Reading

At Stockton School I parked near the entrance on the street although there was a small parking space for teachers nearby.

The first grade room was in a new addition to the building and was truly lovely. Fluorescent lights, beige colored walls, floors of inlaid linoleum, yellow half curtains, a low mirror by the entrance for pupils' inspection, fresh bulletin boards of the current month and season.

Supplies were in abundance in teachers' materials and toys for pupils. There were even six unwrapped packages of ditto paper – a real treasure, as this is usually practically nonexistent by the middle of the second semester in most schools. There was a piano, record player, filmstrip machine, three high stacks of wooden puzzles, plus shelves filled with boxed games.

The teacher had put a morning story on the board but I erased it and printed Easter Poems. When the teacher aide came in I learned it was a slow group so additional easy work was added to be done.

The teacher aide explained that the first grades had an aide all day, which was a part of the Parent Teacher Program. She said the principal wanted the front bulletin boards to be changed monthly, which the regular teacher maintained. The two others were done by the aide – one a large, beautiful one of Spring, and another medium-small attractive one presenting the colors.

21 were present, one absent. The teacher aide took care of the lunch and milk orders.

The children were using Holt Rinehardt reading materials which has two readiness booklets and four preprimers prior to the regular reading books. As I took groups for reading, the teacher aide helped students individually in a back section of the room.

The first group of five youngsters were in "Pets and People"; the third preprimer, level 5. They were starting the booklet. All paid attention and were able to read the words.

Four were in the next group, reading "Books and Games", a second preprimer, level 4. Here one child was unable to read even one word, and never paid attention. Because of this the child was asked to keep a finger on the place, but this was not done.

It was a rainy day so at recess the class remained in with the teacher aide while I went to the lunchroom, then the teachers' room.

The third group of six read in "Can You Imagine", the fourth preprimer, level 6, and were able to do the reading and answer questions.

Most seatwork papers were starred before lunch time. The teacher aide went to get the lunches for the students, which were brought back to the room. She remained with the class while I went to the teachers' room to eat. This was a very large, clean room on a second floor. There were two stoves, a refrigerator, and a dozen teachers eating there at a long table. One small group of four sat at a smaller table, but they were outsiders doing survey work.

After lunch the teacher aide left for lunch. The class finished the seatwork, which was starred, and there were word games, exercises and record games.

Learning they were to attend a movie late in the day, Easter card material was cut, explained and finished earlier than planned. Several made delightful bunnies and eggs as decorations on their messages.

The movie was part of the school's ESEA Reading Program, presented one day weekly in the auditorium, and lasted 45 minutes. Three were shown. "Animals at Work and Play" depicted them at play, getting food and making homes. The second, "People Working & Playing" captured and held the attention of the children as it showed planes and plane jobs with men working. The third movie contained music and several reading words, which were often repeated for reinforcement.

After returning to the room the teacher aide helped the children get into coats and boots and took them to the outside door while I collected my teaching materials and checked the room order.

In the morning I had been apprehensive about going to this school as I had often heard children and teachers comment on the difficult behavior of the 7th and 8th grade pupils – fighting, bothering smaller children, damaging cars, etc. However, the atmosphere was pleasant and inviting. The teacher aide explained the school changed immediately when it was converted to 6th grade only and the upper classes went to another school.

Chapter 128

Disney Terminology Reviewed

Teachers and teacher aides at Disney Magnet School were pleasant and friendly; the children, already present at 8:30, were quietly and busily occupied with various self-help activities in a free period until 9:15. The pupils near me had selected table setting, puzzles, or art work – some tracing concrete forms, others drawing on papers with crayons or pencils. I sat down at one table and drew outlines of butterflies. Immediately increasing numbers of youngsters joined me, requesting papers to color. One child brought a big supply of colored felt pens from a supply cabinet which were then used to complete the work. From their papers I surmised they were 5-year-olds, which another teacher affirmed.

One teacher helped me review the school's terminology. An area from wall-to-wall, about the size of six usual classrooms, was called a "Pod", having 12 teachers. The Pod was divided into four "families", (classes) each having three teachers, with one larger group having four teachers. There were quite a number of teacher aides, some of whom also drove children to and from school on the buses. The teachers in the Pods, I was told, worked together on planning the teaching activities; attendance was kept by teachers of the different families (classes).

After tidying up the various tables pupils of each family (class) sat together on the carpeted floor before one of the teachers, and participated singing a number of activity songs for about 20 minutes.

Next, oral language time lasted about thirty minutes. I was handed two ditto sheets, one a colored picture of Old Mother Hubbard and the other the poem, with suggested oral activities to be followed. This was finished quickly and I took out my Kindergarten set of thinking word questions to use, consisting of rhyming and opposite word categories. The group was divided contest-wise, and shortly interest was high, with first one side ahead and then the other. Several asked to remain inside, skipping recess to continue the contest, but I said we might have time to continue it later. Children of all grades enjoy thinking games.

Recess lasted from 10:30 until 11:00. Teachers and teacher aides accompanied the children outside. The play area was spacious – probably on top of the basement parking area. A favorite play center consisted of five wooden sections, comprised of two-by-fours arranged in alternate criss-cross layers, whereby youngsters could climb, or walk, up, over, under or between them. There were a few slides, one a double one, where two youngsters slid down arm in arm. The floor of this section was heavily padded with heavy rubber at least one inch thick.

After recess there was a special treat of guitar music played by a mother who knew many favorite songs that delighted the group. Near the end of this I went to a teachers' washroom but left quickly to escape the thick smoke inside.

At 11:30 the students were given math dittos. The twenty-two in my charge could display correct numbers of fingers for numbers I called from two to ten so I was not surprised at their ability to cut, color and paste pictures to the correct numbers. These papers were starred when finished and the youngsters proudly put them in their individual drawers to take home later. It always impressed me that these little 5-year-olds were aware of the locations of their individual school drawers, some distance away, as well as where their coats were hung in this very large area. It would have been interesting to observe these habits being taught early in the school year.

There was a 45-minute lunch period for the children. Some carried their own lunches; all ate in a room nearby, where teachers and teacher aides helped them obtain hot lunches and supervised the room during the lunch period.

Teachers' lunches were served at a counter in another part of the room and they ate in a small adjoining room.

Finishing lunch early I returned and noted the abundance of equipment (in addition to books and play materials) in the open areas of the Pod Room. There were record players, records, tape recorders, filmstrip machines, blackboards, chart stands, colored construction paper, crayons, scissors in every section, plus three pianos, five electric wall clocks, miscellaneous file cabinets and long, open closets for children for coat hanging.

After lunch there was a finger play and song period. One song, especially fun to watch demonstrated, was "The Ants Go Marching".

This teacher appeared to enjoy this period as much as the children. Some pupils left for a gym period.

Nap Time was at 1:00 and blankets were brought out and put at various places on the carpeted floor. The children laid on, or snuggled under, these, most falling asleep very soon. There were numerous requests throughout the period for washroom visits, but most slept, or rested peacefully. I remembered my surprise at this one hour rest period when I first came to the school, until it was explained to me that many children rose early in the day to ride for long periods of time, sometimes an hour, both to and from school.

At 2:00 everyone prepared to leave. Coats and mittens were put on, home notes pinned to outer coats, and various lines were quietly formed before multiple exits from the school. A teacher handed me a list of children's names with the bus numbers they were to board as she walked by. I checked this and realized a wrong list had been given to me. All teachers had already left, but past experience taught me not to panic, that the children most likely knew which buses to board. However, to be certain, I checked with each driver to make sure the correct pupils entered the various buses. Teachers returned to the school and left a little later.

Returning to Disney after a year's absence had been a pleasant experience as I was familiar with their overall program and blended into it easily, but after one or two days in Disney I always felt the need to be back in a traditional schoolroom teaching a regular grade. Schedules were already established; classes joined together two or three times throughout the day, with three to five teachers overseeing the pupils, who sat on the floor. For any special activities, like gym, music, ballet, social studies, science, etc. pupils left for another location. I carried sufficient work materials to keep pre-school through 7th graders busily occupied and I liked to teach the three R's, grade and return seatwork, have physical activities, mental games, art, music or short drama skits in the regular room. I liked planning and being in charge of my own class with varied activities throughout the day.

Chapter 129

Individual Help in Gym

At Morris School I was given a choice of a 4/5 grade or an EMH class. I chose the EMH. Twelve students had been enrolled; two had moved; one was absent, leaving nine present. Only one student had been bused in. All had breakfast in the school at 9:00.

As the students walked to the third floor one large black boy waited and walked slowly up with one very little 5 year old who had great trouble climbing the many steps and did so slowly, one step at a time, pulling his left foot up step by step.

The classroom was very attractive – colorful, neat, with a warm atmosphere. Both pupil's work and teacher educational items appeared on the bulletin boards.

After roll was taken three students left to attend a Speech Class. The boys changed to gym clothes in a nearby washroom, but I stayed close by to keep the noise down. Soon the gym teacher called for them.

As I had put seatwork on the boards before the children arrived, I soon joined them to watch the gym exercises. When I entered the small group was sitting in a little circle on the floor with the gym teacher. The teacher was explaining, and demonstrating, the jumping exercise to be done. "Stand on your toes, knees are bent; use the arms as levers – jump!" He repeated this three times; then the class jumped three times.

Running was next. "Stand on your toes; raise the knees high to get longer steps; the body should be upright, forward; bend the arms and swing them forward and backward to produce good action." The pupils practised the arm movements while down on their knees. The little 5 year old was unable to do this; his friend, the 10 year old, also had trouble controlling and coordinating his body movements.

The class practised moving their legs up and down while remaining in one place, arms bent at elbows, swinging back and forth.

The gym teacher demonstrated the proper way to run the length of the gym saying, "Watch my toes, knees and arms." He took one child at a time for running and commented how the running could be improved. "On your toes, bring the knees higher!" But most runners continued just running.

The little 5 year old tried to follow directions. He could not run, but walked stiffly on tip toes, waving his arms. No one laughed.

Next, they stood together in a circle, putting their arms straight forward at elbow level. They were to jump, raising the knees to touch the outstretched hands. Half the class had difficulty doing this. The teacher helped each one individually, slowly, one leg at a time. This helped tremendously and their coordination improved greatly.

The teacher demonstrated the exercise several times slowly, then faster, the pupils then following suit. They enjoyed this, laughing a lot, as the individual attempts at high speed were both interesting, different and funny.

Relay racing was explained next. Pupils were to carry a soft ladle, to be handed to the next participant at the other end of the gym. Nearly every time the runner had to be reminded to go to the end of the line after handing over the ladle. But soon the others waiting turns slid ahead maintaining correct order.

After gym it was recess time. Nearly everyone needed help zipping jackets or tying shoes. One was helped into a pant suit. The little 5 year old went down the steps much faster than up. The bigger boy was asked to stay with him outside, protecting him, which he did.

But it was another little girl that had trouble. She fell from the swings, causing small cuts on her lip and chin, but once inside she stopped crying. One older student persisted in explaining to me that the mishap had not been her fault to such an extent that I began to wonder.

Pizza was served for lunch with cole slaw, apple sauce and milk.

After lunch four students read from a "C" Level Merrill Phonics Workbook. Others said letter and blend sounds.

When the board assignments had been completed, and graded, pupils chose two art papers to color, some of which were very good.

After cleaning up the room, getting into outer clothing, and waiting for the dismissal bell to sound, oral thinking games were enjoyed and several were alert to answer quickly and correctly.

It had been a different kind of day, but pleasant once the boisterous actions and voices lessened as the day continued.

Chapter 130

Quiet Corridors
Gym – 6 Groups

The 2nd Grade room at Oscar Mayer School was dingy in appearance, with minimum, unimpressive pupil art work pinned up a few places. But two blackboards were free of papers pasted over them, so I covered one and a half with challenging, interesting assignments, just finishing as the 9:00 bell rang and children entered.

They seemed to blend into this particular room, and I expected them to be a little below average in abilities and behavior, which proved to be a correct analysis. Only one of 24 listed pupils was absent; three paid the regular lunch fee, two a lesser amount; 13 had free lunches; six brought six cents for milk. Later in the day it developed half of the class had no crayons for art. A top class invariably comes to school well supplied with pencils, paper, crayons, scissors and paste, plus an alive interest.

After two students had been sent to get the milk a little girl appeared by my desk. "Teacher, may I go to my locker and get my milk money?" I nodded and when she returned had her join the others. As the milk was put on a shelf I inquired when they usually drank it. "Whenever we want," answered one child nearby. From a small boy across the room came a voice with authority, "They are supposed to have it after lunch!" They drank it after lunch.

At 9:15 the majority left for other rooms for reading. The incoming students seemed more quiet. All read at 1A level; three groups of five were at the same story, the fourth group being much slower, but they were able to read.

At recess time I had coffee and a roll and sat with four other teachers in the teachers' lunchroom. I commented they were fortunate to be in this school, adding it was my favorite. One teacher said she had heard that before and asked me to explain. I answered the teachers were friendly, the school was a modern one with supplies, and the children seemed to be from families who were interested in their welfare. All agreed they were happy and fortunate with their jobs.

Helen Marie Prahl

Back in the classroom one youngster said they had gym at 1:15 so I listed the time to follow in order to include Bingo and art. Most were able to complete one or two assignments before lunch, at 11:30. As I ate with them one little girl confided in me, "You know the worst thing a kid can ask is how old their teacher is." I told her that didn't bother me, adding I was 39. "I know," she continued, "but that's the worst thing they can ask. A lot of kids ask that. I never do." A few days later when I substituted in another room near by I noticed their teacher and understood why the age question might surface. She was a dark haired beauty, thin, graceful, about 24 years old.

After lunch, class toilet visits, and water fountain stops, the board work was read, row by row, so all could understand it even if it had not been done individually. Next, Milton Bradley's Contraction and Abbreviation Bingo Game cards were distributed and played for 25 minutes. This went very slowly but was very helpful for them in reinforcing reading skills. Art work samples were then shown and outlines selected. This ended in extremes, the first ones finished being very sad examples, but many others later turned in very fine work.

The gym class was composed of two second grade classes. These were divided into six groups that sat on mats in six different parts of the gym, where they later took turns practising six different activities which were first explained and demonstrated by the gym teacher.

Group I took three running steps, jumped on a two-foot high mini trampoline, and off, rolling over and then up on their feet.

Group II students were to do Frog Head-stands on mats, then roll over, but all had fun doing somersaults back and forth.

Group III used the Balance Beam. Pupils were to walk part way across, hands spread out even with shoulders to balance bodies. After four steps a student was to bend a right knee until the knee and leg were flat on the beam. Slowly the pupil rose, walked to the end, and jumped off lightly. The small, thin youngsters appeared to be more adept at performing this feat successfully.

Group IV used the Stall Bars, which were stable, horizontal wooden poles. Students were to jump up, feet landing on one ledge, the left arm grasping hold of a higher round bar. Without using the right hand they were to make small feet-jump steps across, proceeding with the left hand only. Few did this correctly but it was a good

410

exercise requiring foot and arm coordination. One big boy demonstrated this very well but he fell from the balance beam two times.

Group V used a long sturdy rope which hung from the ceiling having a large knot at the end, three-fourths as large as some children's heads. The rope was to swing back and forth naturally. A pupil would grasp hold of the knot and swing across, above the floor, from one mat to another one, then drop his hold. They were told to let go of the rope and not swing it hard to endanger another's head.

Group VI used Still Rings which hung from the ceiling. They were to jump up, grasp hold of two rings with their hands, then pull up their legs and put their feet through and round hoops to their knees, letting the body hang for a minute; then up with the body, and slide out and down. The instructor necessarily helped them scramble into these rings and again out of them.

All of the exercises looked like such fun and all seemed to enjoy themselves.

After gym there was a walking math class. While the regular class had been doing art work I had put math on one board. Having seen a sample math paper of a child to be in the class, the work prepared was quite simple adding and subtraction. When the eight children entered I first explained the importance of the decimal point, then wrote one thousand dollars in figures on the board. Above the figures I wrote horizontally, "one", "ten", "100", and "1,000", further explaining place value. At first not one could write one hundred dollars, but after fifteen minutes of board work, they were much more at ease with this work. They then completed the board assignment.

As the home room class returned one boy immediately continued his usual talking. I took a piece of paper from his hand and wrote on the back of it, "I will not talk in here". The talking changed to crying, again without ceasing, until I finally stopped to learn the reason. Tearfully he held out the math paper for me to see. Evidently his math teacher had requested the problems to be completed as home work and I had written in ink on the back of the same paper for him to be quiet. "But I can't give it to her with this on!" he wailed.

"Why not?" I asked. "You probably talked all period in there too. You can do both sides for homework. I bet she would be glad to see both sides of that paper."

The child had talked incessantly all day. At lunch another child had informed me he bothered the regular teacher as well with his constant chatter, explaining the teacher "put him outside sometimes". During art work period when he had again interrupted the work I was doing I asked the students to put up their hands if he bothered them. Three-fourths of the class had hands up so I asked him to look around. This he did not want to do but finally looked. When hands were put down – up went his hand.

"Tommy is bothering me. He bothers me all the time. He keeps telling me to be quiet!"

The next day I again substituted in this room. This boy brought in the homework – done on two separate sheets! And he remained quiet all day! This really impressed me as I had felt he was hyperactive and required this outlet. But when, by chance, his mother learned of it, the talking ceased immediately.

Once home I thought again about the discussion I had had with the teachers about why I liked this school. Yes, the teachers were friendly and the physical structure of the school was new; children are children wherever one is. But I had forgotten one very important factor. The entire atmosphere of the school was friendly, quiet and orderly – and this in spite of walking reading classes mornings and walking math classes in the afternoon. There was no uproar or confusion; no disorder. Pupils waited quietly, *in line*, outside rooms until asked to enter. Not one ever barged in noisily. And at recess and closing times there was no turmoil, pushing or running.

Sometimes I had noticed the Principal or Assistant Principal observing the order. What I should have told those teachers was that they had an exceptionally good Principal, one who was interested in his work, because any school atmosphere always reflects the Principal's attitude, interest and expectations. This school was a top one in all areas.

Later when substituting here I learned the Principal had transferred to a high school.

Chapter 131

Top Class

At McCutcheon School I was assigned to a "good" room of 2nd graders, well behaved, smart, interested students.

The teacher of this class had to be one of the best I had known of in a long, long time. Twelve assignments were printed on two long blackboards, covering nearly two sides of the room. The Lesson Plan Book was unbelievably clear and neat – beautiful. And daily, functional work of 12 board assignments were carefully printed there for the entire week! Her desk was neat; the drawers contained much material she had obviously purchased to capture and hold the interest of her students. Much of the art work on the walls was as good as that of 6th graders.

The students were white, black and Oriental. 38 had been listed; 10 had moved. Only one was absent. Three paid reduced lunch prices, one full price; others had free tickets.

Two groups of ten each read in a 2A American Company book. All were attentive, good readers. One group of seven, much slower, read in a Harper Company book, "In Sunshine & Shadows", at 1A level.

The students did their work quickly and kept me busy grading and keeping up with them until I had a few students who had completed the work help grade the papers.

As work was completed they took art work to do which they also did very well.

After closing when the class left I remained and put work on the board for the next day. And a few days later I stopped in to visit this fine teacher. She appeared to be in her early 30's, but had not taught long in the Chicago Schools and felt she might be replaced the following year but was not unhappy about this as had taught in California and felt she would like to return there.

As work was completed they took art work to do which they also did very well.

Helen Marie Prahl

Any school system, any class anywhere, would benefit greatly by having this teacher; of this I was certain. It made me feel good to know there were such fine, interested, hard-working individuals in the teaching profession.

Chapter 132

Assyrian Bilingual

A Bilingual (Assyrian) class at Trumbull School was one of the most difficult I ever taught. All remained in the room as there was no walking reading or teacher of Assyrian. I thought bilingual meant students were taught two languages, but here was a group merely speaking one language other than English.

The difficulty was two-fold – the abundant energy of the children, plus the wide range in reading abilities, first through third grades. Three were new with no English and no writing abilities.

None of the 29 were absent and all received free lunches. The teacher had left a detailed time schedule, lesson plans, and board work. But with the super-energetic students it was all I could manage to keep them quiet and occupied while four reading groups had reading turns. Although the first period had been for gym (while I had added boardwork to be done), there was no recess on Fridays so we did barely manage to finish the reading before lunch.

At noon I graded all the seatwork and realized then that very few had completed the work. Efforts had not been channeled to do the assignments, which explained the continual verbal outbursts and reprimands, which tend to drain a teacher's energy.

After lunch math and three spelling tests were given, followed by art – only for those submitting math and reading seatwork papers. Several pupils having sat the morning time out now became busily occupied. There was little time left for the popular bingo game (Milton Bradley's Contractions and Abbreviations) which they really enjoyed.

But here again several did not listen to instructions but punched every word, so their cards were taken away as punishment for a number of games. Others called out as winners when this was not true. Their over-enthusiasm crept into this activity as well for they had punched words not called. Once they realized only called words were accepted this stopped. Because the 30 minutes left were so short and the reading range so great it was not possible to go slowly enough for some students. These were given a choice to sit by 2nd and 3rd grade readers but a few preferred to use their own cards.

The class needed another 30 minutes to better master and enjoy this fine educational game. And there was no time for the oral thinking games in which I felt they would excel and enjoy as much as the bingo.

Even as the cards were collected and the room was put in order for closing, five or six persisted in being vocally troublesome, so each was told to write an essay on school behavior. As all teachers know, any penalty work assigned at closing time is completed as by magic, so as the children walked quietly from the room all such papers were handed to me. I smiled at their "essays". The wording was the same on each, "I will not talk".

Returning, I graded the spelling tests, in which the top two groups did very well.

Once home it was necessary to take a hot bath to relax. I then recalled someone in the morning had commented it was a "hard" room but "I had a teacher aide". One never came, but except to help maintain silence there was little she could have done except help students with the seatwork. Once it was explained I could help no more.

These students had been wholesome, robust, active. It would have required a few days for us to adjust. After that, when things went smoothly without behavior interruptions, more could have been achieved. But with such a class – bursting with pent-up energy – and such a wide range of abilities – teaching here would remain a great challenge. They had a very good teacher who was doing her best. She had needed a day off which was understandable. Had it not been a Friday so would I.

Chapter 133

Top Reading Scores

Being assigned a First Grade class at Boone School and finding no reading books in the desks I assumed it was a low reading group and was putting easy work on the board when a teacher informed me I was on recess duty at 8:30.

At 9:00 it was refreshing to note not one of the 33 pupils was absent, but surprising to see that even in this far northwest neighborhood four had moved since the beginning of the school year, seven months previously.

Four students brought lunch money but paid this at noon themselves. Several went home during the one-hour lunch period; some brought lunches.

Two boys were moving books from a wall cabinet to the reading circle. The books indicated the class read at expected levels so I added more challenging board work.

The children read in Houghton Mifflin books. 18 read at "D" level (1A) and were nearly finished with the book; 8 read at "C" level; 7 were at "B" level, but were not at all at ease with it. The first two groups were fine readers, fast, steady and read with understanding. All pupils had corresponding workbooks, pages of which had been completed, graded and deleted, but these were 30 pages behind the current reading stories in the books.

In the afternoon a teacher appeared and took five students to a bilingual class in Russian. Another took one child for help in reading.

The school had a warm, relaxed, inviting atmosphere and classrooms were decorated with bright window curtains and colorful, cheerful bulletin boards. The main school corridor had 19 large paintings and reprints, all beautiful and especially interesting, a few donated by 8th grade classes. Teachers were friendly and there was a large, comfortable teachers' room on the 2nd floor with a TV that was turned on softly at noon, and coffee was available. Some teachers brought in hot lunches from the lunchroom.

The teacher had left a time schedule and the students were quiet and kept busily occupied completing the work. They had been well trained to perform room duties as caring for the books, which were put away before closing time, erasing the board, straightening the desks and chairs, picking up floor papers, and in the halls lockers were not slammed and they walked in straight, quiet lines.

Teaching in this school had been a special privilege and that evening when I learned this school had topped all city schools in reading scores I was not surprised. Without discipline or absenteeism problems the school could make good, steady progress.

Chapter 134

Show & TELL
Asleep in Africa

Two parents were waiting by the classroom door at Nettelhorst School as I approached. They informed me their child had a bookcase filled with seatwork which he never turned in. Evidently the teacher had contacted them so I took the work to leave for her.

A new school clerk had told me the assignment was for a 2nd grade, but neighboring teachers assured me it was a very smart first grade class.

Work was put on the boards, plus thinking questions to be answered about two stories to be read to them.

27 pupils were listed in the Attendance Book; two were absent. Two paid for lunches. No time sheet was apparent so a note was sent to another teacher requesting recess and lunch times.

It was a delightful class, good readers, but they liked to keep talking so I showed them art work the quiet students would do later. This quieted them somewhat but constant reminders were needed.

The room was in a new section of the building and was very inviting. Bulletin boards were bright and cheery with both educational and children's work displayed. Clean, flowered half curtains were at the high windows; children's art work brightened the section above one of the two blackboards.

One room corner was for group reading; other areas were sectioned off – one with math items, one for individual reading, one with dioramas, one offered clay, one had painting easels. It was truly a beautiful, neat, well-organized room.

One child left to read with a 2nd grade class. Two students from 2nd grade came in to read with the top group of five, who read in "Cloverleaf", by Houghton Mifflin.

During oral reading I asked one student why he read SO noisily.

"When the other teacher is here we have to. The room is so noisy," he answered. Turning to the class I asked those who like noise to raise their hands. None went up, and they stayed reasonably quiet for awhile longer.

All but one were good readers; he did now know any of the one syllable words ending in "e", but was not interested in learning the useable rule; he only wanted to continue his oral word reading. The others applied the rule and utilized it to figure out the new words. One workbook page was completed and starred for each child.

The next group of 13 were half finished in "Getting Ready to Read". All did two pages correctly in their workbooks of which they had two.

Ten students read in "Footprints", a preprimer, and also completed workbook pages.

The lunch bell rang. Eight pupils received free tickets; two had paid; others brought lunches or went home.

At 12:45 the PM bell sounded, but softly, not clamoring.

After lunch there was a period of Show & Tell wherein students were to show and discuss items they had brought to school. Although many from this talkative class had brought items they seemed only interested in showing them, not TELLING about them, so the basic purpose of the period, of overcoming shyness and learning to speak easily before others, was not accomplished. I merely managed to get them to name the items and say where they got them. Only one child added anything else.

Child: "These pictures (snapshots) we took in Africa."

Teacher: "Were you with them?"

Child: "I was sleeping."

But he added his father had taken the pictures, which were so good that a company had made them into post cards. They were 5 x 8 in size, very impressive, of elephants, leopards, giraffes and tigers.

Seatwork papers were starred and art work distributed. The room became heavenly quiet as the art was being completed.

Two boys so insisted on using paints that I told them to get water for the brushes. One had been wetting his tongue to moisten his paints. When a third returned with water in a small container, another child called out, "That's mine!" The boy hesitated, wondering what to do.

"Is that right?" I asked. "Is it hers?"

The boy nodded. I asked the girl if he could use the container for his brushes. But she answered firmly that the teacher had said it was her very own dish, so the boy left, disposed of the water, and used crayons – which really produced far better art pictures, even though I could feel his keen disappointment.

At the sound of the soft closing bell most youngsters started preparing to leave. But one of the painters delayed everyone for five or ten minutes. Obviously this little artist dwelt in eternity, not time, and in his own private, silent barrier as well, for he seemed not to have heard the bell or anyone preparing to stand in line, but was still painting as we started to leave.

Chapter 135

Slower Class
Black is Beautiful

As I was putting seatwork on the board for the 2nd graders assigned to me at Hawthorne School another teacher entered and told me it was a very slow "impossible" class, adding the substitute of the previous day had refused to return. The teacher explained she had had the class the previous year, that some could not even copy boardwork, and added there would be much fighting in the room. She warned me one boy in particular would be especially difficult, as did the principal, who later stepped in admonishing the class to behave.

I changed the seatwork to an easier level and waited for the class to come in. They entered a mixed-up room; chairs were every which way, and it took a while to get the pupils quiet and into their seats.

The boardwork was read by everyone in unison and a box of eight star figurines shown. They were told they could select any outline to be starred on each completed paper, plus receiving extra stars for being quiet and staying in their seats.

As soon as the roll was taken and lunch money collected, I arranged the desks in straight, orderly rows, and as expected, this seemed to make a great difference, the youngsters responding accordingly to the orderliness of the room. The five who had sat in isolated locations conformed when becoming a part of the group seating arrangement and maintained reasonable behavior, which they had agreed to when their desks had been relocated. All papers on the floor were picked up; it looked like a different classroom.

A few started copying board assignments and receiving stars for them, which inspired others to follow suit. Soon there were several standing in line with papers.

Seven youngsters came to the reading circle and read from a 1B Ginn soft cover booklet, all of whom could read the material, except one Oriental boy. I searched for a lower level booklet for him but could not find one. I knew this would bother me later but I did not have time to stop and write a note to send to a first grade teacher. I realized it would take considerable time to locate such a room number; further, not one child in the room appeared mature enough to take such a message along the corridor. Days later the child's face stayed in my thinking so I knew I would have to revisit the room and give him one of the books I had sent for to share with beginning non-readers of foreign backgrounds.

At recess time the class formed a quiet line and waited in the hall for the 2nd bell before leaving, which seemed to me showed behavior improvement.

On their return two children passed out treats that had been brought. A little girl had a box of chocolate cookies, a boy an expensive container of mixed nuts, which he said he had bought with his own money. In sharing he passed out handfuls so had none left for himself and three others. Fortunately, I saw great supplies on several desks and gave some to the overlooked ones and the donor.

The gym period was for 45 minutes before lunch, which I was not able to talk them into skipping so a second reading group could read, so the reading was postponed until after lunch.

At 11:50 the papers were checked. Seven had not done any work so were told they could not leave until one paper was done. Lunch tickets were distributed to those in line, and when the bell rang they left; a few others went home as this school had a one-hour lunch period.

One girl wasted time by continued crying, but finally added one line to the few lines on her paper. One boy insisted some one "stole" his paper. I had seen half of his math done on a paper on top of his desk so asked him to copy the subtraction work. He insisted loudly he did not know how, so I put tiny circles by the top figures, telling him to cross out the number of circles specified by the lower number. This quieted him and he finished quickly. At 12:05 the sitters lined up, received lunch tickets and left for the lunchroom.

I ate my lunch in the room and went to run off ditto work on a machine, but only got one as the principal did not want anyone but the special helpers to operate the machine. It had just been fixed and I agreed with her; these machines are overworked and seem to hold up better if used by regular operators.

As the class entered after lunch a mother came with the girl who had cried about not having done any morning seatwork. She was still crying a little so had probably made herself ill. I explained the situation to the mother who said she was Spanish and did not understand; however, even when a child translated the matter to her she still seemed to feel the child should go home. She wanted work to take home which I said was on the board to be copied.

Two other reading groups came up for turns, one being at 1B level and the other in 1A books. Several said their books were at home so there was not much point in asking much about the stories. However, it was easy to tell which ones were able readers from the work that had been read from the board, as well as the finished seatwork. Three boys appeared to read in each reading group, none being able to read at the 1A level; I assumed the teacher felt she was more able to control them in a reading group than at their desks. Personally, I felt it could be detrimental to their reading interest and progress to be "reading" in books so far above their abilities.

One was the boy the principal had warned me I would have trouble with. This boy did try to talk a lot, with an extra-loud voice (the one who had misplaced his math paper at noon), but I assured him he was smart enough to control himself and he did try. The other boy, his "best friend" (of course) I soon found to be one who reacted swiftly, and could not endure any laughter directed to him. This occurred several times and I apologized to him for the class each time as saw how deeply it hurt him.

It happened once during his reading period. I don't recall what he did that made us laugh, but the class laughed and so did I. Nicky's eyes caught mine laughing and he reacted swiftly – throwing his reading book on the floor, going to his desk behind him and throwing his prized, starred seatwork paper and crayons. I rose quickly and went to him. I had let him down by laughing and was sorry. My heart reached out to this child who reacted so swiftly, so completely. He was so little, so lost. As my arms encircled him, holding him close, I remembered the books said he needed love. I felt him relax as I held him tightly and apologized. He needed love; he needed firmness. He needed understanding and acceptance, not laughter. I told him he was smart enough to go to college but he would have to read all the books in this grade first. He accepted this new thought quickly, returned, sat down and completed his reading.

These were the two boys I had been told would be fighting together several times during the day. Both had a little trouble adjusting to remaining in their seats, but there were never any difficulties of physical combat.

Only five pupils were capable of producing correct seatwork, but all who completed work received stars for the effort involved; many did do very good printing. About five did the easy 1B math work correctly. I was really surprised at their lack of art skills in sample coloring; even after a number of colored samples were shown beforehand. The papers they brought up later were most discouraging. Again, about five had colorful results.

One neatly dressed black boy quietly displayed his work which really did surprise me. It was done completely in black. The paper was of leaf outlines and was truly impressive with its neatness and unusual coloring, which had been done well, the edges far darker than the interiors. As I looked and he stood proudly by, smiling softly, I felt he had surely proved it to be true that "Black is beautiful". He received two stars for the work which I really would loved to have kept.

A neighboring teacher had loaned me a record player and before closing time I played a few records. They loved "How Much is That Doggie in the Window" with its little barks; we danced to the Polka, a child's record specifying the exercises to be done to the music, and then the "Three Little Kittens" quieted them before leaving. Papers were picked up and chairs put on desk tops before the bell rang.

I still enjoyed the memories of the day. They were happy, smiling children, even if they didn't seem to display high abilities. Most likely they would travel through life at a slower pace, but there just might be advantages on that road. No stress. No turmoil. Many people find this only after retirement.

Chapter 136

Korean Boy and Spanish
Girl Top Students

Traveling by busses I arrived at the Hamilton School at 8:35. Two substitutes had signed in at 8:25 and 8:30. The clerk said they were given first grade classes. Mine was a 4th grade and I was glad as felt I could use materials other than those I had been able to use for a while.

The attendance book listed 35; four had left; none were absent. There was walking reading, meaning children changed classes, going to groups who read at their levels, during which time some pupils left and others entered the room. Those remaining were at 4th grade level and the students informed me the entire class read from one book, then worked in workbooks.

There was a Lesson Plan, quite intricate, and for the regular teacher, not for a substitute to understand readily, so I decided to work independently. I asked them to become secretaries, saying I would dictate a business letter for them to write. All seemed agreeable and interested. The letter was short, using their school name, address and zip code, which I asked them to write by themselves. The letter was to a Chicago company; it consisted of one long sentence, a "Thank you", and "Yours truly". They were asked to skip a line and sign their names.

To me, a letter quickly reflects their progress in writing, spelling and English, so I was very surprised as I walked through the aisles noting their work. Although I had told them to put the school name and address to the right top and the business company to the left, after dropping down a space of two, but a handful had done this. It was quickly apparent they were unbelievably weak in spelling and letter-format; many did not start sentences with capitals; 70% misspelled "Gentlemen"; 90% could not spell "truly", some variances being "truly", "trulie", "tury", "thryly", or just skipping it altogether.

When they had finished I wrote the letter correctly on the board for all to see but did not suggest another letter as the allotted time was nearly up. I felt certain they would have done better a second time.

There appeared to be many solid Americans in the class, but the two best letters came from a Spanish girl and a Korean boy; they had but two or three omissions or misspelled words. The boy seemed aware he was weak in spelling, and during the day proved to be tops in the room in every other field.

After the reading period the Milton Bradley Homonym cards were distributed and all enjoyed this game. Had I known then they were weak in abbreviations I would have used those cards as well, but that was revealed later in the day.

Five students had paid for lunch tickets; eight received free tickets, but another boy said he did not have one as we lined up. This caused a great deal of trouble, causing me to try a number of places to obtain a ticket for him. Later it developed he had been in a TESL class when tickets were ordered. Some schools are not as particular about such details, but a ticket was not easily obtained in this one.

I had brought my lunch so ate with the teachers in another room as this school was on "Open Campus", having a free period at noon, and closing at 3:15.

Returning to the room early I studied the cumulative record cards for the children. Fifteen were at 4th grade reading level; nine at third, and seven at second. Math was a bit improved, with 18 at 4th level, nine at 3rd and four at second. For a few minutes I was shocked and suddenly felt I must obtain primary books and help the seven with their reading until I realized they had gone to their own levels in the morning. For the very first time I did appreciate the walking reading.

There was a short math period after lunch in which I dictated dollar amounts for them to write. As I expected, many missed these, but I was surprised at the number who were able to write them correctly the first time. After dictating about five amounts, large and small, but all tricky, I wrote them correctly on the board, stressing the dollar sign was to be written, and emphasizing and demonstrating the importance of the decimal in distinguishing number amounts. We then progressed from easy amounts to more intricate ones, nearly all getting them correct after a few attempts.

After the math exercises I happened to dictate words for them to abbreviate in an oral exercise and was surprised that this seemed a totally unknown area. The majority of words were of American states, most of which they merely guessed – and incorrectly – like

427

"Flo." For Florida, "Vir." For Virginia, and so forth. Had I known this in the morning we could have used the Bradley abbreviation cards then. But time did seem to evaporate very fast during the day. Using the game cards does help youngsters learn reading skills very fast because of the high interest appeal and the repetition is impressive and thorough without being painful. I was always pleased to have room assignments where the cards could be used as they had so much educational value to offer and were always so well received.

There was a fire drill warning, and as it was a cold, damp day, all put on warm clothing to go outside. The class was reasonably orderly and quiet during this exercise.

There was time for a short art period which all obviously enjoyed but only two or three finished as the time was so short. The last period was a gym class, which is always important to students in all grades.

While the children were in the gymnasium the principal came in. I had just finished a letter to the regular teacher telling her what we had done, which I handed to him to read. I also showed him a few unfinished art papers I felt were of interest and he seemed to agree. I was both surprised and pleased that he visited. It was the only time I recall being visited while substituting; evidently principals assume things will go satisfactorily. When I started teaching I used to request the principal to come in and make suggestions, and always felt it contributed to a more closely knit faculty and school when a few such visits were made during the year. But I long ago gave up expecting them.

The children had just enough time after gym to change to warmer clothing before the going home bell rang. They were really a very pleasant class to have been with. Several asked me if I would be returning but I had but one more day to work that month and felt I would like to visit another school.

After boarding a bus and riding a few blocks I noticed the school ring of keys remained in my purse. As I was carrying two heavy satchels of materials I continued the journey home, then called the school office at 3:50. There was no answer so I called the engineer's phone. Fortunately a janitor answered and said he would watch for my car in ten minutes by the entrance. He was really a fine person as he walked outside to the car before I could park it and go inside. I always felt schools were blessed when they had good, understanding janitors; they didn't seem too plentiful, so I always appreciated the ones I encountered.

Chapter 137

My Story Name is Kevin

Southbound Outer Drive traffic from Fullerton to North Avenue, a distance of seven blocks, took fifteen minutes! At 8:45 I signed in at Sabin School and was assigned a "smart" 2nd-3rd grade by the Principal. After taking the three school satchels to the third floor I returned to the incoming entrance to bring up the students.

There were but 24 pupils in this classroom, evenly divided between boys and girls, and they were reasonably quiet and well behaved. No discipline problems. There had not been time to put much board work up for them so two word games were assigned while I took the roll and wrote more work for them.

The very old school building had new shiny, brightly-checkered linoleum covering the corridors, which gave it a softer, more inviting atmosphere. But the room itself was bare – like a ghost room. The thirteen cabinets on two sides of the room were completely empty. Walls were bare of decorations or teaching materials. The teacher's desk contained a minimum of essential materials – writing paper, stapler, chalk, crayons, Lesson Plan Book. Student folders were in a small filing drawer beside the desk. A few teacher's books were on top.

The old-fashioned, high windows on one side were decorated with mosaic crayon art work by the class, which looked most attractive against the outside light, the same as mosaic windows. The room ceiling was very high, twelve or fifteen feet. The walls were clean and newly painted in a soft bright green. There was fluorescent lighting from the ceiling, and front and side blackboards.

There were three reading groups, ranging from first to third grade. The children were aware of the levels, and equivalent grades, of the books. All books were new, clean and kept in the pupils' desks. All were proud of their reading, and all read well in their books.

In looking at the children I suddenly thought it would be nice to have letters from them so as I wrote my name on the board I told them about myself and then asked them to write a letter to me, saying anything they liked – about school, themselves, their homes. One child wrote such a captivating paper that I asked the entire class to do the same, on the same-sized smaller sheets, to be placed on the blank bulletin board. These came out very well, far superior to the letters to me. They were interesting and decorated with crayon pictures. The first little chap had written –

My Story

I am 8 years old.

I have 3 brothers and 1 sister.

I am in Level 7.

I am small.

I like school.

I like lunch too.

My name is Kevin.

Their letters indicated they liked school, lived nearby, and as I had informed them golf was one of my hobbies, most shared their interests, ranging from tennis, bike riding, swimming and dancing. One had five brothers and five sisters; one tiny girl said she lived with her mother and grandmother and had 25 "cuzns". Several had asked help in spelling words but as it was a "closed campus" school, and out at 2:30, time was at a premium and I told them to do the best they could with it. Past experience had taught me that spelling words for them could take an hour's time.

Several interesting assignments were put on the board which were completed by quite a number, and starred, which really pleased them. As usual the Contraction and Abbreviation Game, with which a few were familiar, was a welcome hit, the boys scoring six games ahead of the girls.

There was barely time for some fast art work to be put on the corners of the bulletin board, some children producing impressive work in this area.

Two assignments had not been done so these were left on the board, with an explanatory note to the teacher, in case he wanted to use it the next day.

This had been another pleasant day, my only regret being I had not been able to help with the spelling as they had requested. But there was so much to do in such little time. In teaching time really flies.

Chapter 138

Top Class
Too Far Away

When the call came at 7:00 for Oriole Park School, of which I had never heard, I was suspicious, but of course Sub Center had hung up before I was able to check the address. Finding it was 7400 west I considered calling back and objecting to go that far as from experience I had learned those schools can be very difficult to find.

But I felt it might be an interesting experience so I left a little earlier. The practical route seemed to be Peterson Road but once at 7400 west I turned right instead of left. Then for one hour I was lost on icy seldom used roads. My car compass had stopped functioning a week earlier so on unknown streets, even the direction was unknown to me.

At 9:15, quite shaken after riding nearly two hours, I checked in at the school and was assigned to a split first and 2nd grade. Walking into the room I felt at once the trip had been worth it, which proved to be correct. The children were truly lovely – a primary grade (which I had not had for some time) of interested, alert, well-behaved youngsters.

They waited quietly while I put seatwork on two blackboards and two groups read before recess, one afterwards. All used Houghton Mifflin material and those in books read well. Finding some were in preprimers (preparing to read) I added board seatwork for them on my lunch hour (after grading completed seatwork papers).

I learned from the other six teachers that many parents in the neighborhood chose to send their children to private schools since the busing had started, not being concerned with the incoming pupils, but uneasy that their own children might be bused out.

The children were so likeable that I agreed to return a 2nd day, when I took the expressway. This day went very smoothly as the work was ready when the children arrived. And knowing them I experimented by putting some 3rd and 4th grade seatwork up for the 2nd graders. One child had 100 on the 4th grade work, several had but few errors, and many mastered the 3rd grade assignment.

Helen Marie Prahl

Having taught them was a special memory which soon erased the first difficult traveling experience, but the school was too far distant for time and gasoline money to return again.

Chapter 139

Oral Reading Simultaneous
by Class

In Hibbard School I was assigned to the most dismal, drab, uninviting room imaginable. There were but two faded and colorless commercial pictures on the walls. One large bulletin board, covered with white paper held a few crayoned pictures made months earlier by students. Pin points indicated seatwork had been removed, probably to be replaced soon as parental meetings were scheduled for the following week.

The children were primarily Spanish, Mexican and Oriental and reasonably quiet. None were absent. At noon some went home; others ate in school, but they had their own lunch tickets, or brought lunches.

The teacher had left a beautiful time schedule with work to be accomplished throughout the day but after studying it I felt more seatwork might be needed at times for some students so I wrote two thinking multiple choice assignments on the board.

Although reasonably quiet the pupils liked to whisper a lot so the desks were moved into straight rows which helped.

The class informed me they all read orally from the same 3rd grade book at one time, but I took them in two sitting groups at the back of the room listing the slow readers as they read one or two paragraphs each. It was easy to see that their male teacher had each read but one sentence as from habit a few cut in during pauses in the oral reading. Nearly all read well enough but many were word readers without understanding.

In the afternoon I called the seven slow readers to the back to read again. And their eyes lit up at once as they were very eager to read again, especially in a group at their own level. In the morning one Indian boy had read in a 2nd grade book, alone, and been painfully slow. I had asked him why he was such a lazy reader, whereupon he had awakened and speeded up, so I had him join the slow group and he read at their speed. Before leaving I wrote the teacher I had separated these few, saying they enjoyed reading together and really wanted to improve.

Before school closed the Indian boy came to me saying he had several books at home and would practise reading faster there. I wrote his teacher his behavior would most likely improve if he let him read with the small group as his interest had been revived. He had been a talker, sitter, and minor trouble maker.

Several students asked me to return again when their teacher was absent. I felt this was probably due to having the reading in groups as well as the art work I distributed. Most had their own crayons or art pens. It could have been they missed the Bingo games I had mentioned but our time vanished. There had been Social Studies and Spelling Test papers to grade which absorbed it.

Only one student shone academically in this group in all the work. Unfortunately a few Oriental boys did faster (incorrect) work, but because of their completed papers, were the ones sent on errands when the office called for helpers. The clerk had forewarned me in the morning this class was contacted for helpers at times. Oddly enough, these two boys later admitted to me that they were the ones usually sent to help with office jobs!

One alert student had written a clever answer to one involved Social Studies question but I was too busy to record it. It appeared this class had a far greater potential than was yet being displayed as their basic understanding of the language was not as yet mastered.

Chapter 140

No Oral Reading

The third and fourth grade class at McPherson School was a good, solid one in the three R's.

But the school had walking reading and the class that entered the room from 9:15 until 10:30 for reading was a different story. There were three reading groups at levels "G", "F" and "E", all using Harcourt Brace Books.

It seemed puzzling that no one in any group knew the exact reading page, or story until I learned they NEVER had oral reading. When questioned as to what they did in the reading period they said the teacher "gave them tests to get them up to grade level."

The three students at "G" level, "Widening Circles", read well orally and with understanding. Of the 13 at level "F", "Going Places, Seeing People", ten read well; two poorer ones paid little or no attention after they read, while one could not read orally at this level. All said they read the textbook at home at any page they chose, and did seatwork in school.

The ten at "E" level, "Kittens and Children", were extremely poor, weak readers, not only knowing no basic reading skills, but not even knowing the regular 2nd grade word reading methods. They could not recognize words if "ed", "ing" or "ly" were added; letter sounds were forgotten, dividing words into syllables appeared foreign to them; compound words were frightening. It was truly a sad situation.

Their workbooks revealed they had skipped about, working here and there. No pages were graded. "Do you work on these at home?" "Yes, the teacher says we can do whatever we want to in them." One thing was obvious – there was no regular reading program being presented here.

Report cards in a desk drawer indicated Reading Levels to range from B, C, D, F (mostly) and G with a written statement "should be at Level J".

Every child in this group desperately needed oral reading practise and a complete review of reading skills *daily*. Unable to read orally they certainly would be far less able to complete seatwork which required understanding.

This was one of the most unfortunate situations I had encountered in years. I felt having no oral reading in primary grades, no skill review, and not checking workbooks was an outright disgrace to the teaching profession.

Six word skills were presented and discussed but these require constant reinforcement. Few children are able to absorb them easily or quickly. The board work was read to them orally, thus enabling the children to select correct answers for questions, proving their ability to think well. As they left my heart ached for them.

When the regular home room students returned they informed me if was their recess time, whereupon we all left for a short break. On their return they quickly did all of the board work, the majority producing perfect papers. This must have been an accelerated group; they were also well behaved.

After lunch the papers were graded and there was art and Milton Bradley Homonym Bingo Games. It was inspiring to be with this class – but the memory of the pitiful, neglected walking reading class still haunted me.

Chapter 141

Sight Problems
Oral Thinking Game a Hit

Although Substitute Center called me by 7:30 for Bell School and I was up and dressed, I did not arrive at the school until 8:30. My watch had stopped running or I would have realized how late it was getting. There was but one opening left – for an 8th grade. A lady at the office desk, whom I later learned was the Principal, asked me what grade I was qualified for, and when I told her primary grades they checked and rechecked the list but there was nothing else available. The Principal told the clerks they should always ask the substitutes what grade level they were trained to teach.

As I climbed the three flights of stairs my heart was heavy; this was what I had always dreaded – being assigned to an 8th grade class. It was not until the day was over that I learned it was a split 6-7-8th grade. Entering the room I was awed by seeing the many typewriters. My heart started beating very fast; they would finish everything I had to offer in minutes by using typewriters!

However, the seatwork I had for the upper grades was good; it was interesting, challenging, and fun, so as I wrote four assignments on the board on the one side of the room the fear disappeared, and as it was a "late Wednesday" when the pupils entered at 9:15 all the work was ready for them as they entered. Five boys and two girls came in, two being late, one an hour late.

As they walked into the room, looking surprised to see a substitute, and starting to talk, and run out, I suddenly realized this was Bell School – the one that had pupils with physical handicaps – the deaf, blind, those in wheelchairs. Most likely it came to me when I saw two of the boys going to the board to read, standing but inches from the board, squinting at the words. I knew then they didn't see too well and I wondered if they could do the work I had written on the board. It took about ten minutes to quiet these few boys so I could take the roll but I did start a contest of finding who could write the most words starting with the letters "BR". Two or three started to list words but others had to be reminded several times to get started. One

Helen Marie Prahl

child gave up after while; he seemed unable to do this; later I learned he was a top speller and an unusually fine artist. Two pupils listed 24 words and were given prizes as awards, which consisted of small booklets.

One girl, who was a few minutes late, explained she had been taking primary deaf children to their rooms. At recess, lunch, and closing times she also left early to perform this service. She was a very kind, thoughtful, considerate child, displaying motherly characteristics. In the room she was quiet, cooperative, and dependable. The pupils relied on her as referee in contest games throughout the day.

At one time this child asked if I would like to read an original mystery story she had written that "her teacher had said was very good". Being too busy at the time I read it later during my lunch hour. The story was displayed on the front bulletin board with a big star on it. I was especially impressed with the neatness; the small handwriting was beautifully uniform, and there were truly captivating little illustrations in the margins. It was wonderful that she could produce such beautiful work with such minimal eyesight. Time flies away in teaching and somehow I forgot to mention the story to her, so before leaving I wrote her a note indicating my appreciation.

I helped everyone get started with the board work as the first assignment was one I felt they would especially enjoy. Most of them continued with this work, especially after seeing the star symbols the ones received who had finished it. The star symbols they selected for the work were of Lincoln, Washington, and the Flag or the Big Star. (Primary children prefer the Bunny, Santa and Pumpkin or Turkey.) I let them have three for doing the first assignment as it consisted of a page of work.

The boy who could not do the "Br" words seemed unable to do this either so he went to a front cabinet, selected a large arithmetic book, which he handed to me, requesting that I dictate mathematical words to him to write on the typewriter. I suggested he write the four ways to do arithmetic work, which he soon reasoned would be adding, etc. This work he enjoyed, and I learned he was very good in spelling. The typewriters had extra large keys so not many words appeared on any line. The books, as well, were all extra large with very large print. The child's typing was done slowly, letter, by letter.

440

All keys were covered with tape so although it sounded like seek-and-pick typing, his had been thinking work.

Some children wore glasses; some did not. Three did their work quickly and quietly but the other boys talked, walked about, laughed loudly, and required constant reminders to be quiet. I felt I was getting the usual substitute treatment I had heard about; later two pupils admitted they always acted like this when substitutes were there. The Assistant Principal had forwarned me of one boy who would be very trying, but this child was absent. Several times during the day different pupils commented they were glad he was absent, confirming, to me, that children enjoy quiet, orderly classrooms as well as teachers.

After recess they requested a word game so I wrote "America" on the board, saying I had found 37 little words in this word, adding it had been accomplished during three different times when I turned to it. They seemed unable to be quiet with the words they thought of so I quickly added four more to my list of ones they mentioned. The plan was to read the words orally, when finished, so everyone could add others' words, and see how many we could list together, but we never got back to do this.

Different board work was selected to be done by different children during the rest of the day, and stars were put on as the pages were brought up to be checked.

At noon they were given their tickets which had been purchased earlier and all ate together in the lunchroom. I returned and practised typing on one of the typewriters. These seemed strange as the type was so extra large and my machine at home had elite type, the very smallest. Their machines' type was three times as large as I averaged five words to a line, whereas at home I typed 15 or more on most lines.

Twice during the morning another teacher had come in to look for students who were to come to her room for a science study period, but they were not present. The third time she appeared in the afternoon to collect homework assignments she waited quite some time, standing her ground most firmly, insisting the papers had not been turned in as one student said. After much persistence on her part the boy finally went to his desk to search for the work – and after more time finally delivered the papers to her.

During the interim I was informed this was the teacher of a child who had appeared in our room three times and had been somewhat of a problem. He had come in carrying pencils and paper, obviously to do classwork, but each time had persisted in loud talking and causing a disturbance, always sitting by some other boy and refusing to move. And although he had been told on his last visit to remain in his regular classroom, he had gleefully returned again in the afternoon and was present when the science teacher entered. Realizing at once that he would not be misbehaving under his regular teacher I asked her to take him with her, which she did.

When work papers were completed the pupils enjoyed the Homonym Milton Bradley Card Game, and they seemed to never tire of it, even requesting to continue the play until the entire card was covered completely instead of restarting each time there was a winner. The usual art work I had did not appeal to them, and I realized it was difficult for them to distinguish the many small lines to be colored. However, some did enjoy the cutout designs I had, and two boys created very interesting art pages from them, providing interesting backgrounds for the small figures. The top artist in the room did such unusual work I considered sending it to a newspaper until I realized he had used both sides of the paper for the work, which would handicap good photograph reproductions.

How they enjoyed the Oral Question and Answer Game! I had spent six weeks one summer collecting and typing this work and had sheets for every grade level. They kept asking to continue it until the bell rang! They seemed spellbound, all ears and very alert. This oral thinking contest was something they could do, and do well, as they were very alert, and smart. I read clearly; the answers came very fast, too fast for individual turns so Mary, the author of the mystery story, was made referee to keep score for the winning side. It became very exciting and stayed nearly a tie. They were good thinkers and responded rapidly in this area.

Suddenly it was closing time. As I walked down the three flights with them I was pleased to realize I was no longer hesitant about this grade level. I also realized they, too, were pleased, and secretly quiet, about not receiving any homework, but I felt everyone should have a holiday once in a while.

When the outer school door was opened they ran like the wind and I watched in wonder as they took off – so free, so free. Next time I would remember to introduce physical exercises in a handicapped class, and music, and oral word activities.

Chapter 142

Love Me Too

It was surprising to be called at 7:00 instead of the usual 8:30 time of the past few weeks. The school was Sauganash, far north and west and I felt it would be a different type of experience to be in a school far away from the busy city. The neighborhood was lovely with many trees, spacious lawns and beautiful homes. The streets were open and free with very few parked automobiles.

Walking in I welcomed the thought of a quiet class in these elegant surroundings. The assignments for a 3rd and a 4th grade class were put on the boards before a mother entered at 8:30. The teacher's absence cancelled their conference so I told her I would observe her boy's behavior and ability and contact her later.

At 9:00 the class entered and as six or seven noisy black students pushed, shoved and rushed past me I suddenly remembered the city's busing system. There was yelling, stamping, banging chairs to the floor, talking in groups and all at once. Noise and black students, unruly students, I was used to, but the sudden change here in this lovely quiet neighborhood seemed shocking and out of place.

Quieting them quickly I overlooked the half-mouthed defiance and took the attendance. 29 were present, not one absent. Board work was explained, paper and pencils distributed.

The three groups read well in Houghton Mifflin readers. Two students were to go to another first grade room but the teacher was absent so I found books and they also read well at that level.

There was constant talking. At one time I walked quietly toward the noise and found four boys sprawled on the floor, doing math from a back board and talking aloud. The instigator was the white boy whose mother had been in that morning because she was not pleased with his report card. This boy needed reminders throughout the day to stop talking and to do his work. He was a sitter, a dreamer, and completed but one of the five assignments. Perhaps his pencil and paper toying, and plain sitting, might have escaped my notice had I not told his mother I would observe him, but even though he was forewarned of this it did not change his attitude or habits.

At noon some children went home; some ate in school. I joined another substitute and two teachers in the Teachers' Room for lunch. There were only five teachers in this school, I learned, all teaching two split grades, plus two part-time teachers, one having a Kindergarten class. All teachers had three to five reading levels, plus added discipline problems, both related to the busing.

The other substitute had a 2nd and 3rd grade class which she said was the worst she had ever had, adding she was already exhausted. The other teacher explained her class had had three substitutes in three days as none would return.

Part of my lunch time, and from 1:00 to 2:00 was spent grading papers. All the board work was then gone over orally as none had had perfect papers. One black boy, paying no attention, displayed such insolence that he was sent to the office.

At 2:00 there was an Assembly Program. It was surprising to enter and see the small group of pupils sitting on the floor. Noise was rampant and I held back my class, saying to the Principal, who stood nearby, that I could control them but not all the others. She walked to the front to calm them and my class sat. I carried a chair ahead and turned it to face them.

But it was three very little ones that I soon took out, one by one, until the entire group was manageable. All were first graders. Their substitute teacher had come to enjoy the program, but after the removals she turned to observe behavior also. Once the program started it held pupils' attention without further interruptions.

Back in the room there was time for some art work, a few Homonym Bingo games and competitive oral English thinking games which proved very lively, even capturing the interest of several sitters.

I was asked to return the next day and as this class also had had so many substitutes during their teacher's absence I agreed. Besides, there was something very likeable, very appealing about them. Possibly it was the challenge that attracted me.

The 2nd day went much more smoothly with both class and teacher adjusting to each other. The entering noise did not seem so overwhelming; all but one accepted me without verbal comment; most produced seatwork.

The boy whose mother wanted a report continued to sit out his time both days, turning in but one assignment again. The black boy

445

with an extremely difficult attitude said he had two sisters, grown and married. I felt he was probably over-indulged at home until I slipped behind him and put my arms around him, whereupon he melted and loved the attention. Then I realized he, like all problem children, was really starved for love.

As the class left that day one handsome boy made some impertinent remark to which I said I wished I had heard that before his mother had stopped in that afternoon. Walking out he continued his flippant remarks. Outside I saw his mother. She said he was probably being disrespectful to both of us, adding they were planning to arrange for him to have psychiatric treatments. She said his mother had died very suddenly years before and she was his foster mother.

So here too, in this lovely, tranquil appearing neighborhood there were personal relationship problems. Here too more love was needed.

Chapter 143

Easter Baskets

At 8:00 I signed in at Hibbard School and seatwork was put on the boards before the 2nd graders entered.

In this school the students kept their own free lunch cards for which they were responsible, thus relieving teachers of this sometimes trying endeavor.

All four reading groups read two stories before 10:30, when I learned there was no recess on Fridays - but that gym was from 11:00 until 11:45.

Having brought Easter Basket supplies which were shown the class, there were fast, quiet washroom trips before the art work was started. Everything went smoothly. Step by step I demonstrated how to fold, then cut, and waited while the majority did likewise, a few stragglers being helped. Colored decorations were added and one third had brightly colored handles stapled on before gym time, the remaining ones I added during their gym time.

Lunch was next so the baskets were put out of reach on a front table as other classes entered the room to eat lunch. I remained at the teacher's desk and graded the morning seatwork papers of reading and math while eating. The work was done satisfactorily but all had not submitted papers. There had not been time to check this due to making the Easter Baskets.

The class returned promptly from gym so baskets were filled with colored straw and children lined up to select chocolate bunnies, wafers, cookies and candies.

Next, two huge boxes of Awards and supplies (pencils, erasers, crayons, scissors, etc.) were emptied on a long desk and students lined up five times to make selections. This added surprise appeared to be as enjoyable to them as making the baskets. I had had the boxes of supplies a very long time and was as pleased to see the items disappear as they were to select them. All beamed with delightful anticipation as they waited turns.

There was time for the English Bingo game which was slow going at first, but once a few students won then interest increased.

447

About ten minutes were left for an oral thinking game, where I had to drop from 2nd grade to kindergarten level for them to think of correct answers. These combined rhyming, beginning sounds, opposites, etc. The boys had won the Bingo games but here the girls were catching up score-wise until closing time.

Chairs were put up but there was a lot of paper on the floor as no one had been able to find a large clean up broom.

Because the compass on my car had frozen I inquired directions of a passerby but soon found myself traveling a wrong direction. After driving around a block, I realized the flashing lights of a policeman's car were directed at me.

Handing him my driver's license I quietly asked, "Why, Officer? Is it because I turned in the bank's driveway to turn around?"

"No", he answered. "You made a left turn on..."

"I'm not in familiar territory here and someone misdirected me. I'm sorry. I just finished teaching at a school nearby."

The words were slow. I was deeply tired. The day had been constantly filled with activity. But it had been a good day, no friction of any kind. It was too bad there had to be a driving ticket to mar this particular day - my last teaching memory.

I handed him the requested driver's license which he studied. I was too exhausted to react to anything. All my resources had been used up. Maybe he sensed that - or something. Maybe the love for the profession, for the children, protected me. It was true I had given all so the class could enjoy the day and take home Easter Baskets and happy memories. Most likely I was still enveloped in the aura of that love which protected me as no ticket was forthcoming.

Slowly I drove home, carried the school satchels inside, and went to bed.

I knew the next day I would be rested and start enjoying the freedom of retirement together with memories of children and teaching that would be with me forever.

About the Author

After 3 years of college I worked in Yellowstone National Park one summer as a waitress. Then California called me, then Florida, Washington D.C., and finally Chicago where I became a secretary.

Eventually I finished college and became a teacher in Chicago. I enjoyed working with children and bringing them up to expected grade levels.

Golfing is a sport I worked hard at to improve my game. Summers I am on a course daily.

Chicago, on Lake Michigan, is a beautiful city where I choose to live, work and play golf.

Printed in the United States
18642LVS00003B/67